DOUGLAS STREATFEILD-JAMES wrote the first and second editions of this book. After graduating from Oxford University in 1989, he spent six years in the army where he honed his map-reading skills to 'adequate' and learned that being cold, wet or hungry was definitely to be avoided. During periods of extended vagrancy, he trekked in South America, canoed across France and motorcycled across Europe. Douglas is the author of *China by Rail* also from Trailblazer and Lonely Planet's *Goa* guide.

HENRY STEDMAN researched and wrote the planning sections and the western half of the GR10 for this edition. He studied economics at Bristol University but not even the undoubted thrill of neoclassical endogenous growth theory could keep him from his current calling as a travel writer. He is the author of half a dozen titles including Trailblazer's guides to *Kilimanjaro* and *Trekking in the Dolomites* and *Coast to Coast, The Bradt Guide to Palestine* and the *Rough Guides* to *Indonesia* and *Southeast Asia*.

KEITH CARTER updated the eastern half of the GR10 for this edition. His interest in the great outdoors was kindled on a school trip to Snowdonia which hooked him for life. Work became what he did between walks and he has since explored almost every corner of the British Isles with occasional forays into France, Austria and the USA. He is the author of *Offa's Dyke Path* and co-author of *Pennine Way*, both from Trailblazer.

STEPHEN LORD covered the western half of the GR11 for this edition. Stephen enjoys trips that combine the outdoors with his interest in culture and languages. In the last few years he has walked several of the French pilgrimage routes and the Via de la Plata in Spain. He is the author of Trailblazer's forthcoming *Adventure Cycling Handbook*.

Trekking in the Pyrenees
First edition: 1998; this third edition 2005

Publisher
Trailblazer Publications
The Old Manse, Tower Rd, Hindhead, Surrey, GU26 6SU, UK
Fax (+44) 01428-607571   Email: info@trailblazer-guides.com
www.trailblazer-guides.com

British Library Cataloguing in Publication Data
A catalogue record for this book is available from the British Library

ISBN 1-873756-82-8
EAN 978-1-873756-82-9

© **Trailblazer Publications 2005**
Text and maps

Editor: Henry Stedman
Series editor: Patricia Major
Typesetting and layout: Henry Stedman
Proof-reading: Anna Jacomb-Hood
Photographs (flora): © Bryn Thomas except for:
C1 row 1 right, row 2 centre and right, C2 row 2 centre, row 3 right,
C3 row 1 centre, C4 row 2 centre © Henry Stedman;
C1 row 2 left, row 3 centre, C2 row 2 right, row 3 centre, row 4 right,
C3 row 2 left, row 3 centre, C4 row 2 left © Douglas Streatfeild-James
All other photographs: © as indicated
Colour maps and illustrations on pp50-2: Nick Hill
Trail maps and index: Jane Thomas

The quotation from *A Moment of War* (Laurie Lee) on p294 is reproduced
by permission of Penguin Books

Warning: mountain walking can be dangerous.
Please read the notes on when to go (pp19-20) and on mountain safety (pp34-7). Every
effort has been made by the author and publisher to ensure that the information contained
herein is as accurate and up to date as possible. However, they are unable to accept
responsibility for any inconvenience, loss or injury sustained by anyone as a result of the
advice and information given in this guide.

Printed on chlorine-free paper by
D²Print (☎ +65-6295 5598), Singapore

TREKKING
IN THE
PYRENEES

DOUGLAS
STREATFEILD-JAMES

THIRD EDITION RESEARCHED & UPDATED BY
HENRY STEDMAN, KEITH CARTER & STEPHEN LORD
WITH ADDITIONAL RESEARCH BY
BRYN THOMAS & MURIEL CARBONNET

TRAILBLAZER PUBLICATIONS

Acknowledgements

From Doug: Thanks to the following readers who have written in with helpful advice and recommendations: James Carty, Jonathan Roger, Peter Easton, David Collinge, Angela and Phil Rostance, John and Donna Peterson, Gary Spinks, Dr NA Malcolm-Smith, Vicens Olmos i Blanch, Bob Moore. Thanks also to Sarah Jane Streatfeild-James for the photograph opposite p171, Greg, Jane and Freddie Knott for the photos opposite p65, Pete Hawkins, Gill Harrington, Ed Elton, Luke Southwell, Sarah Newby and Dean Sewell, Simon Mills, John Critchley, Richard Friend, Alison Gould, John Darley, Heather Ann Jilks, Trevor Crippin, EJ Neather, Wim Busschers, Paul Ellis, Robert Turner, Jeremy Smallwood, Richard Mattey, Richard Bell, Neil and Rossella Hardy.

From Henry: I'd like to thank Jo and Simona Rogowski for their company for much of the walk; James Larty; Patrick Sichère; Maziarz Sandrine and Ayerdi Bruno for their help and friendship; and to Mark, Ian and James for the beer.

From Keith: Warm thanks to the friends I made whilst on the trail, especially to Richard Fisher who was a good companion when I needed one and a source of valuable information, and to Philippe Prud'homme who kept me on the straight and narrow in the Eastern Pyrenees. Thanks, too, to Angela and Phil Rostance, dedicated GR10 groupies both, who kindly gave me hospitality and company on my last day. Also thanks to Manuel Galleo and his Spanish friends who guided me across Canigou, and to Mari-Josi Ordronneau for an enjoyable stay at the Refuge De Mariailles.

Thanks, too, to my editor and all at Trailblazer who helped to complete my contribution to this book and to Annie my wife who was with me in spirit every step of the way.

A request

The authors and publisher have tried to ensure that this guide is as accurate and up to date as possible. Nevertheless things change. If you notice any changes or omissions that should be included in the next edition of this book, please write to us at Trailblazer (address on p2) or email us at ⌨ info@trailblazer-guides.com. A free copy of the next edition will be sent to persons making a significant contribution.

Updated information will be available on the Internet at
www.trailblazer-guides.com

Cover photo: Ordesa Canyon, Spain © Bryn Thomas

CONTENTS

PART 4: CENTRAL PYRENEES

Hautes Pyrénées, Haute Garonne, Ariège, Aragón, Catalonia
Facts about the region
General description 153 – Hautes Pyrénées, Haute Garonne and Ariège 153
Aragón and Catalonia 155 – Food and drink 156 – Getting there 156

Central Pyrenees – GR10

Excursions around the GR10

Central Pyrenees – GR11

INTRODUCTION

From the rolling foothills of the Basque Country to the bare rocky peaks of the Maladetta Massif, the Pyrenees have something for everyone. Deep green valleys characterize the western end of the range, while dusty brown slopes speckled with vineyards are distinctive in the east. The harsh, empty landscape of the Central Pyrenees can be forbidding and beautiful by turns, with its passes, gorges, caverns and waterfalls.

The Pyrenees offer all that's best in walking: fantastic scenery, great places to stay, good weather and, above all, variety. Serious trekkers will relish the chance to seek out the untouched valleys of the high mountains. Those who prefer an easier pace can stay closer to civilization, enjoying the culture of the area through which they are walking. The region can provide the best of both worlds. Stay high in the mountains for days on end if you like, either camping or using the excellent mountain refuges that are available on both sides of the border. When you decide to venture down, the hills are scattered with beautiful villages, ideal places for an overnight stop. Try the local wine and cuisine, relax and regain strength for the next day on the trail.

There's a wide variety of other activities, too. If you like to break the day's trek for an hour or two, there are literally hundreds of perfect lakes in which to cool your feet or, if you're hardy enough, to swim. The clear mountain tarns are ideal for a day's fishing, and the ancient churches are worth a visit in their own right. For the adventurous there's everything from mountain biking and paragliding to rafting and rock climbing.

Traditionally the Pyrenees have been compared to their nearest neighbours, the Alps, and because of their inferior height have somehow remained off the walker's 'wish' list. The result is an area of mountains which has, for the most part, escaped the commercialization that has occurred elsewhere; a place where there is still scope to explore an area of untouched natural beauty.

USING THIS GUIDE

In this guide the region is split into three sections: Western, Central and Eastern Pyrenees. The introductory chapters cover getting to the mountains and what to expect when you get there. Thereafter, the information about each area is to be found at the start of the appropriate section. If, for example, you are planning to go to the Basque country (Western Pyrenees) you will find information on trains, planes and buses in Part 1. Information about local bus services once you arrive is to be found at the beginning of the section itself or in the relevant village section in the trail guide.

Trail maps

The sketch maps in this book are designed to be used in conjunction with large-scale contour maps, not to replace them. The maps are drawn to make route planning easier by showing the detail which other maps do not: **walking times**, **accommodation**, **viewing areas**, **water points**, difficult **route junctions** and other useful observations. Everywhere to stay that is within easy reach of the trail is marked – be it a top hotel or an empty shack. Further details about each place can be found in the text.

Routes and walking times

The routes are described from west to east, the direction in which most walkers tend to tackle longer treks through the Pyrenees. A good reason to follow the trend if you're walking the GR10 is that it involves a long uphill stretch on most mornings and with an early start you can complete much of it in the shade. If you plan to walk from east to west allow for the fact that the timings on the maps may vary slightly in the opposite direction.

Note that the time given along the side of the map refers only to the time spent walking, so you will need to **add 30-40% to allow for rest stops**. Remember that these are **my timings** for the section; every walker has his or her own speed. With the earlier editions of this book, several readers commented that they found these timings on the fast side. The times are, however, consistent so you should err on the side of caution for a day or two until you see how your speed relates to my timings on the maps. When planning the day's trekking, count on between five and seven hours actual walking, and allow for an occasional rest day.

Trail profiles

At the start of each section we've included a simple route profile showing altitude for the main places on the corresponding map and the time taken to reach them. As noted above, times are walking times only and you should add 30-40% to allow for rest stops.

> ### Spelling and vocabulary
> Consistency becomes very difficult in a book like this where three languages (French, Spanish and Catalan) are involved as well as Anglicizations. Well-known place names presented no problem but the situation became confusing when, for example, on a single map sheet Orbaiceta was also spelt Orbaitza and Orbaizeta. Words used only in a small region, *gave* (stream) for example, were simple, but others commonly used throughout the Pyrenees are often spelt differently in different places. The word *étang*, for example, is used for many lakes in the French Pyrenees; in Catalan it's *estany*, in Aranes (Val d'Aran region) it's *estanh* and in Basque it's *ibón*. Likewise the word refuge: in French *refuge*; in Spanish *refugio* and in Catalan *refugi*.
>
> Accordingly I have spelt everything exactly as it appears on the maps that walkers are most likely to be using, with no attempt at standardization, and I have, as far as possible, used the French and Spanish word or phrase appropriate to the region.

PART 1: PLANNING YOUR TREK

With a group or on your own?

INDEPENDENT TREKKING: OFF THE BEATEN TRACK

If you're an experienced mountain trekker, and enjoy long days through deserted valleys, you'll find plenty of memorable treks in the Pyrenees. In order to get away from the crowds, you'll have to venture a little off the beaten track but within a relatively short distance there are some wonderful places to discover. Miles into the mountains, you can pitch your tent amidst magnificent scenery and if you are lucky have the place all to yourself in the morning. There can be disadvantages: camping can be miserable in poor weather, and what with food, cooking gear and a tent, you'll have to carry much more in your rucksack. For most trekkers, however, the effort is amply repaid.

INDEPENDENT TREKKING VIA GÎTES D'ÉTAPE & REFUGES

If the thought of spending your holiday hauling a huge backpack around the mountains doesn't appeal, fear not. There are enough facilities along the major paths to bring independent trekking within the reach of everyone. From early June to late September the main routes through the Pyrenees are well served by *gîtes d'étape* (lodges) and *refuges* (mountain huts), where food and accommodation are available. If you use these throughout your trip, you can cut down substantially on the amount of kit you need to carry – a light sleeping bag is all that is needed for overnight gear. Quite apart from lightening the load, there are other perks: a hot shower at the end of the day, delicious local food, and even cold beer.

Staying in lodges is obviously more costly than camping, and it's less flexible, too. There may be occasions in peak season when you have to adjust your plans in order to be sure of having somewhere to stay. In two or three areas along the GR10 and several sections of the GR11 where no accommodation is available, walkers are forced either to camp or make use of *cabanes* (shepherds' huts). These areas, almost entirely towards the eastern end of the range, are clearly marked in the book.

GROUP TOURS AND GUIDED WALKS

The decision of whether or not to trek with an organized group may rest on several factors, but if you enjoy the company of other people and would prefer to leave the route planning to someone else, a group walking holiday may be for you. There can be great advantages in joining a group: you may, for example, have specialist guides who can point out local flora and fauna. These are often

PLANNING YOUR TREK

local people who can tell you about the area you are passing through, and groups that are led by professional mountain guides may be able to follow a mixed itinerary of trekking and other adventurous activities such as rafting or climbing. On the mundane side, if you are going with friends whose stamina and trekking skills vary, the provision of transport ensures that the slower ones can take a break while the rest enjoy a full itinerary. Trekking companies offer various permutations: you can be part of a large or small group; you may be accompanied by a guide throughout the day or simply pointed in the right direction to enjoy the walk by yourself.

The drawback in taking a guided walking holiday is that you may find yourself tied to a fixed itinerary and to a large group of other people. An alternative to being part of a group is to get a trekking company to tailor an itinerary just for you. Several companies do this and will make bookings for all transport and accommodation in advance of your arrival.

TREKKING AGENCIES

Many specialist agencies offer guided treks. While most of them have standard walking tours, several also cater for special interests or abilities.

Trekking agencies in the UK

● **Exodus Walking Holidays** (☎ 0870-240 5550, 💻 www.exodus.co.uk), Grange Mills, Weir Rd, London SW12 0NE. Exodus run a wide range of small-group guided treks, including eight days in the High Pyrenees with an ascent of Pico Aneto, eight days walking from a lodge based in the Central Pyrenees, eight days of 'tough' walking through Gavarnie and Ordesa and a two-week stroll on the central part of the GR10. They also do a week-long scrambling tour on both sides of the border for those with a head for heights, and, unusually, a number of winter-walking trips.

● **Great Walks of the World** (☎ 01935-810820, 💻 www.greatwalks.net), Salcombe House, Long St, Sherborne, Dorset DT9 3BU, offer two Pyrenean treks. Their 15-day High Level Route runs from Etsaut to Gavarnie; the Pyrenean Summits Trek is a high-level traverse of the eastern Pyrenees with ascents of the three highest peaks in the massif – Aneto, Posets and Monte Perdido.

● **Headwater Holidays** (☎ 01606-720099, 💻 www.headwater-holidays.co.uk), The Old School House, Chester Rd, Castle, Northwich, Cheshire CW8 1LE; Headwater offer an eight-day high Pyrenees walk in the Central Pyrenees, based in the picturesque Val d'Azun.

● **HF Holidays** (☎ 020-8905 9556, 💻 www.hfholidays.co.uk), Imperial House, The Hyde, Edgware Rd, London NW9 5AL. HF Holidays use St Lary in the central Pyrenees as a base for one- and two-week guided walking holidays, on both French and Spanish sides. In addition to their Classic Walking holidays, they also offer trips specializing in flora and fauna, a 'rambles' trip for those who like taking things more easily, high trails, winter walking and snow-shoeing.

● **Naturetrek** (☎ 01962-733051, 💻 www.naturetrek.co.uk), Cheriton Mill, Cheriton, Nr Arlesford, Hampshire, SO24 0NG. Naturetrek run birding and

botany tours to the Spanish and French Pyrenees. Groups of 10-16 people are accompanied by an expert naturalist on: an eight-day butterfly tour, an eight-day birding and botanical trip, an eight-day family holiday and a natural-history tour.
● **Pyrenean Mountain Tours** (☎ 01635-297209, 🖥 www.pyrenees.co.uk), 2 Rectory Cottages, Rectory Lane, Wolverton, Tadley, Hampshire, RG26 5RS. This small company runs summer and winter mountain walking trips from its base in Luz-St-Sauveur. They organize both guided and non-guided walks and can plan an itinerary to individual requirements.
● **Pyrenees Adventures** (☎ 0870-1904125, 🖥 www.pyradv.com), see France below.

Trekking agencies in Continental Europe
● **France** La Balaguère (☎ 05.62.97.46.46, 🖥 www.balaguere.com), Route du Val d'Azun, Arrens Marsous, 64503. La Balaguère is probably the biggest of the trekking companies operating guided and self-guided walks in the western and central Pyrenees. **Pyrenees Adventures** (☎ 04.68.20.73.34), 6 route de la Boulzane, 11140 Puilaurens, specialize in guided walking and trekking trips, accommodation, and a host of other outdoor activities.

● **Germany** STB-reisen GmbH (☎ 06128-982513, 🖥 www.stb-reisen.com), Platter Str 87, 65232 Taunusstein. This company specializes in all aspects of French tourism, including walking holidays. **Wikinger Reisen GmbH** (☎ 02331-904741, 🖥 www.wikinger.de), Kölner Str 20, 58135 Hagen. Wikinger offer 7-, 13- and 15-day walking tours to the Eastern Pyrenees.

● **Netherlands** SNP Travel (☎ 024-3277 000, 🖥 www.snp.nl), Bijleveldsingel 26, 6421 AT Nijmegen. SNP offer individual walking and cycling tours all over Europe. **France Individuelle** (☎ 020-688 0066, 🖥 www .france-individuelle.com), Danzigerkade 10, 1013 AP Amsterdam, offer walking tours in the French Pyrenees and give you the option of hiring a donkey to help transport your kit.

Trekking agencies in North America
● **Wilderness Travel** (☎ 510-558-2488, toll free ☎ 1-800-368-2794, 🖥 www .wildernesstravel.com), 1102 Ninth St, Berkeley, CA 94710, offer a 11-day trek from Bilbao to Barcelona.
● **Butterfield & Robinson** (☎ 416-864-1354, toll free 1-800-678-1147, 🖥 www. butterfield.com), 70 Bond St, Suite 300, Toronto, Ontario, M5B 1X3. Butterfield organize a couple of six-day walking, riding and biking family trips, both of which are based in Catalonia, including a straightforward 12km walk.
● **World Expeditions** (☎ 613-241-2700, 🖥 www.worldexpeditions.com), 78 George St, Ottawa, Ontario K1N 5W1; (☎ 514-844-6364) 1705 St Denis St, Montreal, Quebec H2X 3K4. World expeditions offer a 7-day walking tour of the Cathar castles and another week on the pilgrim trail to Santiago de Compostela.

Trekking agencies in Australasia
● **Exodus** Peregrine Adventures (☎ 03-9663 8611, toll free ☎ 1300-854 444, 🖥 sales@peregrine.net.au), 258 Longdale St, Melbourne, Victoria 3000; also 5th floor, 38 York St, Sydney NSW 2000.

● **In the French Pyrenees** (☎ 0500-500301, 🖳 www.acenet.com.au/~pyrenees), PO Box 469, Bowral, NSW 2576; office address, 22 Toongoon Rd, Burradoo, NSW 2576. Patrick Arrieula, a native of Béarn, offers walking and gourmet tours in the French Pyrenees around the Béarn and Basque areas. The tours are run in May and October, usually over nine days. Patrick can also offer tours for private groups with a tailor-made itinerary.

Getting to the Pyrenees

The Pyrenees are accessible by road, rail and air: you can reach the mountains from almost anywhere in Europe in a matter of hours. A good public transport network facilitates getting right into the mountains.

BY AIR

For the Basque country, the closest airport is Biarritz, although Bordeaux is much better served and is only three or four hours by train from the mountains. Pau airport is useful for access to the western part of the central Pyrenees, as is Lourdes, although direct flights to either of these from outside France are rare and you may have to go to Paris and get a connection. The best-served airport near the French Pyrenees is Toulouse, which also has excellent connections into the mountains themselves. Perpignan airport gives the best access to the Mediterranean coast. In Spain, Bilbao is a good option if you intend to start walking from the Atlantic coast, and Barcelona is worth considering for access to Andorra, Ax-les-Thermes and the Catalan Pyrenees.

From the UK

Prices Scheduled flights direct from the UK to one of the Pyrenean airports, using a major airline such as Air France (☎ 08450-845 111, 🖳 www.airfrance .com), British Airways (☎ 0870-850 9850, 🖳 www.britishairways.com), or Iberia (☎ 0845-601 2854, 🖳 www.iberia.com), all tend to cost around £200 (although flights to Barcelona are slightly cheaper). Fares on the '**no-frills' airlines** – Easyjet (☎ 0870-600 0000, 🖳 www.easyjet.com), Flybe (☎ 0871-700 0535, 🖳 www.flybe.com), and Ryanair (☎ 0870-333 1242, 🖳 www.ryanair.co .uk) – can be much cheaper, and it's quite possible to get a return ticket for under £100 (and sometimes much, much cheaper) if you book far enough in advance and take advantage of special offers. Note that these airlines positively encourage you to book online; an extra charge may be made if you book by phone. **Websites** such as 🖳 www.traveljungle.co.uk, 🖳 www.cheapflights.co .uk, 🖳 www.ebookers.com and 🖳 www.expedia.co.uk are often the easiest way to find the best fare though they do not usually include the 'low cost' airlines.

● **Bordeaux** Flybe operate flights from Bristol to Bordeaux four times a week. British Airways has three direct flights every day from Gatwick. Air France has a daily flight (except Sundays) between Gatwick and Bordeaux.

● **Biarritz** Ryanair has twice-daily flights from Stansted to Biarritz. Air France has daily flights between Biarritz and Paris.

● **Pau** Ryanair operates the only direct flight from the UK (Stansted) to Pau, and Air France has five to seven direct flights a week from Paris to Pau.

● **Lourdes** There are no direct flights from the UK, but Air France has flights from Paris (two each on Monday to Friday, one each on Saturday and Sunday).

● **Toulouse** British Airways has three flights every day from Gatwick and a daily flight from Manchester. Easyjet operates two per day from Gatwick, Air France operates no direct flight, but has flights via Paris and Nantes. Flybe also operate flights to Toulouse, from Birmingham (three times per week), Bristol (three times per week) and Southampton (four times per week).

● **Perpignan** Ryanair has a twice-daily service from Stansted, Flybe from Birmingham and Southampton (though these were not running in the winter). Air France has four flights from Paris to Perpignan (three on Saturday).

● **Barcelona** BA has flights every day from Heathrow (eight to nine per day) and Gatwick (three from Gatwick), and two flights a day from Birmingham, and five weekly from Glasgow. Iberia operates several flights a day from Heathrow. Easyjet operates four flights per day to Barcelona from Gatwick, five on Saturday, as well as two daily from Stansted and three per day from Luton (four at weekends).

Ryanair don't actually fly to Barcelona, but do fly to nearby Girona three or four times a day.

● **Bilbao** British Airways has two daily flights from Heathrow, and Iberia operates two daily services from Heathrow. Easyjet has a daily flight from Gatwick, and a twice-daily service from Stansted.

From Continental Europe
There are direct flights from some of the major European cities into Toulouse but to get to any of the other Pyrenean airports, you will almost certainly have to go to Paris and change. The best people to try for information (apart from your local travel agent) are Air France and the national airline of the country from which you are flying.

From the USA, Canada and Australasia
There are no direct flights from the USA, Canada or Australasia into the Pyrenean airports, so you'll have to go to Paris or another European airport. Check with a travel agent to see which airlines are offering the best connections.

BY RAIL

The French rail network is excellent, providing fast services to the major cities in the foothills of the Pyrenees and regular connections, either by train or by bus, to some of the towns and villages in the mountains. Combined with the 300km/h Eurostar service from London to Paris, rail travel from the UK to the Pyrenees is an attractive option. With an early start from London, and a good connection, you can be in Hendaye by mid-evening, and the cheapest fares start at just £100 return.

TOULOUSE – PRACTICAL INFORMATION

Toulouse is the most frequently-used access point for those flying to the Pyrenees. The reasons for this are twofold: the city's airport is served by regular flights from around Europe, and public transport connections into the mountains are very good. Because of inconvenient flight timings, however, many trekkers are forced to stop over in Toulouse for at least one night. This is no great hardship. Toulouse is a lovely city with plenty of good restaurants, shops, and museums; a couple of days here at the end of a walking trip may be just the way to relax after some strenuous trekking. If you do need to stop in Toulouse, the following information may assist:

Where to stay

● **Near the airport** The area around the airport is like a gigantic business park, with no shops and, apart from the airport itself, only one place to eat. Cheap accommodation is available within 10-15 minutes' walk of the terminus at a *Formule 1* (central reservations ☎ 08.91.70.54.10, 🖵 www.hotelformule1.com – easy to book online) which is next to the autoroute. The price isn't bad: €29 for a room. The only place for dinner is at another hotel on the far side of a bridge over the motorway.

You could get a taxi from the airport to the hotel, but it's also possible to walk: there is a route along the service road next to the airport which leads to the hotel (thereby avoiding the need to walk along the hard shoulder of the motorway) – ask for directions.

● **In the city** Despite the temptation to book into the nearest hotel to the bus or train station, it's worth going further afield to find a good place to stay. I'd recommend the *Hôtel du Taur* (☎ 05.61.21.17.54, 🖵 www.hotel-du-taur.com) 2, rue du Taur, which is literally just off the Place du Capitole, the main square in the city. The hotel is very comfortable and the location is excellent. Double rooms cost from €47 single, €52 double.

Local transport

Toulouse airport is some 10-15km from the city centre, in a suburb called Blagnac. The cheapest way to get to and from the airport is by the airport shuttle service, which runs to and from the main bus station which is next to the main railway station in the centre of Toulouse.

Buses run approximately every 20 minutes, the first bus heading out to the airport at around 05.00 and the last bus running at about 20.20. Going from the airport into the city, the first bus goes at about 07.35 and the last bus at about 00.15. At weekends the first and last buses are respectively later and earlier. For more information on timings, contact the bus company (☎ 05.34.60.64.00, 🖵 www.navetteviatoulouse.com). A one-way ticket costs €3.90; a return €5.90; under 25s (€3.90/4.50 single/return).

Tourist office

The tourist office (☎ 05.61.11.02.22, 🖹 05.61.22.03.63, 🖵 www.ot-toulouse.fr/English) is in the Donjon du Capitole, just to the east of the Place du Capitole.

Moving on

From Toulouse it's easy to get trains to Perpignan, Bagnères-de-Luchon, Ax-les-Thermes, Lourdes, Pau, Bayonne or Hendaye. Each of these places is a transport hub from which local transport links can be used to get into the mountains.

By way of example of fares, a one-way train ticket from Toulouse to Bayonne is €33.

TGV

Although there are a large number of daily trains, the most convenient method of rail travel to the Pyrenees is by TGV (*train à grande vitesse*) – the French high-speed rail network. Travel by TGV costs a bit more than on a slow train, and reservations are required, but the comfort and speed more than make up for this.

Bayonne, Biarritz, St-Jean-de-Luz, Hendaye, Pau, Lourdes, Tarbes and Toulouse are all served by the TGV. From Paris to any of these cities takes around six hours.

Other services

Although only the stations listed above are served by the TGV, there's a range of normal services too, including some direct trains from Paris and elsewhere that go right into the heart of the mountains: St-Jean-Pied-de-Port, Bagnères de Luchon, Ax-les-Thermes and Banyuls-sur-Mer are the main stations involved. Details of services from main railheads into the mountains are given at the beginning of each relevant section of the book. Fares are cheaper on normal trains than on the TGV.

Discounts

Passengers on all services can save money by travelling off peak (*periode bleue*) or by buying tickets well in advance. There are numerous money-saving schemes and the offers seem to change from month to month, so it's worth asking when you enquire about or book your ticket. Recent offers have included:

● Children aged 4-12: 25% discount
● Young people aged 12-25: 25% discount (50% if travelling off peak)
● Senior travellers (over 60 years of age): 25% off for off-peak travel
● Découvert Séjour: 25% off fares as long as you stay for a Saturday
● Tickets booked eight days in advance: 25% discount
● Tickets booked 30 days in advance: 40% discount
● Discovery 2: 25% discount for two people travelling together

---

Rail information

Rail Europe (a subsidiary of SNCF; 🖳 www.raileurope.com) provides a quick, efficient service by which you can order rail tickets and passes and have them mailed to you at no extra charge. Contact details in the UK are: **Rail Europe UK** (☎ 08705-848 848), 178 Piccadilly, London W1. The website 🖳 www.raileurope.co.uk has excellent information and gives details of service agents worldwide. Insurance and car hire can also be arranged through this organization and there's an associated company which books accommodation.

For information about **Eurostar services**, see **www.eurostar.com**. SNCF (the French railway company) have a site at **www.sncf.fr**. The timetable section is particularly useful.

Travel agents who specialize in rail travel, such as **Ffestiniog Travel** (☎ 01766-512400, 🖳 www.festtravel.co.uk), Harbour Station, Porthmadog, Gwynedd LL49 9NF, sometimes get different special offers from those available on the Internet so it may be worth comparing prices.

BY CAR

Travelling by car to the Pyrenees can be cost effective if there are two or more of you and may be an attractive option if you've got a lot of gear. Having your own transport also gives you the flexibility to explore the region more widely. Travelling from the UK, you have a choice of the Channel tunnel (☎ 08705-353535, 🖳 www.eurotunnel.com) and the cross-Channel ferries to the ports of northern France, though you're then faced with a long drive southwards. A convenient way of avoiding this marathon is to take a direct ferry to northern Spain. **Brittany Ferries** (UK ☎ 08703-665 333, 🖳 www.brittanyferries.com) operate twice-weekly services from Plymouth to Santander (18 hours, currently departing on Wednesday and Saturday), and **P&O Ferries** (UK ☎ 08702-424 999, 🖳 www.poferries.com) have twice-weekly sailings from Portsmouth to Bilbao (35 hours), dropping to once a week in low season. It takes about three hours to drive from either port up to the area of Irún and Hendaye.

BY COACH

It's a long haul from the UK to the Pyrenees by coach, and the bargain fares available from low-cost airlines make coach travel seem unnecessarily masochistic. One advantage, however, is that there's usually last-minute availability, which may not be the case with flights, and the coach company may be flexible with return dates if you decide to stay longer. Between April and October, Eurolines (☎ 0870-514 3219; 🖳 www.eurolines.co.uk), 52 Grosvenor Gardens, Victoria, London SW1, have services to Perpignan (20 hrs, £109 return), Bayonne (19 hrs, £116 return), Lourdes (via Pau and Tarbes; (21 hrs, £116 return) and Toulouse (20 hrs, £116 return); however, some of these operate in the peak season (July and August) only, so check in advance.

Visas

Visas are not required by members of other EU countries or by US or Canadian nationals who plan to be in either France or Spain for less than 90 days. All other nationalities require a visa. Note that in the Pyrenees the 90-day rule becomes superfluous; since there are no border controls you could easily claim that you've just come across the mountains for a few days and will be returning shortly.

Budgeting

Budgets for trips to the Pyrenees can vary widely. If you head off into the wilderness on arrival, and come back to civilization only to catch the train home, the costs will be very low. If, on the other hand, you make a point of trying some of the local restaurants and of having a couple of beers in the evening, your expenditure will be considerably higher.

CAMPING

If you plan to camp in the hills every night, you can get by on as little as £5/US$9 per day – all you will need to buy is food. Realistically, though, assuming that you might want to eat at a local café occasionally, and every now and again stay in a campsite where there's a shower, you would be wise to bank on £10/US$18 per person per day.

GÎTES

Staying in *gîtes d'étape* (lodges) and *refuges* (mountain huts) en route is more expensive. If you buy food every night and cook for yourself using the facilities provided in most gîtes, you should make do on about £12-15/US$21.50-27 per day. If, however, you eat the meals provided by the guardian and possibly splash out on a glass or two of wine to go with your supper, your costs are likely to come to £20-25/US$36-45 per day. You can stay below this if you really try hard but a drink or two in the evening soon puts the price back up.

EXTRAS

Although there are few additional expenses on a walking holiday, set aside some cash for the inevitable extras – postcards, snacks, and a few really good meals along the way.

When to go

The walking season in the Pyrenees starts in mid-June and ends in late September. It is quite possible to walk outside this period but the weather may be unpredictable and you cannot guarantee that all the normal summer walking facilities will be available.

Note that if you are walking in mid-June and are relying on lodges for overnight accommodation, it will be necessary to ring ahead to check whether each place is open. See p39-40 for more on climate and temperatures in the Pyrenees.

SNOW-FREE PERIOD

In late May many of the lower routes (ie much of the GR10) should be fine but there's always the risk of a late snowfall which would cause problems. It's not so much that the routes would be impassable but that the route markers, many of which are painted on the rocks, become invisible under even a light layer of snow. Note that higher passes (ie over 2000 metres) may not be free from snow until early or even mid-July. The routes that involve crossing particularly high passes are marked in this book. If you're planning to try them in June/early July you'll need to check with a tourist office or, better still, with the guardian of a nearby refuge, as to whether the route is passable before setting out. Ensure when you ask that you get clear advice as to whether the route is passable to walkers *without special equipment*, as some guardians may make the assumption that you have climbing gear. The alternative is to equip yourself with an ice axe, crampons etc to enable you to make the crossing safely. (For more details, see the section on mountain safety, on pp34-7).

GÎTES AND REFUGES

Gîtes and refuges tend to have wardens in permanent residence only from mid-June to late September. If you plan to be walking outside this period, you should phone in advance before relying on using them.

❏ FURTHER INFORMATION
General websites

Sites which can be helpful for planning a trip include the following:
● There are a couple of fantastic Pyrenees-specific sites: Friends of the Pyrenees have their own website, **www.pyrenees-pireneos.org**, covering treks, refuges and all things Pyrenean. And then there's **www.pyreneesguide.com**, covering the same kind of ground in a similarly comprehensive and informative manner. Both of these are great places to start your online planning.
● There's also a reasonable cycling website, **www.bikepyrenees.com**.

Websites for the French Pyrenees

● The **French Tourist Department** site, at **www.franceguide.com** is another good place to start, and has an updated list of events as well as a variety of other background information; **www.france.com** offers a similar style and mix of news, chat, and tourist information.
● For an insight into the **Pays Basque**, look at **www.infobasque.com** where you'll find full details of Basque news and events, as well as some tourist information. More formal and business minded, but interesting nevertheless, is **www.euskadi.net**, the official website of the Basque government.
● For refuges in France see Club Alpin Français: **www.clubalpin.com/fr**.

Websites for the Spanish Pyrenees

● The **Spanish Tourist Office** has a site at **www.spaintour.com**. There's little specific detail about the Pyrenees, but it does have information about general subjects such as exchange rates and travel around Spain. There's also a link to another useful site: **www.spain.info**.
● **Catalonia's** own site, **www.publintur.es**, is well designed and offers a guided tour of the region, complete with insights into culture, history and what's on offer to visitors.
● Ariège has its own website, **www.ariege.com**, and it's a goodie, with lots of information on the bears that have settled in the region. On a similar subject, **www.parc-pyrenees.com** has a thorough run-down on all matters to do with the national park.
● For refugios see **www.refugiosyalbergues.com** which has links to other sites.

NATIONAL HOLIDAYS

Summer holidays in both France and Spain tend to fall between mid-July and mid-August, and make a considerable difference to the availability of accommodation. This can work both to your advantage and disadvantage: you can guarantee that all facilities will be open during the period, and that transport services such as local buses into the mountains will be running; equally, you may find that the most popular lodges will be very full. If you're planning to get off the beaten track and camp rough, this will of course be less of a hassle.

❏ **FURTHER INFORMATION**
National tourist offices
● **Australia French**: (☎ 02-9231 5244, 🖳 info.au@franceguide.com), 25 Bligh St, Level 20, Sydney, NSW 2000.
● **Belgium French**: (☎ 0902 88 025, 🖳 info.be@franceguide.com), 21 ave de la Toison d'Or, B-1050 Brussels. **Spanish**: (☎ 02-280 1926, 🖳 bruselas@tourspain.es), ave des Arts 21, B-1000 Brussels.
● **Canada French**: (☎ 514-288-2026, 🖳 canada@franceguide.com), 1981 Avenue McGill College, Suite 490, Montreal, Quebec H3A 2W9. **Spanish**: (☎ 416-961-3131, 🖳 toronto@tourspain.es), 2 Bloor St West, 34th Floor, Toronto, Ontario M4W 3E2.
● **Denmark French**: (☎ 90 13 90 93, 🖳 info.dk@franceguide.com), NY Ostergade 3,3, DK-1101 Copenhagen K. **Spanish**: (☎ 33 15 11 65, 🖳 www.spanien-turist.dk, copenhague@tourspain.es), NY Ostergade 34,1, 1101 Copenhagen, K.
● **France Spanish**: (☎ 01.45.03.82.50, 🖳 paris@tourspain.es), 43 Rue Decamps, 75784 Paris.
● **Germany French**: (☎ 0190-57 00 25, 🖳 info.de@franceguide.com), Zeppelinallee 37, 60325 Frankurt Main and (☎ 30-590 03 90 11), Franzosische Botschaft, Ambassade de France, Pariser Platz 5, 10117 Berlin. **Spanish**: (☎ 069-72 50 33, 🖳 frankfurt@tourspain.es), Myliusstrasse 14, 60325 Frankfurt Main; (☎ 030-882 6543), 180 Kurfurstendamm, 10707 Berlin; (☎ 0211-680 3981), Grafenberger Allee 100, 40237 Dusseldorf), and (☎ 089-538 9075), Schubertstrasse 10, 80336 Munich.
● **Ireland French**: (☎ 01-679 0813, 🖳 info.ie@franceguide.com), 10 Suffolk St, Dublin, IRL 2.
● **Netherlands French**: (☎ 0900-112 23 32, 🖳 info.nl@franceguide.com), Prinsengracht 670, NL-1017 KX Amsterdam. **Spanish**: (☎ 070-346 5900), Laan Van Meerdervoort 8-8a, 2517 AJ, The Hague.
● **Spain French**: (☎ 807-117181, info.es@franceguide.com), Plaza de Espana 18, Torre de Madrid 8º Pl Of 5, 28008 Madrid.
● **UK French**: (☎ 09068-244123, 🖳 info.uk@franceguide.com), 178 Piccadilly, London W1J 9AL; **Spanish**: (☎ 020-7486 8077, 🖳 info.londres@tourspain.es); note that visits to the office in London are by appointment only.
● **USA French**: (☎ 212-838-7800, 🖳 info.us@franceguide.com), 444 Madison Avenue, 16th Floor, New York NY 10022; also California: 9454 Wilshire Blvd, Suite 715, Beverly Hills, CA 90212-2967 (☎ 310-271-6665, 🖳 info.losangeles@france guide.com), and Chicago: 676 N Michigan Ave, Suite 3770, Chicago, Il 60601-2819 (☎ 312-751-7800, 🖳 infochicago@franceguide.com). **Spanish**: (☎ 212-265-8822, 🖳 www.okspain.org, nyork@tourspain.es), 666 Fifth Avenue 35th, New York, NY 10103. There are also Spanish tourist offices in Chicago (☎ 312-642-1992); Los Angeles (☎ 213-658-7188) and Miami (☎ 305-358-1992).

Route options

The route that you choose will depend on your level of experience, the time available, and what you particularly want to see. There are a variety of footpaths through the mountains but worthy of special mention are the three trans-Pyrenean routes. For an overall **route map** see inside back cover.

GRANDE RANDONNÉE (GR) 10

The GR10 is one of the network of French long-distance paths which cover much of the country. Generally, these routes are well marked and maintained by local volunteers, and the GR10 is no exception. Throughout its 700km course from the Atlantic to the Mediterranean there are only a few places where route-finding causes any real difficulty. Likewise in all but a few areas, the GR10 is well supplied with facilities en route. Day stages tend to start with a climb out of a valley and end with a descent into another valley in order to reach a gîte d'étape or guest house where walkers can stay the night. For many, this may sound unlike what they had in mind, and indeed, during the mid-summer holiday there can be a lot of people following the same path. There are, however, benefits: route finding is scarcely ever a problem, leaving plenty of time to enjoy the scenery. If you're walking by yourself and concerned about the safety aspects, it can be reassuring to know that the path you are following is relatively well trodden, and that if you encounter a problem you will most probably be able to get help from fellow walkers. Finally, since there are good facilities along the way, there's no need to carry your life on your back. You can really keep the weight to the minimum and know that you've got somewhere to stay in the evening.

GRAN RECORRIDO (GR) 11

The GR11 is the Spanish coast to coast path which runs through the mountains of Navarra, Aragón and Catalonia. It's much newer than the GR10, and passes through countryside which is far wilder and more remote. There are fewer villages and practically no lodges on the way, so camping and carrying several days' worth of provisions are necessary. The route is, by and large, well marked but route-finding is made trickier by the inaccuracy of the Spanish maps. Nonetheless, the GR11 passes through some incredibly beautiful areas and has much to recommend it.

HAUTE RANDONNÉE PYRÉNÉENNE (HRP)

The HRP is the classic high-level coast to coast route. It attempts to follow the ridge of the mountain range from Atlantic to Mediterranean, crossing between

France and Spain as the land dictates. Trekkers on the HRP may still find snow in the high passes in early to mid-June, and an ice axe is necessary in certain places in early summer. There are few places where the route descends to the valleys, so that food and a tent must be carried throughout. The HRP should be attempted only by experienced mountain trekkers.

High-route walkers tend to be rather dismissive of the GR10 (*tranquille* is the word they use) and there's no doubt that the scenery is much wilder and more mountainous along the HRP than on the lower paths. In some ways, ironically, the GR10 is harder work; the HRP tends to stay on the ridge of the mountains, only coming down where necessary, whereas the GR10 literally climbs and descends into every valley in order to stay much closer to civilization.

OVERALL

Walkers intent on trekking from coast to coast tend to decide on one or other of the three options above and to follow the route religiously. This is as much for practical reasons as for others: there are separate guidebooks for each of the routes, and few maps show all three routes in relation to each other. There's no reason why, with a little planning, you shouldn't take the best of each route. I met a group of walkers who had hired a guide to take them on an individual route across the Pyrenees, combining elements of the GR10, GR11 and HRP as seemed most interesting at the time.

This book gives a complete description of the GR10 (ie all the stages from the Atlantic to the Mediterranean) and also describes about two-thirds of the

---

❑ ROUTE MARKINGS

Regular way marking along the GR10 and GR11 generally means that route-finding is simple. The fact that much of the way is so well marked can, however, sometimes cause a problem: when walkers encounter a stretch of path with no markings, they assume that they must be in the wrong!

GR10/GR11

The route of the GR10 is indicated with red-and-white waymarks, which may be painted on trees, rocks or buildings. A white line next to a red line marks the way. If the pair of lines has a stem beneath it so that it seems to form a 'flag', there is a turning ahead (in the direction of the flag). A red-and-white cross indicates that you have come the wrong way. There are variations but these are usually fairly self-evident: a pair of lines which clearly bend left or right may indicate that you should follow the path around a corner.

GR10/GR11
ROUTE

GR11 markings are also in red and white and are very similar to those on the GR10.

WRONG
WAY

OR

TURN LEFT
AHEAD

HRP

HRP markings, usually dark red, are not so formalized; in some areas they're clear and in others they're non-existent.

GR11. In addition, connections with some of the best sections of the HRP are included, as are a few interesting variants and suggested itineraries. Of course it's impossible to cover all the options, and the most interesting way to travel is also to do a bit of exploring for yourself off the beaten track.

What to take

The basic essentials
What you decide to pack in your rucksack will depend largely on the sort of walk that you intend to do. If you plan to camp, you will need a tent, cooking gear and all the other bits and pieces, whereas if you're going to be staying in refuges and gîtes, you can make do with much less. The overriding principle, however, is to keep your baggage as light as possible. Be brutally objective about which items you really need and which ones you can do without. Remember that if your pack feels heavy when you try it on at home, it will feel a great deal heavier after you've hauled it up a couple of steep hills. There is a standard procedure amongst all but the best organized GR10 walkers: within the first week most people make for a post office in order to send home large bundles of surplus items.

What to pack it all in
Unless you're going on an organized trek where the company is going to move your baggage for you, you'll need a good **rucksack**. A compromise needs to be struck between getting one big enough to hold all your gear, and one so big that you end up filling it with unnecessary items; a rucksack of about 65 litres' capacity should be ample. It's a good idea to get one with a couple of external zip-up pockets; being able to put a few essential items (water bottle, snacks, waterproof jacket etc) in pockets separate from the rest of your gear means that you can get to them quickly and easily. You don't need a state-of-the-art backpack with loads of adjustment straps but whatever you buy should be robust and feel comfortable.

A **small day sack**, a little rucksack of, say, 20 litres' capacity, can also be invaluable for carrying camera, film and other essentials if you go off sightseeing or for a day walk. This smaller bag should be frameless so that it can be squashed up in the top of your rucksack when you don't need it.

Sleeping bag
Even if you plan to stay in gîtes every night, you'll need a sleeping bag of some sort, as gîte owners insist on the use of a bag to keep the mattresses from getting dirty. At the most basic level, since almost all gîtes provide blankets, you could probably make do with just a **sheet sleeping bag**. On the other hand, if you take only a sheet bag you'll have a chilly night if you ever come across a place without blankets or have to spend a night in a cabane, let alone outdoors. The best compromise, if you plan to stay in gîtes, is a light (one- or two-season)

sleeping bag. If you're going to be camping, you'll probably need a three-season bag. Whatever bag you end up with, ensure that you have a 'compression sack' into which it can be packed, so that it takes up a minimum of space. A **liner** of some sort is a good idea to protect the bag itself.

A **sleeping mat** is essential if you're planning to camp but is a waste of space if you're going to be using gîtes or refuges. If you're heading for a part of the GR10 where there's a lack of accommodation, you have a dilemma: do you carry a sleeping mat which will be used only on two or three occasions, or rough it out for a couple of nights? A compromise would be to buy a small 'thermarest' style inflatable mattress; alternatively, cut down a foam sleeping mat so that you have a section just big enough to cushion your hips and shoulders.

Footwear and foot care
A good pair of walking boots is essential. Pyrenean footpaths are made up of sharp, loose stones, so ensure that your boots have good ankle support and sturdy soles, with enough protection so that you don't feel every pebble. There are many places, too, where paths pass over large areas of rocks, requiring a certain amount of boulder hopping; boots with good grip on the soles inspire a lot more confidence and are safer.

Choosing boots The choice of boot is a matter of personal preference: whatever is most comfortable for you is best. Make sure that the boots fit well; they should not be so loose as to allow rubbing on the heel but there should be enough room at the front so that on long downhill sections you don't get battered toes. If you plan to wear gaiters (not necessary but useful in some cases) ensure that the boots will take them, and if you're going to wear crampons (these shouldn't be necessary but see Mountain Safety, pp34-7) again check that they will fit.

● **Socks** Some people swear that wearing two pairs of socks, a thin inner pair and a thick outer pair, is the best way to avoid blisters; others simply go for a single pair of thick socks. Whatever you choose, ensure that they are natural fibre or at least a good ratio mixed fibre as they are better for your feet and are easier to keep clean.

● **Foot care** There are many ways to protect your feet, but unfortunately none of them is foolproof. Some people prepare for a walking holiday by rubbing white spirit into their feet; over three or four weeks, this hardens the skin and thus helps to prevent blisters. Another good way to avoid blisters is to put zinc oxide tape/plaster (available at any chemist) on the patches that are likely to cause problems – heels and toes in particular. The tape, rather than your skin, then takes the friction of the boot. There are numerous other products on the market, including 'moleskin', 'foot cushions' and special blister treatment packs available from sports stores.

The best way of looking after your feet is to wash and dry them thoroughly and give them every opportunity to breathe, wearing sandals or flip-flops in the evening. Ensure that your socks are clean and dry, and that your boots fit well. Lace them firmly particularly towards the ankle to give good support.

Packing your kit
Everyone has their own way of packing a rucksack, but a few general pointers may be helpful:

● **Waterproof it!** Almost inevitably there will be times when you and your rucksack get soaked. If the clothing and sleeping bag inside the rucksack get wet too, the results will be at least uncomfortable and at worst dangerous. Spending a night in damp clothes and a wet sleeping bag could easily lead to hypothermia. Ensure that your gear is thoroughly waterproofed. Rucksack liners (large heavy-duty plastic bags) can be bought from camping stores. Put everything inside the bag and fold or tie the top; if there's not enough room to get the sleeping bag and clothes into the same liner, get two or more.

● **Have a system** Develop a system so that you know where your stuff is inside the rucksack. For easy access, keep items that you want to get to quickly (guidebook, waterproof etc) near the top of the bag. Put all items in separate plastic bags if they're going to be packed outside the main liner.

● **Food** Fresh food goes off quickly in the heat; chocolate melts. To avoid this bury your edibles deep inside your rucksack. If you're going to be carrying a lot of food, put it all in a large container (eg a plastic biscuit box) and pack this halfway down your rucksack. Try to put the rucksack in the shade when you're resting.

● **Extra footwear** It's a good idea to carry a second pair of shoes, to allow your walking boots time to air in the evenings. Whatever you choose, ensure that they're light. Flip-flops or 'trekking sandals' allow your feet to breathe; trainers take up more space but are more practical if you're going to be wearing them to go sightseeing.

Clothes
In general, the summer months in the Pyrenees are warm, so you don't need to bring lots of kit and, unless you're planning to camp at altitude, you won't need too much warm clothing. For everyday walking in the Pyrenees, the standard gear for most people is shorts, T-shirt, and sun hat.

● **Shorts/trousers** Most people wear shorts but if you're prone to sunburn loose cotton trousers are more sensible. Whatever you choose to wear, ensure that they're robust, and light enough to dry quickly after washing or if you get wet.

● **Shirts** Although T-shirts are good for trekking, you should pack at least one long-sleeved shirt. This is useful for wearing in the evening when the temperature drops, and also during the day if your arms and neck get sunburnt.

● **Warm gear** You need to carry at least one item of warm gear: a fleece jacket or a jumper is ideal. A set of thermal underwear takes up very little space in a rucksack and, if you're camping or staying in a cabane, can make all the difference between a comfortable night and an uncomfortable one. For those camping at altitude, or in the very early or late season, other warm gear is necessary – a woolly hat and gloves are essential.

● **Underwear** Three changes of whatever you usually wear is fine.

● **Sun hat** This really is a must. The sun can be bakingly hot, particularly when it is reflected off the rocks on all sides. A broad brim protects the vulnerable nose and the back of the neck. It doesn't matter if the hat looks silly as long as it does the job.

● **Socks** Three changes of socks should be enough; if you're planning to wear an inner and outer pair this obviously means six pairs of socks in total.

● **Swimsuit** Not essential though it could be a good idea to have one. The lakes are very cold but some people brave them, and some towns have swimming pools, which are very welcome after a hot day's trekking.

● **Towel** Make this a small towel, preferably quite thin, so that it takes up as little space as possible and dries quickly.

● **Waterproof** A waterproof is essential if you're going to be trekking through the Basque country, where it can be very wet. Even in the rest of the Pyrenees, although it really doesn't rain too much, when the skies open they do so in a serious way. Some walkers also go for a pair of waterproof trousers though for the time that you use them it's debatable whether it's worth carrying the extra weight. The alternative to a waterproof jacket is a poncho which covers you and your rucksack. This is certainly much cheaper; a poncho costs only a few euros and it packs up very small. Most French walkers use them.

● **Gaiters** Gaiters are not essential. For those walking in the Basque country in particular, there are likely to be rainy days when they will come in handy, or mornings when they will protect against rain-soaked undergrowth.

Toiletries
Keep these to a minimum. You'll need to bring soap and a small bottle of shampoo. Loo paper is provided in most gîtes but not in many refuges; bring a roll just in case. If you're going to be camping, bring a lighter too, so that you can burn the used paper. Ensure that you pack a tube of high-factor sun lotion to protect your face and neck, in particular. Lip balm is also useful.

Some sort of travel detergent is essential for washing clothes. Camping stores stock biodegradable clothes washing liquid which will not pollute natural water sources.

While biting insects are not really a problem in the Pyrenees, repellent can be useful as some areas are inhabited by horseflies, which have a painful sting.

Medical kit
There are excellent medical facilities available in France and Spain, so you're not trying to pack a complete operating theatre but just enough remedies to sort out minor problems. You should be able to fit all of this in a small waterproof box. Take along paracetamol for headaches and aspirin for inflammation of the joints; both can be used as general pain killers. Plasters/band aids are useful for small cuts, and antiseptic cream or wipes will help to prevent infection. A small bandage can have a number of uses, and if you think that your knees might give

you trouble, elastic knee supports are invaluable. Imodium is useful if you have diarrhoea. Water purification tablets are necessary – see p37-8 for details. Bring ample supplies of any prescription drugs which you need; if you have contact lenses pack plenty of cleaning solution.

General items

● **Essential** No one should go out in the mountains without a compass. Other essential items include: sunglasses; a torch (most walkers choose to carry a head torch) and a spare set of batteries; a loud whistle to summon assistance in an emergency; a small sewing kit; a penknife; two one-litre water bottles; a map case.

● **Useful** A long-burning candle is a good idea if you plan to spend much time camping or in cabanes as you'll save battery power that way; matches or a lighter; a few metres of string for use as a clothes line; a universal bathplug (many washrooms in gîtes don't have plugs, which can make clothes washing tricky); a small pair of binoculars; a diary; an address book; a pack of cards.

Extra walking gear

A walking stick or pole is extremely useful, mainly for taking some of the shock off your knees when you're going downhill, but also for keeping unfriendly dogs at bay and helping you keep your balance when you're fording streams. You can buy wooden walking poles in many of the small villages throughout the mountains; alternatively you can go for the modern approach and get one or two extendible ski-style poles.

From mid-June to late September an ice axe is not necessary on most of the routes described here. Note, however, the point made on pp35-7 ('Snow Free Period') that some of the higher passes may not be free from snow until as late as early-mid July. If you're planning on following a route that includes high passes (ie over 2000m) before early-mid July, either bring an ice axe and crampons or be prepared to alter your itinerary if it turns out that there is still snow on your route.

Some people buy a waterproof rucksack cover, which fits over the outside of the pack and keeps it dry during showers; it's no substitute for waterproofing gear inside the bag itself. If you're going to be walking off the beaten track, and if you're not carrying a tent, you might also choose to take a survival bag. If you get into trouble, this can be guaranteed to give protection against the elements and, being brightly coloured, will be visible to searching helicopter crews.

Finally, even if you're not planning to camp at all, take a small amount of food with you for emergencies. Keep this separate from your daily snacks and open it only if you really need it; make sure that the food you choose to carry will keep for several weeks.

Cooking gear

In France, the blue Camping Gaz cylinders, both the old type and the new resealable version, are available just about everywhere. Methylated spirits (*alcool à brûler*) is sold in hardware stores and supermarkets. Coleman/Epigas cylinders are less easy to obtain. You can buy a suitable gas bottle with the right screw thread in some French hardware stores; the French use them for blowtorches. Although these cylinders work OK, the bottles are very tall, so they're not particularly practical. Special mention is made in this book of stores where Epigas (or the French equivalent) is available.

In Spain there are long sections of the GR11 where it's hard to get hold of any fuel at all. Some campsites and refuges sell the old-style (puncture type) Camping Gaz cylinders, but few if any sell the new-style cylinders and Coleman/ Epigas refills are equally rare. There are several villages where supplies of all types of camping fuel are available (eg Torla and Benasque) but these are few and far between. A possible solution to this problem is to use a multi-fuel stove which can burn petrol.

Provisions

If you're going from gîte to gîte you'll need very few provisions – just snacks for the day. You can stock up on these at each small village that you come to. Apples, chocolate, peanuts and raisins are all good choices. You can also ask the owners of the gîte or refuge if they can provide sandwiches or a packed lunch.

Keen campers all have their favourite foods. In general you want the burden to be as light as possible, so dried foods are best: instant soups, pasta and mashed potato all make for a filling meal; rice is good too, but it takes quite a long time to cook. A little tin of meat or a few spices add flavour. Most people also carry coffee or tea, and some bring powdered milk which can be made up and used on breakfast cereal. Dried sausage (*saucisson*) is obtainable everywhere and is tasty as well as easy to carry. Excellent ewes' milk cheese (*fromage de brebis*) can often be bought at shepherds' huts high up in the mountains.

Lightening your load

One method, which lots of GR10 walkers hit upon to lessen the load they have to carry, is to post parcels ahead to strategic points, where they can be picked up en route. The early stages of the GR10, for example, have plenty of accommodation, whereas the later sections do not. Why carry a camping stove for the first three weeks when you can pick it up from a post office near the spot where you're actually going to need it? If you plan to walk the whole of the GR10 you will have to use at least ten maps. Take three or four at a time, and pick up the rest along the way, at the same time posting the used maps home. A trekker I met while researching this book, wrote:

'I learnt much about the French postal system along the way. The posting of my most valuable tramping equipment by ordinary post from Bidarray to Luchon was successful, even if it did take them a little time (10 minutes) to find the parcel. However, I then posted substantially the same parcel contents on to Banyuls, again by ordinary post. A postal employee apparently carefully removed the label from my parcel and stuck it to a fake parcel, the contents of which were useless. My tip to your readers is that, when posting valuable items in France, be sure that you register and insure the parcel. It is only by this means that you can reasonably certain of it being delivered correctly. It is not unreasonably expensive to do so.

I also posted several parcels from various places back to Australia. They contained mostly used guidebooks, exposed photographic film and literature on local detail. Three out of six of these have not arrived ... again the lesson is don't use ordinary post.'

Andrew Craig (Australia)

Money – see also p58

Most lodges and refuges do not accept credit cards or travellers' cheques. **Cash** is always a safe option for paying your bills so carry plenty of local currency to avoid frequent trips down from the mountains to find a bank.

At most banks there's usually an **ATM** (cash dispenser), enabling Visa, MasterCard, Cirrus, Maestro, Eurocard and EuroCheque cardholders to withdraw local currency directly from their home bank account. Visa (Carte Bleue), is the most widely recognized **credit card** in France and MasterCard comes a close second. Rather than using a credit card in the ATM, use your **bank card** (debit/cheque guarantee card) which will probably have one of the electronic money symbols (Cirrus, Maestro etc.) shown on it; with a credit card you'll get a cash advance on your credit card account and you may have to pay interest on this money. The location of ATMs and banks is noted in the guide section of this book.

Travellers' cheques (American Express, Thomas Cook or any of the other well-known brands) can also be useful. If you cannot get to a bank, remember that in France all but the smallest post offices will change money. Note that you will not find anywhere to change money on Saturday afternoons and Sundays.

Photographic equipment

Film is easily available in both France and Spain but you should bring enough to ensure that you don't get caught short when the perfect shot presents itself. There is generally plenty of light, so 100ASA film should be fast enough. Ensure that you bring a spare set of batteries for your camera as many cameras stop functioning completely when the power goes.

RECOMMENDED READING

The Pyrenean classics

Some of the most famous books about the Pyrenees date from the 19th century or early years of the 20th. If you can find any of these you'll be doing very well indeed; but they're fun to look out for and would make fascinating reading (quite apart from the fact that they're very valuable).

The classic text is *Souvenirs d'un Montagnard* by Count Henry Russell, but Charles Packe's *Guide to the Pyrénées*, published by Longmans in 1880 comes a close second. Only slightly less rare is Hilaire Belloc's *The Pyrénées*, published initially by Methuen in 1909. The Pyrenees were the subject of a vast number of travelogues published around the turn of the 20th century, many by otherwise unknown authors. Most of these accounts tend to be fairly repetitive but they can be quite fun reading, at times.

General guidebooks

There are a number of good guidebooks on the market if you intend to go exploring away from the mountain trails. Cadogan Guides' *Gascony and the Pyrenees* is detailed for the French Pyrenees as far east as Ax-les-Thermes, while the excellent Rough Guides' *The Pyrenees* gives equal coverage on both sides of the border and along the length of the range. *Discover Pyrenees* by Berlitz is a good general guide if you've got your own transport and the time to explore.

Walking guidebooks

Cicerone have guides to various parts of the Pyrenees, for walkers and mountaineers, including *The Pyrenees* (Kev Reynolds) in their full-colour Mountain Guides series.

The classic book about the HRP High Level Route is Georges Véron's *Pyrenees High Level Route*.

There are numerous guidebooks in French, but the classic guides are the *Topoguides* which are published by the Fédération Française de la Randonnée Pédestre. Four guides cover the entire GR10, but they're quite expensive.

In Spanish, the most comprehensive guide to the GR11 is the *GR11 Senda Pirenaica*, produced by the Comité Nacional de Senderas de Gran Recorrido. The fourth edition (last published in April 2000, ISBN: 84-8321-066-5) is in two parts: a guide book with lots of information about the routes/wildlife/history of the region etc, and a separate folder containing 47 route maps, one for each day stage.

Flora and fauna

There are a number of well illustrated guides on the market; what you buy will depend largely on how heavy a manual you are prepared to carry in your rucksack! Collins do several suitable books: the *Collins Field Guide – Birds of Britain and Europe* is comprehensive, but may be a little too weighty for most walkers; the *Collins Nature Guide* of the same title is handier.

Flores del Pirineo (Editorial Pirineo) is a good colour guide available in some bookshops in the Spanish Pyrenees. The names of flowers are given in English.

Other books

Fiction There's not a lot here to choose from. Ernest Hemingway's novel *Fiesta* is largely set in Pamplona, in the foothills of the Navarrese Pyrenees, and his characters briefly visit Burguete (near Roncesvalles). The description of Pamplona during the festival of San Fermin (the bull running) is classic. If your command of the French language is good, pick up a copy of the novel *Ramuntcho* by Pierre Loti; the fictional village of Etchezar is modelled on Sare in the Basque Country.

Non fiction In *The Man who Married a Mountain* (Bantam, 2005), Rosemary Bailey follows in the footsteps of Count Henry Russell, to create this fascinating portrait of the 19th century mountaineer and writer (see opposite) and his contemporaries.

Laurie Lee's *A Moment of War* contains a brief description of his passage across the Pyrenees to join the Republican forces during the Spanish Civil War, and an absorbing account of what he found when he got to Spain. Of a completely different genre, speleologist Norbert Casteret's book *Ten Years Under the Earth* details his incredible exploits in the 1920s and 1930s. Casteret was responsible for proving that the Garonne had its source in the Maladetta, discovered the highest ice cave in the world (in the Ordesa National Park) and found the oldest statues in the world, in a prehistoric cave dwelling. The fact that his equipment often consisted of no more that a handful of candles and his bathing costume somehow makes his story all the more fascinating!

The most recently-published travelogue is *Backpacks, Boots and Baguettes: Walking in the Pyrenees,* by Simon Calder and Mick Webb (Virgin Books, 2004). It's the entertaining account of their travels along the GR10 through France from the Atlantic to the Mediterranean and includes good background and historical information – as one would expect from the travel editor of *The Independent* and a BBC Radio 4 producer. Well worth reading before you go.

Other travelogues include Roger Higham's *Road to the Pyrenees*, published in 1971, which details his exploration of the Pays Basque and Béarn. JM Scott's *From Sea to Ocean, Walking along the Pyrenees*, published in 1969, makes most coast to coast walks nowadays seem rather tame; the author sets off with little clear idea of his exact route but makes plenty of interesting discoveries along the way. In *Clear Waters Rising* by Nicholas Crane, one chapter deals with the Pyrenean section of the author's epic walk across Europe.

There are numerous books in French, most of which seem to be aimed at the tourist market. Editions Sud Ouest have published well-written books about everything from Pyrenean legends to the French Resistance, and local cuisine. There are lots of books, too, about the Cathars.

MAPS

France

The Institut Géographique Nationale (IGN) produce excellent maps. If you intend to stay in the French Pyrenees you need only decide whether you want to carry 1:50,000 scale maps or 1:25,000.

● **1:50,000 IGN/Rando Éditions** cover the entire length of the range, with footpaths, gîtes, refuges and cabanes marked. On the French side, the sheets are numbered 1-11, but No 9 is not required if you're sticking to the GR10. These maps are more than sufficient if you plan to stick to the main paths but you should bear in mind that they are not always entirely accurate. New forest and mountain trails are constantly being built, gîtes and refuges open and close, and the GR10 occasionally changes course. Each map sheet also has a list of useful telephone numbers on the bottom.

● **1:25,000** The IGN **Serie Bleue** of 1:25,000 maps covers the whole of France, and has much greater detail than the 1:50,000 series. If you're hoping to go exploring these may be the maps you need but, unless you plan to spend a long time off the beaten track, don't bother. You will need a minimum of 18 maps to cover the whole of the Pyrenees, and quite apart from having to carry them, this is likely to make a large dent in your budget.

Spain

● **1:50,000 IGN/Rando Éditions** If you're only planning to nip across into Spain for a quick excursion, some of the French IGN maps give coverage across

---

(Opposite): Some of the most impressive scenery in the region is in the central Pyrenees. **Top**: Just south of the border with France, the village of Torla (see p270) is the gateway to the Ordesa National Park. **Bottom left**: The Brèche de Roland, see p122. **Bottom right**: Ordesa Canyon, see p272. (Photos © Bryn Thomas).

the border. The Aigüestortes National Park, for instance, is largely covered by Map No 6. The process of extending IGN coverage across the border, which seems to have been started because Spanish mapping was so poor, is continuing, with about 75% of the Spanish side covered on Map Nos 25, 24, 23, 22, 21, 20 (working west to east).

● **Comité Nacional de Senderas de Gran Recorrido** The guidebook *GR11 Senda Pirenaica*, produced by the Comité Nacional de Senderas de Gran Recorrido, comes complete with a pack of 47 maps, one for each day stage of the GR11, with a few extra sheets detailing some route variants. These are by far the most accurate maps available of the GR11, as well as being the most convenient to carry. They don't, however, show much apart from the route itself, so they're no use if you want to go exploring.

● **Editorial Alpina** Editorial Alpina produce a series of booklets and maps which cover almost the whole of the Spanish Pyrenees. The booklets, which are in Spanish, give useful local information and contain a walking map for the area. The maps are notably hazy on detail (containing, for example, no depiction of vegetation) and there are occasional glaring inaccuracies (on one map the scale bar is the wrong size for the particular scale of map!). Almost as confusing is the fact that they are produced in different scales – a 1:25,000 map may abut a 1:40,000 map. If you've come across the border from France and have been using the 1:50,000 series, you may well find yourself using three different maps, all with different scales, in quick succession.

Having said this, the Editorial Alpina maps are widely used, and once you get used to them they are generally adequate. At least 18 maps are required to cover the Pyrenees, although the series does not have a sheet covering the western end of the mountains – the first map is of the Roncesvalles area.

● **Spanish Military Survey Maps** Very few people carry these but they are worth considering if you are planning to do a lot of walking in the Spanish mountains. Although they are sometimes very dated, they give accurate contour, building and vegetation detail, which is lacking in the Editorial Alpina series. Whereas Editorial Alpina maps can be bought locally in the Pyrenees, the Military Survey maps cannot, and they're not easy to get hold of in the UK either, so order them well before you leave. Because the map sheets are small, you'll need 20 or more of the 1:50,000 maps to get from coast to coast. 1:25,000 scale military survey maps are also available but are unsuitable for walking because they contain less footpath information.

● **Institut Cartographic Catalunya** Also worth looking out for are the excellent 1:50,000 maps produced by the Institut Cartographic Catalunya. The 11 sheets cover only the area from Andorra to the Mediterranean but are far better than the Editorial Alpina maps for the same area. In the UK they can be ordered through bookshops from Cordee.

(Opposite): **Top**: The Chemin de la Mâture, near Borce (see p106), was carved out of the rock face in the 18th century to allow access to the extensive forests above the Aspe and Ossau valleys. (Photo © Douglas Streatfeild-James). **Bottom**: The medieval town of St-Jean-Pied-de-Port (see pp84-7). (Photo © Henry Stedman).

Where to buy maps

IGN maps should be available at any large travel bookstore and are on sale throughout France. Spanish maps are harder to obtain, and even in the Pyrenees you may find that the shops have sold out of the very map sheet you need so get them before you travel.

Stanfords (☎ 020-7836 1321, 🖥 www.stanfords.co.uk) 12-14 Long Acre, London, WC2E 9LP, is the best place in London to buy maps. They have all the above in stock, although they need advance warning to get the 1:25,000 Spanish Military Survey Maps.

The Map Shop (☎ 01684-593146, 📄 01684 594559, 🖥 www.themapshop.co .uk), 15 High Street, Upton upon Severn, Worcestershire, WR8 0HJ, provides an excellent service if you're short of time. For a small fee they'll mail any map to you, first class.

Mountain safety

GENERAL

Mountain walking is potentially a hazardous activity. Even straightforward sections walked in mid-summer can become difficult or dangerous if you encounter unexpected problems such as poor weather, tiredness or injury. While this book is designed to cover summer trekking routes which are within the ability of most people, any walker must always be aware of the possibility that conditions may change unexpectedly. The following paragraphs highlight some areas which should be considered before starting your trek.

WEATHER AND EQUIPMENT

The weather can change extremely quickly in any mountain region, and the Pyrenees are no exception. While a well-planned trek making use of gîtes along the way can allow you to travel light, you should still be prepared for problems, should they arise. Ensure that you have warm clothing in case the weather turns bad, and take great care to keep your set of warm clothes dry. If this means that, first thing in the morning, you have to get back into the damp clothes you were wearing the day before, do so.

TREKKING ALONE

One of the golden rules of mountain walking is that you always walk in company if at all possible. Sometimes it just doesn't work out that way but there are still things you can do to minimize the risks. Carry a brightly-coloured piece of clothing or a bright plastic survival bag that can attract attention to your position if necessary. Carry a whistle and remember the international distress signal (six sharp blasts from a whistle, followed by a minute's silence).

WEATHER FORECAST SERVICES

There are telephone numbers that you can call in any area to get the latest weather forecast. Bear in mind, however, that the service for, say, Haute Garonne is trying to predict the weather for a wide area of which your corner of the mountains is only a small part. The problem is exacerbated because the weather in the mountains is much less predictable than that lower down.

Often the guardian of a refuge or gîte is a better source of information about local conditions than any recorded message. The latest forecast is often written up in gîtes or in campsites. For forecasts in the following areas telephone:

Western Pyrenees
● **France** Pyrénées Atlantiques (☎ 08.36.68.02.64); mountains (☎ 08.36.68.04.04)
● **Spain** Pays Basque (☎ 807-170 331); Navarre (☎ 807-170 331)

Central Pyrenees
● **France** Hautes Pyrénées (☎ 08.36.68.02.65); Haute Garonne (☎ 08.36.68.02.31); Ariège (☎ 08.36.68.02.04)
● **Spain** Aragón and Catalonia (☎ 807-17.03.80)

Eastern Pyrenees
● **France** Pyrénées Orientales (☎ 08.36.68.02.66)

Lastly, if at all possible, tell someone where you are planning to go. This is not so important if you're sticking to the GR10 or any one of the large mountain trails, but if you're going to go exploring by yourself it's essential.

EXPERIENCE

No great level of experience is required to walk the GR10 – it's well marked and there's plenty of shelter along the way. If you're thinking of doing the HRP or of going off the beaten track, you will definitely need to be a confident map reader with a sound knowledge of high-level trekking. Remember that although the route ahead may look simple in bright sunshine, in rain and mist it's very easy to get lost even on a relatively straightforward section.

Do make sure that you are fit. The GR10 may not be technically difficult but there's an awful lot of climbing and descending and, if your body isn't used to it, the first few days will be painful. Knee and ankle strains can often be avoided by ensuring that you've done some training before you set out on your trek.

SNOW

As already mentioned above (see p20), although the walking season in the Pyrenees starts in mid-June, there may well still be snow on the high passes until early or even mid-July. While it's often possible to cross snow and ice safely with the right equipment and with a proper knowledge of how to use it correctly, if you're equipped only for summer walking attempting such crossings could be dangerous. In particular, two hazards stand out:

EMERGENCY HELP

Several different organizations are involved in mountain rescue. In France responsibility in a particular area may fall upon the **Peloton de Gendarmerie de Haute Montagne** (PGHM), the **Compagnie Republicaine de la Sécurité** (CRS), or the local **pompiers** (fire brigade). Emergency medical assistance is from the **Service d'Assistance Medicale Urbain** (SAMU). In Spain, groups range from specialist mountain rescue organizations to the local **bombers** (fire service). Key telephone numbers are given below, but if you're carrying a map in the Éditions Randonnées Pyrénéenes series, you will find extra numbers for local services listed next to the map key.

Western Pyrenees
● **France** PGHM Oloron-Ste-Marie (☎ 05.59.10.02.50); SAMU (☎ 15); Gendarmerie (☎ 17); Pompiers (☎ 18)
● **Spain** Bombers de Navarra (☎ 112); SOS Aragón (☎ 112)

Central Pyrenees
● **France** CRS Gavarnie (☎ 05.62.92.48.24); PHGM Pierrefitte-Nestalas (☎ 05.62.92.71.82); PHGM Luchon (☎ 05.61.79.28.36); CRS Luchon (☎ 05.61.79.83.79); PHGM Savignac (Ariège) (☎ 05.61.64.22.58); SAMU (☎ 15); Gendarmerie (☎ 17); Pompiers (☎ 18)
● **Spain** Bombers de Aragón (☎ 062); Bombers de la Generalitat de Catalunya (☎ 085); Bombers de Andorra (☎ 112,) SOS Aragón (☎ 112)

Eastern Pyrenees
● **France** PGHM Osséja (☎ 04.68.04.51.03); CRS Perpignan (☎ 04.68.61.79.20); SAMU (☎ 15); Gendarmerie (☎ 17); Pompiers (☎ 18)
● **Spain** Bombers de la Generalitat de Catalunya (☎ 085)

● Residual areas of snow may start to melt from the underneath. As the rocks on the mountain side warm up they can melt the snow in contact with them. In this way, a gap can open up between the rocks and the snow/ice above. Melt water running down the slope may enlarge any cavity, until there is a substantial gap between the crust of snow on the surface, and the rocks below. If the crust of snow gets too thin a walker could fall through. At best this would be extremely disconcerting. At worst it could result in serious injury.

● Stopping yourself from sliding on a steep snow slope is likely to be impossible if you do not have an ice axe. The last sections of snow to melt are those on slopes which receive the least sunshine. Often these slopes are steep and there are inevitably rocks at the bottom of the slope. Should you slip while crossing such a snow slope there will be little chance of stopping yourself sliding at great speed and hitting the rocks below, again with chances of serious injury.

Having highlighted these two particular hazards, it has to be said that many trekkers do walk across sections of snow in the early summer, and few experience problems. The difficulty comes in gauging what's safe and what isn't. This guidebook is about summer trekking only, and it would be inappropriate to try to offer further guidance, beyond the following points:

● Before starting in early or mid-summer on a route that involves crossing a high section (ie over 2000m) ask for local advice about conditions. Possible sources of information include the guardian at a refuge, staff at a tourist office (or Bureau des Guides), or other walkers. Make it clear (if such is the case) that you are not equipped with anything beyond walking gear – in case anyone assumes that you're carrying mountaineering equipment.

● Although an ice axe is essential for crossing very steep sections of snow and ice, walking poles are extremely useful for stabilizing yourself on less steep sections of snow. Note that walking poles will not help in stopping you if you fall and start to slide.

● If you're trekking very early in the season, take appropriate equipment and know how to use it.

● If in doubt about the safety of any section or your ability to cross it, turn back.

MOUNTAIN RESCUE SERVICES

There are mountain rescue services on both sides of the border. Remember, if you are involved in an accident and need to summon the rescue services they will need an exact location of where to find the casualty. **See Emergency Help, opposite, for emergency contact numbers.**

Mountain rescue helicopters serve the most popular areas of the Pyrenees. The sign for a person on the ground to alert a helicopter that they need assistance is to hold both arms above their head in a 'Y' shape; so **never** wave both your arms at a passing helicopter unless you need help.

Health precautions

POSSIBLE PROBLEMS

The Pyrenees are not high enough to cause altitude sickness but they are plenty high enough to cause problems if you have not prepared physically for your trek. As long as you are in good health when you start there are likely to be few problems. Sunburn is a potential danger.

Water purification

Water from the taps of any lodge or gîte in Spain or France will be of drinking quality, and all refuges have a tap or pipe (usually outside) where drinking water is freely available. The only question, therefore, is whether or not to purify water taken from mountain streams; some trekkers do and some don't. The generally received wisdom is that if there may be livestock grazing further upstream it's best not to drink the water without purifying it. Since flocks of sheep can be found grazing well above 2000m in the Pyrenees this effectively means that you have to purify almost all except spring water which is taken directly from the side of the mountain.

Water may be purified either by boiling or by using chemical methods. If you're going to boil it, technically you should do so for around five minutes in order to kill all bugs. For chemical purification there are generally two types of products available: chlorine or iodine based. Although both are pretty effective against bacteria, iodine is more reliable in getting rid of other pathogens and is the better option. Either get hold of a product such as Potable Aqua – where you simply add tablets to your water, or buy some 2% Tincture of Iodine from a chemist. Add five drops of the tincture to each litre of water and allow it to stand for twenty minutes. It's not particularly good for you to drink large quantities of iodized water, so try to use chemical purification only as a last resort.

TREATMENT UNDER EU REGULATIONS

Members of EU countries should complete an E111 form, which entitles them to treatment by the state-run health services of other EU countries.

In the UK the form is available from any post office. However, any UK resident who applied for an E111 before 19 August 2004 needs to apply for a new one for travel in 2005. E111s are now issued to individuals whatever their age but it is only necessary to complete one application form. Take the form with you on your travels, and take a photocopy as well; a hospital or clinic may demand to keep a copy of a patient's E111 when they are treated. The form does not mean that you will get free treatment on the spot, and you may find that you are expected to pay something. Theoretically, however, you should be able to claim most of the costs back when you get home although reports indicate that it can be a slow and complicated process.

During 2005 the European Health Insurance Card (EHIC) will be issued automatically to anyone with one of the new E111s. For further information call ☎ 0800-555777, or visit 🖥 www.postoffice.co.uk.

TRAVEL INSURANCE

An E111 form is no substitute for proper medical cover on your travel insurance. Should you need to be brought home for treatment, or if you call out the mountain rescue services, you may find yourself faced with a large bill. Many travel insurance policies make an extra charge to cover sporting activities, and trekking often comes into this category. If you don't tell them that you're going to be trekking, your insurance could well be invalid when you come to make a claim.

PART 2: THE PYRENEES

Facts about the Pyrenees

GEOGRAPHICAL BACKGROUND

Stretching from the Atlantic to the Mediterranean, the Pyrenees form a natural barrier some 450km long between Continental Europe and the Iberian Peninsula. At the eastern and western ends of the range, the mountains descend to the coastal plains in a series of foothills, while the central area of the Pyrenees boasts a number of impressive peaks – the highest of which is the Pico de Aneto (3404m). The tiny principality of Andorra lies in the middle of the mountains, near the eastern end.

CLIMATE

The summer climate of the Pyrenees is warmer than many people imagine. The mountains are, however, subject to a number of climatic factors, which make for marked regional variations in weather along the range.

The east–west factor

Although the range is only 450km long, there is a great contrast in climate at each end. In the western Pyrenees, the weather is governed by systems coming in from the Atlantic, often bringing rain and cloud. While this means that you're more likely to get wet at some stage, it also contributes to a fabulously green landscape.

The eastern end of the range gets much of its weather from the more stable Mediterranean climate; good conditions are pretty much guaranteed but trekking can be hot and dusty work.

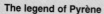

The legend of Pyrène

According to legend, the Pyrenees are named after Pyrène, the daughter of a king who ruled the area. His court, it is said, was in the cave at Lombrives, near Tarascon-sur-Ariège, the largest and most spectacular cavern in the region.

Hercules, engaged in the Twelve Labours imposed on him by jealous Juno, noticed the young and beautiful Pyrène, and they fell in love. He stayed for a while in the royal household promising to return for Pyrène after accomplishing his next task. Soon afterwards, however, Pyrène discovered that she was pregnant, and fled into the woods to escape her father's anger. As she wandered through the trees, she was attacked by a lion, and cried out to Hercules to help her. Although he was far away across the world, he heard her cry and came as fast as he could. He arrived too late, however, and found her dead. In anguish he threw up a range of mountains as her tombstone, and named them after her – the Pyrenees.

❏ **Typical temperatures in South-West France (May to October)**

Aquitaine (western Pyrenees): May 18°C, June 23.7°C, July 27.2°C, August 25.7°C, September 24.2°C, October 19.7°C

Midi-Pyrénées (central Pyrenees): May 19.1°C, June 26.4°C, July 27.6°C, August 27.2°C, September 25°C, October 19.3°C

Languedoc Roussillon (eastern Pyrenees): May 20.1°C, June 26.5°C, July 28.4°C, August 28.1°C, September 26.1°C, October 21.1°C

The north–south divide

The Pyrenees form a divide between the weather systems of Continental Europe and the Iberian peninsula; in summer, conditions are notably more stable and sunnier in the Spanish mountains than in their French counterparts. If you are caught up in a spell of bad weather in France, it's worth considering going south. Travelling only a few kilometres across the border can take you from rainy, misty France to bright sunshine in Spain.

Altitude

The other major factor governing the climate is altitude. With mountains of over 3000 metres in height, wind and weather conditions can vary greatly.

Typical summertime temperatures are given above but note that these are figures for the whole of the *département*, and thus will not account for reduced temperatures in the high mountains. Note too that, as in all mountain ranges, conditions can be very unpredictable; you can easily go from extreme heat to extreme cold in just a short space of time.

Storms

The Pyrenees, particularly on the French side, are prone to rain storms in the late afternoons; thus most people try to make an early start and complete the day's walking by the early afternoon. If the skies are clear you have plenty of time to dawdle, but it is comforting to be within easy reach of your destination should the weather start to change.

HISTORICAL OUTLINE

For centuries, the Pyrenees have been a natural and cultural watershed, and the history of the region is every bit as complex and intricate as its topography. While great empires and cultural movements lapped at the base of the mountains, small pockets could remain unaffected. Individual kingdoms constantly altered shape and influence through local alliances. The border as we see it today did not become fixed until 1659, with the signing of the Treaty of the Pyrenees.

Because specific areas often have a story all of their own, a synopsis of the local history is given at the beginning of each section of the book. This historical overview aims only to give an outline of important events in France and Spain which had their inevitable effect on the kingdoms of the Pyrenees.

Prehistory

Some of the oldest remains in Europe have been found at the foot of the Pyrenees. Bones uncovered in a cave at Tautavel, near Perpignan, are believed to be those of an ancestor of homo sapiens, who lived around 450,000 years ago. The significance of the find can be appreciated when you consider that the next nearest remains so far unearthed in the area, belonged to a cave culture which lived over 400,000 years later. Even this is pretty early, though, and the cave paintings which have been found at, among other places, Niaux, near Tarascon-sur-Ariège, are immensely significant. The people who painted these images lived somewhere between 10,000 and 30,000 years ago.

To put all of this in perspective, Neolithic culture, during which man began to grow crops and to keep animals, reached the mountains about 7000 years ago, and little is known about the people who lived here at the time. There are few remains of the Neolithic Pyreneans, although a scattering of dolmens and stone circles suggests the area was widely settled.

Pre Roman

Coming into surer territory, it seems likely that from about 1000BC onwards, the Celts drifted through the Pyrenees from central and northern Europe. It's possible that the ancestors of the Basques arrived at about this time, too; Roman historians, writing several centuries later, speak of a tribe called the Vascones who were settled in the Pyrenees. At the same time as the Celts were spreading down from Central Europe, the coastline provided access for trading nations. The Greeks, Phoenicians and Carthaginians all set up bases along the Mediterranean coast.

The Romans

In 238BC the Carthaginians invaded Spain, and twenty years later Hannibal used the peninsula as a springboard for his forces, during the Second Punic War. He lost, and the Romans began the long process of incorporating 'Hispania' into their empire. In all, it took them nearly a century to bring the warlike people to some sort of peace, and even then, pockets of the North-West remained effectively out of their influence. It has been suggested that the Basque country was one of these 'independent' areas and thus, while the language of the rest of Spain became Romanized, the Basque language remained unchanged.

At the same time as the Romans were bringing the peninsula to heel, they were also at work to the north of the Pyrenees. By around 50BC the northern slopes were safely under control and incorporated in the Roman province of Aquitania. This was about as near as the Pyrenees have ever got to being united under one rule. The high mountains were still the preserve of the local tribes but the land on both sides and all along the range was firmly Roman.

As Roman power began to wane, however, both Hispania and Gaul suffered a gradual disintegration. The Romans, struggling to protect their homeland from invasion, gradually withdrew their garrisons from the west, leaving the area vulnerable to attacks from the north. In AD409 a huge force passed through the western Pyrenees, and Roman control of the area effectively came to an end. The Romans called for assistance from the Visigoths, who managed to quell the other tribes and became the de facto rulers of the peninsula.

To the north of the Pyrenees, the Visigoths held power for half a century or so, before being pushed back over the mountains by the Franks. The loose-knit collection of tribes in France was brought into some sort of order, towards the end of the fifth century, by the Frankish chief, Clovis, who founded the Merovingian line. Despite this nominal centralization of power, however, the local rulers in the Pyrenees retained almost total autonomy.

The Moors and Charlemagne

While France was slowly descending into chaos, Spain, under the Visigoths, wasn't doing much better. The new rulers inherited what was left of the Roman infrastructure and basked in their good fortune. Consequently when the Moors invaded from North Africa in 711, the Visigoth armies were chronically unprepared. In the space of less than five years, the Moors came to control almost all of the peninsula. A brief attempt to push beyond the Pyrenees, met with defeat at Poitiers in 732, and thenceforth the Muslim sphere of influence remained to the south of the mountains. The Pyrenees became the centre of the Christian resistance to the Moorish occupation, and the unique culture that we can still find in many parts of the mountains is partly attributable to this. Romanesque architecture, which began to flourish in about the 11th century, has some of its finest and earliest examples in the Spanish Pyrenees.

At the same time as the Moors were seizing the peninsula, power was changing hands in France. In 750, Pepin the Short became king of the Franks and founded the Carolingian Dynasty. In 771, following the deaths of both his father (Pepin) and his brother (Carloman), Charles the Great – Charlemagne – became the king. In the 43 years of his rule, Charlemagne extended the French empire to include most of Europe. In doing so he almost succeeded in bringing the Pyrenees back under central control with the formation of the Spanish Marches, a buffer zone to the south of the mountains. Notably Charlemagne also suffered his most famous defeat in the Pyrenees. Answering the request of a Moorish emir for assistance, in 777 Charlemagne crossed the mountains and campaigned on his behalf. While returning to France in 778, however, the rearguard of his army was ambushed and slaughtered by the Basques, near Roncesvalles. The tragedy was immortalized in the medieval lay, the *Chanson de Roland*.

The early Middle Ages

By the start of the eleventh century the scene had changed dramatically. South of the Pyrenees, the Moors were weakened by the collapse of the Umayyad Caliphate, which had been the central power in Muslim Spain. Although it was not until the Battle of Las Navas de Tolosa in 1212 that the tide really turned in favour of the Christian monarchs, fledgling states such as Navarre now had much greater freedom, and began to develop.

Central control had weakened in France too, as Charlemagne's heirs gradually lost their grip over his vast empire. The break-up of the established order on both sides of the Pyrenees allowed the ambitions of local rulers to take flight. Catalonia, which had been part of the Spanish March formed by Charlemagne, now came into its own, and Aragón, under a powerful local lord, became a distinct state. On the northern side of the mountains, Foix and Béarn were but two of the regions which were effectively self-governing.

The High Middle Ages

The Capetian dynasty came to power in France in 987 but initially little was achieved to bring the autonomous states together under central rule. Things looked promising in 1137, when Eleanor of Aquitaine, the heir to the largest of the provinces, became the wife of the French monarch, Louis VII. Fifteen years later, however, the marriage was annulled and she married Henry, Count of Anjou, who became Henry II of England in 1154. This effectively put a whole new twist into the plot, as it brought the whole of Aquitaine under English control.

It should not be supposed that this put all the land north of the Pyrenees into English hands, for much of it was already held by the Spanish. Navarre stretched over today's border and included what we now know as Basse-Navarre, and much of Rousillon and Cerdenya were also in Spanish hands. In 1137 the kingdom of Aragón and the county of Barcelona were united, and James I of Aragón subsequently ruled over a huge chunk of the southern and eastern Pyrenees.

One other event is worthy of special mention from this time: the brutal suppression of the Cathars. The Cathars were a non-violent Christian sect, with a strong following in the eastern Pyrenees. Both for their nonconformist doctrine, and because they posed a threat to the power of the Catholic Church, the movement was branded heretical. After failing to persuade Raymond of Toulouse to do the dirty work, Pope Innocent III declared a crusade against the Cathars. The armies employed were those of professional treasure seekers, such as Simon de Montfort (see p284), father of the Simon who initiated the first English parliament. For 30 years the Languedoc region was ravaged by these armies, and terrorized by the clandestine operations of the Inquisition. The last Cathar stronghold, at Montségur, fell in 1244; 225 Cathar *parfaits* (priests) were burnt to death.

Late Middle Ages

The late Middle Ages were characterized throughout Europe by the establishment of the state, and the slow move towards central government. In a gradual succession of victories, which started with Las Navas de Tolosa in 1212, the Christian monarchs of Spain succeeded in pushing the Moors southwards. Despite almost incessant struggles between the individual states, the marriage in 1469 of Isabella I of Castille and Ferdinand II of Aragón effectively joined the two largest kingdoms in the land. By the end of the century, they had ejected the Muslims from southern Spain, and had managed to bring all of the other kingdoms under their control. The arrangement was a loose one, however, and individual kingdoms such as Navarre and Catalonia retained a large degree of autonomy for centuries. The founding of the nation, however, coupled with the discovery of the New World, set the scene for Spain's growth to become the most powerful nation on earth.

In France, the Hundred Years War (1337-1453) was fought to expel the English from the Continent. Although individual rulers in Aquitaine and

Gascony remained powerful during this period, Charles VII's eventual success in expelling the English, signalled the beginnings of a recognized monarchy.

The 16th-18th centuries

The French state grew stronger throughout the sixteenth century but continued to be racked by problems. In the South-West this took the form in particular of religious dissent, and the Protestant courts of Bordeaux and Béarn resisted the influence of the Catholic monarchy. Béarn eventually provided the answer: Henry of Navarre (at this stage Basse-Navarre was in French hands). By Salic Law, Marguerite de Valois, sister of the late Henry III, could not inherit the throne which was offered to Henry of Navarre provided he became a Catholic. 'Paris is worth a Mass' he observed of his conversion and he was crowned Henry IV in 1589. To end the religious wars still ravaging the country he introduced, under the Edict of Nantes (1598), laws confirming the rights of Protestants (mainly Huguenots) and religious toleration towards them throughout Catholic France. He is still remembered by the French as one of the best monarchs in the country's history. In 1610, he was assassinated by a religious fanatic but by this time central control of the nation was well and truly established.

Meanwhile Spain reached the height of her power during the sixteenth century, with the addition of enormous wealth from her empire in the New World. By the close of the century, however, the golden age was already coming to an end, and the defeat of the Spanish Armada in 1588 effectively marked the downturn in Spanish fortunes. During the first half of the seventeenth century there were regular border disputes with France, resolved only with the signing of the Treaty of the Pyrenees in 1659. The treaty, which finalized the border as we see it today, was consolidated by the marriage of Maria Theresa, the daughter of Philip IV, to Louis XIV, in 1660.

Forty years later, a much simpler solution to Louis's territorial ambitions presented itself. In 1700, following the demise of the last of the Spanish royal line, Louis accepted the Spanish throne on behalf of his grandson, Philip V. Louis's comment at the time, 'Il n'y a plus de Pyrénées', proved to be prematurely optimistic. Unable to countenance the prospect of the French and Spanish united under one royal household, the other major European nations took up arms; the War of the Spanish Succession (1701-14) ended in defeat for France and Spain. In the aftermath of the war, Philip V abolished the individual parliaments of all of the Spanish states apart from Navarre and the Basque Provinces.

The French Revolution and the Napoleonic Wars

The turmoil of the French Revolution (1789-99) inevitably spread south across the Pyrenees with the influx of refugees. Events took a more direct turn in 1795, when the French Army crossed the border and took several towns, including Bilbao and Figueras. Their withdrawal was negotiated with the concession of a part of Spain's overseas territories, and from this time an alliance was maintained between the two countries. While France under Bonaparte went from strength to strength, Spain suffered a number of humiliating defeats, including the ending of its naval power at Trafalgar in 1805.

In 1808, under the pretence of a joint operation against Portugal, French forces entered Spain, and promptly occupied a number of cities. While the Spanish people rose against the French invaders, the royal family were relieved of the throne, which Napoleon gave to his brother, Joseph. The Peninsular War (1808-14) which followed, saw French and British forces competing for control of Spain and Portugal. In 1813 Wellington's victory at Vittoria forced the the French to retreat northwards through the Pyrenees, hotly pursued by the allied forces.

The 19th and early 20th centuries

For the French, the period following the end of the Napoleonic wars was one of confusion, with the reintroduction of the monarchy, followed by the founding of both the second and third republics. In the Pyrenees, far from the politics of the capital, the spa towns became fashionable, and *Pyrenéisme* began, with the first real interest in the mountains themselves. Towards the end of the nineteenth century all the major peaks were climbed, and colourful characters such as Henry Russell wrote some of the most famous literature about the mountains.

Spain suffered a much more turbulent fate during this period. From 1833-9 the First Carlist War was fought over the succession to the throne, and between 1868 and 1874 the monarchy was suspended after a rising of army officers. In 1874, after another brief Carlist uprising, a monarch was restored to the throne, and a government was formed. This rather shaky system lasted until 1917, when it collapsed. Spain remained neutral throughout the First World War, experiencing its own internal violence and confusion.

The Spanish Civil War

The 1920s and 1930s failed to produce any suitable solutions to Spain's internal conflict and, following elections in 1936, the army under General Franco seized power. The Spanish Civil War (1936-9) racked the country and ended in the deaths of tens of thousands, and the flight into France of tens of thousands more. In the early part of the war, idealistic young foreigners passed through the Pyrenees to join the Republican forces; by the end of the war, shattered Republicans crossed the mountains seeking refuge in France. This last dash to safety was made, by many in mid-winter, across the high passes of the central Pyrenees. Thousands died in the attempt.

The Second World War

Spain remained neutral throughout the Second World War and consequently the Pyrenees were a natural escape route for allied personnel and those who wished to join the Free French forces. The French Resistance was particularly strong in the South-West, and escape routes were operated at great risk by guides all along the length of the mountain range. Some of the best *passeurs* were Spanish farmers and shepherds who had fled from their homes during the Spanish Civil War.

Since the War

The period since the end of the war has seen fundamental changes, particularly to the south of the mountains. In the wake of the Nationalist victory, thousands of former Republicans were put on trial and whole regions that had supported the Republican cause were penalized. In the Basque country, for example, speaking Basque in public was no longer allowed. In this adverse political climate, and with the economy so badly mishandled that Spain spent most of the next two decades in recession, many refugees opted to remain in France rather than return to their homes. On Franco's death in 1975, the nation voted overwhelmingly for democracy and in 1978 the Basque country and Catalonia were given a large degree of autonomy.

THE ECONOMY

Despite the fact that a succession of writers over the last century described life in the mountains as a rural idyll, the truth is that the *montagnards* (mountain people) of the Pyrenees endured a hard lot with little reward. The economy was, until recently, almost entirely based on farming. Trans-humance, the custom of following livestock up or down the mountain according to the season, was a way of life well into this century.

Things have changed radically but not without cost to local life. In the Spanish Pyrenees hamlets have been deserted, and many mountain villages now have only a handful of inhabitants. With the growth of industry, jobs in the factories provided more money and an easier living, attracting most young people away from the rural economy. The abundance of hydroelectric power on both sides of the mountains has made the foothills of the Pyrenees a good place for energy intensive industries, such as aluminium smelting. Related industries have flourished too, and Toulouse is a major centre for aircraft construction.

In the mountains themselves, farming is still a way of life but tourism is now a major earner. You can instantly tell a village which has captured the tourist trade in some way; unlike the others nearby, there is building work in progress and a sense of rejuvenation.

THE PEOPLE

The range of mountains that has separated Spain from the rest of Europe throughout history has thrown up many strange affiliations. In some cases villages to the north and south of the Pyrenees share common language and culture, while there is rivalry between valleys on the same side of the mountains. However high the passes, there has been considerable intermingling between communities ever since the area was settled.

Place names emphasize the links: Marcadau (meaning market) was on one of the main trading routes; the Hospice de France and Hospital de Venásque were set up to shelter travellers on either side of the high Venásque Pass, and St-Jean-Pied-de-Port is named after the pass to which it provides access.

The montagnards all along the Pyrenees are a tough and independent lot to whom borders have never been particularly important. Smuggling has been a way of life for centuries and, according to recent reports, is still big business with the movement of duty-free cigarettes from Andorra. There are concessions, of course, to the government and to tourists but you still get the feeling that diehard Pyreneans will do exactly what they want, regardless.

Separatism

With this tradition of toughness and independence it's not all that surprising that there are calls from some parts of the community for self rule. The most vociferous group calling for independence are the Basques, some of whom, under the guise of the organization ETA have resorted to terrorism to achieve their aims. Most of the Spanish Basque community were perfectly satisfied when, in 1978, the Pais Vasco was granted autonomous status, effectively being allowed to govern itself. A small tearaway group, however, opted to continue the violence and since then have shot and bombed their way into the news. There is no equivalent of ETA among the French Basques.

Demands for greater autonomy can also be heard from the Catalans, and there is a common bond between the inhabitants of Spanish Catalonia and the villagers who live on the French side of the mountains.

LANGUAGES

Obviously most people speak either **Spanish** or **French** (many villagers speak both – which is handy if you plan to be walking on either side of the border and don't speak both languages yourself). There are two other main languages: Basque and Catalan. **Basque** is unique and is the oldest language still in use in Europe. Basques on both sides of the border speak the same language, which they call Euskara. During Franco's time, the use of Basque was forbidden but following his death it was granted equal status under the 1978 constitution; nevertheless, despite concerted attempts to keep the language alive, it appears to be losing ground. A recent survey in Spain showed that only 26% of the two million Spanish Basques speak Euskara as their first language.

Like Basque, **Catalan** was banned by Franco but was given equal status with Castilian after 1978. Although the Catalan movement for greater autonomy seldom gets into the news, being overshadowed by the violence of the Basque separatists, it is still a force in local politics. Recent moves to force offices and government departments in Catalonia to use Catalan are meeting with resistance from many people.

GEOLOGY

The formation of the Pyrenees was not a single incident but the culmination of several; hence the geology of the area is complex. In outline, however, the mountains were caused by a huge, slow-motion crash between the Iberian Peninsula and the rest of Europe. This collision of the continental plates began around 200 million years ago and is still continuing today.

Formation

The oldest rocks located in the Pyrenees date from around 500 million years ago when a range of mountains, known to geologists as the Hercynian Range, was formed. The range covered much of Central Europe, and the Massif Central is one remnant of it.

With the constant movement of the earth's crust, part of the mountain range was torn down over the next two hundred million years, and the rocks that had formed the centre of the range were covered by a shallow sea. Gradually layers of sediment were laid down on the sea bed over the top of the Hercynian rock.

Around 220 million years ago, the direction of movement of the earth's crust (the so-called 'tectonic plates') changed, and they began to be forced inwards. It is thought that this change in direction may have been caused by the collision of the continent of Africa with the land mass of Europe. Between about 58 million years ago and 24 million years ago, the inward movement caused a number of sections of land to be crushed up against Europe. Among these were the Italian peninsula, causing the formation of the Swiss Austrian Alps, and the Iberian peninsula, causing the formation of the Pyrenees – thus the Alps and the Pyrenees are contemporaneous.

The rocks in the Pyrenees are much older than their Alpine counterparts, for, as the Iberian peninsula squeezed up against Europe, it was the old Hercynian rock covered with its layer of newer sedimentary rock that was forced upwards. In some areas, the new covering of sedimentary rocks proved malleable and bent with the movement, thereby remaining above the older rock. At the point of greatest pressure, however, along the central axis of the range, the sedimentary rocks often did not bend but shattered, exposing the older, Hercynian, rocks beneath.

Erosion

The fact that all this occurred 24 to 58 million years ago means that the mountains we see today must be looked at with an understanding of the erosion which has occurred since. In many places the younger, softer rocks, even if they remained on top, have been eroded, partially or entirely.

The Quaternary Period, which is the period of the last 1.6 million years up to the present day, has seen a series of ice ages. Glaciers hundreds of metres thick fundamentally altered the shape of the landscape to leave it pretty much as it is today. U-shaped valleys, arêtes (sharp, mountain ridges), cirques (deep, bowl-shaped hollows at valley heads), moraines (deposits of rocks and debris) and hanging valleys are all legacies of glaciation, and are clearly seen throughout the Pyrenees.

Flora and fauna

FLORA

The Pyrenees are well known for their spectacular flora. The huge number of species (160 of which are indigenous) is due in part to the range of climates experienced in the mountains.

Campanula (Bell flower)
Campanula scheuchzeri

Common Monkshood
Aconitum napellus

Pyrenean Iris
Iris latifolia

Trumpet Gentian
Gentiana acaulis

Sow Thistle
Cicerbita plumieri

Violet
Viola cornuta

Foxglove
Digitalis purpurea

Mountain Houseleek
Sempervivum montanum

Rosebay Willowherb
Epilobium angustifolium

Fringed Pink
Dianthus monspessulanus

Pink
Dianthus deltoides

Mallow
Malva moschata

Merendera
Merendera montana

Alpine Aster
Aster alpinus

Devil's Bit Scabious
Succisa pratensis

Field Gentian
Gentianella campestris

Chives
Allium schoenoprasam

Alpenrose
Rhododendron ferrugineum

Sheep's Bit
Jasione montana

Woolly Thistle
Cirsium eriophorum

Dragonmouth
Horminum pyrenaicum

Alpine Clover (Trefoil)
Trifolium alpinum

Bladder Campion
Silene vulgaris

Edelweiss
Leontopodium alpinum

*Geranium
cinerium*

Carline Thistle
Carlina acaulis

Heather (Ling)
Calluna vulgaris

Herb-Robert
Geranium robertianum

Garlic Thrift
Armeria alliacea

Pyrenean Buttercup
Ranunculus pyrenaeus

St John's Wort
Hypericum perforatum

Yellow Rattle
Rhinanthus minor

Sea Holly
Eryngium bourgatii

Marsh Marigold (Kingcup)
Caltha palustris

Senecio
Senecio pyrenaicus

Yellow Monkshood
Aconitum anthora

Reflex Stonecrop
Sedum reflexum

Rock Rose
Helianthemum nummularium

Birdsfoot-trefoil
Lotus corniculatus

Yarrow
Achillea millefolium

Cotton-grass
Eriophorum angustifolium

Rowan tree
Sorbus aucuparia

Highland (lower levels)

At the lower levels (below about 1800m) there is great variety. Rosebay willow herb, valerian and white cloud adorn the banks of streams; the hillsides are visited by trumpet gentians and the woods are good places to find bright pink martagon lilies, purple foxglove and granny's bonnets.

Sub-alpine

At the 'Sub-alpine' level (between about 1800m and about 2400m), one of the commonest flowers is the dark blue Pyrenean iris, but there are many others. Look out for saxifrage, sedum and the highly distinctive mountain houseleek. Sometimes it's the smallest flowers that are the most colourful: they include the purple-fringed alpine aster, the day-glo maiden pink and deep blue spring gentian.

Alpine

Above 2400m it's a case of survival of the hardiest, as these tiny flowers spend at least half the year buried under the snow. They are small, wiry and surprisingly colourful: alpine clover, hawkweed and alpenrose are all common sights.

TREES

Some of the most extensive beech woods in Europe are in the Pyrenees. Oak, birch and hazel also grow in abundance, as well as several varieties of pine trees. Most notable of the pines is *Pinus Uncinata*, which grows up to 30 metres in height and can survive at altitudes to up to 2600m. It is one of the longest-living trees in the world; some are 600-800 years old, some even older. Keep an eye open for scarring on the trunks of older trees; the shepherds used to tap trees for sap, which was used to fuel the lanterns in their huts at night.

FAUNA

Mammals

The most famous inhabitants of the mountains are the **brown bears**. Up to the late nineteenth century there were plenty of bears in the Pyrenees but chronic overhunting, coupled with deforestation made them all but extinct by the middle of this century. In an effort to reintroduce the species, several Slovenian brown bears have been released into the mountains over the last couple of years. Reports suggest that there are now around 15-18 bears living in the Pyrenees. See p188.

Other well-known mammals in the mountains include **marmots**, beaver lookalikes which make their home in the rocks and have a high-pitched cry that sounds similar to a bird call. They're inquisitive creatures, and it's not unusual in the less well-walked valleys to find one or two of them perched on the rocks checking you out as you pass by. Marmots were actually hunted to extinction in the Pyrenees during the last century but were reintroduced, and large colonies are now flourishing on many of the rocky slopes.

Another creature native to the Pyrenees is the **izard**, a relative of the chamois. It is found on high mountainsides through the range, and has distinctive narrow upright horns with backward pointing tips. Izards are hunted in late

THE PYRENEES

September each year, but recently a greater threat to the species has been an unknown disease which has affected the eyesight of many of the animals. Not to be confused with the izard, the **mouflon** is a type of wild sheep which was originally an inhabitant of these mountains but had to be reintroduced from Sardinia. Although they stand about the same height as izards, mouflon are easily distinguishable by their large curved horns and because they tend to be found in herds on the lower slopes.

Perhaps the most peculiar inhabitant of the mountains is the **desman**, a small aquatic mammal belonging to the mole family. It has webbed feet and a long snout which it uses like a snorkel while hunting for its food. The desman eats fish and makes its home in a burrow in the bank of a stream on the lower slopes of the mountains (below about 1800m).

Other common mammals of the Pyrenees include deer, foxes, squirrels, badgers and wild boar.

Reptiles
Just about the only animal you should avoid (apart from the bear, of course) is the **Pyrenean viper**. There's no particular danger of getting bitten, and I saw only one (alive) in five months, but watch your step on the likely sections of the route. There was also great excitement in 1992 when a new species of frog, *Rana pyrenaica*, was discovered living in the high mountain streams.

Birds
The Pyrenees are home to a wide variety of birds including many that you'd be lucky to see elsewhere in Europe. Most interesting of these are the raptors. Probably the best known is the **lammergeier (bearded vulture)**, which can grow up to a metre in length, with a three-metre wing-span. Loners by nature, they nest

LAMMERGEIER

in the high crags and cliffs of mountain ranges, producing only one or two young each year. Lammergeiers have a peculiar way of feeding: they scavenge the bones carrying them to a great height, before dropping them to break open as they hit the ground. They then swoop down to eat the bone marrow. The adult lammergeier's shape and colouring are distinctive. The wings are long, pointed and slightly swept back, and the tail is diamond-shaped and tapering to a point. The adult bird has black wings and tail, with a golden-coloured underside, legs and hood. Particularly apparent on the head is a band of black which covers the eyes and runs to the front of the head where it ends in a 'beard' – hence the name. Young lammergeiers are much harder to identify, as they remain a dark buff colour with only a pale grey underside until full adulthood. Lammergeiers are now very rare in Europe, existing only in Spain, the Alps and south-east Europe. There are estimated to be very few pairs left in the Pyrenees.

The **griffon vulture** is much the same size as the lammergeier but is far more common. It, too, nests on crags and cliff faces, using any available ledge or crevice. The bird's in-flight silhouette is notable for the broad parallel-sided wings, the feathered 'fingertips', and the short, almost square

GRIFFON VULTURE

tail. In colouring, the body of the adult is pale fawn as is the forward part of its wings. The tips and trailing edges of the wings and the tail are black. Seen from

EGYPTIAN VULTURE

below, this bar of pale colour formed by the body and the front edge of the wings is distinctive. The head is white with a cream ruff around the neck. The griffon vulture often soars at great height and in the company of others.

The **Egyptian vulture** is one of the smallest in the vulture family with an average length of 60-65cm and average wingspan of 1.5 metres. When at rest the visible plumage of the adult is almost all white, with a large white ruff. The face is yellow and the beak long and curving, giving the head the appearance of being long and thin. In flight, the body, tail, and forward edges of the wings are white, while the trailing

edges of the wings and the wing-tips are black. In silhouette, the wings are slightly pointed, and the tail is diamond-shaped. The immature Egyptian vulture is dark brown with a mottled body and forward edges of the wings.

Like the others of their family, Egyptian vultures nest on cliff faces though usually in a hole in the cliff where both adults look after a single egg. The Egyptian vulture feeds off carrion but only after its larger brothers have fed first.

The majestic **golden eagle** is one of the rarer birds in the Pyrenees but can still be seen. Adults grow up to 90cm long with a wing-span of around two metres. The adult colouring is almost entirely dark brown

GOLDEN EAGLE

THE PYRENEES

BLACK KITE

with golden tinges on the forward parts of the wings and the head. The tips and trailing edges of the wings, as well as the tail, are brown. In flight, the wings, which broaden perceptibly towards the wing-tips, are canted slightly forwards and upwards, and the tail is long, broad and almost square at the end. Immature golden eagles are also dark brown in the main but have a very distinctive white panel on the under side of the wings and a white base of the tail. They can soar for long periods and are adept hunters, eating smaller birds, rabbits and other small mammals. They nest on cliffs or in trees, building a huge eyrie to which they return year after year.

The **black kite** is a migratory bird that is versatile in its ability to adjust to a number of habitats including river estuaries and towns. Adults grow to around 55cm in length with a wing-span of around 160cm. The adult bird is actually dark brown in colour rather than pure black. In flight it has slightly bowed wings and a long tail with a shallow fork. The black kite has a regular high-pitched cry. It feeds on small animals and carrion and will also scavenge from rubbish tips.

Bonnelli's eagle grows to a length of around 70cm with a wing-span of 160-170cm. The adult bird has grey-brown upper plumage, with a mottled white neck and underbelly. Seen in flight, the under-sides of the wings are predominantly grey-ish white with a prominent band of black, and black edging at the trailing edge and wing-tips. In silhouette the wings are slen-der, and the tail is long and square-ended with a black tip. The immature bird is gen-erally light brown in colour. Like the gold-en eagle, the Bonnelli's eagle is becoming increasingly rare.

BONNELLI'S EAGLE

Among the many other species of birds to be found in the mountains, two are particularly notable. The **ptarmigan**, which grows to around 35cm in length,

PTARMIGAN

makes its home on the mountain tops. It is notable for its dual appearance, cunningly swapping its brown and white summer-time costume for a winter plumage of pure white wings and body with a black tail. In summer the female is distinguishable from the male by her slightly darker colour, and in the winter the male has a black stripe across the eye, while the female does not. The ptarmigan nests on the ground and typically lays 10-12 eggs.

The largest member of the grouse family, the **capercaillie** is found much lower down the slopes, below the treeline. These large turkey-sized birds live in pine forests and feed on shoots and berries. Capercaillies can fly (often noisily), and they will rest in trees but nest on the ground. Females are reddish-brown and grow to around 60cm in length, whereas males grow up to 90cm and have a dark plumage with a red comb. The males are highly territorial and have a ritual to deter intruders which includes puffing themselves up, spreading their tails and going through an elaborate series of calls. If this fails, the male will attack energetically. One handbook of birds notes: '…the male gives out his curious love-notes in early spring; at this time he shows off somewhat like a Turkey-cock, and becomes so excited that at a certain phase of the 'song' he is temporarily deaf and blind. His encounters at this season with his rivals are fierce and bloody; and on the continent savage old birds have been known to attack persons…'

CAPERCAILLIE

The **alpine chough** (length 40cm, wingspan 73-90cm) is a medium-sized black crow and makes a similar but higher-pitched call. Their long, curled beaks are usually pale in colour, and their legs are a bright ruddy-orange. Common above 1500m they are generally seen in pairs or small groups. A gregarious species, they are not shy of humans and are known for playful, aerobatic flying and are a pleasure to watch. They nest on or around rock faces and crevices.

NATIONAL PARKS

Parc National des Pyrénées

The park, which was created on 23 March 1967, has a central zone of 457 square kilometres and an outer zone of 2063 square kilometres. It contains a wealth of flora and fauna including, apparently, 571 species of algae! Of more interest to most visitors are the spectacular birdlife and other wildlife. Of the 107 species of mammal present in France, 75 can be found in the Pyrenees. At the last count there were estimated to be 9 pairs of bearded vultures, 52-54 pairs of royal eagles and over 200 pairs of Griffon vultures. Among the park's other occupants are izards (around 5000), marmots and even bears. For more information, see their excellent website: 🖥 www.parc-pyrenees.com.

● **Rules** Dogs are not allowed in the park (even on a lead), and mountain biking is forbidden. Strictly speaking, **camping** is not allowed in the park but it is generally tolerated as long as certain rules are followed. Pitching a tent is permitted for one night only, as long as the location is more than one hour's walk from the park boundaries and from any paved road. Tents are not supposed to be put up before the early evening (ie 6-7pm) and are to be down by 9am. Obviously no litter or damage to the surrounding area is tolerated, and fires are not allowed. Refuges in the park generally have a small area near the building where camping is permitted. **Fishing** is allowed in the park (as elsewhere in the Pyrenees) as long as you have a fishing permit, which can be bought from any tabac. The fishing season runs from March to September.

● **Information** For more information, visit 🖥 www.parc-pyrenees.com or contact the **park office** directly (☎ 05.62.44.36.60), 59 route de Pau, 65000 Tarbes.

THE PYRENEES

Parque Nacional de Ordesa y Monte Perdido

From its tentative beginnings in 1918, when an area of around 20 square kilometres was designated a protected zone, the park now covers 156 square kilometres with a peripheral zone of a further 190 square kilometres. Included within this area is the spectacular Ordesa Canyon and its smaller neighbour, the Añisclo Canyon. To the north, Ordesa shares a border with the Parc National des Pyrénées.

● **Rules** Fires are not allowed, and **camping** is permitted only in certain areas – near the Refugio de Goriz, around Refugio San Vicenda and in the area of Ermita de Pineta. As long as you are sensible, you can probably get away with putting up a tent elsewhere just for a night. However, leave no litter.

● **Information** For further information visit 🖳 www.ordesa.net.

Parque Nacional d'Aigüestortes i Sant Maurici

Designated on 21 October 1995, this park has a total area of 488 sq km of which 141 sq km is the inner area. Sant Maurici lake is near its centre.

● **Rules** Fires are not allowed, and camping is permitted only near refuges. Bathing in the lakes and rivers is against the rules.

● **Information** The park office is in Espot (☎ 973-62.40.36)

Réserve Naturelle de Néouvielle

The reserve is a protected area rather than a designated national park, but it's subject to most of the rules already listed above for other places. Camping is limited to one site near the Lac d'Aubert.

Practical information for the visitor

LOCAL TRANSPORT

France

Public transport in the French Pyrenees is good, although bus services tend to run only to the larger villages. If you're planning to travel to or from the mountains by public transport, it makes sense to use, as a start or finish point, one of the following towns and villages which are served by buses or trains:

● **Western Pyrenees** Hendaye, Bidarray, St-Jean-Pied-de-Port, Borce/Etsaut, Arrens-Marsous

● **Central Pyrenees** Arrens-Marsous, Cauterets, Luz-St-Sauveur, Gavarnie, Barèges, Vielle Aure, Bagnères-de-Luchon, Seix, Aulus-les-Bains, Mérens-les-Vals

● **Eastern Pyrenees** Mérens-les-Vals, Mont-Louis, Arles-sur-Tech, Banyuls-sur-Mer

Spain

Public transport in Spain is less regular than that in France and there tends to be only one or possibly two buses a day into the mountains:

● **Western Pyrenees** Roncesvalles, Ochagavia, Sallent de Gallego

● **Central Pyrenees** Torla, Bénasque

ACCOMMODATION

There is a wide variety of accommodation available, and this book attempts to give a selection of the best of each sort. While the larger villages generally have some very pleasant hotels and *chambres d'hôte* (guest houses), the choice of accommodation in the mountains, as you would expect, is much more limited: *gîtes d'étape* (lodges) and *refuges* (mountain huts) are the two main options. In mid-summer, try to ring in advance and reserve a place at any of the above. Not only will this ensure that you have accommodation at the end of a full day's walking but you may also find that you get preferential treatment if you can give a couple of days' notice (ie a better bed, or even a room to yourself). There are a few areas along the GR10 where no accommodation is available, and where the only option other than camping is to stay in a *cabane* (shepherd's hut).

Hotels

Spending the occasional night in a hotel is well worth it. After the dormitory conditions of the gîtes d'étape, you can enjoy privacy, a proper bed, and no snoring neighbours – guaranteed! Moreover, almost all Pyrenean hotels have a restaurant where you can try excellent local food, and a glass or two of good wine, which should, after all, be part of the general experience of travelling through France or Spain. The great thing about all this is that small hotels are often not all that much more expensive than the gîtes. Treat yourself!

Chambres d'hôte and casas rurales

Another option is staying in a local house. In France, staying in a chambre d'hôte is often no cheaper than a night in a small hotel, and since food is usually not available, they don't represent any great bargain. In Spain, *casas rurales* (called *casas de pagès* in Catalonia) can be much better value and are definitely worth checking out – although, again, you are often expected to bring your own food.

Even if staying in a local house does cost you a little more, you may judge it to be money well spent. It's an interesting experience and allows plenty of opportunity to chat to the owners about the area through which you are passing.

Gîtes d'étape

The name says it all: these are lodging houses which have been set up along the routes of major footpaths, and which tend to form the start and end point of the day stages. They vary in quality, facilities and efficiency. Some are run as full-time businesses in the summer, in which case you can expect everything to be in good shape. In other places the gîte is not much more than a camping barn.

Accommodation is almost always in a dormitory, often with one or two large platforms, on which mattresses have been laid side by side. Try to get the space near the window, as in mid-summer with a full complement of walkers, it can get a bit stuffy at night. Food is usually available but again it pays to ring in advance and confirm this. There are almost invariably kitchen facilities though the standard can vary greatly. A night's accommodation (*la nuitée*) in a gîte costs around €10; breakfast generally costs €5, and an evening meal (*repas*) normally costs about €12-15. Half board (*demi-pension*), therefore, costs around €27-30.

THE PYRENEES

> **Discounts at refuges**
> If you intend to use refuges regularly during your trek, you can save money by joining one of the large mountaineering organizations. Most of the French refuges are owned by the **Club Alpin Français** (CAF), membership of which gives an instant discount of up to 50%. In addition, there is an agreement of réciprocité between the CAF and many other mountaineering groups. Unfortunately, the cost of membership (£24.50) of the British Mountaineering Council (see below) and the Reciprocal Rights Card (£32.50) that entitles you to a discount at French CAF refuges comes to over £50, and with most of the refuges in the Pyrenees *not* owned by the CAF, it makes little sense economically to join just from your Pyrenees trek unless you're deliberately going to go out of your way to stay at their refuges, which will entail deviating from the GR routes regularly. The details of the agreement are renegotiated every year. The agreement also includes many refuges in the Spanish Pyrenees.
>
> To find out more, contact your national mountaineering association. In the UK this is the **British Mountaineering Council** (☎ 0161-445 4500 ☐ www.thebmc.co.uk) 177-179 Burton Rd, Manchester, M20 2BB. You could also try contacting the Club Alpin Français (☎ 01 53 72 87 00, ☐ www.clubalpin.com), Commission de Gestion des Refuges et Chalets, 24 avenue de Laumière, 75019 Paris.

While the gîtes can be crowded in mid-summer (they tend to open only from early June to late September), and they are by no means cheap, there are certain obvious advantages. Showers, a bed, and shelter from the elements are some of them; in addition, you get to meet other walkers, try local cuisine, and get information from the gîte owner.

Refuges

Refuges in the Pyrenees may either be staffed (ie with a guardian) or unstaffed.

Staffed refuges Staffed refuges are to be found along the most popular walking trails. Some of these places are quite large – Wallon can take a hundred people in peak season, and there are many others which can accommodate 50-60 people. Conditions are rather like those in a gîte but because of the remoteness of the refuges (supplies must be brought up either by helicopter or by mule), prices are slightly higher and facilities rather more basic. A night in a refuge costs from around €9, breakfast about €5, and supper €14; thus demi-pension is usually in the order of €28-30. Prices in Spanish refuges (*refugios*) are similar. Very few refuges have a shower, and in many the loo is a draughty lean-to shelter away from the main building. Bring your own loo paper – it isn't provided.

Although the largest refuges have a guardian (and sometimes staff) to handle the large numbers of visitors, they are only there during peak season. Guardians are in residence from early June to late September and, if feasible, Christmas, Easter and a few weekends in between. When the guardian is not in residence, a small section of the refuge is generally left open for passing walkers.

Even in peak season it is acceptable to pay for accommodation only and to provide your own meals; cooking areas are set aside where you can use camping stoves safely. Unlike gîtes, however, there are no kitchen facilities provided.

Unstaffed refuges A number of smaller refuges throughout the Pyrenees do not merit a guardian – even in peak season. They have basic facilities and a conscience box; place your donation in the box before you depart, and ensure you leave everything clean for the next users.

Cabanes

The last sort of shelter available in the mountains are the cabanes. These are marked on IGN maps (as are gîtes and refuges), and in the later stages of the GR10 they occasionally offer the only accommodation available. Cabanes are generally shepherds' huts which are available for use by walkers. There is no charge for using them but it is expected that walkers will leave them clean.

There is always the risk that others may want to use the same cabane as you do, and if you arrive to find that there are already trekkers, shepherds or hunters in residence, you'll just have to go elsewhere, or sleep outside. Try to ensure, therefore, that you arrive at your chosen cabane with plenty of time and energy to go elsewhere if necessary.

Cabanes vary greatly in quality, and brief remarks on each are given in this book. At the most basic, a cabane may be a dark, dirty and smelly shelter for no more than two or three people. There are, however, a few cabanes which are kept in very good condition, and which occupy excellent positions in otherwise deserted countryside. The best of these can be great places to spend a night.

Camping

French and Spanish campsites are generally excellent, with good facilities and a pleasant atmosphere. Prices vary considerably according to the standard of the site (they are rated by stars) and the popularity of the area. Tariffs are worked out in one of two ways: some charge separately for the tent site (*emplacement*) and for the occupants, whereas others have a flat rate for two walkers with a small tent. Pretty much all the campsites have showers and proper toilets.

Rough camping is feasible in the mountains themselves but, if you're near anyone's land, ask first. For details on camping in the national parks, see p54.

LANGUAGE

Many of the locals speak both French and Spanish, but English speakers are rather less common. Getting by in English is easy enough, but don't expect to find out a lot about what you're eating, or whether the path is clear ahead. Learning a little French or Spanish before you go will considerably enhance your trip, and it's well worth carrying a small phrase book. If all else fails, head for the nearest tourist office, where you'll find someone who can speak English. See p312 for phrase lists.

HOLIDAYS AND FESTIVALS

There are numerous holidays and festivals throughout the Pyrenees. It's best to get information from the French and Spanish tourist offices (see p21) or their websites (p20) before you travel. Some of the larger festivals are as follows:

Festivals – Western Pyrenees
● **13 July – Celebration of the Tribute of the Three Cows**, Ronçal. This treaty, which allows the neighbours from the Ronçal and Barétous valleys to graze their animals on each other's land, is one of the oldest in the world. See p99 for further details.

● **Mid-July – Bull running** The most famous festival in Spain takes place in Pamplona, Navarre.

● **Early August – International Pyrenean Folk Festival**, Oloron-Ste-Marie.

Festivals – Central Pyrenees
● **July – Jazz Festival,** Germ.

● **Mid-July – Jazz-Altitude**, Luz-Saint-Sauveur.

● **Late July – Theatre Festival**, Gavarnie.

● **Mid-July – Tour de France** This famous cycle race passes through the central Pyrenees.

● **Late August – Floral Festival**, Bagnères-de-Luchon.

Public holidays
● **France** There are two major holidays during the walking season: Bastille Day on 14 July, and the Feast of the Assumption on 15 August.

● **Spain** In the walking season there are public holidays in mid-June (Corpus Christi), 24 June, 25 July, 15 August (Assumption), and 12 October.

Office hours
● **France** Working hours are much the same as in the UK, except that shopkeepers usually take a long break from midday until about 3.30pm, then shops stay open until about 7pm. Banks also take a short midday break and tend to close completely over the weekend. Post offices are open from around 9am to 6pm, and are also open on Saturday mornings.

● **Spain** The Spanish have a more relaxed attitude to life. Shops come to life at around 9am and work stops for a long siesta from midday onwards. Around mid-afternoon there are signs of activity, and shops stay open late into the evening.

MONEY

❏ **Rates of exchange**

	Euro
Aus$1	€0.60
Can$1	€0.64
NZ$1	€0.55
UK£1	€1.45
US$	€0.78

For up-to-the-minute rates of exchange check
💻 www.xe.com.

Currency
France and Spain were among the first European countries to take the **euro (€)** and the franc and peseta ceased to be legal tender in July 2002. The euro is divided into 100 cents. Euro notes come in denominations of 5, 10, 20, 50, 100, 200 and 500 notes; there are 1, 2, 5, 10, 20 and 50 cent coins, and 1 and 2 euro coins.

Tipping
● **France** A service charge is included in restaurant bills so a tip is not expected. Taxi

drivers expect a tip of a euro or so, whatever the length of the journey.
● **Spain** For waiters and taxi drivers 5-10% is about right, or the small change in a café or cheap restaurant.

ELECTRICITY

Electricity on both sides of the border is 220V, and the plugs are of the two round-pin variety.

POST AND TELECOMMUNICATIONS
Postal services
Postal services in France and Spain are efficient. You can save time, however, by buying stamps in tabacs.

Although it's largely been superceded by email now, having poste restante sent to any of the large post offices is still easy. Letters or parcels should be clearly addressed with the surname in capitals and underlined, then sent to Poste Restante, Bureau de Poste, Name of town, Post code (given in the guide section of this book). You will need to produce some proof of identity to be able to pick up your mail. Along the GR10, good places to collect poste restante are:
● **Western Pyrenees** Hendaye, St-Jean-Pied-de-Port, Lescun, Arrens Marsous.
● **Central Pyrenees** Cauterets, Luz-Saint-Sauveur, Vielle Aure, Bagnères-de-Luchon, Seix, Ax-les-Thermes.
● **Eastern Pyrenees** Arles-sur-Tech, Banyuls-sur-Mer.

Phone, fax and email
Most though not all public telephones in France and Spain use phone cards. In France, *télécartes* are available at tabacs and at post offices. In Spain *tarjetas telefónicas* can be bought at small shops and post offices. To make a domestic call within France, note that you should always dial the full ten-digit number even when calling within the same area.

To make an international call from France dial 00 and then the country code (44 for the UK, 1 for USA & Canada) followed by the area code (minus the 0) and the number you require. French phone boxes which have the symbol of a blue bell on the side receive incoming calls. From Spain dial 07 before the country code.

Most post offices have a **fax** machine available for a small charge, but otherwise try a hotel or bookshop (*librairie*).

Email and internet facilities are still surprisingly rare in the Pyrenees. Currently there are internet cafés at Hendaye, St-Jean-Pied-du-Port, Borce, Cauterets, La Guingeta d'Àneu, and Torla.

FOOD

One of the greatest pleasures of walking in the Pyrenees is the chance to sample a variety of French and Spanish food. Pyrenean cuisine is generally simple, delicious and very filling – preparing people for the strenuous mountain lifestyle.

Throughout the Pyrenees, meals often start with a thick and filling soup, with huge hunks of potato and other vegetables. In France this soup is known as *garbure*. A plate of *charcuterie* (cold meats, usually served with some salad) is another excellent way to start a meal and to taste some of the delicious locally-made *saucisson* (sausage). Main courses are generally meat or fish. In France, *poulet Basquaise*, chicken in a thick dark sauce, is a favourite in the western Pyrenees. *Piperade*, a tangy mixture of tomatoes, onions, peppers and garlic may be served with pork or chicken, or in an omelette. Another traditional dish is *boudin* – black pudding sausages which are often served with cooked apple chips.

In Spain, sausages are also common; in the Valle d'Aran, spicy *butifarra* sausage is a speciality. The Spanish are also keen on stews – huge, filling and generally made with lamb or chicken. In the same area, one of the more unusual dishes is to try izard (a relative of the chamois); the dark, strong-tasting meat is served up in a thick wine sauce. Mountain trout is very popular on both sides of the Pyrenees and is guaranteed absolutely fresh from the nearest river or lake.

The other food trekkers are likely to eat frequently is cheese. *Fromage de brebis*, made from ewe's milk, can often be bought from shepherds themselves, who make it in their huts, high on the mountain side.

DRINK

The quality of Pyrenean wine varies greatly – try them all in order to discover one you like. From the table wines of Irrouleguy in the Basque country to the sweet aperitif wine produced in Banyuls on the Mediterranean coast, there should be something here to satisfy everybody.

Beer is reasonably priced and just the thing after a hot day's walking. The French tend to stick to beers such as Pelforth, Amstel and Kronenbourg – try Pelforth Brune if you like dark beer. The Spanish have several brews worth trying from the ubiquitous San Miguel to Estrella Damm and others.

There is an array of local aperitifs and digestifs, from Izarra in the Basque country to Ratafia in the Valle d'Aran.

THINGS TO BUY

The best things to bring away from the Pyrenees as souvenirs are the local foods and wines. A whole cheese makes an excellent gift, although there may be a strong temptation to keep it for yourself. Wine is another good option, as are locally-produced honey and liqueurs.

SECURITY

Travelling in the Pyrenees is very safe, and generally you can leave your belongings in a gîte or refuge without worrying. It's common sense, however, to take some standard precautions. Don't leave valuables lying around, and keep your passport and money with you at all times.

MINIMUM IMPACT TREKKING

With areas of outstanding natural beauty throughout the world under attack, the onus is on every visitor to the Pyrenees to do their own bit in helping to preserve the landscape. There are several ways in which you can assist without creating any great difficulties for yourself – it's just a matter of following a few simple rules.

Don't leave litter

The following observation was seen on a noticeboard in Mérens-les-Vals: 'A bit of orange peel lasts six months before decomposing. Silver foil lasts eighteen months, textiles last 15 years, and a plastic bag ten to twelve years. An aluminium drinks can will last for 85 years on the ground, or 75 years in the sea. Scrap iron takes more than two centuries to be broken down. It takes the soil five years to recover from unauthorized dumping. Think about it.'

Some people persist in leaving rubbish along the main trails and near the refuges. Everything that you take up into the mountains should either be eaten, buried if it's biodegradable, or carried with you to the nearest village where you can find a bin. It is not possible to dump your litter at refuges as they have to deal with their own rubbish. Guardians, however, have supplies of plastic bin bags which they give away free to encourage walkers to take their litter with them.

Don't pick the flowers

However tempting it may be, leave the flora completely intact for the next people to enjoy.

Stay on the main trail

Increasing numbers of visitors are travelling to the Pyrenees in the summer – particularly to the busiest areas of the Central Pyrenees. This is causing severe erosion along the paths. The staff of the national parks and the local population elsewhere can cope with carrying out erosion control on one path but not on several where walkers have made separate ways up or down the hillsides.

Burn used lavatory paper

Used lavatory paper is an unsightly health risk. If you're camping rough or just have to answer the call of nature along the way, burn the paper rather than leaving it to rot in the open air. Bury the faeces.

Don't pollute water sources

If there's a latrine available, use it. Don't defecate within 20 metres of a water source.

When washing yourself or your clothes using detergents, don't pollute streams or lakes. Carry the water well away from the water source, and after using it dispose of it at least 20 metres from the original source.

THE PYRENEES

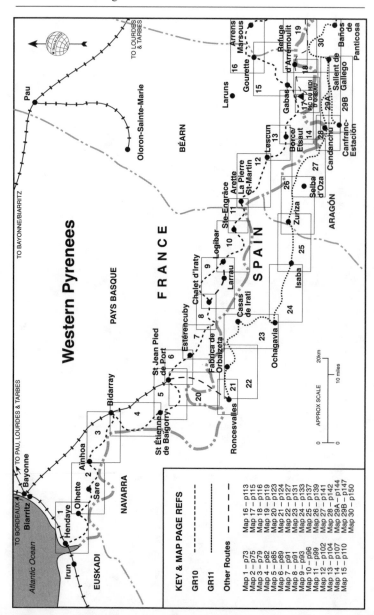

Western Pyrenees

TO BAYONNE/BIARRITZ

TO LOURDES & TARBES

Pau

Oloron-Sainte-Marie

BÉARN

FRANCE

PAYS BASQUE

Bidarray

St Jean Pied de Port

Estérencuby

Chalet d'Iraty

St Étienne de Baïgorry

Roncesvalles

Fabrica de Orbaizeta

Casas de Irati

Larrau

Logibar

Ste-Engrâce

La Pierre St-Martin

Arette

Lescun

Borce/ Etsaut

Candanchú

Canfranc-Estación

Sallent de Gallego

Baños de Panticosa

Arrens Marsous

Refuge d'Arremoulit

Gourette

Gabas

PIC DU MIDI D'OSSAU

Laruns

ARAGÓN

Selba d'Oza

Zuriza

Isaba

Ochagavia

SPAIN

NAVARRA

EUSKADI

Bayonne

Biarritz

Irun

Hendaye

Olhette

Sare

Ainhoa

Atlantic Ocean

TO BORDEAUX

TO PAU, LOURDES & TARBES

KEY & MAP PAGE REFS

GR10	·—·—·—·
GR11	··············
Other Routes	– – – –

Map 1 – p73	Map 16 – p113
Map 2 – p75	Map 17 – p115
Map 3 – p79	Map 18 – p116
Map 4 – p82	Map 19 – p119
Map 5 – p85	Map 20 – p123
Map 6 – p89	Map 21 – p124
Map 7 – p91	Map 22 – p127
Map 8 – p91	Map 23 – p131
Map 9 – p93	Map 24 – p133
Map 10 – p96	Map 25 – p137
Map 11 – p99	Map 26 – p139
Map 12 – p102	Map 27 – p141
Map 13 – p104	Map 28 – p142
Map 14 – p107	Map 29A – p144
Map 15 – p110	Map 29B – p147
	Map 30 – p150

APPROX SCALE

20km

10 miles

PART 3: WESTERN PYRENEES

Facts about the region

GENERAL DESCRIPTION

The Western Pyrenees are defined here as the area from the Atlantic coast, inland as far as the eastern edge of the French département of Pyrénées Atlantiques. The département, which comprises the provinces of **Pays Basque** and **Béarn**, is mirrored to the south of the border by the Spanish Basque country, the autonomous region of **Navarra** and the western part of the region of **Aragón**.

Although the extent of the area is easy to sum up in a few words, its history and culture are impossible to pigeonhole. Unlike the Central Pyrenees, where high mountain ridges have defined areas much more clearly, this region of low hills and confused topography has allowed a mixing of communities. The border between France and Spain, finally settled by the Treaty of the Pyrenees in 1659, may have made a formal definition of nationality but local affiliations have never lost their importance. Nowhere is this clearer than in the case of the Basques – one of the most fiercely nationalistic communities in the world.

The Western Pyrenees, watered amply by weather systems from the Atlantic, are an area of incredible greenness and fertility. While the hills here in

---

 Trekking in the Western Pyrenees – Highlights
● **France** On the French side of the Western Pyrenees, the GR10 is particularly memorable for passing through a succession of beautiful villages. **Biriatou**, **Aïnhoa** and **Sare** are examples of typical Basque villages, with their ancient churches, *frontons* (pelote courts) and colourful old houses. Further to the east, in Béarn, the mountainside hamlet of **Lescun** is considered by many to be one of the most beautiful spots in the Pyrenees. All visitors should make a point of seeing **St-Jean-Pied-de-Port**, the capital town of Basse-Navarre, with its 15th-century walls, and imposing citadel. Also worthy of a special mention is the 11th-century church in **Sainte-Engrâce**, which is held to be one of the best examples of early Romanesque church architecture in the Pyrenees. The western sections of the GR10 aren't just notable for the villages through which they pass: there are stunning views of the **Kakoueta and Holzarté gorges**, and the **Chemin de la Mâture** is one of the most memorable sections of the whole GR10.
● **Spain** On the Spanish side of the border, although the villages are not particularly exciting, special mention must be made of the monastery at **Roncesvalles** and of **Ochagavia**, a lovely little village of red-roofed houses. Several sections of the GR11 through the Western Pyrenees are also particularly impressive. Notably, the following stages: Isaba–Zuriza; Selba d'Oza–Candanchú; Candanchú–Sallent de Gallego; and Sallent de Gallego–Balneario (Baños) de Panticosa provide some challenging walking through quite amazing natural scenery.

no way approach the dramatic presence of the mountains in the Central Pyrenees, they've a grandeur of their own. The deep valleys, beautiful villages, and slow, friendly way of life are perfect for anyone who isn't too worried about going very far, or very high but would rather explore and enjoy an area of natural beauty and unique culture.

THE BASQUE COUNTRY

Politics and history

The **Basque Country** (Euskalleria in Basque) spreads out on both sides of the French–Spanish border. The ancient divisions of Labourd, Basse-Navarre and Soule, with a population of around 250,000, make up the French **Pays Basque**; Guipúzcoa, Vizcaya and Alava provinces, with a population of around $2^1/2$ million make up the Spanish **Pais Vasco**. While each area has its own character (the coastal provinces, for example, have a proud maritime history) much cultural heritage is shared.

Basque identity is tied up in a question of origins. The Basque language, Euskara, which has no known related tongue, is claimed by linguists to be the earliest of European languages. No one is quite sure where the ancestors of the Basques came from; some historians suggest that they were the earliest Celtic settlers, others that they came from North Africa, still others that they may have been a lost tribe of Israel. Whatever the answer, it is clear that Spanish and French Basques can trace their ancestry back to some of the earliest settlers of the Iberian peninsula.

The Basques are a proud and independent people who have asserted their individuality from the earliest times, their bloody revenge on Charlemagne in 778 being only one example. The French Basques formally became part of France when, in 1790 the Pays Basque and Béarn were brought together into a new département – the Basses Pyrénées. In 1970, despite local attempts to get departmental status for the Pays Basque, the département was renamed the Pyrénées Atlantiques; attempts to gain a level of self-government through a departmental administration are still continuing. In Spain, the Basque provinces enjoyed some autonomy until the Spanish Civil War, when Franco plotted the devastating bombing of Guernica, and thereafter removed their independence. In 1979 they were granted autonomy by the Spanish government, and although the majority of Spanish Basques are quite happy with the arrangement, it has proved insufficient to pacify a tiny minority who have resorted to terrorism, under the banner of ETA.

For the walker

The Basque Country is a region of deep, emerald-green valleys and squat farmhouses tucked into the folds of the hills. The half-timbered houses have remained in the same families for generations, and on the lintel over the front door of each

WESTERN PYRENEES

(**Opposite**): Traditional food shop, St-Étienne-de-Baïgorry. (Photo © Henry Stedman).

is recorded the year in which it was built and the name of the family. Huge, rough-cut corner stones and thick wooden shutters give an air of indestructibility, while fresh whitewash and brightly painted woodwork lend a sense of house-proud homeliness.

Food and drink

The local cuisine consists largely of huge, nourishing dishes with plenty of calories to see you through a tough day in the hills. *Jambon de Bayonne* (cured Bayonne ham) is the most famous speciality, and may be served with *piperade*, a sauce made from peppers and tomatoes. *Poulet Basquaise* is also very popular. *Fromage de brebis* (ewes' milk cheese) is made by farmers and shepherds throughout the region. *Gâteaux Basques* are a popular dessert to take up any space which might be left. *Irouleguy* is the most famous of the local wines, while *izarra* is the local liquor.

Beer drinkers trekking through the Pays Basque should try the local brews which, although not widely advertised, are often available if you ask for them by name. Some caution is required if you're planning an early start the following morning; *Akerbeltz* and *Oldarki*, the two most widely available brews, both weigh in at about 6% alcohol by volume.

BÉARN

Politics and history

Although Béarn may be less well known by name than the Pays Basque, it too has a proud history. Nowhere in the Pyrenees is the cross-border tradition more clearly seen than here. On 13 July each year, at the Col de La Pierre St-Martin, the communities of the Roncal valley (Spain) and Barétous valley (France) celebrate the Tribute of the Three Cows. The tradition goes back to 1375, and is thought to be the earliest peace treaty still in force in Europe.

For many years Béarn existed as a semi-independent and powerful statelet. Its proud boast is having been the birthplace of King Henry IV (1553-1610), who was born in Pau, son of Antoine de Bourbon and Jeanne d'Albret, Queen of Navarre. Henry acceded to the throne in 1589 and is remembered as one of the best rulers in French history. Although Béarn was quite clearly a part of the French state from this time, it maintained a surprising level of autonomy for years to come.

For the walker

Beyond the village of Sainte-Engrâce, which stands at the eastern extent of the Pays Basque, Béarn is a transitional zone between the hills of the coastal belt and the high mountains of the Central Pyrenees. There is a striking contrast between the rich greenness of the Basque country and the limestone moonscape that surrounds the Pic d'Anie (2504m). This area of karst (limestone) forma-

(Opposite) The ancient game of pelote (see p77) is ingrained in the Basque way of life and no Basque village is without its court, which may be an outdoor court (*fronton*) as shown here or an indoor one (*trinquet*). (Photos © Greg and Jane Knott).

WESTERN PYRENEES

tions boasts some of most memorable views in the Pyrenees – the Aspe and Ossau valleys, the Cirque de Lescun, the Chemin de la Mâture and the Pic du Midi d'Ossau (2884m).

NAVARRA

Politics and history
In its day, Navarra was one of the most important kingdoms in the Pyrenees, and stretched across the mountains to include what is today the French district of Basse Navarre. The rise of Navarra as an independent kingdom started with its first king, Iñigo Arista (824-852), and the kingdom reached its peak around the 11th century during the reign of Sancho el Mayor (1004-1035).

Navarra was a springboard for efforts to push the Moors out of Spain, and in 1212 it was the king Sancho el Fuerte who led the charge in the Battle of Las Navas de Tolosa, where the Moors were routed. The power of the kingdom began to wane in the fifteenth century, the decline accelerated by a dispute between two leading families.

In 1479, Navarra became divided; the Spanish lands were annexed by Ferdinand of Aragón, while the northern half of the territory went to Catherine of Foix. Catherine's grandson was Henry of Navarre, who subsequently became Henry IV of France. In 1512, Spanish Navarra was formally annexed by Castille/Aragón, although it remained semi-independent until 1841, when it finally became a province of Spain.

For the walker
Navarra is largely undeveloped and consequently this is an area to consider if you like the idea of getting away from things – including other walkers, and most facilities. The sections of the GR11 (the Spanish long-distance path) which pass through Navarra are hardly exciting; there are lengthy stretches along rough forestry roads and in places the route is poorly marked.

They do, however, provide a logical itinerary across this part of the Pyrenees with far fewer walkers than on the French side of the border, and occasional highlights – such at the monastery at Roncesvalles, and the pretty villages of Ochagavia and Isaba.

ARAGÓN

Politics and history
The Romans started mining activities in several places in the Pyrenees but the high valleys remained largely untouched by them or, later, by the Moors. Christianity appears to have reached the mountains in the seventh and eighth centuries, and at the end of the eighth century the region came under the control of the Franks when Charlemagne created the Spanish March.

With the slow disintegration of Charlemagne's empire, and the gradual retreat southwards of the Moors, the kingdoms of northern Spain began to sort themselves out. Aragón, initially an area of the March under a nominated governor, began to emerge as a separate entity from the eighth century onwards, and from the ninth century became linked by marriage to neighbouring Navarra.

Even after the union of Aragón and Castille in 1479, the kingdoms of Aragón, Catalonia and Navarra retained a large degree of self-rule, and it was not for some time that border questions were settled.

Walking in Western Aragón

In comparison to Navarra, the sections of the GR11 through western Aragón begin to feel truly mountainous. Although the scenery is not as dramatic as that to be found to the east, in the central area of the Spanish Pyrenees, there are several spectacular day stages. In some ways you get the best of all worlds here: great scenery and fewer other walkers than you'll encounter on the sections through the Ordesa region, which follow.

GETTING THERE

Getting to the Western Pyrenees

● **Air** There are airports in Bordeaux, Biarritz and Pau, as well as Bilbao in Spain.
● **Train** TGVs run from Paris to Bayonne, Biarritz, Hendaye, Pau and Tarbes.
● **Coach** A summertime coach service to Bayonne is operated by Eurolines from London. See p18 for more information.

Getting to the walking

● **Western end** Starting the GR10 from its western end is easy. For those flying to Bordeaux or Biarritz there are numerous daily trains from both places to Bayonne, Hendaye and Irun. Those flying to Pau can also get a train west to Bayonne and Hendaye, although there's also easy access to the mountains by catching a bus south. Alternatively, you can catch a direct TGV from Paris to Hendaye.

To get into the hills further eastwards there are various possibilities:
● **Bidarray** (p78), **St-Étienne-de-Baïgorry** (p83), **St-Jean-Pied-de-Port** (p86). There are five daily trains from Bayonne along the branch line, via Bidarray (NB the name of the station is actually Pont Noblia) and St-Martin-d'Arossa to St-Jean-Pied-de-Port. The journey takes an hour, and a one-way ticket costs €7.70. The first train from Bayonne to St-Jean currently departs at 08.55; the last train departs, between July 11 and Sept 5 at 19.58 and for the rest of the year at 18.03. From St-Martin-d'Arossa there is an SNCF bus service to St-Étienne-de-Baïgorry. If you miss the train, a taxi from Bayonne to St-Jean-Pied-de Port will cost about €65. Europcar has an office in rue Hugues, opposite Bayonne railway station.
● **Borce/Etsaut** (p105) From Pau there are regular trains to Oloron-Ste-Marie, from where there's an SNCF bus service to Borce and Etsaut (approx 5 daily).
● **Gabas/Bious Oumette/Lac de Bious Artigues** (p109) There are few **buses** passing through Gabas. In July and August the Pic Bus runs twice daily (excluding weekends and holidays) between Laruns, to the north, and the Col du Portalet, to the south. Currently, the morning service departs from Laruns at 08.45, calling at Gabas (09.10) and at the Camping de Bious-Oumette (09.20) on its way south; on the return journey (departing from Portalet at 10.20) it stops only at Gabas (10.50). The afternoon service departs Laruns at 15.20 call-

ing at Gabas (but not Bious-Oumette) at 15.45 and returns (departing from Portalet at 16.25) via both Bious-Oumette (17.10) and Gabas (17.20); the fare is €3. The company that runs the Pic Bus also operates **taxis** (☎ 05.59. 05.30.31). A taxi from Laruns to the Lac de Bious-Artigues costs around €30.

● **Gourette** (p112) Buses operate during the peak season (ie July and August) between Gourette and Pau via Laruns and Les Eaux Bonnes. There are currently two services each way every day.

● **Arrens-Marsous** (p114) There is one bus a day (except Sundays and holidays) between Tarbes and Arrens-Marsous via Lourdes (bus station) and Pierrefitte Nestalas (from where there are connections to Cauterets, Luz-St-Sauveur and, indirectly, Gavarnie). From Tarbes to Arrens takes one and a half hours; from Lourdes to Arrens takes just over one hour.

Car hire
This will obviously not be ideal for most people, as it's very expensive to hire a car and then go walking for several days. If you want to have a very flexible itinerary it may, however, be suitable.

● **Lourdes** Avis (☎ 05.62.42.12.97) has an office at the railway station

● **Pau** Avis (☎ 05.59.13.31.33), avenue Didier Daurat, Budget (☎ 05. 59.62.72.54), avenue Jean Mermoz, Europcar (☎ 05.59.92.09.09), 115 avenue Jean Mermoz.

Western Pyrenees – GR10

The starting point for both the GR10 and the HRP is the quiet resort town of Hendaye on the border between France and Spain.

HENDAYE
✉ code 64700

Hendaye sits on the northern bank of the Bidassoa River, the waterway which marks the border between France and Spain. Across the river, the tenement buildings of Fontarabie and Irún do little to tempt the visitor further southwards and it has to be said that Hendaye is hardly exciting. Stock up on provisions, have a good meal and possibly a quick swim – and then go.

Orientation and services
The town is divided into two parts: Hendaye Ville, which is the area around the railway station and near to the border bridge, and Hendaye-Plage, which is 2km to the north. As its name suggests, the latter of these is the area to find the beach as well as a multitude of small hotels and the nearest of the

campsites. Although there are several shops around the seafront, the large stores, including two supermarkets, are to be found nearer the ville.

There's a daytime **bus service** running to and from Fontarabie across the border. It goes every half hour from the traffic circle behind the beach, past the railway station and on to Fontarabie. **Taxis** wait outside the railway station or can be booked: try Tino Taxis (☎ 05.59.20.56.79 / 06.09.72.86.67) or Agur Chingudy Radio Taxis (☎ 05.59. 20.85.82).

The **post office** is on rue des Aubepines (Mon-Fri 09.00-12.00 & 13.30-16.30, Sat 09.00-12.00), just to the south-east of the traffic circle in Hendaye-Plage. Next door is the **tourist office** (☎ 05.59.20 00.34, 🖥 www.hendaye.com), where they provide a useful free map of the town. There's an **internet café**, Cyber Basque, up the hill from the station at 39 boulevard du Gen-de-Gaulle. It's open daily, 09.00-02.00.

There is a row of **banks** and bureaux de change opposite the railway station, and there are also two branches with cash dispensers near the Place de la République. Note that many banks in Hendaye are closed on Mondays.

Europcar have an agent in a garage just to the east of the railway station (☎ 05

.59.20.70.86) and **Avis** have an office opposite the station (☎ 05.59.20.79.04).

For **supplies** before starting your walk, the best place is the enormous Champion supermarket on rue Iran-datz. They sell the blue camping gaz here (both the old and new style cylinders) but do not stock Coleman Epigas. If you need Epigas, try the Bricotruc branch on the upper level (ie above the supermarket). They sell large bottles of gas designed for use with blowtorches, although the thread size should be suitable for Epigas stoves.

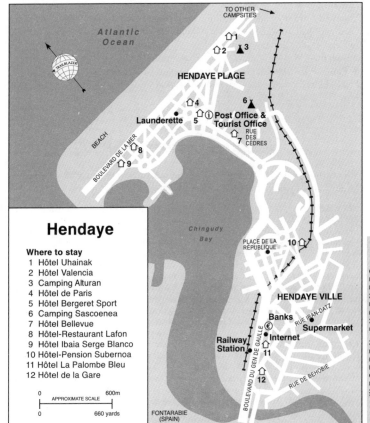

Hendaye

Where to stay
1 Hôtel Uhainak
2 Hôtel Valencia
3 Camping Alturan
4 Hôtel de Paris
5 Hôtel Bergeret Sport
6 Camping Sascoenea
7 Hôtel Bellevue
8 Hôtel-Restaurant Lafon
9 Hôtel Ibaia Serge Blanco
10 Hôtel-Pension Subernoa
11 Hôtel La Palombe Bleu
12 Hôtel de la Gare

0   600m
APPROXIMATE SCALE
0   660 yards

WESTERN PYRENEES

Where to stay

As one would expect in a resort town, there is no shortage of accommodation.

● **Hendaye-Plage** The undisputed top place in Hendaye-Plage is the *Hôtel Ibaia Serge Blanco* ☆☆☆☆ (☎ 05.59.48.88.88, 🖥 05.59.48.88.89). Rooms in high season start at €126/158 sgl/dbl. Close by, and actually on the sea front, is the *Hôtel Restaurant Lafon* ☆☆ (☎ 05.59.20.04.67, 🖥 05.59.48.06.85), a large, friendly boarding house where double rooms start at €63-65, with breakfast €6. Better value is the *Hôtel de Paris* ☆☆ (☎ 05.59.20.05.06, 🖥 05.59.48.02.82), 68 blvd Leclerc, which is on the traffic circle just back from the seafront. Rooms start at €35 – great value – and there's a pleasant shady terrace where you can sip your beer and mentally prepare yourself for the walk ahead.

Then there's *Hôtel Bellevue* ☆ (☎ 05.59.20.00.26, 🖥 www.hotelbellevue-hendaye.com) along the road at 36 blvd Leclerc, with rooms from €43 and a view overlooking the river-mouth that is, if not *belle*, certainly rather interesting.

Other hotels of a similar standard and price in Hendaye-Plage, include the *Hôtel Uhainak* ☆☆ (☎ 05.59.20.33.63, 🖥 05.59.48.13.72; rates from €56-71 sgl/dbl); *Hôtel Valencia* ☆☆ (☎ 05.59.20.01.62, 🖥 05.59.20.17.92; rates €50-68) and the friendly *Hôtel Bergeret Sport* ☆☆ (☎ 05.59.20.00.78, 🖥 05.59.20.67.30; rates from €122/140 demi-pension/pension for 2 people).

● **Hendaye Ville** In the Ville, many places open from 18.00 only (unless there's a café). There are several places that are conveniently close to the railway station. *Hôtel La Palombe Bleue* (☎ 05.59.20.43.80) is the cheapest of these, but prices have risen recently: double rooms now start at €34. Directly opposite the station is the *Hôtel de la Gare* ☆☆ (☎ 05.59.20.81.90), where

double rooms start at €43. If you're looking for something cheaper, you could try *Hôtel/Pension Subernoa* (☎ 05.59.20.08.33), on rue Subernoa. It's quite far from the station and is a bit dingy but has basic double rooms from €45 during high season.

There are several campsites but they are all a fair way from the railway station. The nearest to the station is *Camping Sascoenea* ☆☆☆ (☎ 05.59.20.05.44, 🖥 05. 59.20.55.77) where it costs, in high season, €18 for two people and a tent. There is a restaurant on site. *Camping Alturan* ☆☆☆ (☎ 05.59.20. 04.56) is the next nearest to the town centre and is located just behind the beach on Hendaye-Plage; it costs from €9.

Although there are several other campsites around Hendaye, they are all much further out and the prices only minimally lower. The following are pleasant enough: *Camping les 2 Jumeaux* ☆☆ (☎ 05.59. 20.01.65; 🖥 www.camping-des-2jumeaux. com) where one person with a tent can stay for €15; *Camping Ametza* ☆☆☆ (☎ 05.59. 20.07.05; 🖥 www.camping-ametza.com) – more expensive but it has a swimming pool; *Camping du Moulin* ☆☆ (☎ 05.59. 20.76.35) – almost the entire clientele are in camper trailers – very residential; *Camping Les Acacias* ☆☆☆ (☎ 05.59.20.78.76) – again they're rather surprised to see a real live backpacker – most people here have brought the kids' bikes, the barbecue etc and are well settled in.

Where to eat

Nearly all the hotel restaurants have reasonable food but particularly worth a try are the restaurants of the *Hôtel Bergeret Sport*. For Chinese and Thai food, try *Le Jardin de Jade*, on Boulevard de la Baie de Chingudy. For cheap eats, *La P'tit Bouff* on ave des Allées in the Ville serves pizzas, baguettes and burgers.

HENDAYE → OLHETTE   [MAP 1, p73]

Officially the GR10 starts on the seafront by the casino building (now the Residence Croisière), heads down to the roundabout and onto rue Citronniers, continues along the waterfront before weaving its way along boulevard du Général Leclerc, rue Subernoa, chemin Biantena and rue Errondenia. For a slightly more scenic route, however, take the newly established waterfront promenade along boulevard de la Baie (rather than following the busy boulevard du Général Leclerc), turning up along rue Pellot. The red-and-white GR markings (see p23) initially appear at that first roundabout near the casino, though the first obvious ones are on chemin Biantena, as you leave the town. Wherever you come across the first one, there's no doubt that by the time the path leaves the

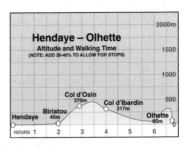

Hendaye – Olhette
Altitude and Walking Time
(NOTE: ADD 30-40% TO ALLOW FOR STOPS)

outskirts of the town they are well established and easy to spot.

At the top of rue Errondenia the GR10 turns right, following the lane past a farmhouse on top of a small hill and on to a track that appears on your left, with a building site opposite. Turn left and follow the track over a knoll and down an access lane to the main road (N10). Cross the road and head off to the right on an overgrown footpath that initially runs parallel to the road before turning sharply right and down the hill (south). Follow the GR10 markings closely as it takes you back onto tarmac past a few farmhouses, then descend steeply. At the bottom, follow the lane, turning right to an underpass below the autoroute, beyond which the lane leads towards **Biriatou**, which you reach about two hours after starting from the seafront. Here, *Hôtel les Jardins de Bakea* ☆☆ (☎ 05. 59.20.02.01, 🖳 www.bakea.com) charges €51 in high season for a double room. Squeezing between the church and Auberge Hiribarren, take a left on the lane as the GR10 curves round the village below the church then turns right off the road. The path now climbs steeply up a rough footpath under electricity pylons to just below the Rochers des Perdrix, and then contours around the hillside to the **Col d'Osin (370m)**. At the col there's a yellow sign, OLHETTE 3H 20, and there are good views over the next section of the walk. Descend to the Col de Poiriers, where there's a turnoff to the lake, before climbing steeply again along the side of a wood, and then towards the summit of Mandalé (573m), keeping an eastward direction and ignoring the paths to your right (south) leading beyond the gully below. The path skirts north around the top of this hill and then descends to meet a tarmac road, beside which is a large and busy *venta,* a traditional market area straddling the border, which in days gone by offered duty-free bargains for shoppers from both France and Spain. These days, with the advent of the EU, the sales pitch has turned to discounted items and bulk selling – tacky souvenirs, discount alcohol and cigarettes. It's a far from attractive spot; there are, however, two or three places to eat. Follow the shop-lined road downhill to the **Col d'Ibardin (317m)**, which you'll get to about four hours after starting from Hendaye.

From the col (the road junction at the bottom of the slope), walk north for 50 metres along the tarmac, before turning right near a signpost: OLHETTE 2H 10. After a short but steep climb the GR10 joins a track which turns sharply to the left (it's the only path going downhill from this junction) and descends along the valley side. Just before meeting a minor road (at point A on Map 1), the path

WESTERN PYRENEES

> ### Route maps
> ● **Scale and walking times** All the following trail maps are drawn to a scale of 1:100,000 (10mm = 1km/0.625miles). Walking times are given along the side of each map, and the arrow shows the direction to which the time refers. Black triangles indicate the points between which the times have been taken. Note that the time given refers only to the time spent walking, so you will need to **add 30-40% to allow for rest stops**. Remember that these are **my timings** for the section; every walker has his or her own speed. With the first edition of this book, several readers commented that they found these timings on the fast side. The times are, however, consistent so you should err on the side of caution for a day or two until you see how your speed relates to my timings on the maps. When planning the day's trekking, count on between five and seven hours actual walking, and allow for an occasional rest day.
> ● **Up or down?** The trail is shown as a dotted line. An arrow across the trail indicates the slope; two arrows show that it is steep. Note that the arrow points towards the higher part of the trail. If, for example, you're walking from A (at 900m) to B (at 1100m) and the trail between the two is short and steep it would be shown thus: A—>>—B.
> ● **Refuges, gîtes and cabanes** Everywhere to stay that is within easy reach of the trail is marked. See the text for more details about each place.
> ● **Other information and symbols** Altitudes are given on the map in metres. Places where you can get water are shown by a 'W' within a circle.

cuts down into a dip and, turning eastwards, continues downhill through the trees on the north side of the little valley. At the eastern end of the valley (near spot height 115m on the map) the path meets an old paved way leading south-eastwards to the Spanish border. Turn right and follow the old road alongside a rushing stream; just before arriving at **Inzola** there are four or five stepping stones which can be precarious if the watercourse is in spate. About 200m beyond the stones, you'll see the *Café-Bar d'Inzola*, where food and drink are available but there's no accommodation. (Note you've now crossed the border, something the café capitalizes on by selling 'Souvenirs d'Espagne'.)

From the café, cross a tiny footbridge and climb north-eastwards, following narrow paths up the gullied hillside, to a pleasant grassy col (spot height 273m). From here the GR10 makes a gradual descent northwards along the valley side to the gîte d'étape at Olhette. The *gîte* (☎ 05.59.54.00.98) is open all year and can take 14 people. Conditions are basic but quite adequate, with a hot shower and a small kitchen area. It costs €9 for the night, or €28 for demi-pension. The nearest village of any size is Ascain, which is four km away.

OLHETTE → AÏNHOA [MAP 2, p75]

A sign, SARE 3H 05, outside the gîte, points the walker across the stream and up the opposite hillside. The initial climb is hard-going, particularly in hot weather, and takes nearly an hour as you struggle south-eastwards towards the dominating shape of La Rhune (900m – see p74). There are lots of 'false' paths (though, to be fair, they all seem to join up with the main path eventually), and further up the path frays regularly. Nevertheless, the path is easy to follow,

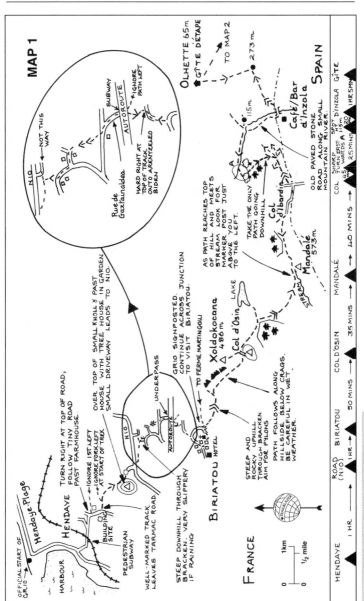

MAP 1

OLHETTE 65m GÎTE D'ÉTAPE

TO MAP 2

SPAIN

Café/Bar d'Inzola

Col d'Ibardin

Mandale 573m.

Xoldokogaina 486m.

Col d'Osin LAKE

TO FERME MARTINGOILI

GRIO SIGNPOSTED. CONTINUE ACROSS JUNCTION TO VISIT BIRIATOU.

AS PATH REACHES TOP OF HILL AND MEETS STREAM LOOK FOR MARKER POST JUST ABOVE YOU TO THE LEFT.

TAKE THE ONLY PATH GOING DOWNHILL

OLD PAVED STONE ROAD ALONG SMALL MOUNTAIN RIVER.

PATH FOLLOWS ALONG HILLSIDE BELOW CRAGS. BE CAREFUL IN WET WEATHER.

STEEP AND ROCKY, UPHILL THROUGH BRACKEN. AIM FOR PYLONS.

BIRIATOU HOTEL

STEEP DOWNHILL THROUGH BRACKEN. VERY SLIPPERY IF RAINING.

UNDERPASS

AUTOROUTE

N10

OVER TOP OF SMALL KNOLL & PAST HOUSE WITH TREE IN GARDEN. SMALL DRIVEWAY LEADS TO N10.

TURN RIGHT AT TOP OF ROAD, FOLLOW TINY ROAD PAST FARMHOUSE.

IGNORE 1ST LEFT IGNORE FORK LEFT AT START OF TREK

WELL-MARKED TRACK LEAVES TARMAC ROAD

BUILDING SITE

PEDESTRIAN SUBWAY

Hendaye

Hendaye Plage

OFFICIAL START OF GR.10

HARBOUR

NOT THIS WAY

N10

SUBWAY

IGNORE PATH LEFT

Rue de Graztainaldea

AUTOROUTE

HARD RIGHT AT TOP OF TRACK ONTO ARENTZUELEU BIDEN

FRANCE

115m.

273m.

1km
½ mile

0

WESTERN PYRENEES

HENDAYE — 1 HR. — ROAD (N10) — 1 HR — BIRIATOU — 50 MINS — COL D'OSIN — 35 MINS — MANDALÉ — 40 MINS — COL — SHARP TURN POST 55 YARDS — SPOT HT. DINZOLA 115m — 25 MINS — GÎTE — IRESHIN

although the variety of painted markers can be a little confusing; there are blue and yellow marks as well as the normal red and white. Near the top, cairns plot the course of the GR10. The consolation in the rather hard first hour is that when you reach the **Col des Trois Fontaines (563m)**, just below the summit of La Rhune, you've pretty much done the day's climbing. At the col, a signpost, SARE

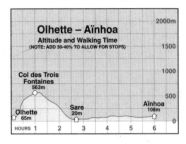

1H 35, indicates the way around the edge of a wood, on the far side of which is a large track leading south-eastwards. After about ten minutes the GR10 crosses a miniature **rack railway** running to the summit of the hill, a popular tourist attraction, then descends along a footpath towards Sare. About halfway down the hill the footpath doubles back on itself by a ruin to join a rock-strewn track which eventually leads down to a tarmac lane. Follow the lane to within the last kilometre or so of Sare, turning off at a sharp right-hand bend to cross a small bridge by a couple of farm buildings; it's not well marked, but if you reach the road at the foot of the lane, you've gone too far. From here the GR10 cuts across the fields for 10-15 minutes on two overgrown footpaths before emerging on a tarmac lane leading into the village.

The Storming of La Petite Rhune

The ridge just to the west of La Rhune was the scene of one of the last engagements of the Peninsular War when, on 10 November 1813, Wellington's forces carried the Heights of the Nive. Among the units taking part were the Rifle Brigade ('the bloody fighting 95th') who formed part of the formidable Light Division. In his autobiography, Harry Smith (later Lt Gen Sir Harry Smith), describes the capture of La Petite Rhune:

'As we started for our position before the great, the important day, the night was very dark. We had no road, and positively nothing to guide us but knowing the bushes and stones over a mountain ridge. Colborne stayed near the Brigade, and sent me on from spot to spot which we both knew, when he would come up to me and satisfy himself that I was right. I then went on again. In this manner we crept up with our Brigade to our advanced picquet within a hundred and fifty yards of the enemy...The anxious moment of appearing day arrived. We fell in, and our attack was made on the enemy's position in seven columns, nor did we ever meet a check, but carried the enemy's works, the tents all standing, by one fell swoop of irresistible victory...Ours was the most beautiful attack ever made in the history of war.'

SARE

Sare is a lovely little place – acclaimed as one of the most beautiful of the Basque villages. While this means that in summer its streets are crowded with tourists, it also means that there are several places to stay and to eat, and Sare is an ideal place to break the day's walk for a leisurely lunch.

There are a couple of small **shops**, useful for stocking up. More information can be had from the **tourist office** (☎ 05.59.54. 20.14) and there's a **post office** too (Mon-Fri 09.00-12.00, 13.30-16.30, Sat 09.00-

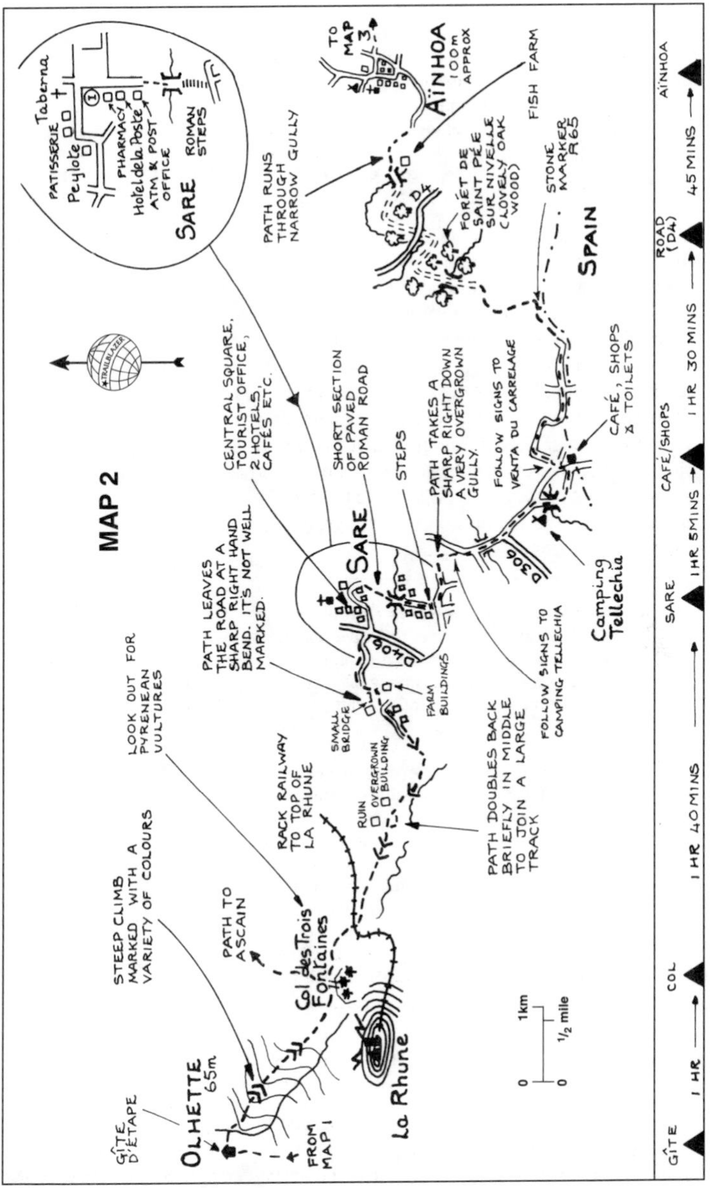

MAP 2

OLHETTE 65m.

GÎTE D'ÉTAPE

FROM MAP 1

La Rhune

Col des Trois Fontaines

PATH TO ASCAIN

STEEP CLIMB MARKED WITH A VARIETY OF COLOURS

LOOK OUT FOR PYRENEAN VULTURES

RACK RAILWAY TO TOP OF LA RHUNE

RUIN

OVERGROWN BUILDING

PATH DOUBLES BACK BRIEFLY IN MIDDLE TO JOIN A LARGE TRACK

SMALL BRIDGE

FARM BUILDINGS

FOLLOW SIGNS TO CAMPING TELLECHEA

PATH LEAVES THE ROAD AT A SHARP RIGHT HAND BEND. IT'S NOT WELL MARKED.

D306

SARE

CENTRAL SQUARE, TOURIST OFFICE, 2 HOTELS, CAFÉS ETC.

SHORT SECTION OF PAVED ROMAN ROAD

STEPS

PATH TAKES A SHARP RIGHT DOWN A VERY OVERGROWN GULLY.

FOLLOW SIGNS TO VENTA DU CARRELAGE

Camping Tellechea

D306

CAFÉ, SHOPS & TOILETS

SPAIN

STONE MARKER R65

FISH FARM

FORÊT DE SAINT PÉE SUR NIVELLE (LOVELY OAK WOOD)

PATH RUNS THROUGH NARROW GULLY

TO MAP 3

AÏNHOA

100m APPROX

SARE

PÂTISSERIE

Peyloko

Taberna

PHARMACY

Hotel de la Poste

ATM & POST OFFICE

ROMAN STEPS

0   1km
0   ½ mile

WESTERN PYRENEES

GÎTE	COL	SARE	CAFÉ/SHOPS	ROAD (D4)	AÏNHOA
1 HR	1 HR 40 MINS	1 HR 5MINS	1 HR 30 MINS	45 MINS	

12.30). On weekdays during July and August there's a regular **bus service** (☎ 05.59.26.30.74) between Sare and St Jean de Luz (just north of Hendaye), from where it's possible to pick up onward transport by bus or train. The service operates only three days a week between April and June, and September and October. There are a couple of local **taxi** operators: try Taxi Ederko (☎ 05.59 54.26.92) or Transport de Personnes (☎ 05. 59.54.27.23).

Where to stay

Top of the pile is the *Hôtel Arraya* ☆☆☆ (☎ 05.59.54.20.46, 💻 www.arraya.com), which has a lovely terrace restaurant and a rather exclusive atmosphere; doubles start at €62. On the other side of the street, the

Hôtel de la Poste (☎ 05.59.54.20.06) is rather more basic; it's open from mid-June to mid-September and has rooms from €33.

The tourist office also lists a number of *chambres chez l'habitant* (chambres d'hôte) which might be worth a try, though you should check where they actually are, before booking. Among those on offer are: *Maison Otsanda* (☎ 05.59.85.93.16) from €46 for a double room, breakfast included; *Maison Argi-Alde* (☎ 05.59.54.20.93) doubles from €36; *Maison Mendian* (☎ 05.59. 54.25.96) doubles from €45.

The nearest campsite to Sare is the *Camping de la Petite Rhune* ☆☆☆ (☎ 05. 59.54.23.97, 🖨 05.59.54.23. 42), which is 1.5km south of Sare. It's €12 for two people and a tent.

The GR10 leaves Sare via an old paved lane, next to which is a sign: AÏNHOA 3H 20. The lane passes over a tiny bridge and ends at a set of steps. At the top of the steps, turn left and continue eastwards for several hundred metres; at the end of this access lane, go right for 300-400m down an overgrown pathway, to meet a larger road (D306). Turn right and follow the road for about 500 metres before turning left down a small lane leading south-eastwards towards the border, following the signs to *Camping Tellechea* (☎ 05.59.54.20.12) a fairly basic campsite which is open only during July and August; emplacement is €3.10 and it's €2.5 per person. Just past the campsite the GR10 turns right along another lane, passes through a farmyard, and rejoins a short stretch of road leading to the border, where there's a venta (market, see p71). Facilities here include a shop, toilets and a café; it's not a very attractive area. From the venta, the GR10 continues towards Aïnhoa almost entirely on country lanes or large farm tracks which are well marked. An initial loop is made to the north before the path heads back to the border near marker stone 63. As the path finally swings northwards towards the D4 road, it passes through an area of attractive oak forest before crossing the main road and heading into Aïnhoa village.

AÏNHOA

✉ code 64250

Aïnhoa is a pretty village centred around a short main street. Sadly, apart from places to stay and eat there are few facilities here which are of much use to walkers. There are several shops selling trinkets, but none of them sells food. There's no bank (the nearest bank is in Espelette, some five kilometres to the north-west) and there's no public transport (the best bet is to hitch a lift or get a taxi to Cambo-les-Bains, and

pick up public transport there). The **tourist office** (☎ 05.59.29.92.60; 🖨 05.59.29 .86.31) is in the Mairie on the main street; they should be able to help with queries about transport. There's also a **post office**. From a sightseeing point of view, Aïnhoa has an open-air pelote court, and a lovely old church.

Where to stay

The top place in town is undoubtedly the *Hôtel Argi Eder* ☆☆☆ (☎ 05.59.93.72.00,

Pelote

Undoubtedly the most famous of Basque games is pelote (*pelota*). Despite the fact that we glibly give it a single name, there are around 20 versions of the game. Its classic form, which is descended from the game of *paume*, is known as *main nue*; as the name suggests, players use their bare hands to serve and return the ball. In other versions, the players use varying forms of *palas* (wooden bats), *pasakas* (leather gloves) or *chisteras*, basket-shaped contraptions made of chestnut and willow, which are attached to the hand with a glove. No Basque village is without its pelote court (see photos opposite p65); this may be an outdoor court (*fronton*) or an indoor court (*trinquet*). The extent to which Basque life rotates around pelote is revealed in the way in which the courts have become central landmarks in towns and villages. You may be told that your hotel is near the *trinquet municipal* or be directed to the avenue du Fronton.

The fastest version of pelote is played using huge basket-shaped gloves called *grand chisteras*. This game, *cesta punta*, is the fastest ball game in the world. Often known by the name of the court in which it is played, *jäi alai*, the game has become popular in Florida, and the many of the best Basque players now pursue their sporting careers in the United States.

05.59.93.72.13). It's rather overpriced, with rooms from €84 to €138, but the facilities include a swimming pool and two tennis courts. Although staying here will be well out of most walkers' price range, if you're after a really good meal try the restaurant – set menus range in price from €20 to €36, and the food is excellent.

Hôtel Ithurria ☆☆☆ (☎ 05.59. 29.92.11, 🗐 05.59.29.81.28) can manage to match Argi Eder on price too: rooms here start at €88. The restaurant looks very good but is expensive; the 'Menu Basque' is inter-

esting, though. Luckily there are a couple of cheaper places to stay in the village: *Hôtel Oppoca* ☆☆ (☎ 05.59.29.90.72, 🖳 www. oppoca.com) has double rooms for €38-49.50, and *Hôtel Ohantzea* ☆☆ (☎ 05.59. 29.90.50) is a friendly place with doubles starting at €45-55 plus €6 for breakfast.

Camping Harazpy (☎ 05.59.29.89 .38) is conveniently close to the centre of the village and is relatively cheap – €3 for emplacement, and €3.75 per person. It's open from mid-June to mid-September.

AÏNHOA → BIDARRAY
[MAP 3, p79]

The GR10 leaves Aïnhoa along the lane running eastwards from the centre of the village and past the Argi Eder hotel. A sign at the start of the lane indicates the route and some likely timings: COL DES VEAUX 3H 30; BIDARRAY 7H. The tarmac road soon gives way to a loose-surfaced track which winds up

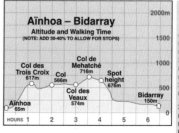

the steep hillside to the **Chapelle de l'Aubepine**, and the **three crosses** which can be seen from certain points in the village. From the chapel, follow a good vehicle track which runs north-east around the side of Ereby (583m). On the north side of the hill look out for a **small sheep shelter**; the GR10 passes next to the building before joining another track heading south-east. Some 1¼ hours after starting from Aïnhoa you'll reach the **Col des Trois Croix (510m)**.

Although the IGN 1:50,000 map shows the route skirting to the north of Atxulegi (617m), the sign (COL DES VEAUX 2H) and the route markers actually direct walkers along the vehicle track which passes to the south of the hill top. The rough road descends to a track junction and then climbs to a col (spot height 566m on the map). Keep an eye out for vultures to the east of the col; they are often to be seen circling above. From here the route is well marked; a vehicle track leads initially along the side of the valley, but it soon narrows to a footpath that descends to the **Col des Veaux (574m)**. Just to the west of the col itself, the path passes some farm buildings and the lovely cow, pig and duck farm that is a friendly *gîte d'étape* (☎ 05.59.29.82.72), which is open all year and can take 14 people: it costs €9 for the night and €12 for the evening meal, and kitchen facilities are available for guests.

From the Col des Veaux, the path heads eastwards, and soon joins the tarmac road leading up to the **Col de Mehatché (716m)**. At the col, which marks the border between the provinces of Labourd and Basse Navarre, the GR10 swings south-eastwards. The ensuing 1.5km are easy – though there are next to no markers along the way – until the path reaches the top of the crags (spot height 676m on the map). From here the GR10 drops steeply towards Bidarray – a descent which many remember as one of the narrowest and most vertigo-inspiring on the GR10, with the initial descent being the steepest. The views are magnificent, but ensure that you leave plenty of time for this section and take it slowly; only three days after starting from the Atlantic, your knees may not have adjusted to the stresses and strains of mountain walking, and this particular section has caused more than its fair share of injuries. Near the bottom of the descent a brief diversion (only a few metres) is possible to visit the **Grotte du Saint qui Sue**, a small cave with an iron cross and a couple of tiny icons.

Just below the cave, the path heads round the back of a farm, following the farm wall to join a tarmac lane. Follow the lane downhill to a bridge over the river, and then east along the valley bottom. After 2km along the river, you come to an old stone bridge; the GR10 does not cross the bridge but cuts uphill to the right, just before it joins a footpath leading directly to Bidarray. Unfortunately route marking here is poor, and some exploration in the undergrowth is required to find the way. The footpath eventually joins another lane which leads to a road junction and the *gîte*.

BIDARRAY
⊠ code 64780

Arriving in Bidarray on foot, it would be easy to think that the village consisted only of the buildings near the gîte d'étape. In fact, Bidarray is split into two parts: the gîte, shop (Mon-Sat 08.30-12.30, 16.30-20.00, Sun mornings only), restaurant, tourist office (closed at the time of writing), post office, church and one hotel are in the upper part of the village, while the lower part, near the River Nive and the D918, boasts a couple more hotels, a campsite and the railway station.

Five trains a day run each way between Bayonne and St-Jean-Pied-de-Port and stop at the small station, which is shown on timetables as 'Pont Noblia'. If you're heading for Saint-Étienne-de-Baïgorry it's possi-

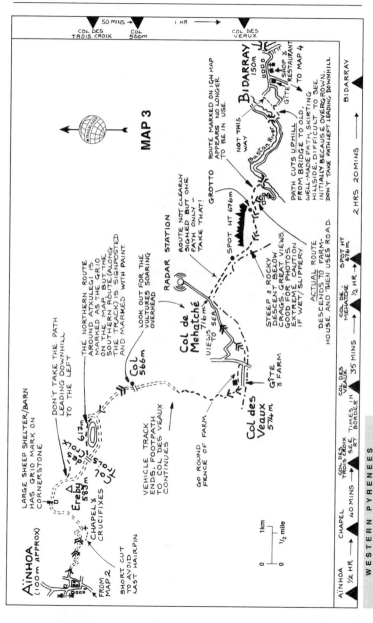

MAP 3

Col des Trois Croix — 50 MINS → **Col 566m** — 1 HR → **Col des Veaux**

AÏNHOA (100M APPROX)

FROM MAP 2

SHORT CUT TO AVOID LAST HAIRPIN

CHAPEL & CRUCIFIXES

Ereby 583m

Col des Trois Croix 617m

LARGE SHEEP SHELTER/BARN HAS GRIO MARK ON CORNERSTONE

DON'T TAKE THE PATH LEADING DOWNHILL TO THE LEFT

THE NORTHERN ROUTE AROUND ATXULEGI IS MARKED AS THE GRIO ON THE MAP, BUT THE SOUTHERN ROUTE (ALONG THE TRACK) IS SIGNPOSTED AND MARKED WITH PAINT.

Col 566m

VEHICLE TRACK ENDS, FOOTPATH TO COL DES VEAUX CONTINUES

GO ROUND FENCE OF FARM

LOOK OUT FOR THE VULTURES SOARING OVERHEAD

RADAR STATION

Col de Mehatché 716m   VIEWS TO SEA

Col des Veaux 574m

GÎTE & FARM

STEEP & ROCKY DESCENT BELOW COL GREAT VIEWS, GOOD FOR PHOTOS. EXTREME CAUTION IF WET/SLIPPERY.

ACTUAL ROUTE DESCENDS TO FARM-HOUSE AND THEN USES ROAD.

ROUTE NOT CLEARLY SIGNED BUT ONE PATH ONLY — TAKE THAT!

SPOT HT 676m

GROTTO

SPOT HT 676m

ROUTE MARKED ON IGN MAP APPEARS NO LONGER TO BE IN USE.

NOT THIS WAY

Baztan River

BIDARRAY 150m

GÎTE   SHOP & RESTAURANT   TO MAP 4

PATH CUTS UPHILL FROM BRIDGE TO OLD, WELL-MADE PATH, SKIRTING HILLSIDE. DIFFICULT TO SEE INITIALLY BECAUSE OVERGROWN. DON'T TAKE PATH LEFT LEADING DOWNHILL.

0   1km
0   ½ mile

AÏNHOA — ½ HR → CHAPEL — 40 MINS → COL DES TROIS CROIX — SEE TIMES IN SRT BORDER → COL DES VEAUX — 35 MINS → COL DE MEHATCHÉ — ½ HR → SPOT HT 676m — 2 HRS 20MINS → BIDARRAY

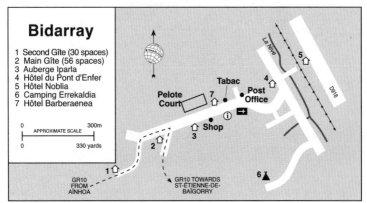

Bidarray

1 Second Gîte (30 spaces)
2 Main Gîte (56 spaces)
3 Auberge Iparla
4 Hôtel du Pont d'Enfer
5 Hôtel Noblia
6 Camping Errekaldia
7 Hôtel Barberaenea

0 ——— 300m
APPROXIMATE SCALE
0 ——— 330 yards

La Nive

Tabac

Pelote Court

Post Office

D918

Shop

GR10 FROM AÏNHOA

GR10 TOWARDS ST-ÉTIENNE-DE-BAÏGORRY

ble to catch a train to Ossès-St-Martin-d'Arrossa (one stop south-east) and then get an SNCF bus service to Saint-Étienne.

The old church in the upper part of the village is well worth looking into. It has massive stone walls, dark wooden pews, and prayer books in unpronounceable Basque.

Where to stay
The *Hôtel du Pont d'Enfer* ☆☆ (☎ 05.59. 37.70.88, 📠 05.59.37.76.60), which takes its name from the ancient bridge in front of it, is very pleasant and has rooms from €40. They own the *Auberge Iparla* up the hill near the shop – the best place to eat in Bidarray, with a set menu for €20.

Directly across the river is the *Hôtel Noblia* ☆☆ (☎ 05. 59.37.70.89) where rooms start at €25 but you'll be lucky to stay in a room at this price – €35 is more normal; the restaurant has menus from €11 upwards. Also worth a try is the *Hôtel*

Barberaenea ☆☆ (☎ 05. 59.37.74.86, 📠 05.59.37.77.55), just behind the pelote court, where rooms start at €32, though again you'll be lucky to get a room at this price. The church bells can disturb your sleep too.

Signposted from the bottom of the hill, and about 1km down the lanes to the south, is *Camping Errekaldia* (☎ 05.59. 37.72.56) where a chambre d'hôte (actually a delightful, great value, self-contained little camping home) is also available for as little as €8 per person. It costs €3 per person in the campsite.

In the upper part of the village is the *gîte d'étape* (☎ 05.59.37.71.34). The main building sleeps 50 but is occasionally booked up by large groups, so they've opened a second building which takes 30, some 200m to the west. Even this is often booked out in summer. If you manage to get in, a night in the gîte costs €9.

BIDARRAY → SAINT-ÉTIENNE-DE-BAÏGORRY   [MAP 4, p82]

The section from Bidarray to Saint Étienne is a long one. With only one possible place to fill up with water all day it's essential that you carry plenty to drink.

From the gîte, head south along the small lane. After 750 metres the GR10 turns right and winds up the hillside on a footpath. The route marking is slack as you cut through a farm (and through a gate at the back) and head uphill, though it becomes clearer as you continue. There is a brief pause in the climbing when the path reaches a grassy shoulder (just north of spot height 602m on the map), but the ascent soon resumes towards the craggy ridge ahead. Though there are no real difficulties, care is required to keep to the right track. In particular, where a path leads off right you should continue upwards instead on a

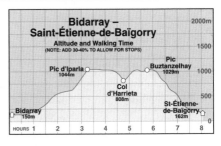

route that curves around to the east of the crag, and into a grassy bowl beside it. The path climbs the side of the bowl, past the ruins of two sheep shelters (the second one hidden behind the crag), and on to the top of the ridge.

If the weather is fine, the next section is excellent, as the GR10 runs along the top of the **Crête d'Iparla**, with spectacular views to the east. About an hour and a half to the south of the **Pic d'Iparla (1044m)**, the path makes a rocky descent to the **Col d'Harrieta (808m)**.

A signpost (BAÏGORRI 4H) directs the way onwards for the GR10. Climb steeply through the beech woods on the far side of the col, and continue south along the ridge, going over the tops of Astaté (1022m) and **Buztanzelhay (1029m)**; the way can be hard to follow for both of these but as with much of this stage, just hug the clifftop and you won't go wrong. Eventually you descend to the Col de Buztanzelhay (843m). From here, cut downhill along a

> ❏ **Water near Col d'Harrieta**
> According to a walker I met after I'd passed the Col d'Harrieta, there is a very good water source nearby. Take the horizontal path (not the GR10) leading south-west from the col, and the spring is within five minutes' walk. Another option, useful in bad weather, is to take the path leading down to the east from the col, which provides the quickest way down from the ridge, and leads to the village of Urdos.

stream, and then head south-eastwards along a ridge, before joining a loose-surfaced vehicle track which winds down the hillside.

After about a kilometre, the GR10 leaves the vehicle track and continues down the ridge on a footpath, which runs through trees to a tarmac lane below. Follow the lane for just under a kilometre to a sharp right-hand bend. If you are planning to continue along the GR10, follow the road southwards for 15 minutes past the gendarmerie towards the centre of **St-Étienne-de-Baïgorry**. If you're planning on staying in the gîte, however, follow the old cart track which descends to the left from near the sharp bend in the road, with the turn-off marked with the familiar 'trekking bear' sign. Though not really part of the GR10, it is marked on the IGN maps and even has the occasional red-and-white waymark towards the end. The track leads to another tarmac lane, which meets a main road (D948). About 20 metres to the north of the junction are the gîte d'étape and campsite.

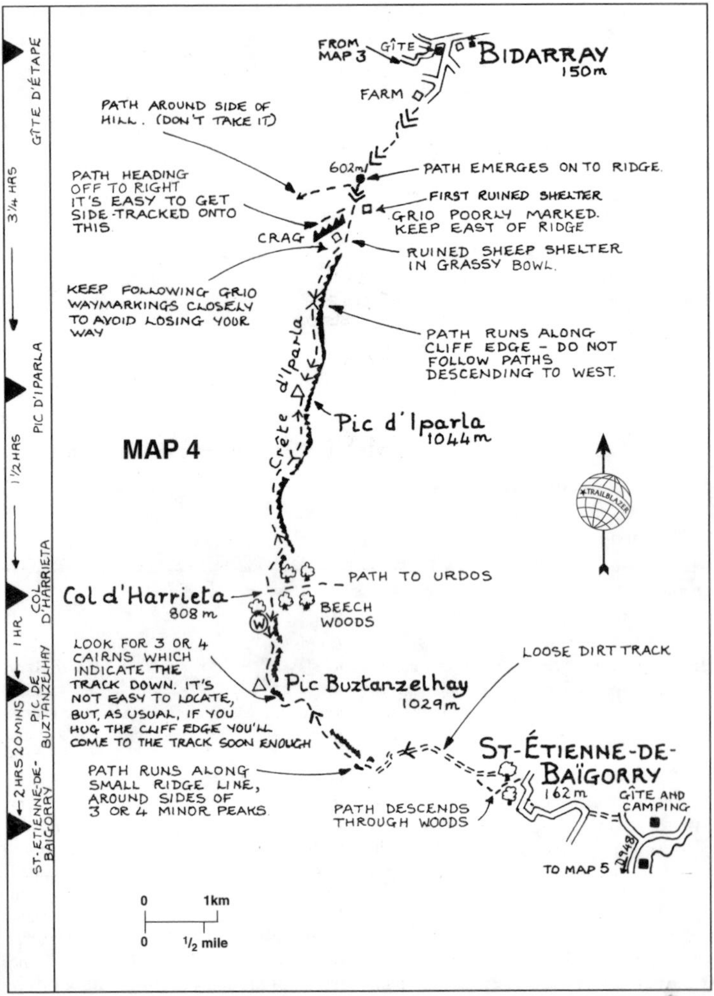
GÎTE D'ÉTAPE
3¼ HRS
PIC D'IPARLA
1½ HRS
COL D'HARRIETA
1 HR
PIC DE BUZTANZELHAY
2 HRS 20 MINS
ST-ÉTIENNE-DE-BAIGORRY
FROM MAP 3
GÎTE
BIDARRAY 150m
FARM
PATH AROUND SIDE OF HILL. (DON'T TAKE IT)
602m
PATH EMERGES ON TO RIDGE.
PATH HEADING OFF TO RIGHT IT'S EASY TO GET SIDE-TRACKED ONTO THIS
FIRST RUINED SHELTER
GRIO POORLY MARKED. KEEP EAST OF RIDGE
CRAG
RUINED SHEEP SHELTER IN GRASSY BOWL.
KEEP FOLLOWING GRIO WAYMARKINGS CLOSELY TO AVOID LOSING YOUR WAY
PATH RUNS ALONG CLIFF EDGE - DO NOT FOLLOW PATHS DESCENDING TO WEST.
Crête d'Iparla
Pic d'Iparla 1044m
MAP 4
PATH TO URDOS
Col d'Harrieta 808m
BEECH WOODS
W
LOOK FOR 3 OR 4 CAIRNS WHICH INDICATE THE TRACK DOWN. IT'S NOT EASY TO LOCATE, BUT, AS USUAL, IF YOU HUG THE CLIFF EDGE YOU'LL COME TO THE TRACK SOON ENOUGH
Pic Buztanzelhay 1029m
LOOSE DIRT TRACK
ST-ÉTIENNE-DE-BAÏGORRY 162m
PATH RUNS ALONG SMALL RIDGE LINE, AROUND SIDES OF 3 OR 4 MINOR PEAKS
PATH DESCENDS THROUGH WOODS
GÎTE AND CAMPING
D948
TO MAP 5
0 1km
0 ½ mile

❑ Walking times on trail maps

Note that on all the trail maps in this book the times shown alongside each map refer only to time spent actually walking. Add 30-40% to allow for rest stops.

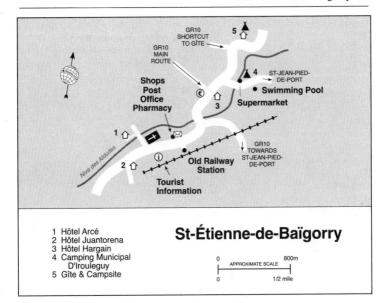

1 Hôtel Arcé
2 Hôtel Juantorena
3 Hôtel Hargain
4 Camping Municipal
  D'Irouleguy
5 Gîte & Campsite

St-Étienne-de-Baïgorry

APPROXIMATE SCALE

0 — 800m

0 — 1/2 mile

SAINT-ÉTIENNE-DE-BAÏGORRY

✉ code 64430

The main part of village of St-Étienne is
actually about a kilometre to the south-west
of the gîte d'étape, but there are buildings
spread out along the road between the two.
St-Étienne's wonderful church is to the
south, and a visit is highly recommended. If
it looks plain and unassuming from the outside, wait until you get through the door and
your eyes have adjusted to the gloom: much
of the interior's decorated, and the three tiers
of galleries add to its unique atmosphere.

Services

Most of the **shops** (including food shops,
pharmacy and a tabac) are in the main part
of the village but there's a large **supermarket**, Écomarché, near the public **swimming
pool**. The **tourist office** (☎ 05.59. 37.47.28)
is open daily 09.00-19.00, Sat 09.00-12.00
and 14.00-19.00, Sun 10.00-13.00. The railway station has been closed for some years,
but there are SNCF **buses** which run the
7km (10 minutes) north-east to St-Martin-
d'Arrossa where there's a railway station.

Where to stay

By far the best (and most expensive) place
to stay in St-Étienne is the *Hôtel Arcé*
☆☆☆ (☎ 05.59.37.40.14, 🖳 www.hotel-
arce.com), which has single/double rooms
from €60/109. The shady terrace restaurant
overlooking the river could be difficult to
prise yourself away from, if you once settle
in; there are menus from €23 and an extensive à la carte menu. Just to the south-west
of the church, on the main road, *Hôtel
Restaurant Juantorena* ☆☆ (☎ 05.59.37
.40.78) is much more reasonable: from
€30/40 for a single/double. *Hôtel Hargain*
☆ (☎ 05.59. 37.41.46) is a small and friendly place; rooms are from €30-40 and the
restaurant looks good too.

The *gîte d'étape* (☎ 05.59. 37.42.39)
charges €10 per night. It sleeps 48 people
and has a small but well-equipped kitchen.
No meals are available. The owner also
runs the *campsite* beside the building,
which is good value at €3 per person.
Camping Municipal d'Irouleguy (☎ 05
.59.37.43.96), a short way to the south-
west, charges €2.50 per person.

WESTERN PYRENEES

ST-ÉTIENNE-DE-BAÏGORRY → ST-JEAN-PIED-DE-PORT   [MAP 5]

A sign (ST JEAN PIED DE PORT 6H 15; MONHOA 4H) points the way out of St-Étienne along the lane heading east from just south of the bridge. The lane runs under the railway line, turns right and from here the GR10 begins to climb along country lanes and foot-paths and after a while along a farm track. It joins a tarmac lane (near spot height 521m) and heads off to the south-west around the west side of

St-Étienne-de-Baïgorry – St-Jean-Pied-de-Port
Altitude and Walking Time
(NOTE: ADD 30-40% TO ALLOW FOR STOPS)

Oylandaroy (933m). It's a rather tedious walk up this road to the Col d'Aharza (734m), and a more interesting option, which is marked on the IGN maps, might be to take the old path which climbs straight over Oylandaroy, passing the chapel which sits on the top.

Go straight over the Col d'Aharza, and about 100m downhill on the far side turn right up a tarmac lane. The lane climbs steeply to start with and then lev-els out, skirting around the eastern side of Munhogain. After a little more than a kilometre, near the Col de Leizarze, follow a footpath to the left. It leads around the hillside to the Col d'Urdanzia (869m), which is marked by a sim-ple iron cross and a tiny shepherds' hut that is usually kept locked.

Follow the small tarmac road north-eastwards from the col for a few hundred metres, before heading left across the grassy slopes to the top of Monhoa (1021m), from where there are excellent views. The path goes straight down the hill's eastern spur and briefly joins the road, before short-cutting down the hill-side to meet the road again lower down the slope. Turn left along the road to the trough, where the nearby red-and-white markings point down a path off the road.

Soon the footpath joins a wide track that snakes down to join, eventually, a tarmac lane. Turn left and follow the signs to Lasse, 2km along the lane, and 1.5km further down the road is St-Jean-Pied-de-Port.

SAINT-JEAN-PIED-DE-PORT

✉ code 64220

St-Jean-Pied de Port is an ideal place to take a day's rest at the end of the first five days' walking. It's a lovely and historic old town with plenty to see and some excellent places both to stay and to eat.

Services

There are several **banks and cash dis-pensers**. In particular there's a large branch of the Crédit Agricole (with ATM) just down the hill from the Hôtel Continental. Opening hours are Monday to Friday

09.00-12.15 and 14.00-17.00, and there's a cash dispenser outside. Just to the north-west of the Crédit Agricole is the **post office**, which is open Monday to Friday from 09.00-12.00 and 14.00-17.00, and on Saturdays from 09.00-12.00. You can also send and receive faxes here (☎ 05.59. 37.90.09). Very near the train station is a **bar-tabac** and **grocery store** (*alimenta-tion*) where, by the toilets, you'll find a small broom cupboard, a computer terminal and the town's only public **internet access** (Mon-Sat 07.15-12.30, 14.30-20.30; €4 per

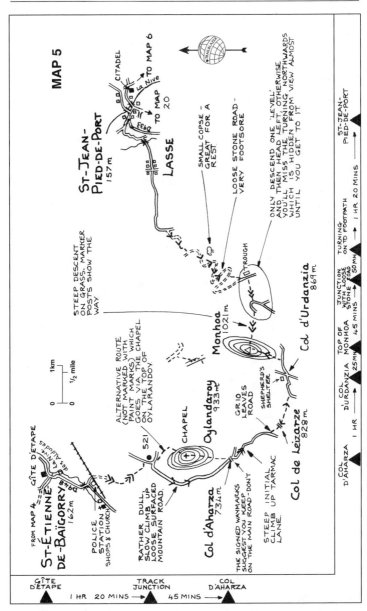

MAP 5

ST-JEAN-PIED-DE-PORT 157m

CITADEL

La Nive

TO MAP 20

TO MAP 6

LASSE

SMALL COPSE - GREAT FOR A REST

LOOSE STONE ROAD - VERY FOOTSORE

ONLY DESCEND ONE 'LEVEL' AND THEN HEAD LEFT, OTHERWISE YOU'LL MISS THE TURNING NORTHWARDS WHICH IS HIDDEN FROM VIEW ALMOST UNTIL YOU GET TO IT

STEEP DESCENT ON GRASS. MARKER POSTS SHOW THE WAY

TROUGH

Col d'Urdanzia 869m.

Monhoa 1021m.

ALTERNATIVE ROUTE (NOT MARKED WITH PAINT MARKS) WHICH GOES VIA THE CHAPEL ON THE TOP OF OYLARANDOY.

521

CHAPEL

Oylandaroy 933m.

Col d'Urdanzia

GR.10 LEAVES ROAD

SHEPHERD'S SHELTER

0   1km
0   1/2 mile

FROM MAP 4 - GÎTE D'ÉTAPE

ST-ÉTIENNE-DE-BAÏGORRY 162m

des Aldudes

POLICE STATION SHOPS & CHURCH

RATHER DULL, SLOW CLIMB UP LOOSE SURFACED MOUNTAIN ROAD.

THE SIGNED WAYMARKS SUGGEST YOU KEEP ON THE MAIN ROAD - DON'T

Col d'Aharza 734m.

Col de Leizarze 828m.

STEEP INITIAL CLIMB UP TARMAC LANE.

GÎTE D'ÉTAPE	TRACK JUNCTION	COL D'AHARZA
1 HR 20 MINS →	45 MINS →	

COL D'AHARZA	COL D'URDANZIA	TOP OF MONHOA	JUNCTION WITH LOOSE STONE ROAD	TURNING ON TO FOOTPATH	ST-JEAN-PIED-DE-PORT
1 HR →	25 MN →	45 MINS →	50 MN →	1 HR 20 MINS →	

WESTERN PYRENEES

hour, €2.50 for 30 minutes). As for the **railway station**, St-Jean is at the end of a branch line from Bayonne, and there are five trains per day in high summer going in either direction. A ticket one way costs €7.70 and the journey takes an hour.

Due east of the train station, the **Champion** supermarket has every type of food you could possibly want. At the other end of the town, almost opposite the *gîte d'étape*, the new **LiDL** supermarket is similarly well stocked. Probably more convenient than either of these, however, are the two small general stores on the rue d'Espagne in the centre of town. Near the *gîte d'étape* is a **launderette** which is open Monday to Saturday (half day closing on Saturday). They charge €5 per load, plus €3 for drying.

For camping equipment there's Maya **sports store** on avenue de Jaï-Alaï. They sell both the old (puncture) and new (resealable) type blue Camping Gaz cylinders. If you're interested, St-Jean is also one of the better places to pick up walking sticks and berets.

The **tourist office** (☎ 05.59.37.03.57, 🖹 05.59.37.34.91; Mon-Sat 09.00-19.00, Sun 10.00-16.00) has plenty of information about various activities in the area. Opposite is La Maison de la Presse, which sells all the IGN maps. For those who are walking the pilgrimage route to Santiago (see p121), the **Pilgrims' Welcome Centre** (☎ 05.59.37.05.09) is at 39 rue de la Citadelle and is open from mid-May to late September.

Where to stay

St-Jean draws a large number of tourists during summer, so there are plenty of places to choose from.

The most upmarket place in town is the *Hôtel des Pyrénées* ☆☆☆ (☎ 05.59 37.01.01, 🖹 05.59.37.18.97, 🖳 Hôtel.Pyrénées@wanadoo.fr) where prices start at €92 for a double room. Of much the same standard but rather more relaxed and friendly is the nearby *Hôtel Continental* ☆☆☆ (☎ 05.59.37.00.25, 🖹 05.59.37.27.81), where rooms start at €64. The *Central Hôtel* ☆☆ (☎ 05.59.37.00.22, 🖹 05.59.37.27.79) is another fairly smart but relaxed place, with rooms starting at €53.

Coming down to earth slightly, the *Hôtel Etche Ona* ☆☆ (☎ 05.59.37.01.14) is pleasant, with rooms from €56, and the *Hôtel Itzalpea* ☆☆ (☎ 05.59.37.03.66, 🖹 05.59.37.33.18, 🖳 itzalpea@wanadoo.fr) is also good news, with rooms starting at €37, and a restaurant serving very reasonably priced food.

If you're dying of heat exhaustion as you enter St-Jean, you could do far worse than to stay at the *Hôtel Camou* (☎ 05.59.37.02.78), the first hotel that you pass as you enter the town. It's peaceful and friendly and has the added attraction of a small swimming pool. Rooms start at €37-40.

There are a number of budget places to stay. A couple of hundred metres further down the road from the Hôtel Camou is the *gîte d'étape* (☎ 05.59.37.12.08), which is run by Mme Etchegoin, a friendly and helpful woman. It's €9 per night here, and breakfast is available for an extra €4. The gîte takes only 12 people, so ring in advance if possible. Mme Etchegoin also has a few chambres d'hôte available (€38 for two people including breakfast).

Even better, however, *L'Esprit du Chemin* (☎ 05.59.37.24.68; 🖳 www.espritduchemin.org) is a recently-opened gîte at 40 rue de la Citadelle, in the old walled part of the town. It's a fantastic place – clean, central, friendly, with great food and wonderful hospitality from the Dutch owners who are also great sources of information. They charge €10 per night including breakfast. Nearby, the cheapest place in St-Jean is the *Refuge des Pélerins* (☎ 05.59.37.05.09) at 55 rue de la Citadelle. It's only for pilgrims who are walking the Santiago route (pilgrims must show their 'pilgrim passport'; those who are starting in St-Jean can buy one from the Pilgrims' Office at No 39 for €2). There are 16 beds in the refuge, showers and a kitchen. On proof of 'pilgrim status', it costs €7 per night.

There are a couple of campsites close to the town centre. To the north is the *Camping de l'Arraday* ☆☆ (☎ 05.59.37.11.75), which charges €1.50 for emplacement, and €1.70 per person. Near the fronton municipal is the *Camping Municipal*

WESTERN PYRENEES

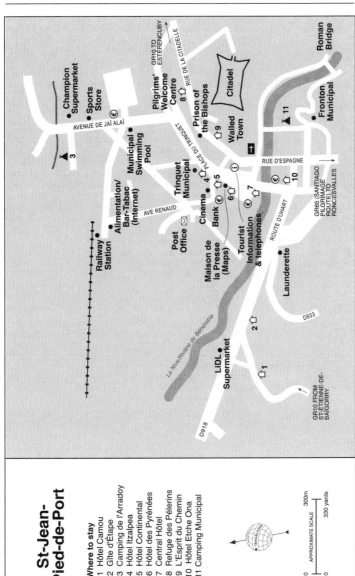

St-Jean-Pied-de-Port

Where to stay
1 Hôtel Camou
2 Gîte d'Étape
3 Camping de l'Arradoy
4 Hôtel Itzalpea
5 Hôtel Continental
6 Hôtel des Pyrénées
7 Central Hôtel
8 Refuge des Pèlerins
9 L'Esprit du Chemin
10 Hôtel Etche Ona
11 Camping Municipal

0   APPROXIMATE SCALE   300m
0   330 yards

WESTERN PYRENEES

Plaza Berri (☎ 05.59.37.11.19) which is popular because of its location close to the shops and cafés. The tariff here is €2 per person and €2 for emplacement.

What to see

The paved streets of the walled town are well worth exploring. Popular places to visit within the walls include the **Citadel** on top of the hill (you can't get in, but there are good views from the outer walls), the imposing **south gate** of the town, and the **church** which stands just inside it.

The **Prison of the Bishops**, half-way up the hill between the gate and the citadel, isn't especially interesting but the upper floors of the building house a display of photographs which give the visitor an insight into the Basque way of life. Entry to the prison and display is €3 (open July and August only).

The weekly **market**, which takes place on Mondays on the Place du Trinquet, is well worth looking out for. It's a focal point for farmers and artisans selling local produce – cheeses, wines, honey, linen and more. Also thoroughly recommended is the chance to see a game of **pelote**. During the summer there are fairly regular games, which are well advertised around town, and which take place either at the trinquet municipal (the indoor court) or at the fronton municipal (the outdoor court). Entry can be reasonably costly (€10 to get in to see a game in the trinquet municipal) but it's well worth it.

ST-JEAN-PIED-DE-PORT → RONCESVALLES   [MAP 20, p123]

For a description of the pilgrimage route to Roncesvalles, the **Chemin St Jacques**, see p122.

ST-JEAN-PIED-DE-PORT → ESTÉRENCUBY/PHAGALCETTE
[MAP 6 opposite; Map 7, p91]

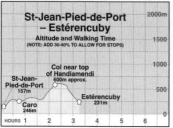

St-Jean-Pied-de-Port – Estérencuby
Altitude and Walking Time
(NOTE: ADD 30-40% TO ALLOW FOR STOPS)
Col near top of Handiamendi 600m approx.
St-Jean-Pied-de-Port 157m
Caro 246m
Estérencuby 231m
2000m 1500 1000 500 0
HOURS 1 2 3 4 5 6

It's a fairly short walk to Estérencuby and, with the stage following this one so long and exhausting, many trekkers choose to continue beyond Estérencuby up the hill to Phagalcette, where a *gîte d'étape* has been established.

From the centre of St-Jean, go straight up the rue de la Citadelle, and leave the old walled town through the gate of St Jacques at the top of the hill. After 400m, at a road junction, there's a blue sign pointing south-east down the D401 (ESTÉRENCUBY 4H 00; CARO 0H 45). A kilometre up the road, follow a brief detour to the right on a footpath, before the GR10 descends into **Caro** along a tiny lane. There's a water point beside the road in the village, though there's no indication of whether it's potable. It would be wise to purify it.

Beyond the village the GR10 remains on lanes for a further 1.5km, until, having skirted around the side of a small hill (spot height 305m on the map), it cuts down through trees to a stream. The path climbs again on the far side of the stream, and enters the tiny hamlet of **Ahadoa**. From here two possible routes present themselves to the walker. Purists will opt to follow the GR10, as it climbs over the top of **Handiamendi (642m)**, and descends on the far side. Those who

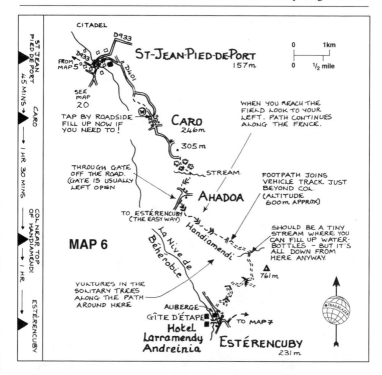

are feeling lazier may choose to head south down the lanes which contour around the base of the hill – a flatter and quicker route to Estérencuby. The 'proper' route over the top of the hills involves a relatively short but steep climb. From the lane junction in Ahadoa a signpost (ESTÉRENCUBY 2H 45) points the way up a clear footpath. At the top of the hill, the footpath goes over a small col, and soon joins a rough vehicle track, where there's a further sign (ESTÉRENCUBY 1H 30). Follow the track as it winds down the hillside into the village below.

ESTÉRENCUBY
✉ code 64220

Estérencuby is a quiet village with a choice of places to stay. The largest hotel, the *Hôtel Andreinia* ☆☆ (☎ 05.59.37.09.70, 🖹 05. 59.37.36.05) with rooms available from €34 (room only), €32 demi-pension per person. The restaurant serves good food and the Menu Randonneur is solid value at €10. The *Auberge Etchegoyen/Carricaburu* (☎ 05. 59.37.09.77), next to the pelote court, has rooms for €28-32; the restaurant has fixed

menus starting at €12 and looks worth trying too. By the way, more than one trekker has suggested that the small 'car-park' opposite (by the hotel's noticeboard) makes a convenient **campsite**, and the hotel, for now at least, doesn't seem to mind – though do ask first! The *gîte d'étape* is run by the Hôtel Andreinia (use the telephone number above). It's small and modern but sleeps only 12, so book in advance if possible. It costs €11 per night, or €24 demi-pension.

Beside the church, a yellow sign, COL D'IRAU 4H 00 & COL BAGARGIAK 8H 30, points the way eastwards up a small lane. Follow the lane uphill for two kilometres, before leaving it, and cutting up the hillside on a narrow, thorny path. At the top of the path, join another tarmac lane which leads across a plateau past the tiny settlement of **Phagalcette**.

PHAGALCETTE

There's nothing up here except birds, sheep, farms and a lovely little gîte d'étape, called *Kaskoleta* (☎ 05.59.37.09.73). Run by the indefatigable Mme Iriarte, the gîte offers some of the best food on the entire path, and some comfy accommodation too. Prices are €12 for bed only, with dinner an extra €13, and breakfast €5. Stop here for lunch even if you're not staying the night.

PHAGALCETTE → CHALET D'IRATY (COL BAGARGIAK) [MAPS 7-8]

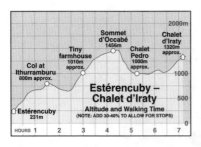

This stage begins where the last left off, as you rejoin the road heading up to the col at **Ithurramburu**. Watch out for the brief short cuts, a couple of which are poorly marked. Several paths meet at the col, but route-finding is no problem as the GR10 is relatively well marked and there's also a sign: COL D'IRAU 1H 45 & COL BAGARGIAK 6H 15. Head south, descending along the side of the valley on a vehicle track. At the southern end of the valley, the track crosses two streams and turns northwards. Within 400m the GR10 turns off to the right and begins to climb up the hillside on a steep footpath. After a tiring ascent, you eventually reach the col; there's a farmhouse here where they sell their own cheese and honey and have a (very) small food store; there's a water point on the outside of one of the buildings too. A sign here used to (it has now been removed) give the following timings: CROMLECHS D'OCCABÉ 1H 30 & COL BAGARGIAK 4H 30.

Follow the tarmac road south-eastwards to the **Col d'Irau**, and climb straight up the side of the hill beyond. There's no path as such but there are wooden marker posts that guide you up on to the ridge. From here you follow a cart track, lined with the occasional handsome stone waymarker, to the south of the nearest hill (1307m) and continue upwards towards the **Sommet d'Occabé (1456m)**. Just north of the Sommet, the path swings eastwards and begins to lose height. Soon you join an extremely-rutted vehicle track that descends sharply through the beech trees (signposted as path numbers '3' and '7'). Approximately one hour after passing the Sommet d'Occabé, you come to a tarmac road, on the far side of which is **Chalet Pedro** (☎ 05.59.28.55.98), a popular spot for day trippers. There's a restaurant, a handful of apartments for rent (minimum period a weekend), and numerous short, marked walks around

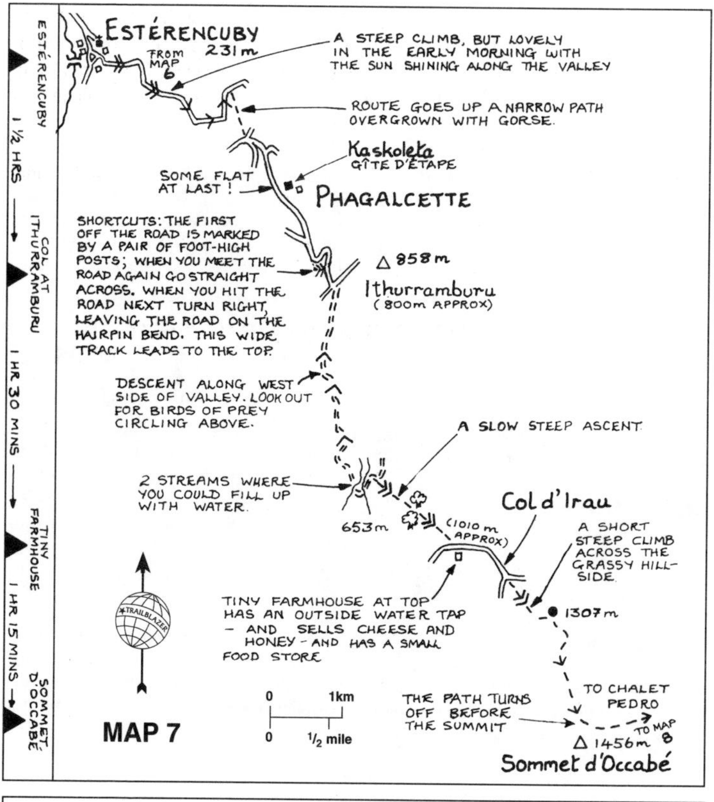

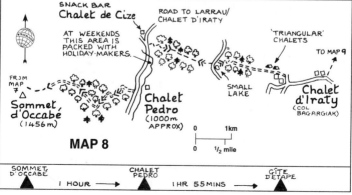

MAP 7

ESTÉRENCUBY 231m
FROM MAP 6

A STEEP CLIMB, BUT LOVELY IN THE EARLY MORNING WITH THE SUN SHINING ALONG THE VALLEY

ROUTE GOES UP A NARROW PATH OVERGROWN WITH GORSE.

Kaskoleta
GÎTE D'ÉTAPE

SOME FLAT AT LAST!

PHAGALCETTE

SHORTCUTS: THE FIRST OFF THE ROAD IS MARKED BY A PAIR OF FOOT-HIGH POSTS; WHEN YOU MEET THE ROAD AGAIN GO STRAIGHT ACROSS. WHEN YOU HIT THE ROAD NEXT TURN RIGHT, LEAVING THE ROAD ON THE HAIRPIN BEND. THIS WIDE TRACK LEADS TO THE TOP.

△ 858m
Ithurramburu
(800m APPROX)

DESCENT ALONG WEST SIDE OF VALLEY. LOOK OUT FOR BIRDS OF PREY CIRCLING ABOVE.

A SLOW STEEP ASCENT

2 STREAMS WHERE YOU COULD FILL UP WITH WATER.

653m

(1010m APPROX)

Col d'Irau

A SHORT STEEP CLIMB ACROSS THE GRASSY HILL-SIDE.

● 1307m

TINY FARMHOUSE AT TOP HAS AN OUTSIDE WATER TAP – AND SELLS CHEESE AND HONEY – AND HAS A SMALL FOOD STORE

THE PATH TURNS OFF BEFORE THE SUMMIT

TO CHALET PEDRO

△ 1456m
Sommet d'Occabé

TO MAP 8

TRAILBLAZER

0   1km
0   ½ mile

ESTÉRENCUBY

½ HRS

COL AT ITHURRAMBURU

1 HR 30 MINS

TINY FARMHOUSE

1 HR 15 MINS

SOMMET D'OCCABÉ

MAP 8

SNACK BAR
Chalet de Cize

ROAD TO LARRAU/ CHALET D'IRATY

AT WEEKENDS THIS AREA IS PACKED WITH HOLIDAY-MAKERS.

'TRIANGULAR' CHALETS

TO MAP 9

FROM MAP 7
△ Sommet d'Occabé (1456m)

Chalet Pedro
(1000m APPROX)

SMALL LAKE

Chalet d'Iraty
(COL BAGARGIAK)

TRAILBLAZER

0   1km
0   ½ mile

SOMMET D'OCCABÉ

CHALET PEDRO

1 HOUR

GÎTE D'ÉTAPE

1 HR 55 MINS

WESTERN PYRENEES

the local hillsides. There is a sort of *gîte* here (€10 per night) but it has only eight beds; if you haven't booked in advance you may be disappointed. For most walkers, Chalet Pedro is just a great place to stop for lunch, a cold drink or an ice cream. It's also a good place to fill up the water bottles: the tap on the end of the main building (currently hidden behind a small marquee) dispenses spring water.

Follow the road north from Chalet Pedro for about a kilometre. The road suddenly splits into two and then three. As it does so, you may be able to make out the markings straight up the hill to the right. If not, keep on the right-hand road until you come to a sign pointing to the track zig-zagging up the hill. Both paths reunite and climb south-eastwards across the wooded slopes of a hill, before descending to the road on the far side, where there's a small lake. As you cross the road, you are passing from Basse Navarre into Soule, the easternmost of the Basque regions. The path immediately climbs again, zigzagging through the woods and then following a vehicle track to the top of the hill, where there are a couple of modern, wedge-shaped ski chalets. Continue eastwards past these to a road and track junction. Take the road heading east to reach the chalet and gîte, 700m away.

CHALET D'IRATY
✉ code 64560

Chalet d'Iraty is primarily a ski resort, which is turned to other uses in summer. In common with most ski resorts, it's a rather drab and ugly place when there's no snow, but it's a convenient overnight stop for walkers.

The registration/booking for the *gîte* is done at the **tourist office** (☎ 05.59.28.51.29) in the main complex of buildings. A night in the gîte, situated behind the tennis courts, costs €12.50, with breakfast €6.50, and with two large buildings available the capacity must be at least 50 people. Despite this,

it's still worth booking in advance (especially at weekends) as they frequently hold events such as mountain-biking competitions. The buildings themselves are modern, with good washing and kitchen facilities. There's a cheap but unexciting *restaurant/bar* near the information office and also a small **épicerie**. The nearest *campsite* is a couple of kilometres down the road; it would be easier to pick up provisions on the way past the main buildings and find somewhere to camp just to the south of the Pic des Escaliers (ie just beyond Iraty).

CHALET D'IRATY → LOGIBAR   [MAP 9]

Just east of the information office and the restaurant, turn left down a tarmac road – leaving it for a loose stone road on the left at the first hairpin. This in turn you leave for the right-hand (eastern) of two paths heading up the southern side of the **Pic des Escaliers**. The path is steep at first but it soon levels out and becomes a pleasant walk across the grassy hillside to the top of the ridge, from which there are excellent views to the north.

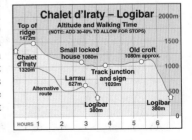

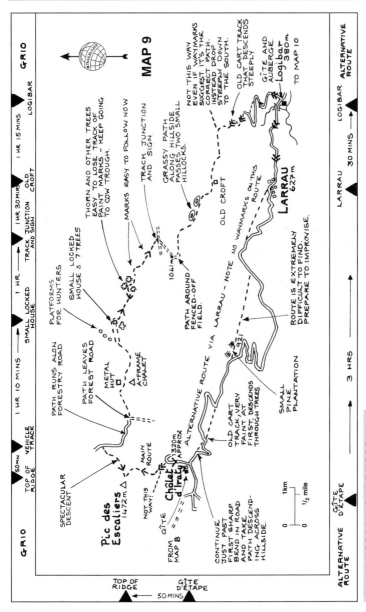

MAP 9

94 France – Pays Basque and Béarn

Iraty to Logibar – alternative route
The GR10 from Chalet d'Iraty to Logibar takes about $6^{1}/_{2}$ hours, and there are two areas where route-finding can be time-consuming in bad weather. Those who want to take a short cut could consider the alternative route that is marked on the IGN 1:50,000 map, via the village of **Larrau**. Much of this alternative route is along the road but it has some advantages – it's much quicker (about $3^{1}/_{2}$ hours) for a start.

The main attraction of taking the shorter route, however, is that Larrau has a campsite, restaurant, two hotels and a shop, whereas there's only the gîte and auberge in Logibar. The route described below is the main route (GR10).

After a spectacular but not particularly well-marked descent you reach a rough forest road. Follow it to the right for about 700m, before a signpost, LOGIBAR 5H, directs you to go left down another track.

At the first sharp bend in the new track, the GR10 continues straight ahead (east-north-east) on a footpath which leads around the grassy hillside. (Look for the beginning of the path to the right by a small post – don't go over the top of the hill!) The path continues, passing in front of a number of platforms used by hunters who shoot wood pigeon (*palombe*) in the spring and autumn.

After about an hour you come to a small locked **house** with an outbuilding; descend past the house and under the seven large trees below it, and join a track just beyond the trees.

The track rises over a spur and then descends to an area of scrub which is laced with paths made by cows and sheep. It's easy to lose the markers here but pay really close attention to them and you should emerge below a **cow trough**. Veer right here down into a small grassy dip along a wide, grassy track, before leaving it for a smaller path to the left, currently marked by two red-and-white poles, whereafter sticking to the trail becomes much easier. The path begins to climb again, emerging eventually at a track junction by a small col (just north-east of spot height 1041m on the map). A yellow sign, LOGIBAR 3H 15, points the way to the next section of the path.

Follow the vehicle track along the top of the hill to a fenced-off field. The GR10 avoids the field by passing down a muddy cart track to the right-hand side, before taking a footpath which skirts the bottom of the enclosure. Follow this footpath south-eastwards along a spur, past two small hillocks, and eventually to an old gate, beyond which is a **croft**.

With the black-and-white village Larrau to your right, round the hill and follow a wide track. Eventually, the path begins a steep descent south down towards the valley bottom. (Ignore markers painted on a tree at the start of the descent which many people mistakenly interpret as suggesting that you should carry on traversing round the hill on a minor path. You shouldn't.)

After a steepish descent, you join a tarmac lane very briefly before short-cutting down the hillside on another footpath. These short cuts are easy to miss, but all being well you should eventually arrive on the road just below **Logibar**.

WESTERN PYRENEES

LOGIBAR

✉ code 64440

Logibar really only consists of a single building, the *Auberge Logibar* (☎ 05.59.28.61.14), which is a combination of an inn, restaurant and gîte d'étape.

The gîte takes 36 people, has reasonable kitchen facilities, and costs €11 per night. Double rooms in the auberge cost €26. Food at the restaurant is adequate and reasonably priced. Logibar is popular with day trippers, because it is the nearest parking place for a visit to the famous Gorges d'Holzarté.

LARRAU

✉ code 64560

Larrau is the nearest place with a shop, and is 2.5km up the steep road from Logibar; try hitching a lift as it's a 40-minute walk. *Hôtel Etchemaite* ☆☆ (☎ 05.59.28.61.45, 🖻 05.59.28.72.71) has rooms for €42-58, while *Hôtel Despouey* ☆ (☎ 05.59.28.60.82.) charges €28 for a room. The former also has the only restaurant in town which is beautiful but eye-wateringly expensive, though their €15 set menu is tremendous value. The *campsite* just below the village charges around €5 for a one-person tent.

LOGIBAR → SAINTE-ENGRÂCE [MAP 10, p96]

Cross the Gave de Larrau and immediately turn left to a wooden bridge, which spans the river flowing from the Gorges d'Holzarté. On the far side of the bridge, next to a clear sign (SAINTE-ENGRÂCE 7H; PASSERELLE D'HOLZARTÉ 0H 50) the path divides, with the 'real' GR10 heading directly uphill, and the alternative route, via the spectacu-

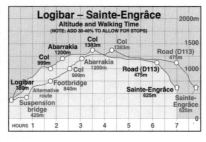

lar **Gorges d'Holzarté**, going right. The alternative route (see p97), which rejoins the main path after about 2¹/₂ hours' walking, is more interesting but takes about an hour longer and can be quite wet after bad weather. Both routes are described below.

GR10

From the sign, the GR10 climbs steeply on a small footpath through a wood, before emerging from the trees to climb even more steeply through bracken. On reaching a small level area the path, which to this point has been climbing up the end of a spur, diverts along the north side of the spur. It soon begins to climb again, albeit at a much easier gradient and through trees which offer welcome shade.

The footpath soon becomes a wide stony track which eventually meets a rough road. A yellow sign at this junction simply says 'SAINTE-ENGRÂCE' with an arrow pointing southwards along the rough road. Follow the road south for over a kilometre until it emerges on to an open area of spur and bends sharply round to the left, before starting to descend. On the right here is a rounded hillock (spot height 999m on the IGN map), and there's a yellow sign beside the track: COL D'ANHAOU 1H 45; SAINTE-ENGRÂCE 5H 15. This is the point at which the alternative route rejoins the GR10.

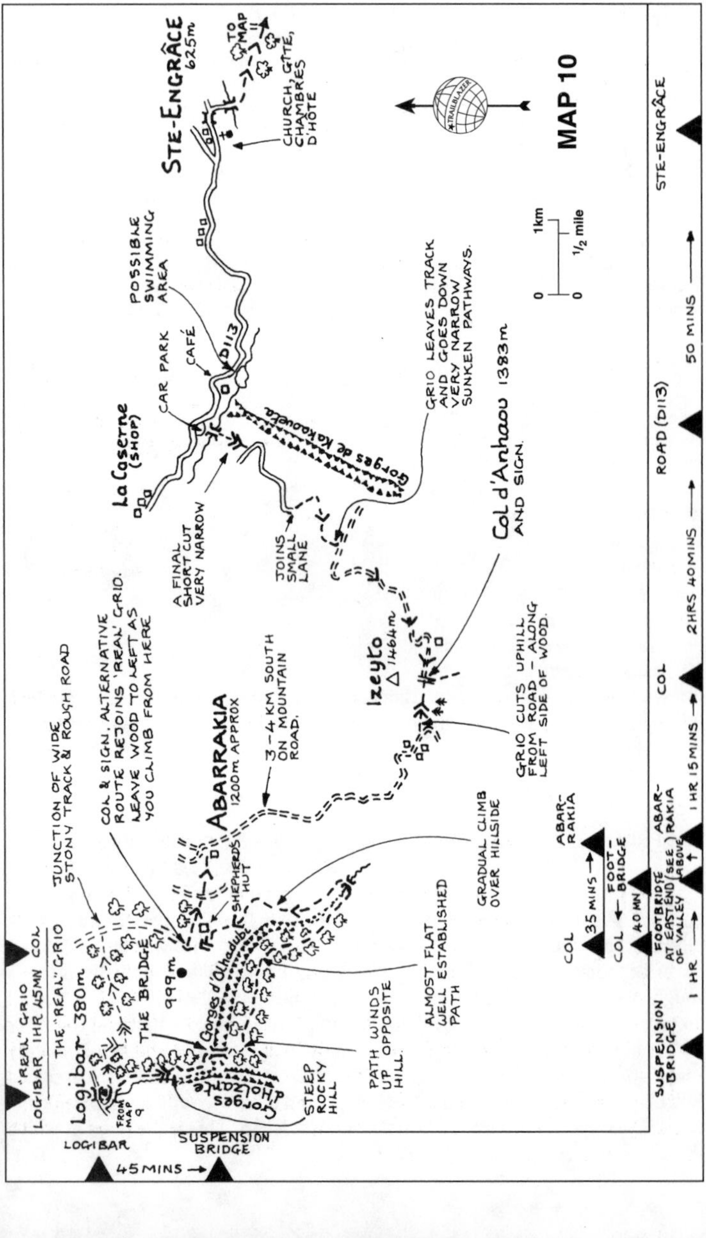

WESTERN PYRENEES

MAP 10

STE-ENGRÂCE

STE-ENGRÂCE 625m

CHURCH, GÎTE, CHAMBRES D'HÔTE

TO MAP

POSSIBLE SWIMMING AREA

La Caserne (SHOP)

CAR PARK

CAFÉ

D113

GR10 LEAVES TRACK AND GOES DOWN VERY NARROW SUNKEN PATHWAYS.

Col d'Anhaou 1383m AND SIGN

Gorges de Kakouéta

A FINAL SHORT CUT VERY NARROW

JOINS SMALL LANE

Izeyta △ 1464m

GR10 CUTS UPHILL FROM ROAD - ALONG LEFT SIDE OF WOOD.

JUNCTION OF WIDE STONY TRACK & ROUGH ROAD

COL & SIGN. ALTERNATIVE ROUTE REJOINS 'REAL' GR10. LEAVE WOOD TO LEFT AS YOU CLIMB FROM HERE

ABARRAKIA 1200m APPROX

3-4 KM SOUTH ON MOUNTAIN ROAD.

SHEPHERDS' HUT

GRADUAL CLIMB OVER HILLSIDE

"REAL" GR10
LOGIBAR 1HR 45MN COL

THE "REAL" GR10

Logibar 380m

THE BRIDGE

999m

Gorges d'Olhadubi

ALMOST FLAT WELL ESTABLISHED PATH

PATH WINDS UP OPPOSITE HILL.

Gorges d'Holzarte

STEEP ROCKY HILL

FROM MAP 9

LOGIBAR

SUSPENSION BRIDGE

45 MINS →

SUSPENSION BRIDGE

1 HR

FOOTBRIDGE AT EAST END (SEE VALLEY ABOVE)

COL 40 MN

COL 35 MINS

ABAR-RAKIA →

ABAR-RAKIA

FOOT-BRIDGE

ABAR-RAKIA

1 HR 15 MINS →

COL

2HRS 40MINS →

ROAD (D113)

50 MINS →

STE-ENGRÂCE

0   1km
0   ½ mile

Alternative route

Turn right, following the sign pointing towards the 'PASSERELLE D'HOLZARTÉ', and climb along a rocky but well-worn trail, which gains height above the gorge. After about 45 minutes it levels out, and as it swings to the left, the **suspension bridge** comes into sight. Crossing it can be a little disconcerting – the whole structure sways and bounces. On the far side of the bridge a tiny footpath zig-zags up the hillside, and after 20 minutes meets a large and nearly level track where you should turn left (south-east). Follow the track for approximately 2.5km to the footbridge which crosses the south-east end of the valley. From here a poorly-defined trail climbs north-westwards across the opposite hillside. Gradually the path becomes clearer and eventually you reach the small grassy col (just to the east of spot height 999m) where you rejoin the official GR10. The shepherd's hut just down from here can provide water to desperate trekkers.

Both routes

The next part of the path is not particularly well marked and varies slightly from what is printed on the IGN 1:50,000 map. From the col (spot height 999m), the GR10 climbs south-eastwards, leaving the wood just to the left, and it passes over a couple of small hummocks to meet a loose-surface vehicle track. Go straight across the track and continue straight up to the hut and sheepfold at **Abarrakia** (and not to the south of it as the IGN map suggests). Join the vehicle track here and follow it southwards for 3.5km; it's not a very interesting walk, although there are excellent views of Chardekagagna (1893m), to the right. After passing two houses and a large animal shed, leave the rough road and climb up a small gully to the left to reach the Col d'Anhaou (1383m). At the col there are a number of tracks, and a sign: SAINTE-ENGRÂCE 3H 30.

Head down the vehicle track on the far side of the col and after a few minutes you come to a small house. All being well, there should be two options from here: either you can take the path down the western side of the **Gorges de Kakoueta**, or take the longer route which circles the gorge and passes down the eastern side. Unfortunately, since the first edition we've been waiting for the eastern path to be properly waymarked and reopened – and we are still waiting. As a result, the remainder of this route description details the path along the western side of the gorge. Follow the vehicle track as it winds downhill below the house. A series of posts indicates short cuts through the hairpins of the track. On the last of these the path runs into a deep-ish channel behind a sheep hut, crosses a stream and joins a wider track on the hillside opposite. After 20m a smaller path heads off right. Join it and go through the barbed-wire gate at the end to enter a dark, shadowy path. Eventually you reach a road, which you follow down to another short cut, again down a 'sunken' path. At the bottom of the valley, cross the river via a concrete bridge and come to the main road. From here it's about three weary kilometres east along the tarmac to the nearest accommodation. Note that there are no shops in Sainte-Engrâce, just a drink seller on the way; the nearest shop is in La Caserne, 2km from the path to the north-west, so if you need supplies you should make for La Caserne before going to the gîte.

WESTERN PYRENEES

SAINTE-ENGRÂCE

✉ code 64560

The commune of Sainte-Engrâce actually incorporates all the hamlets along several kilometres of road but, since the closure of the only other lodge, the only facilities are the gîte and auberge, which are opposite the ancient church. The *gîte d'étape* is run by the *Auberge Elichalt* (☎ 05.59.28.61.63), next door. The gîte takes about 30 people, costs €9 per night and has good kitchen facilities. Demi-pension is €26 and includes, courtesy of Mme Burguburu, a great evening meal. The house next door to the auberge also advertises *chambres d'hôte*. The owners of the auberge can help out with *camping* space – €3 gets you a place in a nearby field and use of the showers in the gîte.

Before leaving Sainte-Engrâce, take a look into the **11th-century church**. The simple interior, bare stonework and rounded vaults are legacies of the Romanesque tradition. Of special interest are the carvings around the tops of the pillars nearest the altar, depicting scenes from everyday life.

SAINTE-ENGRÂCE → ARETTE LA PIERRE ST-MARTIN   [MAP 11]

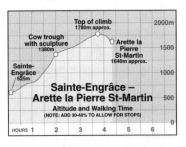

Top of climb
1780m approx.

Cow trough
with sculpture
1380m

Arette la
Pierre
St-Martin
1640m approx.

Sainte-
Engrâce
625m

**Sainte-Engrâce –
Arette la Pierre St-Martin**

Altitude and Walking Time
(NOTE: ADD 30-40% TO ALLOW FOR STOPS)

2000m
1500
1000
500
0

HOURS 1   2   3   4   5   6

Continue down the lane from the gîte and, just beyond a tiny bridge, turn right. After a couple of minutes you cross another small bridge, take a left just before the house and start to climb along a narrow and overgrown footpath. The path soon enters a small gully, which marks the border between Soule (Pays Basque) and Béarn. Follow the gully for 20-30 minutes in an easterly direction, before cutting up the gully side to the left and continuing to climb through the beech woods that cover the hillside. On a number of occasions the path comes to a forest track that snakes around and up the hill. Most of the time you just cross it and continue, though the second time you meet the road you should turn right and look for a small cairn on the left that marks the way forward. Route-marking in this area is not always clear; if in doubt, continue uphill and you should be able to pick up the path again after a while. After about 1½ hours of ascent, the path arrives at a distinctive cow trough; the likeness of a human head, sculpted into the rock beside the trough, wears a hat with 'Le Gardien' written around the brim.

Above the cow trough the path leaves the woods and becomes less distinct as it climbs across the grassy slopes. Although a few posts have now been used to mark the route, many of the markers are painted on low rocks and are hard to see until you get near to them. If in doubt, stand at the edge of

> ❑ **Weather alert**
>
> The route from Sainte-Engrâce to Arette la Pierre St-Martin is not particularly tricky, but in poor weather route-finding on the hillsides around the Soum de Lèche can be problematic. In the event of low mist or rain, less confident walkers might be wise to wait for conditions to clear. If you decide to go ahead, ensure that you have a compass, and that you pay particular attention to the map and route markers.

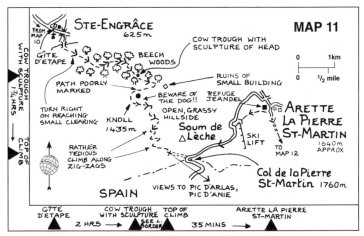

the wood, with the grassy bowl of hillside in front of you, and look at the hill on your right-hand side. The path passes just to the north of this knoll, before turning back on itself and circling around to climb in a south-easterly direction. At a trough on the other side of the hill, head up the southern slopes. Beware of a particularly vicious sheepdog that guards the flock around here and has been known to bite trekkers; to prevent being bitten, avoid both the dog and, just as importantly, try not to disturb the sheep so as not to antagonize him.

Further up the hillside the route becomes more obvious, until it joins a monotonous wide track zig-zagging up the slopes.

Finally, on reaching the highest point of the climb, a bizarre spectacle is seen to the south-east. After the greenery of the Basque country, you're suddenly faced with the bare moonscape of the limestone country around the **Pic d'Anie**.

La Pierre St-Martin

In the centre of the col stands La Pierre St-Martin (St Martin's Stone), which is the site of one of the best-known annual rituals in the whole of the Pyrenees. This ritual has its origins in a 14th-century squabble between the inhabitants of the Barétous valley (France) and the Roncal valley (Spain). The dispute centred on the rights to graze livestock on the high pastures around the col. The best pastures were on Roncalese territory, and hence attempts by the Barétous farmers to graze their herds there were not appreciated.

After a series of violent encounters, a settlement was reached in 1375 with the **Tribute of the Three Cows**. Every year the Barétous villagers would hand over three heifers in return for the rights to use pastures in the Roncal valley. The treaty, believed to be the oldest remaining in force in Europe, is still observed every year on 13 July. It's not like it used to be, of course. Nowadays, the three animals are taken back home after the ceremony. The number of participants has grown, too – to around 3000 people.

Climbing the Pic d'Anie

Despite its imposing size, the Pic d'Anie is a straightforward climb. To get to the peak one can either take the HRP (High Route) from Arette, which approaches from the north-west and rejoins the GR10 at the Cabane du Cap de la Baigt, or follow the GR10 to the cabane and climb from there. For those walking the section from Arette to Lescun, the former is quicker by at least an hour.

The HRP leaves Arette on the same path as the GR10 and splits off after 25 minutes as described above. It is not as well marked as the GR10, but there are markers nonetheless – splashes of dark-red paint indicate the way. The path heads south to the border and then south-east towards the pic across a rocky and boulder-strewn landscape. At the Col des Anies, directly to the north of the pic, directions are painted on a large boulder. From here the route across a limestone plateau is indicated with paint marks and small cairns. The path up the Pic is also visible, a clear diagonal scar on the side of the mountain. It's a steep walk to the top, which you should reach approximately 1¼ hours after leaving the Col des Anies.

I started from the Cabane du Cap de la Baigt and returned to it, before continuing to Lescun; as a rough guide on timing, walking up from the cabane and back took me nearly five hours. Allow plenty of time for the descent: it's over 800m of rocky downhill path from the top of the Pic to the cabane, and this can be hard on the knees.

The Pic itself is a sign of the changes ahead. At 2504m it is the first of the high peaks you'll encounter as you move from the coastal region into the central Pyrenees.

Continue along the track to the tarmac road at the **Col de la Pierre St-Martin (1760m)**. From the col, the GR10 turns northwards (left) and follows the road for about a kilometre. The IGN map suggests you should stay on the roads, but it's quicker and more interesting to cut across the empty ski slopes and under a ski lift. As you cross the small ridge on the far side of the slope **Arette la Pierre St-Martin** comes into sight, with the refuge clearly visible on the left.

ARETTE LA PIERRE ST-MARTIN

✉ code 64570

Arette la Pierre St-Martin must be quite attractive under a layer of snow but it's pretty bleak in summer. Nevertheless, it has reasonable facilities which make it a convenient overnight stop for walkers.

The gîte d'étape is next to the GR10, as it descends into the resort. *Refuge Jeandel* (☎ 05.59.66.14.46) is run by a friendly fellow who's something of a joker. The hostel itself can accommodate 19 people and charges €10 per night or €24.50 for demi-pension. There are kitchen facilities for those who are self-catering, and a small store of supplies for sale (chocolate, pasta,

tinned food etc) although it's worth checking that the shop in the main building of the resort isn't open before you blindly accept his prices. Note that being offered a cold drink as you collapse onto the bench outside the door of the gîte isn't just a show of spontaneous generosity: you'll be charged for it when you leave; check your bill.

The few facilities that exist in Arette during the summer are to be found on the ground floor of the very ugly high-rise building. There's a **cash dispenser**, a small **supermarket**, Proxi (which is open from 08.30 to 12.30, and 16.00 to 18.30), a **launderette**, and a **tourist office** with information on activities including hang-gliding, canyoning and caving. However, it should be noted that the shop appears to open only in mid-summer (ie July and August) when there are likely to be enough walkers passing through to make it worthwhile.

ARETTE LA PIERRE ST-MARTIN → LESCUN [MAP 12, p102]

Leave Arette la Pierre St-Martin along the track heading roughly southwards across the hillside. There are no real waymarks as such but just keep to the road until, after approximately 25 minutes, you come to a small grassy bowl (*pescamou* on the map) and a sign clearly indicating the direction of the GR10. At this point, the GR10 heads off to the left across the grass, while the High Route continues on the road.

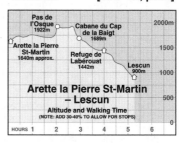

On the far side of the grass the GR10 strikes off across the rocks. Keep a careful eye out for the markers; it's very easy to lose them. Look, too, at how the flora has changed, including Pyrenean irises, as you move deeper into the High Pyrenees. Though the waymarkings are not always easy to see, the path is actually well marked; indeed, there comes a point where, if you don't see a way-mark where you expect to – on an obvious path-side boulder, for example – you start to think, maybe unjustifiably, that you are on the wrong path.

After an hour of meandering across the limestone 'pavement', the path arrives at a large track, crosses under two ski-lifts then drops back onto the rocky terrain. For 30-40 minutes the route continues across the plateau until you approach a large cliff on the right-hand side. Pay particular attention to the markers as they lead up to the cliffs and

> ❏ **Weather alert**
> This section is not difficult but is best avoided in bad weather because it can be hard to follow. You spend at least two hours crossing a bare limestone plateau where it's very easy to mistake the path and wander off along an imaginary line of cairns. If in doubt, wait a day in Arette la Pierre St-Martin for the weather to clear.

not along the more obvious path straight on. After 5-10 minutes the path does the seemingly impossible, cutting uphill (right) to cross the ridge itself. The last few metres to the **Pas de l'Osque (1922m)** are a scramble.

From the narrow ridge of the Pas de l'Osque, you descend along a rocky path into a dip and climb the far side to the **Pas d'Azuns (1873m)**. It's a lovely place to stop for a few minutes and take in the view: on the far side of the valley the Pic d'Ani dominates the scene, and down below you can see the roof of the tiny shepherd's cabin dwarfed by the landscape around it. The path winds down the hillside and after 20 minutes reaches the **Cabane du Cap de**

WESTERN PYRENEES

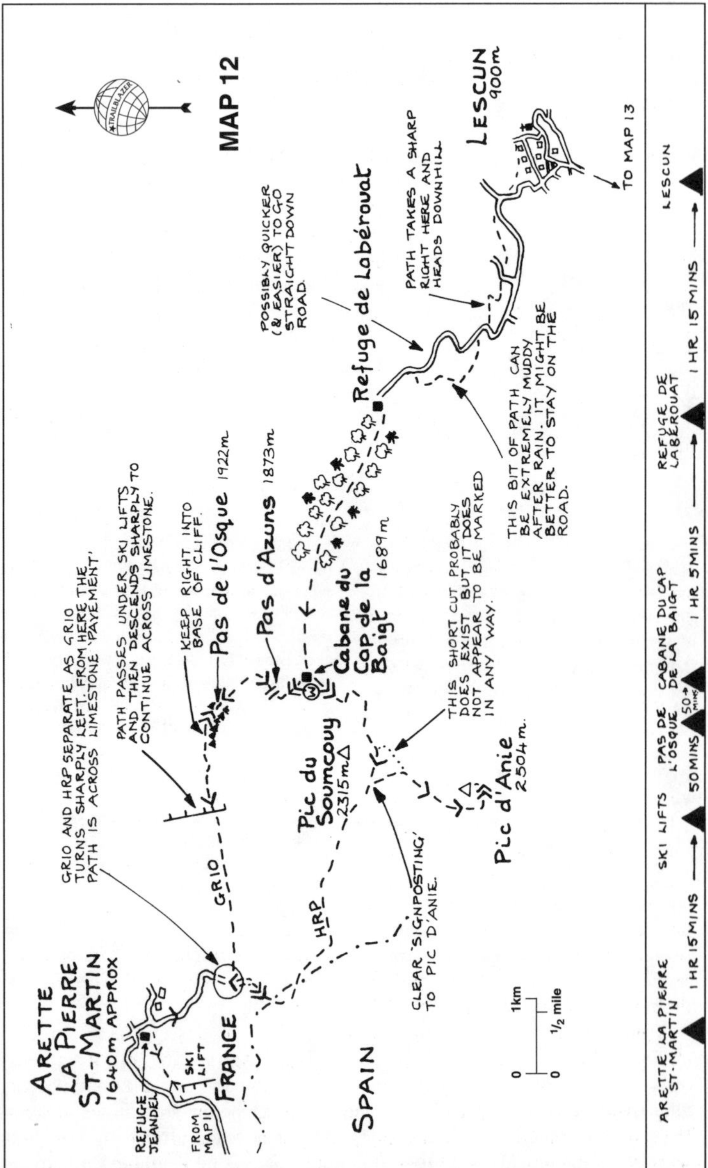

WESTERN PYRENEES

MAP 12

ARETTE
LA PIERRE
ST-MARTIN
1640m APPROX

REFUGE JEANDEL

SKI LIFT

FROM MAP II

FRANCE

GRIO AND HRP SEPARATE AS GRIO TURNS SHARPLY LEFT. FROM HERE THE PATH IS ACROSS LIMESTONE 'PAVEMENT'.

PATH PASSES UNDER SKI LIFTS AND THEN DESCENDS SHARPLY TO CONTINUE ACROSS LIMESTONE.

GRIO

HRP

KEEP RIGHT INTO BASE OF CLIFF.

Pas de l'Osque 1922m

Pas d'Azuns 1873m

Cabane du Cap de la Baigt 1689m

Pic du Soumcouy 2315m

Pic d'Anie 2504m.

CLEAR 'SIGNPOSTING' TO PIC D'ANIE

THIS SHORT CUT PROBABLY DOES EXIST BUT DOES NOT APPEAR TO BE MARKED IN ANY WAY.

THIS BIT OF PATH CAN BE EXTREMELY MUDDY AFTER RAIN. IT MIGHT BE BETTER TO STAY ON THE ROAD.

Refuge de Labérouat

POSSIBLY QUICKER (& EASIER) TO GO STRAIGHT DOWN ROAD

PATH TAKES A SHARP RIGHT HERE AND HEADS DOWNHILL

LESCUN 900m.

TO MAP 13

SPAIN

0   1km
0   ½ mile

ARETTE LA PIERRE ST-MARTIN	SKI LIFTS	PAS DE L'OSQUE	CABANE DU CAP DE LA BAIGT	REFUGE DE LABÉROUAT	LESCUN
◄ 1 HR 15 MINS ►	◄ 50 MINS ►	◄ 50 MINS ►	◄ 1 HR 5 MINS ►	◄ 1 HR 15 MINS ►	

la Baigt (1689m). The cabane is occupied during the summer months and *fromage de brebis* is for sale. There is a water point next to the cabane and a sign which points the way along the GR10 (REFUGE DE L'ABÉROUAT 1H) and to the Pic d'Anie (PIC D'ANIE 2H 15). See p100 for information on climbing the Pic d'Anie.

From now on as you make your way down the valley you'll encounter any number of tourists heading the other way. From the cabane the GR10 goes down the valley and enters a beech wood. Beware: there are plenty of trees here that have red-and-white painted markings upon them ... though they are not way-markings! Thankfully, these marks are usually distinctive in some way (perhaps a red stripe with a white border around it or vice versa).

All being well, after about an hour you come to *Refuge l'Abérouat*; this was closed at the time of writing but used to open in July and August. Below the refuge, the GR10 joins the tarmac road for 5-10 minutes and then diverts to the right on a cart track that can be a quagmire in wet weather. The path rejoins the road briefly before leading off cross-country at the next hairpin bend.

The path joins a tarmac lane, where it turns left and, via a couple more well-marked short cuts, makes its way into **Lescun**.

LESCUN
✉ code 64490

Lescun is a lovely little village, indeed many people remember it as the prettiest spot on the GR10. Perched on a hillside, with the imposing Pic d'Anie towering over it, it seems the quintessential Pyrenean hamlet with winding streets and old stone houses.

Services
Lescun doesn't boast much in the way of services. There's a **post office** (which does not change cash/travellers' cheques) and the **Bar des Bergers** down the hill below the hotel has a tiny stock of essentials including phone cards. There is no bank in Lescun; the nearest bank/cash dispenser is in Bédous, on the way to Oloron-Ste-Marie.

There are 2-3 SNCF **buses** to Oloron every day which run along the valley below Lescun. It's a 5km walk down the hill to get to the bus stop, then 31km on the bus (€4.70 one way). If you need to get out of the mountains it's much better to wait a day and get to Borce and Etsaut, both of which are on the road and are served by the same bus service.

Where to stay
The *Hôtel Pic d'Anie* ☆☆ (☎ 05.59.34.71 .54, 🖷 05.59.34.53.22) is recommended. It's not very grand but it's very comfortable and friendly; rooms are from €32/42 single/double; they also do a set menu for €15. Those not on a shoestring budget should try the hotel restaurant; the food is delicious and portions generous – the €15 menu is worth every euro. The hotel accepts credit cards (Visa & MasterCard) both for hotel and restaurant bills, as well as for payment by those staying in the gîte (see below).

Just across the road is the gîte d'étape – *Refuge du Pic d'Anie*, which is run by the hotel. It's clean and modern with excellent kitchen facilities, and it costs €10 per night. It sleeps only 14, so it's worth booking in advance. The new *Maison de la Montagne* (☎ 05.59.34.79.14) is a fairly new and very comfortable gîte d'étape. It's open all year and charges €11 for the night, €4.50 for breakfast and €26 for demi-pension. There's a **Bureau des Guides** here, and information on a variety of activities in the local area, including walking tours, climbing and canyoning.

Camping Municipal Le Lauzart ☆☆ (☎/🖷 05.59.34.51.77) is about 1km south-west of the village (on the GR10) and has a well-stocked shop on site; an emplacement costs €3.80 plus €2.20 per person.

LESCUN → BORCE/ETSAUT [MAP 13]

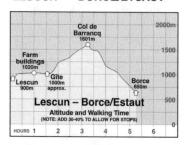

Col de
Barrancq
1601m

2000m

1500

Farm
buildings
1020m

Gîte
1000m
approx.

Borce
650m

1000

Lescun
900m

500

Lescun – Borce/Estaut
Altitude and Walking Time
(NOTE: ADD 30-40% TO ALLOW FOR STOPS)

0

HOURS 1   2   3   4   5   6

Take the road running south-west out
of the village, down to the **Pont du
Moulin**. There's a sign here (ETSAUT
6H 05 & PLATEAU DE LHERS 1H 25)
pointing directly up a steep rocky footpath which short-cuts up to the road
above. Whichever route you take, the
GR10 soon passes the entrance to the
campsite. A short distance further on
there is a road junction; go straight
over, and after a couple of minutes
leave the tarmac on a small path to the left. This path meets and crosses the road
two or three times before coming to a farm access track. Turn left and follow the
track for 300-400m, before taking a footpath which skirts around the farm buildings. Beyond the farm, the path runs through attractive woods for half a kilometre before abruptly doubling back on itself. As you walk southwards along a
shady farm track, the **Plateau de Lhers** spreads out on the left.

After 1.5km the track joins a small tarmac lane, near a farmhouse where
eggs, honey and cheese are for sale. The lane leads on, over a small bridge, to a
road junction. Just south of the junction is a *gîte* and a grassy area suitable for
camping. The gîte is looked after by Mme Nicole Rachau (☎ 05.59.34.77.27)
but there is no guardian in residence so you'll need to make arrangements in
advance if you wish to stay here.

From the road junction the GR10 goes north along the road past three or
four houses, before leaving the tarmac and heading towards a rough-surfaced
vehicle track which can be seen starting to climb the hillside. About 20m along

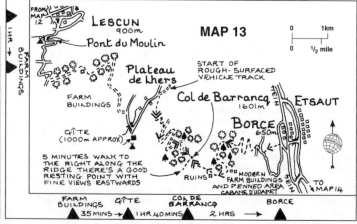

FROM
MAP
12

LESCUN
900m

MAP 13

0   1km
0   1/2 mile

Pont du Moulin

START OF
ROUGH-SURFACED
VEHICLE TRACK

Plateau
de Lhers

FARM
BUILDINGS

Col de Barrancq
1601m

ETSAUT

BORCE
650m

GÎTE
(1000M APPROX)

5 MINUTES WALK TO
THE RIGHT ALONG THE
RIDGE THERE'S A GOOD
RESTING POINT WITH
FINE VIEWS EASTWARDS

RUINS

MODERN
FARM BUILDINGS
AND PENNED AREA
CABANE D'UDAPET

TO
MAP 14

FARM
BUILDINGS

GÎTE

COL DE
BARRANCQ

BORCE

35 MINS →   1 HR 40 MINS   2 HRS →

WESTERN PYRENEES

1 HR →

FROM
BUILDINGS

the track, however, the GR10 bends off to the right uphill across the grass, and then morphs into a footpath that runs through bracken. The path climbs steeply before joining a proper track and after a few minutes this joins a rough road used by logging vehicles. The road climbs in zigzags across the slopes and soon enters the woods, the trees providing welcome shade. Route-finding around here is easier than it used to be, but there is still scope for confusion because the foresters have daubed the trees with red-and-white-painted markers similar to those in the forest above Lescun that you encountered in the previous stage!

Following the rough road (and the occasional short cut marked out between the hairpins), the GR10 cuts straight up the hill on footpaths to the **Col de Barrancq (1601m)** where there's a yellow sign: Borce 2H; Etsaut 2H 20. The col is a good spot for a lunch break, and if you head south-west along the ridge for a couple of minutes, the path leaves the trees, giving a decent view over the valley to the east. The footpath down from the col is steep initially but soon emerges at a grassy plateau. After five minutes you pass some small ruins and quarter of an hour later you come to the **Cabane d'Udapet**, though the GR10 soon cuts steeply downhill on a footpath; lower down the hill, at the edge of the wood, the gradient lessens and the path descends the open hillside in large, gentle loops. At the bottom of the slope, you come to a lane.

Turn left along the tarmac following it down for a few minutes until the GR10 markers clearly indicate a turn off the road for a final short cut down a footpath to the village.

BORCE AND ETSAUT
✉ code 64490
The two villages on either side of the River Aspe offer plenty of accommodation, plus a couple of basic shops. The SNCF bus service to and from Oloron-Ste-Marie is particularly useful and makes the villages a popular place either to start or finish a walking trip; the lodges can get very booked up.

Services
The bar near the gîte d'étape in Borce has a small **shop** (open 08.30-22.00) attached to it where most essentials are available and there's even a free **internet** terminal; there's also a small general store in Etsaut. Etsaut also has a **post office** and there's a **Maison du Parc** (open July & Aug daily 10.15-12.30, 14.00-18.30) north of town which houses exhibitions and has the latest on the region's precious and precarious brown bear population.

The nearest bank and cash dispenser is in **Bédous**, to the north, which is accessible via the SNCF bus service which runs four

---

The Pau to Saragossa Railway
Running through the centre of Borce and Etsaut are the rusting remains of the old railway line which used to run from Pau to Saragossa, via the huge Tunnel du Somport-Canfranc. The international line, built in the 1920s was a major feat of engineering and saw its fair share of history. In February 1939, towards the end of the Spanish Civil War, train loads of fleeing Republicans were transported through the Pyrenees and placed in hastily-constructed refugee camps at Gurs, near Oloron-Sainte-Marie.

The railway itself stopped functioning after a derailment in the 1970s, and services have never been resumed.

times a day in each direction, the bus stop being in the main square in Etsaut. The nearest large town and railway station is **Oloron-Ste-Marie** which is also easy to get to on the bus (five daily).

Where to stay

● **Etsaut** The only hotel in either village is *Hôtel des Pyrenees* ✰✰ (☎ 05.59.34.88.62, ▤ 05.59.34.86.96) with rooms for €26-40. It's pleasant enough and the restaurant is good, with a set menu at €13.50. *La Garbure* (☎ 05.59.34.88.98, 🖥 www.garbu re.net), just off the square, is a new venture housed in a 15th-century farmhouse with its own library and three dining-rooms that charges €11 for a bed in a dorm, and €23 for demi-pension. If that's full, opposite the

hotel is *La Maison d'Ours* (☎ 05.59.34.86. 38), which seems to be owned by the same people as La Garbure and mops up any of their excess guests.

● **Borce** The *gîte d'étape* (☎ 05.59.34. 86.40) is the next best place to stay after the hotel. It's clean and modern, has 18 places, and the charge is a thoroughly reasonable €9 for the night (payable to the lady who runs the bar/shop nearby). There's no food but there are good kitchen facilities. The only problem is that it's right next to the church. Even the double glazing doesn't keep out the noise of the church bell which chimes throughout the night and, in true mountain tradition, repeats every set of chimes twice (eg at 2am it will strike twice, then pause and then strike twice again).

BORCE/ETSAUT → GABAS   [MAP 14]

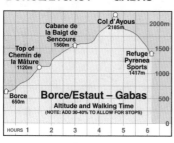

If you're beginning this stage from Borce, take the lane heading south onto the busy N134 past the disued railway bridge, then turn left across Pont de Cebers. If you're coming from Etsaut, take the road leading out of the village to the Pont de Cebers. On the east side of the bridge where the two paths reunite, a sign points along a small side road. Follow the lane uphill a short way and where it bends sharply back on itself continue southwards up a rocky trail. As the path swings to the left, the Fort du Portalet comes into sight on the opposite side of the gorge and the **Chemin de la Mâture** begins.

From the top of the Chemin, follow a level footpath through the woods for 20 minutes past the Grange du Perry, before another 5-10 minutes of steep ascent. A few minutes after this, the path forks and the GR10 goes right (east).

🦌 Chemin de la Mâture

Whatever you may hear about this part of the GR10, nothing quite prepares you for the first sight of the Chemin de la Mâture (the Way of the Masts – see photo opposite p33). The project was initiated by the need for masts for the French navy. The forests of Béarn contained trees of a suitable size and quality, but getting them down from the mountains seemed impossible. This pathway, carved by convicts into the solid rock of an almost vertical cliff, was the solution. From its completion in 1772, huge tree trunks were brought down this slippery and precarious route, before being floated down river to the coast.

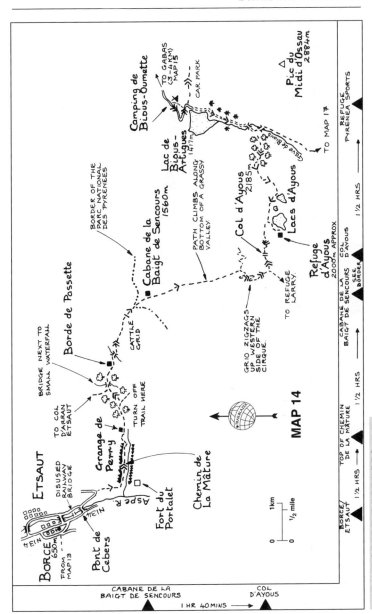

MAP 14

Etsaut 650m
FROM MAP 13
DISUSED RAILWAY BRIDGE
Pont de Cebers
Aspe R.
Grange de Perry
Fort du Portalet
Chemin de La Mâture
TO COL D'ARAN ETSAUT
TURN OFF TRAIL HERE
BRIDGE NEXT TO SMALL WATERFALL
Borde de Passette
CATTLE GRID
BORDER OF THE PARC NATIONAL DES PYRENEES
Cabane de la Baigt de Sencours 1560m
PATH CLIMBS ALONG BOTTOM OF A GRASSY VALLEY
Camping de Bious-Oumette
TO GABAS (3-4 KM) MAP 15
CAR PARK
Lac de Bious-Artigues 1417m
Gave de Bious
Col d'Ayous 2185m
GRID ZIGZAGS UP WESTERN SIDE OF THE CIRQUE.
TO REFUGE LARRY.
Lacs d'Ayous
Refuge d'Ayous 2000m APPROX
Pic du Midi d'Ossau 2884m
TO MAP 17
Refuge PYRENEA SPORTS

0 1km
0 ½ mile

WESTERN PYRENEES

BORCE/ETSAUT — ½ HRS — TOP OF CHEMIN DE LA MÂTURE — ½ HRS — CABANE DE LA BAIGT DE SENCOURS — SEE BORDER — COL D'AYOUS — ½ HRS

CABANE DE LA BAIGT DE SENCOURS — 1 HR 40 MINS — COL D'AYOUS

Ten minutes later, you reach ***Borde de Passette***, a shepherds' croft which at the time of writing had still not been converted into a walkers' lodge despite work starting some years ago. It seems unlikely it will ever be finished.

Beyond the lodge continue climbing along the north-east side of the valley, and after an hour you come to the **Cabane de la Baigt de Sencours (1560m)**. The cabane was completely renovated a few years ago; there's room to sleep four to five people quite easily on the sleeping platform, though it was all locked up the last time we called. The cabane is just inside the boundary of the Parc National des Pyrénées (see p53).

Head south along the valley and, after crossing the stream, you arrive eventually in the bottom of a cirque, below the Pic d'Ayous. The path winds its way up the west slope of the bowl, arriving initially at a small col, which is also on the High Route, and soon afterwards at the **Col d'Ayous (2185m)**. Looking eastwards, the scene is dominated by the Pic du Midi d'Ossau (2884m), which stands isolated from the ridges and peaks around it. After 10-15 minutes' steep descent you come to the **Lacs d'Ayous** and the refuge. The ***Refuge d'Ayous*** (☎ 05.59.05.37.00) is a modern building with capacity for 50 people; accommodation costs €9 per night, or it's €25 for demi-pension.

The area around the Lacs d'Ayous, and indeed the whole area around the Pic du Midi d'Ossau, is popular with holidaymakers and day trippers, so the walk down from here can be crowded, and the path is well worn. After descending across open hillside and then through woods, you come to a track junction next to the Gave de Bious. From here a rough road leads to the **Lac de Bious-Artigues**. If you're planning to spend a day doing the tour of the Pic du Midi d'Ossau (see p114) – and you have a tent – it's best to stay near the lake (or at the campsite below it) as the lake is the starting point for the circumnavigation. Those continuing straight along the GR10 are better off heading down the road to Gabas. (Note that, despite what some editions of the IGN maps suggest, and indeed a red-and-white waymark by the dam's entrance that seems to indicate that you should enter into the woods above the car park, the correct path is, in fact, all the way along the road, apart from a small short cut down to the campsite where you can leave the road to slide down a steep, eroded slope.)

BIOUS-ARTIGUES
✉ code 64440

By the dam and the lake are a couple of small *cafés* and about 500m down the hill is *Camping de Bious-Oumette* (☎ 05.59.05.38.76). The campsite is open from mid-June to mid-September and has a tiny but well-stocked shop. Overnight charges are reasonable at €3.50 per person and €1.30/1.70 for a small/big tent.

Opposite the gate of the campsite is the bus stop for the Pic Bus (see p109). Only the morning service coming from Laruns, and the evening service heading back to Laruns make the detour up the hill to call at the campsite.

GABAS
✉ code 64440

Three and a half kilometres down the hill from Bious-Artigues is the village of Gabas. The *Chalet/Refuge de Gabas* (☎ 05.59.05.33.14) is, since the introduction of a short cut into the village itself, now just off the GR10. There are 34 places in four tiny dormitories and no communal cooking facilities, and they charge €7.10 per night, or €25.50 for demi-pension. Despite being rather cramped, the refuge is recommended for the warm welcome and excellent food provided by the lady who runs it. About 500m down the road in the village itself there are two small hotels. The *Hôtel le Biscau* ☆ (☎ 05.59.05.31.37) has rooms for between €17 and €43, and *Le Chalet des Pyrenees* (☎ 05.59.05.30.51, 🖥 www. lechaletdespyrenees.com) is a new place with a wide range of facilities that charges up to €42 for a room.

There are few **buses** passing through Gabas. In July and August the Pic Bus runs twice daily (excluding weekends and holidays) between Laruns, to the north, and the

Col du Portalet, to the south. Currently, the morning service departs from Laruns at 08.45, calling at Gabas (09.10) and at the Camping de Bious-Oumette (09.20) on its way south; on the return journey (departing from Portalet at 10.20) it stops only at Gabas (10.50). The afternoon service departs Laruns at 15.20 calling at Gabas (but not Bious-Oumette) at 15.45 and returns (departing from Portalet at 16.25) via both Bious-Oumette (17.10) and Gabas (17.20); the fare is €3.

The company that runs the Pic Bus also operates **taxis** (☎ 05. 59.05.30.31). A taxi from Laruns to the Lac de Bious-Artigues costs around €30.

GABAS → GOURETTE   [MAP 15, p110]

[Includes high section – see warning on pp19-20] This section is a long one; try to get an early start so that you can take a decent break somewhere along the way.

The GR10 heads up a short stretch of old road behind the refuge, and joins the D934 going east. Ten minutes along the road, a yellow sign (PLATEAU DE

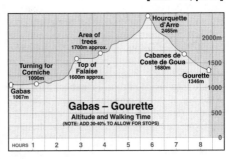

CÉZY 3H, HORQUETTE D'ARRE 6H, GOURETTE 8H 30) points left towards a footbridge. Cross the bridge and follow the path as it enters the wood and climbs along the side of the valley. It soon passes over the top of the spur and starts to descend towards the north. Ahead, through the trees, the Pic de Cézy can be seen. After 15 minutes the footpath meets a forestry track, and the GR10 turns left along it. Don't allow yourself to be confused by the forestry markings painted on the trees, many of which have a single red line – this has nothing to do with the GR10.

After a further 20 minutes you come to another yellow sign: PONT DU GOUA VARIANTE 0H 25 & CORNICHE ALHAS 0H 20 (PASSAGE VERTIGINEUX) – actually, the start of the latter is only about ten minutes away. Much is made of the dizzying walk along the **Corniche Alhas**, and for most people it will come as a bit of a disappointment. The drop beside the path is vertical in places but there's a handrail most of the way and the path is reasonably wide. The alternative to walking along the corniche is to take the other route via the Pont du Goua, a path which drops over 150m to the bridge and then has to gain height again to rejoin the main trail.

For those walking along the corniche, the path leads along the cliff face for 20 minutes before coming down to cross a footbridge below a waterfall. A few

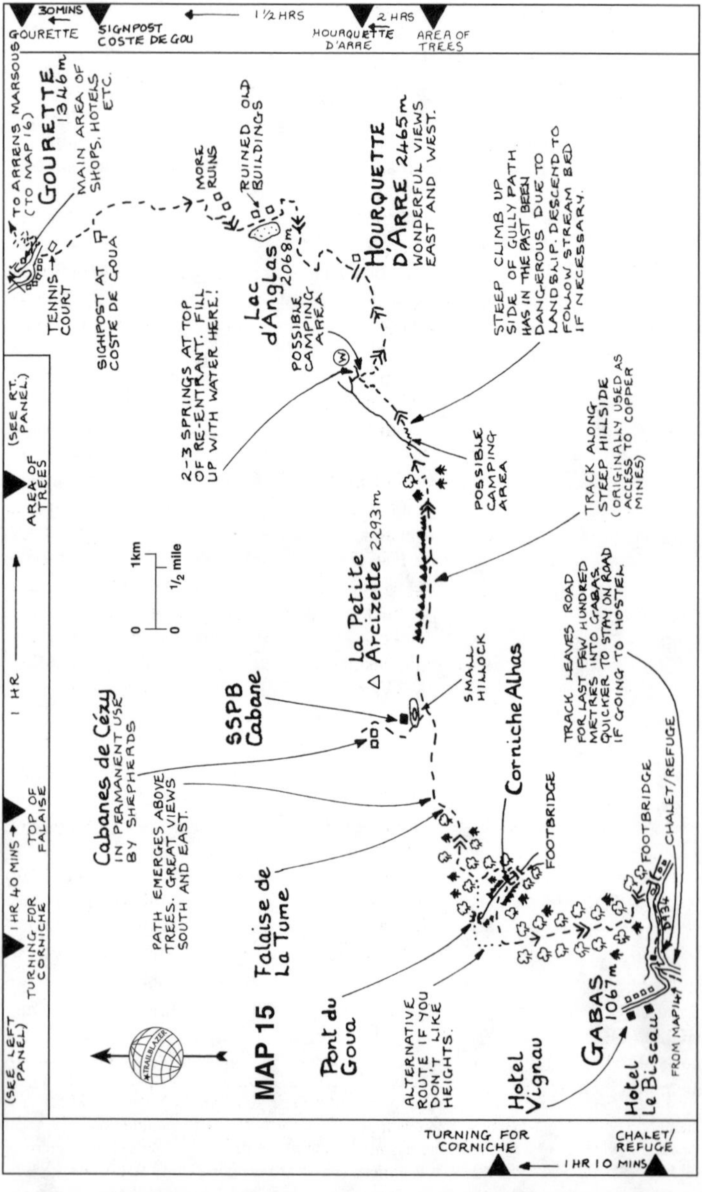

MAP 15 Falaise de La Tume

(TO MAP 16)
(FROM MAP 14)

WESTERN PYRENEES

TURNING FOR CORNICHE

1 HR 40 MINS → TOP OF FALAISE

1 HR.

AREA OF TREES

(SEE LEFT PANEL)

(SEE RT. PANEL)

30 MINS GOURETTE   SIGNPOST COSTE DE GOU   1½ HRS   HOURQUETTE D'ARRE   2 HRS   AREA OF TREES

GOURETTE 1346m.

TO ARRENS-MARSOUS (TO MAP 16)

MAIN AREA OF SHOPS, HOTELS ETC.

TENNIS COURT

SIGNPOST AT COSTE DE GOUA

MORE RUINS

RUINED OLD BUILDINGS

HOURQUETTE D'ARRE 2465m. WONDERFUL VIEWS EAST AND WEST.

STEEP CLIMB UP SIDE OF GULLY PATH HAS IN THE PAST BEEN DANGEROUS DUE TO LANDSLIP. DESCEND TO FOLLOW STREAM BED IF NECESSARY.

Lac d'Anglas 2068m

POSSIBLE CAMPING AREA

2-3 SPRINGS AT TOP OF RE-ENTRANT. FILL UP WITH WATER HERE!

POSSIBLE CAMPING AREA

TRACK ALONG STEEP HILLSIDE (ORIGINALLY USED AS ACCESS TO COPPER MINES)

La Petite Arcizette 2293m.

SMALL HILLOCK

Cabanes de Cézy IN PERMANENT USE BY SHEPHERDS

SSPB Cabane

0   1km
0   ½ mile

PATH EMERGES ABOVE TREES. GREAT VIEWS SOUTH AND EAST.

Corniche Alhas

FOOTBRIDGE

Pont du Goua

ALTERNATIVE ROUTE IF YOU DON'T LIKE HEIGHTS.

Hotel Vignau

TRACK LEAVES ROAD FOR LAST FEW HUNDRED METRES INTO GABAS. QUICKER TO STAY ON ROAD IF GOING TO HOSTEL.

FOOTBRIDGE

CHALET/REFUGE

GABAS 1067m.

Hotel Le Biscau

FROM MAP 14

TURNING FOR CORNICHE

CHALET/REFUGE

1 HR 10 MINS

more minutes along a level path through the trees brings you to a junction where both paths meet.

From here the serious climbing begins. The steep and rocky path eventually rises above the **Falaise de la Tume** and out of the trees. The views are excellent. To the south, on the opposite side of the valley, one can see the route of the Petit Train d'Artouste, and to the south-east the valley floor, the Plaine de Soussouéou, spreads out below. Heading eastwards on a level path, you are confronted by the fascinating sight of the twisted layers of rock which make up La Petite Arcizette (2293m). Soon the path is joined by an indistinct trail coming from the **Cabanes de Cézy**. Although the cabanes are in constant use by shepherds there is a possibility of some basic shelter near here: just to the north of the path junction, on the far side of the little hummock that blocks the Plateau de Cézy from view, is a tiny *cabane* with a roof so low that it looks as though it could actually be a covered sheepfold. On the metal door is a black badge with the letters SSPB. The cabane is left open and according to the shepherds may be used by walkers; it could sleep three to four people.

Continuing along the GR10 from the path junction, after three quarters of an hour you reach a small area of trees and begin the second big climb of the day, towards the **Hourquette d'Arre**. Half an hour above the trees the path crosses to the east bank of the small stream it has been following and begins a steep ascent up a sharp-sided gully. This section along the east bank is prone in places to landslips which sweep away the path. If in doubt, it would be safer to descend to the stream and follow the bank as far as possible. At the top of the gully, the gradient becomes more gradual and the track passes two or three springs. It's an excellent place to fill up with water: you can get it literally from the mountain side.

The path crosses a level area, goes past a tiny tarn and soon begins to climb again. The final approach to the Hourquette d'Arre is very steep, with snow patches at the top, but the views from the col in either direction are magnificent. There's a yellow sign at the col, GOURETTE 2H 30, and nearby a tiny *hut* that could be useful for shelter in an emergency. Heading north across the top of the hill, you soon begin to descend steeply to the **Lac d'Anglas** (*not* the lake you see from the col), which you can see below. Although camping is probably not allowed, it's a lovely spot and people sometimes pitch their tents here.

Continue downhill from the lake on a badly-eroded path for a further hour, towards the **Coste de Goua** and onto Gourette, an ugly and modern ski resort, which soon comes into sight. The path drops down the final hillside to the outskirts of the resort. From here, follow the road downhill to the main area of shops and hotels.

GOURETTE
✉ code 64440

Most of the facilities in Gourette are closed outside the ski season and particularly in the early summer (ie May/June) there is little choice of where to stay and where to eat. In July and August, however, a few more places open up, and the bus service to/from Laruns and Pau also operates. The *Hôtel Au Pène Blanque* ☆☆ (☎ 05.59.05.11.29, 🖥 www.hotel-peneblanque.com) is right next to the main road through the centre of town and is open in July and August; rooms are €48-55. A short distance away, the *Hôtel la Boule de Neige* ☆☆ (☎ 05.59.05.10.05, 🖳 www.hotel-bouledeneige.com) opens mid-July to mid-September and charges €49-54. There's a couple of cheaper hotels down the hill: *Face Nord* (☎ 05.59.05.19. 62) charges €38 per double, and *Le Glacier* (☎ 05.59.05.10.18, 🖳 www.leglacier.fr.st) charges €38-53. The *CAF refuge* (☎ 05.59 .05.10.56) is behind the Intersport shop. The refuge can take 40 people: it's €8 per night, €23 for demi-pension, and is open from early July until the end of August. By contrast, *Club Pyrénéa refuge* (☎ 05.59. 05.12.42), near the Inter-sport shop, is open all summer. It's a large, modern place which charges €15 for the night or €34 for demi-pension. There's also a campsite, *Camping Le Ley* (☎ 05.59.05.11.47), charging €6.40 for one person, €11.25 for two.

Although the bank in the main building of the complex is closed, the **cash dispenser** (Crédit Agricole) remains in use. The **tourist office** (☎ 05.59.05.12.17; Mon-Sat 09.00-12.30, 13.30-17.30, Sun 10.00-12.00, 14.00-17.00), which opens full time only in July and August, is on the ground floor of the main building, though the post office and pharmacy up the stairs in the same complex are usually open in winter only. There are food **shops**, including a small Proxi **supermarket** (Mon-Sat 09.00-12.30, 15.30-19.00, Sun morning only), a sports shop and plenty of *cafés*. During July and August a bus service operates between Gourette and Pau (via Les Eaux Bonnes and Laruns); there are two buses a day each way (from Gourette at 11.30 and 17.00, from Pau at 08.15 and 13.15) plus a further one running between Eaux Bonnes, below Gourette, and Pau, leaving Eaux Bonnes at 06.45, Pau at 18.30.

Entertainment-wise, as well as the bars there's also a **cinema** (Wed-Sat only at 21.00; €5.50).

GOURETTE → ARRENS-MARSOUS   [MAP 16]

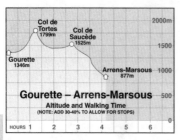

Gourette – Arrens-Marsous
Altitude and Walking Time
(NOTE: ADD 30-40% TO ALLOW FOR STOPS)

From the centre of Gourette, walk back up the road to the tennis courts/ car park area where the GR10 entered the resort. The GR10 goes up a small tarmac lane in front of the large building with 'ASPTT' written on the front, and almost immediately passes a yellow sign: COL DE TORTES 1H 30.

Follow the lane (which soon becomes a stony track) as it twists up the hillside to a point where another yellow sign clearly points the way up a footpath through the trees. The path climbs steeply to the **Col de Tortes (1799m)**, before descending for half an hour to the main road (D918). At the road there's another yellow sign: ARRENS 3H 00; COL DE SAUCEDE 1H 15. Turn right and follow the road south-east for nearly 3km; about three-quarters of the way along the road a small waterfall marks the border between the Pyrénées Atlantiques and the Hautes Pyrénées.

Finally the GR10 leaves the road near a simple sign pointing uphill towards ARRENS. It's an easy walk up to the **Col de Saucède (1525m)**, beyond which the route heads straight down the valley, across rolling pasture land. After three-quarters of an hour the path drops down the side of a small ridge and joins a farm track which in turn leads to a tarmac road running into Arrens-Marsous.

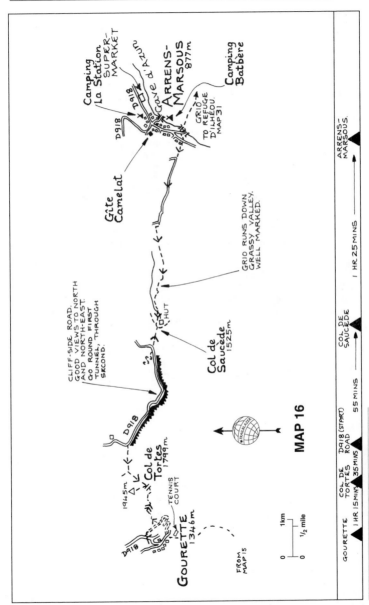

MAP 16

CLIFF-SIDE ROAD.
GOOD VIEWS TO NORTH
AND NORTH-EAST.
GO ROUND FIRST
TUNNEL, THROUGH
SECOND.

GRIO RUNS DOWN
GRASSY VALLEY.
WELL MARKED.

Camping
La Station

SUPER-
MARKET

Gave d'Azun

ARRENS-
MARSOUS
877m

D918

Camping
Batbère

GRIO
TO REFUGE
D'ILHÉOU.
MAP 31

Gîte Camelat

Col de
Saucède
1525m.

HUT

Col de
Tortes
1799m.

1945m.

TENNIS
COURT

GOURETTE
1346m.

D918

FROM
MAP 15

0   1km
0   ½ mile

GOURETTE   COL DE   D918 (START)   COL DE   ARRENS-
1 HR 15 MINS   TORTES   ROAD   SAUCÈDE   MARSOUS
    35 MINS   55 MINS   1 HR 25 MINS

WESTERN PYRENEES

ARRENS-MARSOUS

✉ code 65400

Although there is a hotel in Arrens-Marsous, the nicest place to stay is the *gîte Camelat* (☎ 05.62.97.40.94, 💻 gite-camelat@wanadoo.fr). The pretty and well-maintained building is immaculately clean and has seven rooms which can take 4-6 people each. There's access to a sauna (free access on Tuesday & Thursday, ask at other times) and, since the gîte is run by a chef, the food is fantastic. Staying here costs €15 for the night in a dorm bed, €29 per person for demi-pension, €19 for B&B; in a double it's €37.50 per night room only, €50 B&B, €70 demi-pension for two people.

On the way into Arrens the *Hôtel Le Tech* ☆☆ (☎ 05.62.97.01.60) is the first hotel you pass; it's a grey and impersonal place where unlovely rooms cost €32-41. About 800m north of the village is *Le Gipaet* (☎ 05.62.97.48.12), a second gîte d'étape with great facilities charging €12. The tourist office (☎ 05.62.97.49.49, 💻 www.valdazun.com; Mon-Sat 09.00-12.30, 14.00-19.00, Sun 09.00-12.00, 15.00-18.00) also has the details of three or four *houses* in the village offering chambres d'hôte.

There are several campsites around Arrens-Marsous. The two most central ones are the *Camping Batbère* (☎ 05.62.97.10.50) which is just across the river from the village centre and is next to the sports centre/swimming pool. It's €2.50 per person here, and €1.30 for emplacement.

The village has a few shops including a small **supermarket** (half a kilometre from the centre of the village, past Camping La Station), a **pharmacy** and a fine **local-produce store** in the same building as the tourist office.

Behind the tourist office is a Crédit Agricole **cash dispenser** and you can normally also change money and travellers' cheques at the **post office** (Mon-Fri 09.00-12.00, 14.00-17.00, Sat 09.00-12.00). There's a public **swimming pool** near the Camping Batbère and a cinema (open Tues-Thurs only).

Well worth looking into if you have a spare moment is the permanent **exhibition** about the Pyrenees which is in the gallery area of the tourist office.

There is a daily **bus** (not Sunday) to/from Lourdes and Tarbes.

Excursions around the GR10

PIC DU MIDI D'OSSAU   [MAP 17]

The short, one-day tour around the base of the Pic du Midi d'Ossau is a popular hike through attractive but not spectacular scenery. As well as giving you a break from the routine of the GR10 it offers interesting alternatives: those with the necessary experience can climb the Pic itself (it's not difficult but you'll need a rope and some knowledge of climbing), while others can make an interesting diversion from the GR10 by continuing east from the Refuge de Pombie to the

---

❏ **The High Route**

The Refuge de Pombie is on the High Route (HRP), and an interesting option here would be to join the HRP as it passes through some of the most spectacular scenery in the Pyrenees. See p117 for a recommended route via the Refuge d'Arrémoulit and Refugio de Respumoso to Refuge Wallon, near Gavarnie.

Refuge d'Arrémoulit, near Balaïtous. From Arrémoulit an excellent 1-2 day section of the HRP takes you direct to Refuge Wallon, near Cauterets.

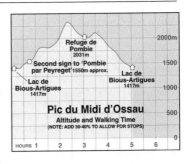

From the Lac de Bious-Artigues, the route goes south up the rough road, towards the Col d'Ayous. At the top of the road, where the GR10 splits off to the right, is a sign, which includes an arrow: POMBIE PAR PEYREGET 2H 30. Follow the arrow left over a small bridge, and cross the plateau on the footpath which runs alongside the stream. After quarter of an hour you come to another sign; again follow the arrow (POMBIE PAR PEYREGET), as the path turns eastwards, climbs up the hillside, and then up a gully. At the top of the gully the path zigzags uphill across the grass to join a footpath running east. After a few minutes you come to the **Lac de Peyreget**.

From the lake the trail climbs eastwards over a low ridge, and descends to a little tarn. Beyond this is an area of boulders which must be negotiated before you reach the **Col de Peyreget (2320m)**. From the col there is a magnificent view eastwards towards Balaïtous. Descending from the col, you soon come to the refuge (2031m). The ***Refuge de Pombie*** (☎ 05.59.05.31.78) can take 50 people indoors. Accommodation costs €13.50 (half-price for CAF and affiliated society members) for the night and demi-pension is €32. Food is available,

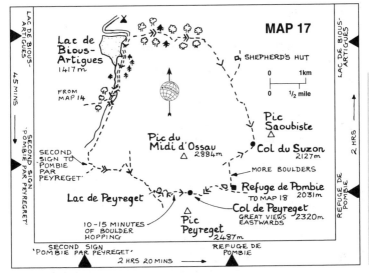

and you're allowed to camp near the refuge. From the refuge the track heads due north, wending its way through a mass of boulders for quarter of an hour before mounting a clear path to the **Col de Suzon (2127m)**. Beyond the col there's a long and gentle descent, mostly on grass, to the **Lac de Bious-Artigues**.

AROUND BALAÏTOUS

At 3144m, Balaïtous is one of the highest peaks in the Pyrenees, and the area around it is utterly unlike the landscape that one encounters on the GR10. Bare rock, perennial snow in some of the gullies and steep drops make the scenery appear savage and forbidding. It's an area which is unsuitable for the inexperienced walker but which offers plenty of excitement. It also provides some interesting variants to the GR10 which, at this stage, loops far to the north.

One of the best options is to leave the GR10 at the Pic du Midi d'Ossau and follow the HRP variant from the Refuge de Pombie, to the Refuge d'Arrémoulit. From Arrémoulit it's possible in a single, albeit long, day to cross the Col de Palas (2517m) into Spain and then cross back into France via the Col de la Fâche (2664m) arriving at the Refuge Wallon. The section from Arrémoulit to Wallon is a long one (9-10 hours' walking) which could easily be broken into two equal stages by stopping overnight at the Refugio de

Respumoso. Whether you take two or three days to walk from Pombie to Wallon, it's still quicker than getting to Wallon via the GR10, and the scenery is superb. This route is described below. Note that both the Col de Palas and the Col de la Fâche may be impossible to cross in early summer because of snow. Even as late as early July it is advisable to check with the guardians of the refuges whether the cols are passable before setting out.

REFUGE DE POMBIE → REFUGE D'ARRÉMOULIT   [MAP 18]

[Includes high section – see warning on pp19-20] Next to the refuge, a sign points the way down towards the valley bottom where the path crosses the main road (D934): CAILLOU DE SOCQUES 1H 30. Head directly east from the refuge, following a clear path which descends across grassy slopes before skirting around to the right hand side of a large area of boulders. After half an hour you come to the **Cabane de Pucheaux** (approx 1730m) and,

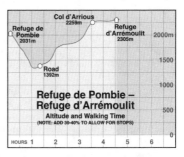

nearby, the **Cabane de la Glère**, both of which are in use by shepherds. Looking down to the left from the Cabane de Pucheaux, a clear path can be seen running along the far bank of the Ruisseau de Pombie. Descend from the cabane, cross the stream at a footbridge, and follow the path eastwards. After about 15 minutes the path crosses back to the south side of the stream via another footbridge, and enters a small wood. From here the path winds gently down the hillside until, after about 20 minutes, it leaves the trees and descends to cross the valley floor before climbing a short way to the road.

On the far side of the road a yellow sign points the way uphill: COL D'ARRIOUS 2H 30; ARREMOULIT 3H. The path makes a couple of sharp turns up the grassy slope before it enters the woods, climbing steeply for the next 20 minutes or so. As the gradient lessens, the path emerges from the trees, crosses a footbridge over the Ruisseau d'Arrious and begins the long climb up the Arrious valley. Half an hour after leaving the trees, you arrive at the **Cabane d'Arrious (1775m)**, which is in use by shepherds. Continue past the cabane and some 45 minutes later you reach a small level area which is a good spot to take a break. Half an hour's further climbing brings you to the **Col d'Arrious (2259m)**.

❏ **Getting to Refuge d'Arrémoulit – the easy option**
For the lazy or those who are short of time, there is a quick way up to this area. A **cable car** runs uphill from the northern end of the Lac de Fabrèges (near Gabas), to the starting point of the **Petit Train d'Artouste**. The narrow-gauge train, normally crammed with tourists, takes 40 minutes to run around the hillside to the Lac d'Artouste, from which it's a 30-40 minute walk up to the Refuge d'Arrémoulit.

WESTERN PYRENEES

A yellow sign at the col indicates a choice of routes: ARREMOULIT (ATTENTION PASSAGE DELICAT) 0H 45; ARREMOULIT 1H 30. Although the 'passage délicat' to Arrémoulit is quicker (it's more direct and doesn't lose height – which the other path does, requiring a climb back up to the refuge) it's not a wise route to take if the weather is poor or if you haven't got a very good head for heights. The 'délicat' section consists of a narrow and uneven ledge above a steep drop (a cable has been fixed to the rock as a handrail). Many people do follow this path but if you're inclined to vertigo it's better to take the longer route which descends to the Lac d'Artouste and then climbs again. The 'easy' path takes around an hour, rather than the 1$^1/_2$ hours that the sign suggests.

Whichever route you choose you soon arrive at the refuge (2305m). The old-style (it dates back to the 1920s) *Refuge d'Arrémoulit* (☎ 05.59.05.31.79) is a tiny place with space for 28 people indoors and a further 16 people in the tent which is erected during peak season. A space in the refuge costs €13.50 (CAF members and affiliated half price), or a bunk in the tent costs €6.50; supper is €14 and breakfast is €4.50. Other drinks and snacks are available. It's cosy and quite charming, though it's due for renovation in 2006.

REFUGE D'ARRÉMOULIT → REFUGE WALLON   [MAP 19]

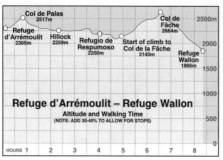

Refuge d'Arrémoulit – Refuge Wallon
Altitude and Walking Time
(NOTE: ADD 30-40% TO ALLOW FOR STOPS)

[Includes high section – see warning on pp19-20] From the Refuge d'Arrémoulit, there are two ways across into Spain – via the Col d'Arrémoulit (2448m) which is visible from the refuge, or via the Col de Palas (2517m), which is hidden from view to the left, as you stand with your back to the refuge building. The route described here is via the Col de Palas. Note that although the route is not difficult it shouldn't be attempted in poor weather or bad visibility, as the way down from the col is indistinct: much of it is over boulders. Being able to see the lake below provides an important reference point which would be lost in poor visibility. Equally, unless you're properly equipped with crampons and an ice axe, the route is unsuitable in early summer when there is still likely to be snow on either side of the pass. If in doubt, ask the guardian of the refuge whether the col is passable.

From the refuge, go a short way around the north-east side of the lake before starting to climb steeply eastwards over rocks and boulders. There are no painted route markings but there are numerous small cairns indicating the way up to the **Col de Palas (2517m)**, which you'll reach after about 50 minutes. Keep an eye on your map and compass to ensure you don't go to the Col d'Arrémoulit, unless of course the weather is threatening – in which case a detour via the (easier) Col d'Arrémoulit is advisable. If you do choose the Col de Palas, there's a water pipe

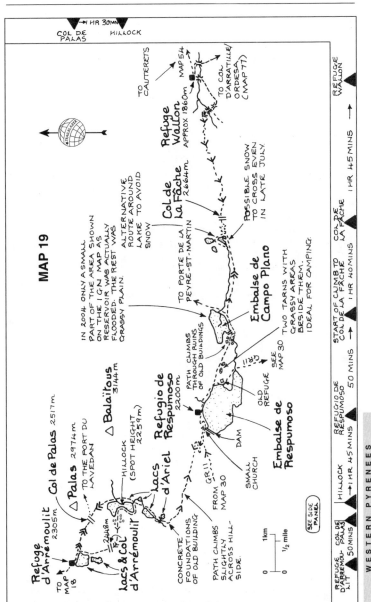

MAP 19

COL DE PALAS
HILLOCK
→ 1 HR 30MN

TO CAUTERETS

MAP 54

TO COL D'ARRATILLE/ ORDESA (MAP 77)

Refuge Wallon
APPROX 1860m

REFUGE WALLON

In 2004 only a small part of the area shown on the I.G.N. map as reservoir was actually flooded. The rest was grassy plain.

ALTERNATIVE ROUTE AROUND LAKE TO AVOID SNOW

Col de la Fâche
2664m

POSSIBLE SNOW TO CROSS EVEN IN LATE JULY.

TO PORTE DE LA PEYRE-ST-MARTIN

△ Balaïtous
3144m

Col de Palas 2517m

△ Palas 2974m

TO THE PORT DU LAVEDAN

HILLOCK (SPOT HEIGHT 2259m)

Refuge d'Arrémoulit 2305m

TO MAP 18

2449m

Lacs & Col d'Arrémoulit

Lacs d'Ariel

Refugio de Respumoso 2200m

PATH CLIMBS THROUGH RUINS OF OLD BUILDINGS

Embalse de Campo Plano

TWO TARNS WITH GRASSY AREAS BESIDE THEM. IDEAL FOR CAMPING.

SEE MAP 30

GR11

OLD REFUGE

Embalse de Respumoso

DAM

SMALL CHURCH

PATH FROM GR11 MAP 30

CONCRETE FOUNDATIONS OF OLD BUILDING.

PATH CLIMBS SLIGHTLY ACROSS HILLSIDE.

0 1km
0 ½ mile

SEE SIDE PANEL

WESTERN PYRENEES

REFUGE D'ARRÉMOULIT ▶ COL DE PALAS 50 MINS

COL DE PALAS ▶ HILLOCK 1 HR 45 MINS

HILLOCK ▶ REFUGIO DE RESPUMOSO 1 HR 45 MINS

REFUGIO DE RESPUMOSO ▶ START OF CLIMB TO COL DE LA FÂCHE 50 MINS

START OF CLIMB TO COL DE LA FÂCHE ▶ COL DE LA FÂCHE 1 HR 40MINS

COL DE LA FÂCHE ▶ REFUGE WALLON 1 HR 45 MINS

leading up the slope that you may find will help you locate the path to the top. The route down from the col is steep and rocky and can be tricky to find in some places although occasional cairns help to keep you on track. After a few minutes the northernmost of the **Lacs d'Ariel** becomes visible. Head down, across boulders, to the lakeside and then go around the eastern edge of the lake. The section around the lakeside is still mostly across boulders and consequently progress is fairly slow. Finally, just next to the small rocky hillock mid-way down the eastern side of the lake (spot height 2259m on the IGN map), you'll come to a good path. Follow this path as it runs level past the first three lakes and then climbs slightly to reach the fourth lake. Just beyond the last lake the path passes the concrete foundations of an old building.

Continue along the same path as it climbs gradually around the hillside and soon you'll see the dam of the Embalse de Respumoso ahead of you. The path continues to climb at an easy gradient for some minutes before sinking down to arrive at the dam, where it meets the GR11 (the Spanish trans-Pyrenean footpath) which has climbed up the valley below (for a description of this route see p151). From the dam the new refugio is visible ahead and is reached after a further 10-15 minutes. The **_Refugio de Respumoso_** (2200m) (☎/🖳 974-49.02.23) is an extremely modern and comfortable place which is open all year and which charges €16 for the night. Drinks and snacks are available and the refuge sells some provisions such as maps, chocolate, biscuits and peanuts.

From the refuge, walk around the side of the lake for a short way and then follow the path as it continues in an east-south-easterly direction past the old refuge, a low building with a Nissen-hut type appearance, which is now firmly locked. As the path climbs and falls it passes two small tarns which have flat grassy areas beside them – perfect (and popular) for camping. Soon the small dam at the end of the Embalse de Campo Plano comes into view. The path descends to a signpost at the (southern) end of the dam and passes around, crosses a bridge, and then skirts the south side of the grassy Campo Plano beyond, to arrive at the bottom of the climb up to the col.

The first part of the climb is at an easy gradient but gradually the path steepens and becomes rocky. After just over an hour of climbing you come to a 'lip', beyond which is a small lake. Even in mid-August there is snow here, and the path around the south side of the lake crosses this. (It is advisable to avoid crossing the snow, which is precarious, by taking an alternative path around the north side of the lake). From the far side of the tarn the path climbs in steep zigzags to a second lip, beyond which there is a short further climb up to the col itself. From the **Col de la Fâche (2664m)** there are wonderful views in both directions.

Hidden behind a rock just to the left as you reach the col is a yellow sign: WALLON 1H 45. The descent to Refuge Wallon is surprisingly gentle and along a well-marked path, although even in mid-/late July three or four patches of snow may have to be crossed. Since the path is hard to miss there is little point in describing it in detail. The timing on the sign at the col is fairly accurate; after approximately an hour and three quarters you arrive at the **Refuge Wallon (1860m approx)**. For details of Refuge Wallon and the possible routes beyond Wallon see p215 and p269.

Western Pyrenees – GR11 (Spain)

The section of the GR11 (the Spanish trans-Pyrenean trail) described here passes through the province of Navarra and the western part of the province of Aragón. Although **Navarra** does not offer the best walking in the Spanish Pyrenees it does make a change from the GR10 and offers a chance to experience something rather different.

Walking on the Chemin St Jacques is not the same as backpacking on the GR10, and the rolling hillsides to the east of Roncesvalles are almost deserted compared with the French hills.

There are drawbacks: poor maps and a lack of both route markings and accommodation, but these are not insurmountable, and it's enjoyable to leave the carefully marked and often crowded French paths behind. **Aragón**, further to the east, contains some excellent walking routes, with the GR11 providing plenty of variety and some truly memorable days.

Route planning

This section describes the pilgrimage route (Chemin St Jacques) across the border from St-Jean-Pied-de-Port to the monastery at Roncesvalles. From Roncesvalles, the section describes a brief short cut to join the GR11 which is then followed through the Western Pyrenees (this part of the book) and the Central Pyrenees (Part 4).

There are numerous places to cross from the French to the Spanish Pyrenees (or vice versa), either to add some variety to your itinerary or simply to make sense of your transport plans. The route across the border from St-Jean-Pied-de-Port is just one of these places. Others (eg via the Col de Palas described above or the Col d'Arratille described in Part 4) are mentioned in the text, where appropriate.

 Chemin St Jacques – The Way of St James

Although pilgrims walking to Santiago de Compostela begin their journey from many places, St-Jean-Pied-de-Port is where the trails tend to converge, and where many walkers choose to make a start. The route to the shrine of St James (the French know him as St Jacques) is an ancient one, known locally as the Chemin St Jacques, and given the status of a footpath – the Grande Randonnée 65.

In mid-summer, walking the Chemin is a truly international experience; some people have travelled across the world to make the pilgrimage. While many pilgrims are devoted Catholics, others complete the walk for a variety of reasons. For most there is an element of spirituality, even if only because walking every day for three weeks allows plenty of time to think. There's no need for it to be a religious experience, though; the GR65 offers some lovely walking across the north-west of Spain.

> **Chanson de Roland and Pyrenean folklore**
> Little is known about the Battle of Roncesvalles, fought in 778, in which the
> rearguard of Charlemagne's army was attacked and decimated by the Basques
> as it crossed the Ibañeta Pass. Nonetheless, the battle is one of the most famous of the
> early Middle Ages, owing to the work of the poet who immortalized it in the *Chanson
> de Roland*.
>
> The poem's central character is Roland, commander of the rearguard, who too late
> sounds his horn to summon help from the main body of the army, a tragic delay that
> leads to the massacre of the élite of Charlemagne's knights. For his part in the tale
> Roland has passed into Pyrenean folklore. In the central Pyrenees, the Brèche de
> Roland (see photo opposite p32) is said to have been formed when the hero, after a
> struggle with the Moors, found himself in a tight corner, and slashed a hole through
> the mountains with his sword, Durandal.
>
> Nearly 10km down the valley is a rock said to bear the hoof prints of his horse,
> as it leapt down from the newly-made hole in the ridge. At the battle of Roncesvalles,
> legend has it, Roland, overcome by the enemy, flung his sword in the air. The spot
> where it landed is still proudly marked by one of the villages on the plain below.

SAINT-JEAN-PIED-DE-PORT → RONCESVALLES
[MAP 20, & MAP 21, p124]

Although the scenery is not particularly remarkable and most of the
walk over the hills into Spain is
along lanes or rough roads, interest
is amply provided by the historical
links of the area and by the presence
of the other pilgrims. The route is
marked in a variety of ways. The
most prominent and frequent markings are the red-and-white paint
markings of the GR65 (the French

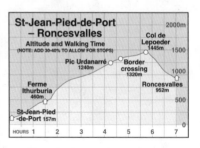

have given the pilgrimage route the status of a long-distance footpath and numbered it the GR65). The other key colour is yellow – yellow arrows painted on
trees, wooden arrows with a carved cockleshell (*la coquille St Jacques*) and a
yellow tip, or yellow stickers on the telegraph poles.

If you arrive in St Jean in the afternoon and feel like making a start that
same day, be warned that you'll need about 2½ hours for the walk up to the
recently-opened Refuge Orisson – though it will help to reduce this stage, a long
(27km) walk to Roncesvalles. From there you can walk the next day to Auberge
Mendilatz and then direct to Ochagavia.

The Chemin leaves St-Jean-Pied-de-Port along the rue d'Espagne, starting
at the mediaeval bridge near the church. This becomes the D428, a winding tarmac lane which climbs steadily to around 900m. A couple of kilometres before
the top of the hill, at **Honto**, there are chambres d'hôte at *Ferme Ithurburia*

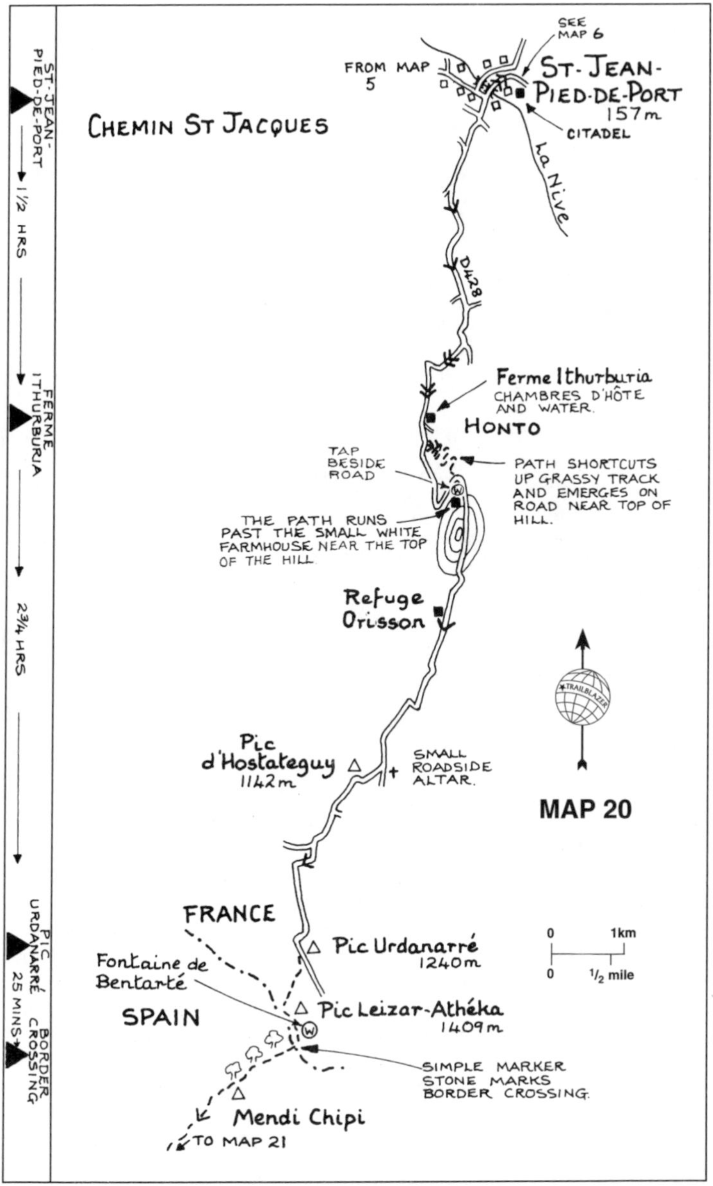

CHEMIN ST JACQUES

FROM MAP 5

SEE MAP 6

ST-JEAN-PIED-DE-PORT 157m

CITADEL

La Nive

D428

Ferme Ithurburia
CHAMBRES D'HÔTE AND WATER.

HONTO

TAP BESIDE ROAD

PATH SHORTCUTS UP GRASSY TRACK AND EMERGES ON ROAD NEAR TOP OF HILL.

THE PATH RUNS PAST THE SMALL WHITE FARMHOUSE NEAR THE TOP OF THE HILL

Refuge Orisson

Pic d'Hostateguy 1142m

SMALL ROADSIDE ALTAR.

MAP 20

FRANCE

Pic Urdanarré 1240m

Fontaine de Bentarté

SPAIN

Pic Leizar-Athéka 1409m

SIMPLE MARKER STONE MARKS BORDER CROSSING.

Mendi Chipi

TO MAP 21

0   1km
0   ½ mile

ST-JEAN-PIED-DE-PORT
→ ½ HRS

FERME ITHURBURIA
→ 2¾ HRS

PIC URDANARRÉ BORDER CROSSING 25 MINS

WESTERN PYRENEES

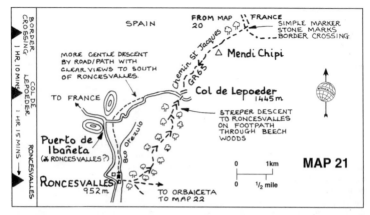

(☎ 05.59.37.11.17). The farm is run by Mme Jeanne Ourthiague; double rooms cost €37 and an evening meal costs €13. There is also a barn and a dormitory for €7-11 per person.

Above Honto, the path takes a short cut, winding up a steep grassy track before rejoining the lane. Near where the path meets the tarmac there's a tap by the roadside, which provides a welcome chance to fill up with water (though it would be wise to treat the water before drinking it).

An hour after leaving Ferme Ithurburia you come to *Refuge Orisson* (☎ 06. 84.49.79.56) with bar, restaurant, small dormitories and camping behind the building. Demi-pension is €28, while camping with half board and a sandwich for the next day is €23.

From here continue along the road all the way to the **Pic Urdanarré (1240m)**, where you finally leave the lane for a footpath. Be cautious here: the path leaves the road at a slight bend and is clear in good weather, but is easily missed in poor light or snow. The signs are small, partly broken, and do not face the road. Look for a cairn, a cross 20m beyond that, and the path going straight up and around the peak.

Beyond this point, the walk becomes more attractive, passing alongside and then through beech woods. Approximately 20 minutes after leaving the road by the Pic Urdanarré, the path passes the Fontaine de Bentarté, which provides another chance to fill up with water. The fountain is usually very reliable but can run very low at the end of a dry summer. Shortly after this the path crosses the border, which is marked by a stone, carved with the word 'Navarre'. From here, the path climbs slowly to the **Col de Lepoeder**. There are two routes at the col, both signposted. The traditional route is slightly shorter but steep in places, passing through beech woods. The alternative route is along a narrow road in open country with good views of Roncesvalles. It is 4km, as opposed to 3.6km for the short route.

RONCESVALLES

The **monastery** at Roncesvalles was built at the beginning of the thirteenth century by Sancho el Fuerte, King of Navarre. Today, it still plays an important role in aiding pilgrims on the Camino de Santiago as the first rest-stop in Spain after their long 27km haul over the Pyrenees. The village still consists of just the monastery, its attendant buildings and two hotels. There are no shops except for the souvenir shop in the monastery, though it does sell phone cards, film and batteries.

Next to the church, in the **chapter house**, is Sancho's mausoleum; the enormous statue of the king, which lies on top of the tomb, is said to be life-size. The stained-glass window in the south wall of the chapter house shows Sancho at the battle of Las Navas de Tolosa (1212). The complex also houses a **museum** and **cloister** open to visitors and a **tourist office**.

The **church** in the monastery is well worth a visit for the impressive daily mass for pilgrims. The service starts at 20.00 on weekdays, 19.00 on Saturday and Sunday. There are usually over a hundred pilgrims in attendance and they receive a special blessing after the service.

Services

Either the baggage delivery service Burricot (☎ (France (33) 06.61.96.04.76) or Pedro Tellechea (☎ 948-76.00.07, mobile 629-87.81.81) can transport you or your bags between St-Jean-Pied-de-Port and Roncesvalles. Burricot charges €0.70/kg and Pedro charges €0.20 either for a backpack or a person. Thus for bags, Burricot is probably cheaper whereas for a taxi service, Pedro should be but they would probably charge the same.

Buses to Pamplona run only on weekdays; taxis cost €45 but may try to charge more on weekends – €50 should be the maximum.

Where to stay

Almost all pilgrims sleep in the accommodation provided within the monastery, a room full of old iron bunk beds, but it is impossible to get in without a card certifying pilgrim status. The other budget option is the *Albergue Juvenil de Roncesvalles* (☎ 948-76.03.02) which has accommodation for 80 people in clean, modern dormitories. They are insistent on a YHA or equivalent card from other countries, and charge €9 for people under 26, €12 for people over 26. It's a good facility and a lot of people who are cycling the pilgrim route but who haven't got a pilgrim card stay there.

The larger of Roncesvalles' two hotels, *La Posada* (☎ 948-76.02.25) has single rooms from €37 and double rooms from €42, and has a restaurant. Being the larger hotel, it gets a lot of tour-bus business. Small and friendly *Hostal Casa Sabina* (☎ 948-76.00.12), next to the monastery, has a few modern and very comfortable double rooms for €37 and a pleasant patio for drinks outside.

Your last chance for accommodation in Roncesvalles itself, which can fill up completely at weekends, is to **camp** in the woods beyond the parking lot to the east of the monastery where the GR65 comes into the village and where the route to Fabrica de Orbaizeta starts. The field to the south of the parking lot is not visible from the road but receives visits from police patrols in the mornings, so you should look as though you are about to leave if they arrive. Washrooms in the monastery are open all night and can be found near the entrance to the youth hostel.

Alternatively, 2km south of Roncesvalles, either by road or by following the unmissable Camino de Santiago signs, the village of **Auritz-Burguete** has two hotels, the *Hostal Burguete* (☎ 948-76.00.05) with singles/doubles from €30/41 (att) and Loizu ☆☆☆ (☎ 948-76.00.08), with rooms from €36/45 (att). In addition, there are several Casas Rurales in Auritz-Burguete, *Casa Loigorri* (☎ 948-76.00.16), *Casa Loperena* (☎ 948-76.00.68), *Casa Pedroarena* (☎ 948-76.01.64) and *Casa Vergara* (☎ 948-76.00.44), with double rooms from €25 to €35. The tourist office may or may not help by making calls for you for a reservation but it is always worth asking them.

Roncesvalles – Where to eat

Pilgrims can eat at the restaurant of either of the hotels in Roncesvalles, where they receive a special set menu for only €7 by buying a ticket beforehand for dinner at either 20.00 or 21.00. There's a chance you might be able to get such a ticket without showing a pilgrim card; otherwise you would pay €11 for a standard three-course meal with wine and bread.

RONCESVALLES → EMBALSE (RESERVOIR) DE IRABIA [MAP 22]

From the monastery, retrace your steps 400m eastwards along the previous day's route, to the point where the GR65 turns uphill on an earthen path, leaving the rough forestry road. Don't follow the GR65, but instead take the forestry road for 15-20 minutes, ignoring a left fork after 10-15 minutes, until the track meets another forestry road. Turn left along the new track, cross a small bridge, and follow the

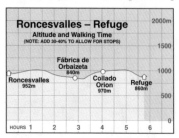

track for a kilometre as it climbs to the **Collado de Nabala** (1000m approx). There's a gate at the col, and just on the far side of it a concrete drainage duct has 'A FABRICA 9K' painted on it, with an arrow pointing north-east.

Follow the forestry track north-eastwards for about a kilometre, scaling a crude stile if a barbed-wire fence is stretched across the track, until it swings south-east and descends to a large trail junction at the base of a small hill (spot height 1048m on the map). A signpost here points left to: 'FA ORBAIZETA'. This is the route to follow. Don't be tempted to take the path, shown on maps, which continues over the top of Latxaga (1204m) and appears to be a short cut to Orbaiceta; it starts off promisingly but peters out near the top of the hill. You then have to traipse back to this junction again.

From the junction, a stony vehicle track leads downhill through the trees for 5-6km. The latter half of the walk alongside the Barranco de Itolaz is pretty and just before arriving at **Fábrica de Orbaizeta** there's a small spring on the left, a good opportunity to fill up with water. Fábrica de Orbaizeta is for the most part a fairly ramshackle collection of buildings, although three or four houses have recently been renovated. Cheese (and sometimes bread) is for sale at one of the houses (there's a notice on the door) and there's a small bar which sells drinks and sandwiches.

ORBAICETA AREA

About a kilometre after the rather rundown village of Fábrica de Orbaizeta there's a new hostel which has transformed walkers' options in this region. As you leave the village head due south on the road and do not follow GR11 signs to the left, continuing until you come to a sharp left turn about 10 minutes later which has a signpost indicating the **Alberge Mendilatz** (☎ 948-76. 60.88, 💻 www.mendilatz.com). Half-board is €24 in the dormitories, and it's €43 in double rooms with two people sharing. It's

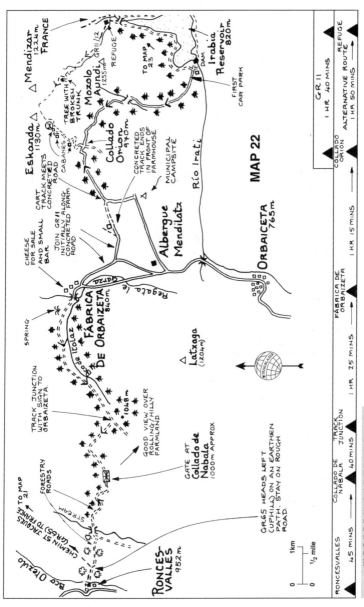

MAP 22

Pamplona

Pamplona, the ancient capital of Navarre, is a fascinating place. Easily accessible from both Roncesvalles and Ochagavia, it makes a memorable excursion from any walking itinerary in this area.

The city is famous for the annual fiesta of San Firmin, which takes place in the second week of July. The week-long festival is well known not only for the bull fights but also for the time-honoured tradition of **bull-running**. According to age-old custom, the bulls are herded through the heavily-barricaded streets to the bull ring, and large numbers of brave (or crazy) participants dare to run through the streets with them. The ultimate adrenalin rush: the aim is to get close but obviously not too close. Every year a few people get it wrong: if they're lucky it's simply a case of severe panic and some bruises but it's not unusual for runners to be badly injured or even killed.

Apart from the bulls, the fiesta is an excuse for a massive party. For a full week the town is packed to capacity and celebrations go on non-stop. If you plan to visit the festival, book somewhere to stay as far in advance as possible; turning up and expecting to find somewhere for the night is sure to end in disappointment. Above all pack some extra stamina. Ernest Hemingway summed up the atmosphere of the event in the novel *Fiesta*: 'The fiesta was really started. It kept up day and night for seven days. The dancing kept up, the drinking kept up, the noise went on. The things that happened could only have happened during a fiesta'.

a big hostel, and they might also let you camp if you ask. Mendilatz is open year-round and is large enough so that you should never have a problem in getting in.

Alternatively, by continuing along this road to rejoin the GR11 you'll come to an unattended municipal campground with water and toilets. If you needed a shop, you'll have to walk 4km south to the village of Orbaiceta, which also has some accommodation. *Camping Irati* (☎ 948-76.60.74) has a restaurant and shop. Casas Rurales include: *Casa Alzat* (☎ 948-76.05.55), *Casa Etzangio* (☎ 948-76.60.14), *Casa Mujurdin* (☎ 948-76.60.46), and *Casa Sastrarena* (☎ 948-76.60.93). Prices for a double room in all the above range from €25 to €30; all of them do breakfast but Casa Sastrarena is the only one where an evening meal is available.

The GR11 and GR12 pass through Fábrica de Orbaizeta and are marked clearly with red and white paint. They leave the hamlet on a concrete road which is followed for over a kilometre until it comes to an end in front of a farmhouse. Continue past the front of the house and beyond it join an old cart track. Follow this through the woods for 20-25 minutes, until it descends to meet a concrete road. Turn left along the road and follow it as it climbs slowly eastwards to the **Collado Orion (970m)**.

At the col there's a road/track junction and sign. From here you have a choice: following the GR11 down to the Embalse, or taking a shorter route, continuing by road down to the dam and either walking north up to the camping spot, or around the south to Casas de Irati and then on to Ochagavia.

GR11

The GR11 leaves the concrete road at the Collado Orion and follows the rough road which zigzags up the hillside to the north of the signpost. After five minutes the track levels out and passes a shepherd's hut on the left. Beyond this it starts to climb again and after a further 5-10 minutes passes, on the left, a small hut with a corrugated iron roof.

Here the GR11 leaves the rough road, descending on a grassy path to the right, and almost immediately passes another hut, beside which is a water source. The path, which is very poorly marked in this area, contours around a spur and, remaining just above the trees, crosses a tiny re-entrant before climbing towards the grassy col between Mendizar (1224m) and Eskanda (1130m). Just below the col a couple of GR markings direct you onto a narrow and overgrown path which contours around the southern slope of Mendizar. About 25 minutes after passing the col, the path, which has remained well above the trees up to this point, descends to meet the treeline. Look for a large tree with a broken trunk, on which there is a very faded GR marker. Go down into the woods near this tree to find the path. It's poorly marked and hard to distinguish at first but soon becomes clearer. After ten minutes' steep descent through the trees the path crosses a stream and becomes much easier to follow. A further 20-30 minutes' walking brings you to the *refuge* at the north end of the Embalse de Irabia. The hut is dirty and basic and could sleep five people at most, but the area is beautiful and if you have a tent it's an ideal spot for (unofficial) camping.

Alternative route – Fábrica de Orbaizeta to Casas de Irati via the dam (southern trail)

The shortest way, which would make sense in bad weather or if you are in a position to get to Ochagavia in one day, would be to go around the south side of the embalse. The day walk from Fábrica de Orbaizeta to Ochagavia would be about seven hours.

From the Collado de Orion, continue south/downhill on the road. At the car park, take the right fork. (The left fork leads around the embalse to the camping area on the northern end). A few minutes later at a second fork, take the path to the left, which goes across the dam. At the end of the dam, take the signed footpath to the left, leading to a beautiful walk around the reservoir on a fairly level, easy path in beech woods.

At the next signpost you come to, take route SL 53, marked CASA FORESTAL. The path goes around another inlet and crosses a footbridge which puts you on the north bank of the Rio Irati, heading east. At the following signpost, go for VIRGEN DE LAS NIEVES, which is a small chapel just above Casas de Irati. The path goes around an abandoned house with a spring behind it. Take the lower path, not the one leading directly past the spring, and continue, heading across the creek where the path forks.

After a few hundred metres, you meet a good track at a horseshoe bend. This is the GR11, and turning right towards Casas de Irati, you will soon see red-and-white markers again. The track follows the Rio Irati for about 3km until you reach Casas de Irati.

EMBALSE (RESERVOIR) DE IRABIA → OCHAGAVIA   [MAP 23]

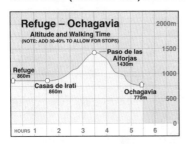

Refuge – Ochagavia
Altitude and Walking Time
(NOTE: ADD 30-40% TO ALLOW FOR STOPS)

Paso de las Alforjas 1430m
Refuge 860m
Casas de Irati 860m
Ochagavia 770m

From the refuge at the northern end of the dam, the GR11 goes 200m south and crosses to the eastern side of the reservoir via the Puente de la Cuestión. On the far side of the bridge a sign points the way southwards: CASAS DE IRATI 1H 05. Note that this timing is wildly optimistic: unless you're jogging it takes about $1^1/_2$ hours. Follow the vehicle track all the way around the eastern side of the lake to the **Casas de Irati**, where there's a spring (this is a good opportunity to fill up with water) a car park and a tiny information booth but nothing else.

In his original research for this guide, Douglas Streatfeild-James had difficulty locating the course of the GR11 at this stage, partly owing to inaccurate maps. He blazed his own trail straight up the hill towards the landmark peak of Abodi Occidentale, of which you will have glimpses. The staff at the information booth told me a few years ago that the GR11 route had been changed – to Douglas's route! They swear that it is easy to find now, but after walking about 1km beyond the bridge along the road you'll find only a sign for the SENDERO LOCAL, well above the road. Nevertheless, around the post are red-and-white stripes that indicate that this is, indeed, the GR11. Get into first gear and begin trudging up the hill, bearing right where the local path bears left, then passing the road again where it makes a switchback to the left, before continuing straight up. The gradient becomes a bit easier as you cross the forestry road but then resumes its uphill course. The path is easy to follow but keep looking up for the markers on the trees as eventually the path forks and the GR11 bears left, going gently uphill on a grassy path before finally turning more sharply uphill after about 1km. As you rise above the treeline the markers disappear. Go straight uphill and this will bring you to the **Paso de las Alforjas (1430m)**, a grassy col with two large dips in the ground. If you have a little time to spare this is a great place to take a break. There are excellent views to the south and north; the route onwards to Ochagavia is all downhill from here.

A sign at the Paso points the way to Ochagavia. From the sign, go southeast past the large flat rock, and beyond it find a small building with a GR marking on the wall. Turn left (south-east) just before the building and follow the path as it gradually descends across the hillside. After a few minutes the path turns directly downhill and passes through a gate before descending a short way further to meet a farm track. The GR11 goes left on the track, which soon narrows to become a stony footpath, skirting the fields.

At the **Borda de Botin** pass a barn to join a vehicle track which runs south for 1500m to a tarmac road. Turn right, and soon you come to the **Santuario de Muskilda**, a pretty church with a conical roof on the tower. The path runs through the buildings and then down a steep and seemingly endless trail to Ochagavia.

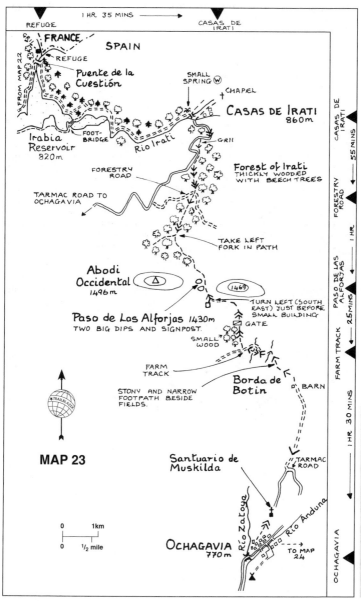

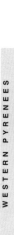

OCHAGAVIA

Ochagavia is a sleepy and beautiful Basque village at the intersection of two rivers. Cobbled stone streets and the habit of leaving doors open to reveal entrance halls with patterned floors made of small cobblestones and lots of heavy, simple woodwork make it an interesting place to stroll around.

The **tourist office** ☎/🖥 948-89.06.41) is open 10.00-14.00 and 16.30-19.30 (except Sundays and hols: 10.00-14.00). The **post office** is near the church (behind the tourist office). There are three **cash dispensers** and one small bank which is open Monday to Friday, mornings only. There is a daily **bus** (not Sundays) to Pamplona, which leaves Ochagavia at 07.00.

A small **shop** on the road to the campground displays Camping Gaz and Epigas canisters in its window, and meths can be found in the **general shop** (very close to the post office) but you may have to ask for it.

Where to stay

Hostal Aunamendi (☎ 948-89.01.89) is right on the main square and has very pleasant single rooms from €41 and doubles

from €60. Also worth trying is *Hostal Ori-Alde* (☎ 948-89.00.27) where doubles are €39. Both hotels have a restaurant.

Ochagavia is one of the prettiest villages in the Basque country, so now may be a good time to stay in a traditional Basque house. There are a number of Casas Rurales, including *Casa Aisko* (☎ 948-89.03.30), *Casa Ballent* (☎ 948-89.03.73), *Casa Dukea* (☎ 948-89.00.62) and *Casa Eloico* (☎ 948-89.04.64). Double rooms in all the above cost €26.

If you are carrying a tent, *Camping Osate* (☎ 948-89.01.84), five minutes' walk from the main square, is a nice spot – quiet, level and grassy with some tree shade; it's a good spot for a rest day. Camping charges are €3.50 per person and €3.50 per tent. There's a reasonable restaurant/bar and a very poorly-stocked shop. The owners' interest in the restaurant and shop dwindles in September, but the campground remains open.

The hotel **restaurants** offer three-course dinners for €13-15 at 20.00, but the **bar** next to the tourist office offers cheaper menus that are available from 21.00.

OCHAGAVIA → ISABA   [MAP 24]

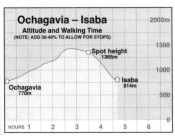

Ochagavia – Isaba
Altitude and Walking Time
(NOTE: ADD 30-40% TO ALLOW FOR STOPS)

Spot height 1365m
Isaba 814m
Ochagavia 770m

The GR11 stage from Ochagavia to Isaba lies mostly along a single rough road. By way of consolation, the Ermita de Idoya is beautiful and Isaba is a very attractive little village in which to stop for the night. Moreover the following day's stage, over Ezkaurre (2049m), is excellent. There is no water on this stage until Isaba.

From the main square in Ochagavia, go up the east bank of the Río Anduña, past the building with 'Exposicion' written on the front of it. Pass to the left of another building which bears the words 'Estacion Pateteria', and, on the wall of the building, a faded GR marking. The road swings right and becomes a rough track climbing north-eastwards. Although there are few route markers throughout the rest of the day, basically you follow this track almost all the way to Isaba.

WESTERN PYRENEES

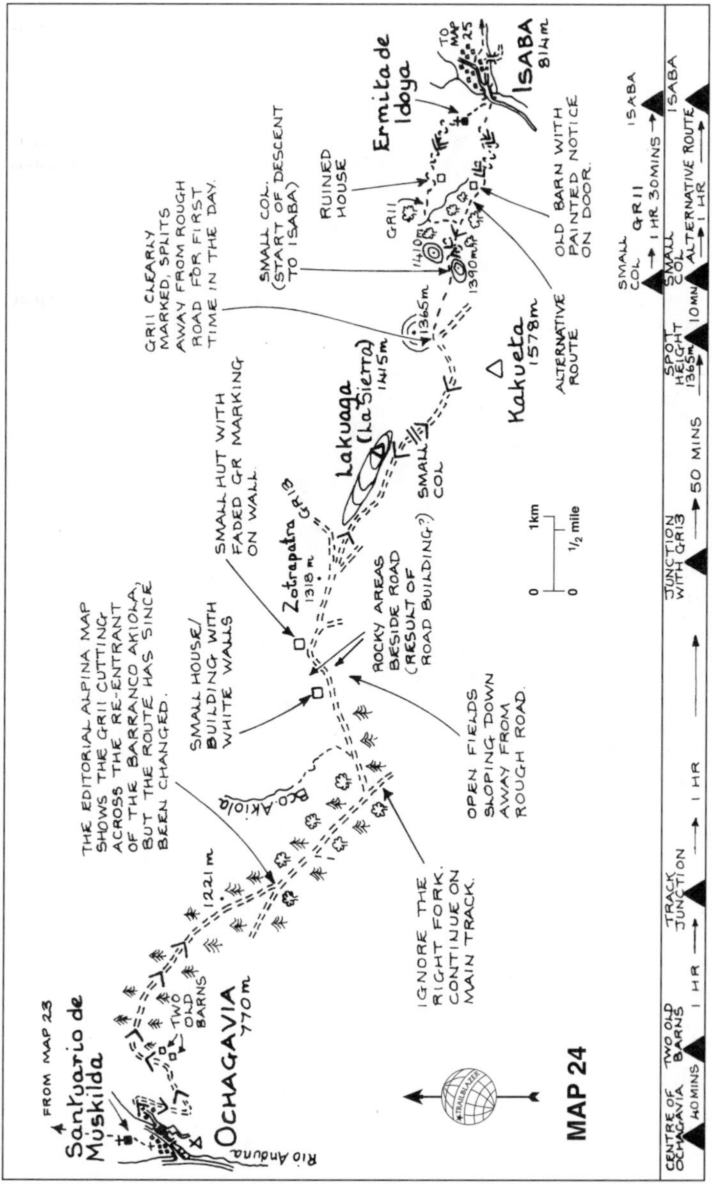

MAP 24

WESTERN PYRENEES

FROM MAP 23

Santuario de Muskilda

OCHAGAVIA 770m.

Rio Anduna

TWO OLD BARNS

1221m.

IGNORE THE RIGHT FORK. CONTINUE ON MAIN TRACK.

Bco. Akiola

OPEN FIELDS SLOPING DOWN AWAY FROM ROUGH ROAD.

THE EDITORIAL ALPINA MAP SHOWS THE GR11 CUTTING ACROSS THE RE-ENTRANT OF THE BARRANCO AKIOLA, BUT THE ROUTE HAS SINCE BEEN CHANGED.

SMALL HOUSE/BUILDING WITH WHITE WALLS.

ROCKY AREAS BESIDE ROAD (RESULT OF ROAD BUILDING?)

Zotrapatra GR13 1318m.

SMALL HUT WITH FADED GR MARKING ON WALL.

SMALL COL

Lakuaga (La Sierra) 1415m.

Kakueta 1578m.

ALTERNATIVE ROUTE

1365m.

1390m. 1410m.

GR11 CLEARLY MARKED, SPLITS AWAY FROM ROUGH ROAD FOR FIRST TIME IN THE DAY.

SMALL COL (START OF DESCENT TO ISABA)

RUINED HOUSE

Ermita de Idoya

ISABA 814m.

TO MAP 25

GR11

OLD BARN WITH PAINTED NOTICE ON DOOR.

0 1km
0 ½ mile

CENTRE OF OCHAGAVIA	TWO OLD BARNS	TRACK JUNCTION	JUNCTION WITH GR13	SPOT HEIGHT 1365M	SMALL COL	SMALL COL ALTERNATIVE ROUTE	SMALL COL	ISABA
← 40 MINS →	← 1 HR →	← 1 HR →	← 50 MINS →	← 10 MINS →	← 1 HR →	← 1 HR 30 MINS →		← ISABA →

WESTERN PYRENEES

The track makes a couple of large zigzags up the hillside and after 40 minutes passes two old barns. At the barns the track swings left and continues to climb at an easy gradient, with occasional shade from blocks of pine trees on either side. Gradually it swings round to the right to head south-eastwards and, about an hour beyond the barns you come to a junction with another rough road. Continue south-eastwards passing, after about 15 minutes, a fork to the right, which you should ignore. Carry on along the main track as it swings around to head in a north-easterly direction. After a further 20 minutes the track leads past a small house on the left and ten minutes beyond this passes another tiny building with a very faded GR marker on the wall. A couple of minutes beyond this building there's another fork. Go left, and follow the track, which now climbs gently in a east-south-easterly direction to meet another rough road (the route of the GR13) at a very sharp bend.

A sign points the way from here straight up the middle road heading east-south-east. This soon passes around the south slope of Lakuaga (La Sierra; 1415m) and then, having descended a little to a small col, passes around the north side of Kakueta (1578m). At a point where the rough road bends sharply right to pass around the east slope of Kakueta, a handful of very clear painted markers direct the GR11 away from the rough road for the first time in the day. Follow the markers down an earthy track to the left before the footpath swings right to pass across a couple of grassy mounds to a small col. From here the GR11 heads down through young beech woods on a well-established path. From the start of this descent there are two alternative routes down to Isaba.

GR11

Some 10-15 minutes after starting down through the trees, as the main path settles into an easy descent, the GR11 turns sharply left off the path without warning and with almost no marking. Keep a careful look out into the trees on the left of the path and you can just make out some red-and-white GR markings painted on the trunks of trees set well back from the path. A red-and-white cross on a tree ahead will tell you if you have just missed the turn. Once you've spotted the turning itself, the GR11 is easy to follow as it doubles back sharply and heads northwards on a tiny earthen footpath. After 20 minutes the footpath crosses a stream and descends steeply through an area of overgrown bushes to pass a ruined building. The path doubles back sharply to the left and, after descending through more bushes, leads steeply downhill though woods. Half an hour after passing the ruined building you come to the beautiful **Ermita de Idoya**. Allow a little time here if possible. The immaculately tended garden, the small church and the whole setting make it a very special place. To continue down to Isaba, go through the arch, past the door of the church, and follow the stony footpath down to the village, which you'll reach 20 minutes after leaving the ermita.

Alternative route

If you miss the GR11 turning 10-15 minutes after starting down from the col, you needn't necessarily turn back to look for it; continuing on down the main path from the col, you soon pass a building on the left of the path, with the words 'Por Favor Cerrar la Puerta' painted on the door. Follow the path which, although slightly overgrown in places, also leads straight down to Isaba, getting you there rather quicker than the GR11 route. Unfortunately, by coming this way you'll miss the Ermita de Idoya.

ISABA

Isaba is an attractive village with a few useful shops, a **tourist office** (☎ 948-89.32.51) and lots of places to stay and eat.

Two **shops** sell meths, and a shop over the road from the phone box sells Camping Gaz and Epigas fuel. A **cash machine** can be found just uphill from the phone box.

The smartest hotel in Isaba is the modern and rather soulless *Hotel Isaba* ☆☆☆ (☎ 948-89.30.00; 🖹 948-89.30.30) which you will see as you enter the village, where a single room costs €49 and a double goes for €65. The more interesting area is the north end of the village, after the sharp left-hand turn in the road. *Pensión Txiki* (☎ 948-89.31.18), on the main road, is a popular place with locals and the bar is open for breakfast at 08.00, about the only place that

is open at that time. Next door but set back in the side street, *Hostal Lola* (☎ 948-89 .30.12, 🖳 www.hostal-lola.com) is another good bet, with doubles for €45-50.

A cheaper alternative is the *Hotel Ezkaurre* ☆ (☎ 948-89.33.03, 🖹 948-89.33. 02), with doubles from €36 to €42. Also worth considering are the dozen or so Casas Rurales in the village. These include *Casa Francisco Mayo* (☎ 948-89.31.66) where French and English are spoken; *Casa Garatxandi* (☎ 948-89.32.61); *Casa Idoya* (☎ 948-89.32.49) and *Casa Inés* (☎ 948-89.31.55). All charge around €26-30 for a double room. An independent *restaurant* has opened up next to the plaza near the church, serving a menu del dîa in the evenings.

ISABA → ZURIZA   [MAP 25, p137]

This is a really enjoyable day, the high point of which is undoubtedly the scramble to the top of Ezkaurre and the steep descent on the far side. Note that after the first hour's walking, there is no water until Zuriza. If the weather is poor, however, or if any member of the party is likely to be uneasy with scrambling it might be wise to take an alternative route, possibly looping to the north, to avoid the crossing of Ezkaurre.

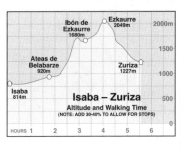

From the main road through Isaba, just above the area of the phone boxes, take a right fork down Calle Barrikata, a narrow cobbled street. Soon the road narrows to a footpath and this brings you to the tiny **Ermita de Belén**, where the path forks. Take the left fork and follow the narrow and occasionally overgrown path for 15 minutes until it descends to meet a rough road. Turn left and go eastwards along it for quarter of an hour, climbing steadily, to arrive at a junction with another rough road, just before a small gorge. A sign here indicates that the area is the **Ateas de Belabarze (920m)**. Cross the bridge and follow the road heading south-east until it comes to an end at a widened car-park area.

Map 25 – Alternative route east from the car park area
If you're feeling adventurous, the route as marked on the Editorial Alpina map should be quite possible but you'll need a compass as the path becomes difficult to follow. From the car park area a footpath climbs straight up the steep earth bank at the eastern end. The path remains fairly clear most of the way up the valley, at least until it has crossed the second stream marked on the EA map. After about 45 minutes it reaches a large open grassy area by the Ibón de Ezkaurre. From here the path is difficult to find and you'll need to set a compass bearing to follow through the relatively small area of trees and up to the col over the grassy hillside.

From the end of this rough road, the GR11 does **not**, as marked on the Editorial Alpina map, continue south-eastwards straight up the valley. Instead it makes a large loop, climbing up the spur to the south, before swinging north, back towards Ezkaurre. (See above for the alternative route from here.) From the car park area, head down the short vehicle track and cross the stream. On the far side, follow the track as it climbs steeply in a north-westerly direction. Ignore two left turns, but at the third left turning, follow the path as it doubles back and climbs in a south-easterly direction. A couple of faded GR markings near this turning help to reassure you that you're on track.

Follow this track as it climbs through trees until, after 10 minutes or so, the line of fencing on the right suddenly bends away from the track, at the corner of the enclosure. Leave the track here and follow a path alongside the fence for 100-200 metres, and as the fence bends around to the right continue with it for another 100 or so metres. The GR11 then splits left, away from the fence, climbing through bracken to join a steep track. This track climbs through trees for 10 minutes to a grassy area, in the middle of which is the ruin of an old building.

The GR11 goes south-west from the ruin and climbs through trees, following a few faded paint markers on the tree trunks. It crosses another grassy area and on the far side joins a very steep old earthen track which climbs in a southerly direction. There are only one or two faded paint markings as you go up this track, but after 10-15 minutes' hard climbing you arrive at another grassy area which also has a ruined building in the middle of it. Head straight across the grass, leaving the building just to your right, and follow the footpath as it runs through pine trees and along the top of a spur. Soon the path levels out and contours along the north slope of the hillside before emerging above the trees at a fine viewpoint from which you can pick out most of the remaining route to the base of Ezkaurre.

Don't allow yourself to be tempted by the two or three obvious paths leading away from this point across the hillside, as they all gradually lose height. The GR11 climbs a little further from this point, to follow a route which stays high, passing above the trees as you go round the side of the Berueta valley before arriving at the grassy col (1650m) at the end of it.

Go north from the col, heading directly over a small hillock, and then passing to the right of a second hillock and straight over a third beyond that, to reach a tiny tarn, the **Ibón de Ezkaurre (1680m)**. Some paint markings on the west

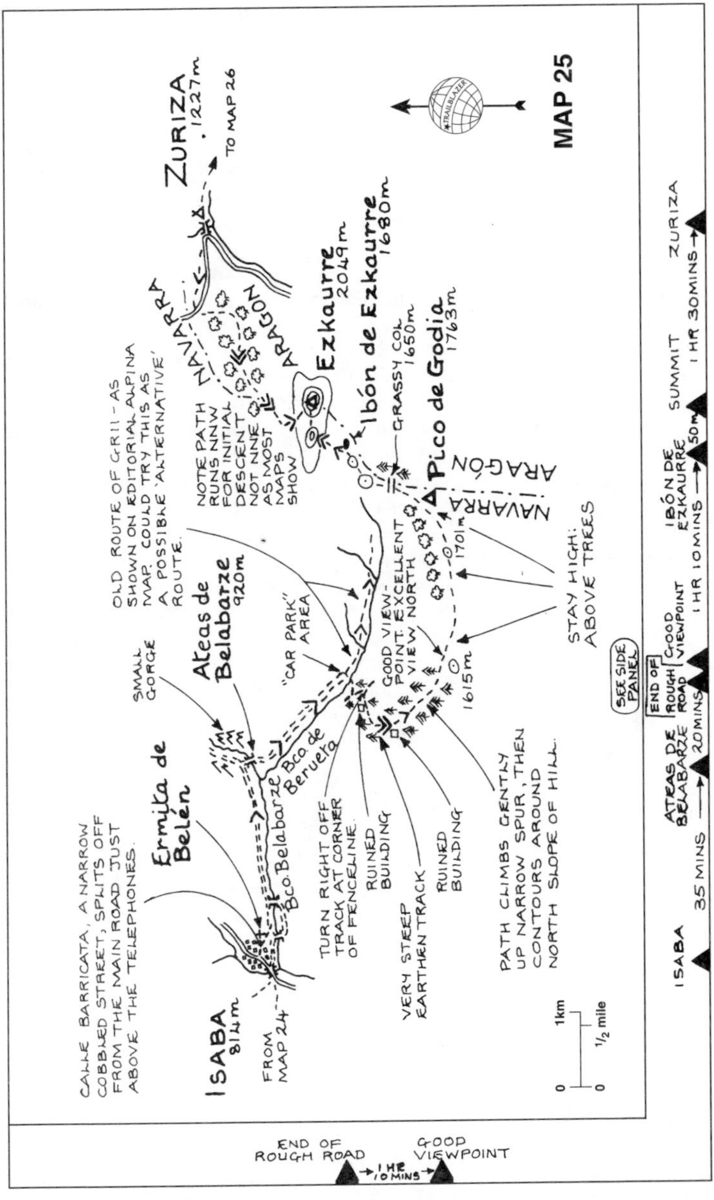

MAP 25

ZURIZA · 1227m.

TO MAP 26

Ezkaurre 2049m.

Ibón de Ezkaurre 1680m.

NAVARRA

ARAGON

NOTE PATH RUNS NNW FOR INITIAL DESCENT NOT NNE AS MOST MAPS SHOW

OLD ROUTE OF GR11 AS SHOWN ON EDITORIAL ALPINA MAP COULD TRY THIS AS A POSSIBLE 'ALTERNATIVE' ROUTE.

GRASSY COL 1650m.

Pico de Godia 1763m.

ARAGÓN

NAVARRA

1701m.

STAY HIGH: ABOVE TREES

1615m.

SMALL GORGE

Ateas de Belabarze 920m.

"CAR PARK" AREA

Bco de Beruela

GOOD VIEW-EXCELLENT VIEW NORTH

CALLE BARRICATA, A NARROW COBBLED STREET, SPLITS OFF FROM THE MAIN ROAD JUST ABOVE THE TELEPHONES.

Ermita de Belén

Bco Belabarze

ISABA 814m.

FROM MAP 24

TURN RIGHT OFF TRACK AT CORNER OF FENCELINE

RUINED BUILDING

VERY STEEP EARTHEN TRACK

RUINED BUILDING

PATH CLIMBS GENTLY UP NARROW SPUR, THEN CONTOURS AROUND NORTH SLOPE OF HILL.

SEE SIDE PANEL

0   1km

0   ½ mile

WESTERN PYRENEES

ISABA	ATEAS DE BELABARZE	END OF ROUGH ROAD	GOOD VIEWPOINT	IBÓN DE EZKAURRE	SUMMIT	ZURIZA
35 MINS →	20 MINS →	1 HR 10 MINS →	1 HR 10 MINS →	50m →	1 HR 30 MINS →	

END OF ROUGH ROAD   GOOD VIEWPOINT

← 1 HR 10 MINS →

side of the tarn point the way to the start of the scramble up the peak. The route up the side of Ezkaurre, mostly up a gully, is clearly marked with red-and-white GR markings. The ascent is not tricky and should be easily within most people's ability though possibly is not suitable in early summer if there's still snow, or if conditions are very wet. Once at the top of the scramble the path swings right to reach the concrete summit cairn of **Ezkaurre (2049m)**.

The descent from Ezkaurre starts in a roughly north-north-westerly direction with a large cairn helping to indicate the way. After ten minutes or so down a steep rocky path the gradient increases and there's an extremely steep section which leads down to a grassy shoulder at the top of a spur but no scrambling is required. Here the GR11 enters a dense beech wood through which it continues to descend very steeply on a narrow but well-worn path. Approximately 40 minutes after entering the beech wood the trail levels off and emerges near the road and a large colourful sign which marks the border between Navarre and Aragón. Turn right down the road for a few metres, before heading off to the left on a footpath that parallels the road for a short distance.

Eventually the path leads you back to the wood, a short distance below the campsite. *Camping Zuriza* (☎ 974-37.01.96) is a large place with good facilities including a reasonably well-stocked shop (though with only puncture-type gas cylinders and meths), bar and restaurant. There's also a guesthouse with 10 double rooms (€27, €36 with attached bathroom), and a hostel with 70 bunks in a clean but slightly crowded dormitory. A bed for the night costs €10; camping is €6 for one person and tent. A three-course dinner with bread and wine is €12.

ZURIZA → AGUAS TUERTAS   [MAP 26, MAP 27 p141]

This is a long stage but is on the whole fairly easy, involving a walk along two beautiful valleys before reaching a third and even more picturesque valley via an easy track up the pass.

From the campsite at Zuriza follow the rough road east-south-eastwards, as it climbs very gently, with the Barranco de Taxera on the right-hand side. After half an hour the road arrives at a car-park area, beyond which it bends sharply to the right and crosses the stream via a concrete bridge. The GR11 splits off to the left before the bridge on a footpath which climbs past a small iron cross and, just above this, a ruined stone hut.

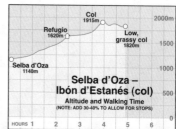

WESTERN PYRENEES

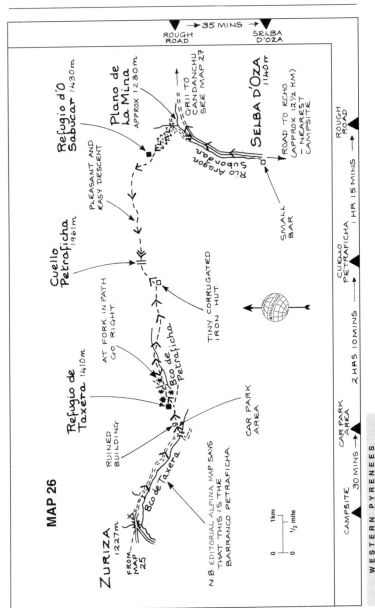

MAP 26

ROUGH ROAD → 35 MINS → SELBA D'OZA

Refugio d'O Sabucar 1430m

Plano de la Mina APPROX 1230m

GR11 TO CANDANCHU SEE MAP 27

SELBA D'OZA 1140m

ROAD TO ECHO (APPROX 12½ KM) – NEAREST CAMPSITE

PLEASANT AND EASY DESCENT

Río Aragón Suborján

SMALL BAR

Cuello Petraficha 1961m

TINY CORRUGATED IRON HUT.

At fork in path go right

Refugio de Taxera 1410m

Bco de Petraficha

RUINED BUILDING

CAR PARK AREA

Bco de Taxera

ZURIZA 1227m

FROM MAP 25

NB EDITORIAL ALPINA MAP SAYS THAT THIS IS THE BARRANCO PETRAFICHA.

0 — 1km
0 — ½ mile

CAMPSITE — 30 MINS → CAR PARK AREA — 2 HRS 10 MINS → CUELLO PETRAFICHA — 1 HR 15 MINS → ROUGH ROAD

WESTERN PYRENEES

Twenty minutes after leaving the car-park area you come to the *Refugio de Taxera* (1410m). The doors to both rooms have long since gone and the floors are thick with animal dung; this is not a place to stay except in an emergency.

From the refuge climb north-eastwards on a footpath which has a few faded red-and-white GR markings. After 7-8 minutes the path enters an area of trees and levels out. After a further 2-3 minutes there's a fork; go right. The path soon leaves the trees and descends across the grassy hillside to pass alongside a stream bed (dry in late July). From here it climbs up the left side of a gully and contours around a rocky slope, before continuing upwards over grass. After passing a small corrugated iron shed on the right, the trail leads around a rocky outcrop and up to the **Cuello Petraficha (1961m)**.

With the exception of the first ten minutes of descent, during which the GR11 heads down a steep and rocky path, the way down from the col is mostly across grassy slopes covered with Merendera and Pyrenean irises. In a couple of places the path becomes indistinct, but look out for some marks on low rocks. Approximately 50 minutes after leaving the col you come to a large grassy area near an old building, the *Refugio d'O Sabucar* (1430m) (which again is doorless and unsuitable for overnight shelter). Although the path is unmarked across this area, continue south-eastwards, towards the road and large barn seen below, and you soon pick up the path again as it descends in long easy zigzags to meet the road at the area known as **Plano de la Mina (1230m approx)**. Turn right (south-west) and walk along the rough road, which soon crosses the river and joins the main road coming up from **Selba d'Oza**. Maps still show a campground at Selba d'Oza but it closed five years ago because the private owner was unable to afford the required investment in a septic tank.

Follow this rough road for about 1³/₄ hours as it climbs steadily east-south-eastwards. Near the end of the valley the road makes three or four long zigzags to climb the steep slope ahead, while the GR11 simply short-cuts up the hillside. At the top you'll look down upon the beautiful plain of **Aguas Tuertas**. Although camping is probably not strictly allowed, there's ample opportunity to do so as long as you're unobtrusive about it. The *refugio* here on our last visit was entirely usable as a place to sleep, with excellent water sources nearby, but the land is used for pasture and all water should be treated before drinking.

AGUAS TUERTAS → CANDAN-CHÚ [MAP 27, MAP 28 p142]

This is a relatively short but quite arduous section, and one well worth taking slowly as there is much to see and enjoy along the way, including the first views of distinctive giants such as Pic du Midi d'Ossau. With time to

Low, grassy col 1820m

Candanchú 1550m

Cuello Causiat 1634m

Ibón d'Estanés (col) – Candanchú

Altitude and Walking Time
(NOTE: ADD 30-40% TO ALLOW FOR STOPS)

HOURS 1   2   3   4   5   6

2000m
1500m
1000m
500m
0

WESTERN PYRENEES

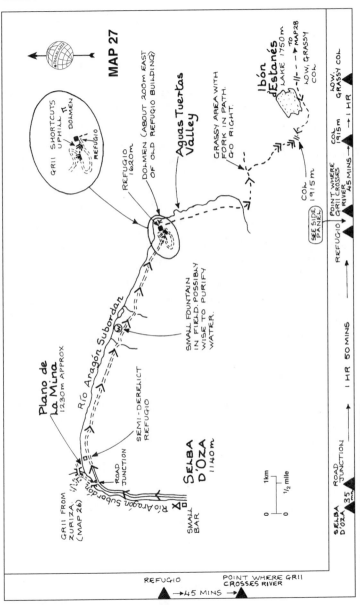

MAP 27

GRII SHORTCUTS UPHILL
DOLMEN
REFUGIO

REFUGIO 1620m
DOLMEN (ABOUT 200m EAST OF OLD REFUGIO BUILDING)

Aguas Tuertas Valley

Plano de la Mina 1230m APPROX

Río Aragón Subordan

SEMI-DERELICT REFUGIO

SELBA D'OZA 1140m

GRII FROM ZURIZA (MAP 26)

ROAD JUNCTION

Río Aragón Subordan

SMALL BAR

SMALL FOUNTAIN IN FIELD POSSIBLY WISE TO PURIFY WATER.

GRASSY AREA WITH FORK IN PATH. GO RIGHT.

Ibón d'Estanés
LAKE 1750m → TO MAP 28

LOW, GRASSY COL

COL 1915m → 1 HR

SEE SIDE PANEL

COL 1915m

POINT WHERE GRII CROSSES RIVER 45 MINS

REFUGIO

1 km
½ mile
0

SELBA D'OZA 35 → ROAD JUNCTION → 1 HR 50 MINS

WESTERN PYRENEES

REFUGIO → 45 MINS → POINT WHERE GRII CROSSES RIVER

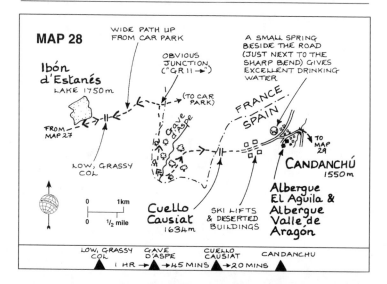

MAP 28

Ibón d'Estanés
LAKE 1750m

WIDE PATH UP
FROM CAR PARK

OBVIOUS
JUNCTION
("GR11 →")

(TO CAR
PARK)

A SMALL SPRING
BESIDE THE ROAD
(JUST NEXT TO THE
SHARP BEND) GIVES
EXCELLENT DRINKING
WATER

FRANCE
SPAIN

FROM
MAP 27

LOW, GRASSY
COL

Gave
d'Aspe

TO
MAP
29

CANDANCHÚ
1550m

Cuello
Causiat
1634m

SKI LIFTS
& DESERTED
BUILDINGS

Albergue
El Aguila &
Albergue
Valle de
Aragón

0 ____ 1km
0 ____ ½ mile

LOW, GRASSY
COL   GAVE
             D'ASPE   CUELLO
                             CAUSIAT   CANDANCHU
▲   1 HR →   ▲   →45 MINS   ▲   →20 MINS   ▲

spare you can continue on to Canfranc-Estación for shopping and supplies.

Follow the clearly-marked path southwards, remaining on the west side of the Río Aragón Subordan. About halfway down the valley the markers disappear, but the route is fairly well trodden and is easy to discern. Near the southern end of the plain the path finally crosses the stream and swings left (east). There are faded markers to indicate this.

From here the path climbs gently for 5-10 minutes to a grassy area where there's a poorly-marked fork. Go right and follow a well-worn trail which begins to climb more steeply and soon arrives at a rocky-sided bowl with a grassy bottom. The GR11 climbs steeply up the east side of this bowl, below a crag that gives welcome shade even in mid-morning. At the top of the climb the path swings left and crosses a rocky **col (1915m)**.

From the col you can see the **Ibón d'Estanés (1750m)**, a popular spot for day walkers and also for campers. The GR11 takes a time-consuming route all the way around the south side of the Ibón before arriving at a **low grassy col** on the south-east side of the lake. From here, you go eastwards down a wide path, much used by day walkers coming up from the car park below. After about quarter of an hour, at a very well-marked junction ('GR11 → ' is painted on a rock), turn right off the large path and follow the footpath which contours south across the grassy hillside.

After about 20 minutes the path enters beech woods and starts descending through the trees before coming to a crossing over the Gave d'Aspe where a waterfall and some large rocks make an excellent spot for sunbathing. Beyond the river the path narrows and crosses a steep scree slope (care is needed) before climbing to the **Cuello Causiat (1634m)**. Descend from the col to a rough road and follow this down through an area of deserted ski lifts and buildings to meet the main road through Candanchú.

CANDANCHÚ

Candanchú is a large and unattractive ski resort which, in common with most other Pyrenean ski resorts, feels like a ghost town during the summer. There are, however, enough facilities here to make it a good stopping point.

There's a reasonable choice of places to stay. At the expensive end is *Hotel Tobazo* ☆☆☆ (☎ 974-37.31.25), although it's not strong on ambience. Prices include meals: €28 per person for bed and breakfast or €38 for a bed and supper. *Hotel Candanchú* (☎ 974-37.30.25; 📠 974-37.30. 50), is slightly cheaper and generally nicer, but doubles are still in the €50-60 range.

There's a choice of good budget accommodation. From the point where the GR11 meets the main road, walk down the tarmac for 150 metres and take the first road on the right (a large sign reading 'ALBERGUE' points downhill), dropping down behind one hotel and taking the first road to the left; a short way down here are two excellent lodges. Both *Refugio-Albergue Valle de Aragón* (☎ 974-37.32.22) and *Refugio-Albergue El Aguila* (☎/📠 974-37.32.91) are comfortable,

friendly and modern, and charge the same prices: €10 for the night, or €24 for media-pensión.

There's a small **supermarket** near the point where the GR11 meets the main road. Next to this is a decrepit-looking **bureau de change** which has a **cash dispenser**.

Candanchú is a possible place to start or end a walk along the GR11 by virtue of the **bus service** which runs five times a day each way from Canfranc-Estación, via Candanchú to Jaca (where there's a railway station). You can get details of bus services from the company's website: 🖥 www.mav aragon.com. If you want to return from the French side, you can walk uphill (via the marked GR65 route) and catch a bus at the customs post at the col du Somport. The walk is only about 40 minutes, and there is a cheap and reasonable *albergue* on the Spanish side of the border to spend the night. There are two or three buses a day from the col down to Oloron Sainte-Marie, a journey of 1¼ hours, and from Oloron, itself a nice place to spend a night, there are trains to Pau. Bus and train details can be found at 🖥 www.ter-sncf.com/aquitaine.

CANDANCHÚ → SALLENT DE GALLEGO   [MAP 29A, p144]

From the area in front of Hotel Tobazo, walk down the main road to the sharp right-hand bend, where the road crosses a bridge over the river. A signpost on the far side of the bridge points the way for the GR11 (and the GR65) up a footpath which climbs away from the road and soon meets another road above. Cross this road and walk up a vehicle track (signposted: 'GR65.3 SANTIAGO, CANFRANC, JACA') which climbs past a Telecoms mast. (Note that if you're using the Editorial Alpina map, the road layout appears to be wrongly depicted on the map.)

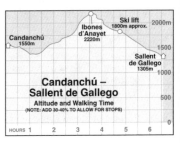

Candanchú –
Sallent de Gallego
Altitude and Walking Time
(NOTE: ADD 30-40% TO ALLOW FOR STOPS)

WESTERN PYRENEES

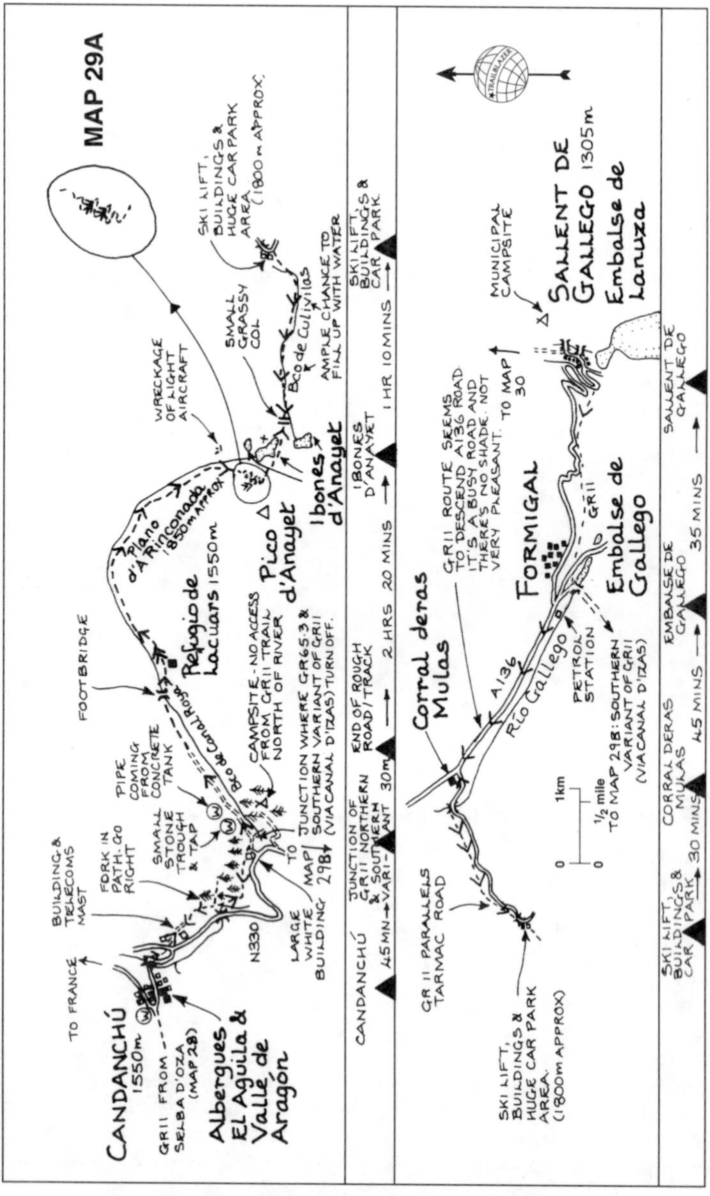

WESTERN PYRENEES

MAP 29A

TO FRANCE

CANDANCHÚ 1550m.
GR11 FROM
SELBA D'OZA (MAP 28)

Albergues
EL AGUILA &
Valle de Aragón

BUILDING &
TELECOMS MAST

FORK IN PATH, GO RIGHT

SMALL STONE TROUGH & TAP

PIPE COMING FROM CONCRETE TANK

Bco CORRAL ROYO

FOOTBRIDGE

Plano d'Arinconada 1850m APPROX.

WRECKAGE OF LIGHT AIRCRAFT

N330

LARGE WHITE BUILDING 1298

JUNCTION WHERE GR11 SOUTHERN VARIANT OF GR11 (VIA CANAL D'IZAS) TURN OFF.

Refugio de Lacuars 1550m.

CAMPSITE - NO ACCESS FROM GR11 TRAIL NORTH OF RIVER

Bco de Culivillas

SMALL GRASSY COL

Pico d'Anayet

Ibones d'Anayet

SKI LIFT, BUILDINGS & HUGE CAR PARK AREA. (1800m APPROX.)

AMPLE CHANCE TO FILL UP WITH WATER

SKI LIFT, BUILDINGS & CAR PARK

1 HR 10 MINS

CANDANCHÚ
45MN → VARIANT 30m

JUNCTION OF GR11 NORTHERN & SOUTHERN VARIANT

END OF ROUGH ROAD/TRACK

2 HRS 20 MINS

Ibones d'Anayet

SKI LIFT, BUILDINGS & HUGE CAR PARK AREA. (1800m APPROX.)

GR11 PARALLELS TARMAC ROAD

Corral deras Mulas

A136

Rio Gallego

PETROL STATION

TO MAP 29B: SOUTHERN VARIANT OF GR11 (VIA CANAL D'IZAS)

GR11 ROUTE SEEMS TO DESCEND A136 ROAD. IT'S A BUSY ROAD AND THERE'S NO SHADE. NOT VERY PLEASANT. TO MAP 30

FORMIGAL

Embalse de Gallego

GR11

MUNICIPAL CAMPSITE

SALLENT DE GALLEGO 1305m.
Embalse de Lanuza

SALLENT DE GALLEGO

0   1km
0   ½ mile

SKI LIFT, BUILDINGS & CAR PARK

CORRAL DERAS MULAS
30 MINS

CORRAL DERAS MULAS
45 MINS

EMBALSE DE GALLEGO
35 MINS

At the end of the rough road go over a small rise and follow an obvious path downhill towards a road bridge over the river. Near the bridge the path levels out and there's a fork – go right (on the lower path). The path climbs, passes over a spur, and then swings left and descends to a large white building, beyond which it joins a rough vehicle track coming up from the road below. Follow this track past a signposted junction where the GR65.3 and the southern variant of the GR11 turn off to the right. Just beyond the junction you catch a glimpse through the trees of a campsite on the other side of the valley. There's no way directly across to the campsite from the path; to get there you need to retrace your steps and walk down the main road a short way.

Continue along the track, which soon passes two possible water points (although there's no indication that the water is fit for drinking). Some 20 minutes beyond the second of these the track, which has been climbing steadily, comes to an end. From here follow the footpath which runs along the north bank of the stream to a footbridge. On the far side of the bridge the path climbs gently up to the **Refugio de Lacuars (1550m)**, one room of which is literally a foot deep in decomposing rubbish, making the refuge unsuitable for habitation.

Beyond the building the path climbs fairly steeply for 20-30 minutes before levelling out briefly and then beginning to climb again at a more gentle gradient. Slowly the trail starts to swing around to head south-eastwards and then southwards to arrive at the end of the valley in a grassy area called **Plano d'a Rinconada (1850m approx)**. To the left of the path on the north side of the bowl is the wreckage of a light aircraft, and a small plaque attached to a rock. The GR11 continues southwards, however, somehow finding a path up the dauntingly steep rock face at the end of the valley. It's a well-made and well-marked trail but hard work. After nearly an hour of steep ascent you eventually reach the top of the climb and beyond this you come to the first of the **Ibones d'Anayet (2220m approx)**. Allow some time here if at all possible. The lakes themselves are pretty and the view northwards of the Pic du Midi d'Ossau is superb. The lakes are a popular day-walk destination, so there are often quite a few people around here picnicking and even swimming. **(For walks/refuges around the Pic du Midi see p108 and p115.)**

The path down from the Ibones d'Anayet is pleasant and easy to follow, much of it running alongside crystal-clear mountain streams – no problem with getting water on this section. Approximately an hour after starting going down, the GR11 arrives at the bottom of a ski lift with a couple of buildings and a huge car park area. Beyond the buildings, next to a small bridge, the GR11 heads off to the left, parallelling the road as it runs down to meet the main road (A136) by a small building, the **Corral deras Mulas**. From here it's a boring trudge 3km south-eastwards to a concrete bridge at the end of the Embalse de Gallego. The road is narrow and busy, so it may be more sensible to follow the track which runs just to the left of the road. This doesn't take you all the way to the bridge but it allows you to escape most of the walk along the road. Just before the bridge the GR11 turns left off the road on to a footpath. From here it follows a well-marked trail, mostly on old farm tracks, to Sallent de Gallego (1305m, see p148).

WESTERN PYRENEES

GR11 SOUTHERN ROUTE:
CANFRANC-ESTACIÓN TO SALLENT DE GALLEGO   [MAP 29B]

If the hotels in Candanchú are full or closed or you need a bank or post office, you might end up walking down to **Canfranc-Estación**, a small town built around the train station and with some history relating to the old nineteenth-century rail tunnel through to France and the enormous 'international' rail terminal which still has trains running down to Jaca.

Candanchú to Canfranc-Estación
From Candanchú, follow signs for the GR65.3 Camino de Santiago downhill, sharing the path with the GR11 for a while before continuing south. On the way note where the path crosses a bridge to join the road for the last 400 metres into Canfranc-Estación: this is where you will rejoin the trail the next day.

Canfranc-Estación
There are various hotels, the first one you come to being a cheap hostal called *Pepito Grillo* (☎ 974-37.31.23), which has beds in dorms for €10 a night and a bar, but no food. **Restaurants** nearby are within five minutes' walk, and there is a pizzeria a few minutes further down, just behind the main road on the right. Closer to the hostal, a lively café/bar serves a wide range of breakfast dishes.

The **post office** also opens at an almost unheard of 08.30 on weekdays, 09.30 on Saturdays. A **bus** stops outside the main entrance to the train station to take you back up the hill if you want to go to Candanchú or up to the Col du Somport (buses into France from there) at 09.50.

Canfranc-Estación to Sallent de Gallego
From Canfranc-Estación, follow the road back up and around to the right, leaving at the bridge you crossed the day before, and after the bridge, go right (south) 300m before the track turns around to head north towards the abandoned house on a small spur over the valley. Bear right as you reach the spur and after five minutes (the path actually runs slightly downhill) you will see a sign pointing to a path up to the right, and straight ahead, a barrage which is where the GR11 Southern Variant from Candanchú crosses over to join the path you will take. A sign reads 'COL D'IZAS 3H 30M', an accurate walking time to the highest point of the day.

After five minutes the path crosses a small but steep landslip. If you choose to climb up and around it, the path is easily rejoined as it is the only path up this steep-sided valley. A second landslide, much larger and older, is marked. The path zig-zags up the side of the mountain and at the top of the landslide the valley opens up to pasture land and broad views. Around 45 minutes later you reach the *Refugio d'a Mallata*. While not exactly charming inside, it is secure against animals and is a passable shelter. Half an hour later, the path crosses the plentiful Barranco d'Izas and backtracks for 20-30 metres before heading up a gentle grassy gully to continue uphill. Exactly where the path leaves the gully is a mystery, but if you cross a path clearly heading up the valley, take it and you'll be back on the GR11. After half an hour you reach the second refuge, which appeared to be inhabited, probably by a shepherd, when we last checked. After here, route markings become sparse but there is a very clear view of the pass, which is marked by a ski lift, an indication of what lies on the other side. The path continues straight but then begins to bear left, staying parallel with the Barranco as it turns north-east. Markers become fewer and farther apart in this grassy area, though if you do see a decent-sized rock, it is that much more likely to have a red-and-white stripe on it.   (Continued on p148)

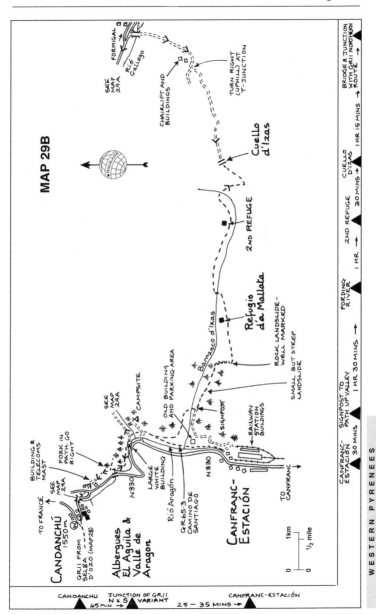

MAP 29B

CANDANCHÚ
1550 m.

to FRANCE

GR11 FROM SELBA D'OZO (MAP 28)

Albergues EL Aguila & Valle de Aragon

BUILDING & TELECOMS MAST

SEE MAP 29A

FORK IN PATH-GO RIGHT

SEE MAP 29A

CAMPSITE

OLD BUILDING AND PARKING AREA

LARGE WHITE BUILDING

Rió Aragón

N330

GR65.3 CAMINO DE SANTIAGO

N330

SIGNPOST

RAILWAY STATION BUILDINGS

CANFRANC-ESTACIÓN

TO CANFRANC

SMALL BUT STEEP LANDSLIDE

ROCK LANDSLIDE - WELL MARKED

Refugio de Mallata

Barranco d'Izas

2ND REFUGE

Cuello d'Izas

CHAIRLIFT AND BUILDINGS

TURN RIGHT (UPHILL) AT T-JUNCTION

SEE MAP 29A

FORMIGAL

Rió Gallego

SEE MAP 29A

0   1km
0   ½ mile

WESTERN PYRENEES

CANDANCHÚ
◀ 45 MIN →

JUNCTION OF GR11
N x S VARIANT
25 – 35 MINS →

CANFRANC-ESTACIÓN
◀

CANFRANC-ESTACIÓN
◀ 30 MINS →

SIGNPOST TO PATH UP VALLEY
1 HR 30 MINS →

FORDING RIVER
◀ 1 HR 30 MINS →

2ND REFUGE
1 HR →

CUELLO D'IZAS
◀ 30 MINS →

BRIDGE & JUNCTION WITH GR11 NORTHERN ROUTE
1 HR 15 MINS →

❏ **GR11 SOUTHERN ROUTE**
Canfranc-Estación to Sallent de Gallego *(Continued from p146)* Carry on north-east for about 5-10 minutes. In this area there are not enough stones for even a tiny cairn so you will need all your forensic skills to distinguish red paint fragments from lichen on the few rocks that you can find. The exact point where the trail turns right is hard to find, but it's well before you meet the steep northern side of the valley. Turn right when the ski-lift is due south-east in your sights. Don't follow the sheep trails contouring the slope but head directly towards the pass, walking towards a rocky area where the GR11 markers resume. The track passes below the chairlift and becomes more distinct, before turning back on itself to approach the pass on a very clear path from the south-west. If you miss the path and wander to the south, you will join this larger path and then turn back (left and uphill) to the pass.

The view from the pass is a shock – the barren slopes of a ski resort out of season, and behind, the hideous new ski village of Formigal. Above this, though, is a splendid view of the Central Pyrenees, including Balaitus (3146m), behind Formigal. The route down is straightforward at first, following a service road on the left side of the bowl, then crossing to the right and taking an obvious and marked short cut, till the road joins another service road at a T-junction. Take the (unmarked) right, dusty road and head uphill for 400m before turning left towards some buildings and chairlifts. Walk behind them and down to the next service road. At this point, pick the best route down depending on whether you prefer solid vehicle tracks or short cuts because at the time of research there was a lot of construction work here (it would be worth enquiring about this before starting out, or avoiding weekdays) and the service roads may change. You need to concentrate on the exit point of the resort, just left (west) of the turn-off to Formigal, as a river prevents any crossing further east than this. Joining the road, the GR11 follows it only for about 500m before turning off into quiet countryside leading into Sallent de Gallego.

SALLENT DE GALLEGO

Sallent de Gallego is a pretty little village with a few shops and plenty of places to stay and to eat. The village looks as though it has doubled in size in recent years due to the development of the ski resort at nearby Formigal, but all new building has been reasonably faithful to the old style and uses the same materials, and the village centre still has a lot of character, especially in and around the Bar Casino which is in the old Ayuntamiento building.

Where to stay

Two-star hotels are increasing in number and steadily raising their standards and prices, catering mainly for skiers and typically charging €60-70 for a double.

The most pleasant place to stay is the *Hotel Balaitus* ☆ (☎/▤ 974-48.80.59), a lovely old hotel in the centre of the village and run by the same family which has owned it for over a hundred years. They also own two more expensive hotels in the village. Hotel Balaitus has a very old feeling to it, with lots of detailed woodwork, wooden floors and antiques on display. Single rooms go for €29 and up, and doubles are from €35, all with attached bathroom. The buffet breakfast for €5 is excellent.

The cheapest place in the village, the *Albergue Foratata* (☎/▤ 974- 48.81.12), has dormitories and offers breakfast but is a simple place, a big drop down in standard from the hotels; B&B here is €17, half-board may be available in summer at nearer to €30.

The small municipal **campsite** is five minutes from the village centre to the north-east. There's no shop or bar here but it is an excellent spot, quiet and on raised ground offering great views. The clean showers were still running nice and hot in October when we were there. The tariff is €3 per person.

Services

In the centre of the village there are several shops (including two **supermarkets**, one of them a Spar on the route out of town to the north-east) and a handful of good places to eat, most offering meals for €13-16. Campstove fuel was not on sale anywhere when we last visited. There are two **cash dispensers** and a phone by the old *ayuntamiento*. The **tourist office** (☎ 974-48.80.12) is open only during July, August and the first half of September and is located in a wooden booth outside the town hall. You can get information on the local area (the Valle de Tena) before you travel from their website: 🖳 www.valledetena.com.

If you're starting or ending your walk in Sallent there's a local **bus service** that might be useful: it runs to Sabiñanigo and Jaca (both of which have train stations). The service is currently run by Automoviles La Oscense SA (Sabiñanigo: ☎ 974-48.00.45; Jaca: ☎ 974-35.50.60) and there are two daily buses each way, departing Sallent at 07.00 and 16.00 and departing Jaca at 10.15 and 18.15. The journey from Sallent to Sabiñanigo takes one hour, and Jaca (the final stop) is quarter of an hour further on. The same company runs buses from Sabiñanigo and Jaca to Pamplona. It's also possible to get a bus from Sabiñanigo to Huesca (approximately one hour) and get a connection there for Barcelona.

If you need a **taxi** try Taxis Domec (☎ 974-48.82.68; mobile ☎ 919-75.75.50).

SALLENT DE GALLEGO → BALNEARIO (BAÑOS) DE PANTICOSA [MAP 30, p150]

[**Includes high section – see warning on pp19-20**] This section is a very long one so it's worth making an early start, in order to allow plenty of time for rest stops along the way. An alternative would be to break the section into two equal day stages, either by camping or by staying overnight at the Refugio de Respumoso (see p151). Head through

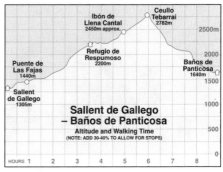

Sallent de Gallego – Baños de Panticosa
Altitude and Walking Time
(NOTE: ADD 30-40% TO ALLOW FOR STOPS)

the main square of the village (with the modern sculpture and climbing wall) and walk up the back street (don't cross the bridge over the river – the GR11 remains on the west bank of the Río de Aguas Limpias).

Where the road comes to an end the GR11 goes up a farm track which remains level for the first few minutes and then begins to gain height gradually. The GR markers, which have been absent on the way through the village, start again as soon as you reach the farm track. After a few minutes the GR11 splits left away from the farm track and climbs up a narrow path to meet the road. Walk north along the road to the **Embalse de la Sarra (1438m)** and, at

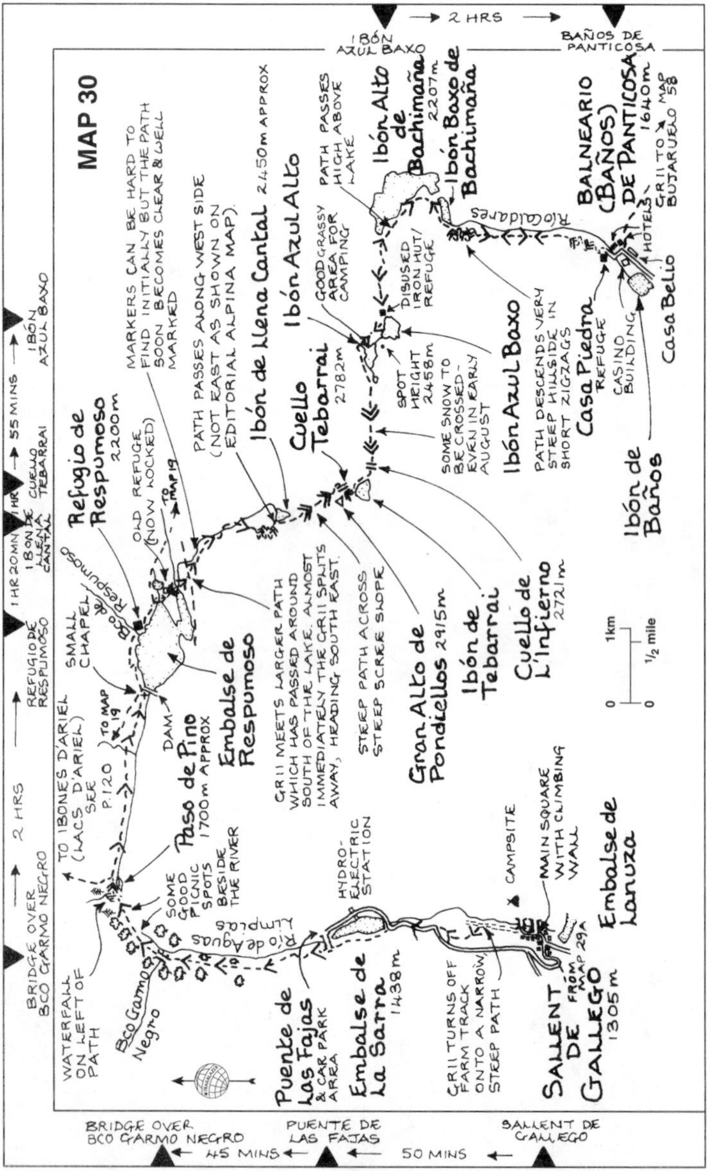

MAP 30

WESTERN PYRENEES

Markers can be hard to find initially but the path soon becomes clear & well marked

Path passes along west side (not east as shown on Editorial Alpina map).

Refugio de Respumoso 2200m

Old refuge (now locked)

Ibón de Llena Cantal 2450m approx

Ibón Azul Alto

Cuello Tebarrai 2782m

Good grassy area for camping

Path passes high above lake

Ibón Alto de Bachimaña 2207m

Ibón Baxo de Bachimaña

Spot height 2458m

Disused iron hut / Refuge

Río Caldarés

BALNEARIO (BAÑOS) DE PANTICOSA 1640m

Hotels

GR11 to MAP Butaruelo 58

Some snow to be crossed even in early August

Casa Bello

Ibón Azul Baxo

Path descends very steep hillside in short zigzags

Casa Piedra Refuge

Casino building

Ibón de Baños

Cuello de L'Infierno 2721m

Ibón de Tebarrai

Gran Alto de Pondiellos 2915m

Steep path across steep scree slope

GR11 meets larger path which has passed around south of the lake, almost immediately the GR11 splits away, heading south east.

Embalse de Respumoso

Dam

Paso de Pino 1700m approx

Small Chapel

Río Respumoso

Río de Aguas Limpias

TO IBONES D'ARIEL (LACS D'ARIEL) SEE P.120

TO MAP 19

BRIDGE OVER BCO GARMO NEGRO ← 2 HRS

Waterfall on left of path

Bco Garmo Negro

Some good picnic spots beside the river

Puente de Las Fajas & car park area

Embalse de La Sarra 1438m

Hydro-electric station

GR11 turns off farm track onto a narrow steep path

Campsite

Main square with climbing wall

SALLENT DE GALLEGO 1305m

GR11 FROM P.120 29A

Embalse de Lanuza

IBÓN AZUL BAXO → 2 HRS — BAÑOS DE PANTICOSA

REFUGIO DE RESPUMOSO ← 1 HR 20MN / HR → REFUGIO DE RESPUMOSO — IBÓN DE LLENA CANTAL 1 HR 20MN — CUELLO TEBARRAI 55 MINS — IBÓN AZUL BAXO

BRIDGE OVER BCO GARMO NEGRO 45 MINS — PUENTE DE LAS FAJAS 50 MINS — SALLENT DE GALLEGO

0   1km
0   ½ mile

the southern end of the reservoir, take a level footpath which leads around the west side of the lake. After 10 minutes the path descends slightly passing, on the right, a car park area near the **Puente de las Fajas**.

From here a clear path climbs along the west side of the valley, starting at a gentle gradient but becoming gradually steeper. Three quarters of an hour after passing the car park area the path crosses a small concrete bridge over the Barranco Garmo Negro and starts to swing round to head north-eastwards. Forty minutes beyond the bridge, at the **Paso de Pino (1700m approx)**, the path climbs around to the north side of a spectacular waterfall. Halfway up beside the waterfall there's a path splitting off to the left, signposted IBONES D'ARIEL 1H 30. (For information about the route over the Col de Palas via the Ariel lakes, see p120.) Continue up the main path, which climbs steadily for a further hour until it reaches the huge dam at the end of the Embalse de Respumoso.

From the dam the refuge building (2200m) is visible ahead, and you'll reach it after a further 10-15 minutes. The *Refugio de Respumoso* (☎/🖹 974-49.02.23) is an extremely modern and comfortable place which is open all year and charges €7 for the night, €11 for dinner, and €3.50 for breakfast. The refuge sells some provisions such as puncture-type gas cylinders, chocolate, biscuits, peanuts etc.

From the refuge the GR11 passes around the side of the lake and then climbs past the former refuge building, which is locked, before descending steeply to cross the Barranco de Campo Plano and the torrent running down from the Ibón de Llena Cantal. Walk up the slope above the streams and you soon meet the well-established trail around the reservoir's southern side. Go left along this path ('GR11' is prominently painted on a rock) but almost immediately turn right off it onto a path heading south-east up the valley. The markings across the grass are vague at first before becoming more distinct. The path climbs at an easy gradient for 20-30 minutes, then ascends steeply to the **Ibón de Llena Cantal (2450m approx)**. From here there's a further steep haul up a scree slope to the **Cuello Tebarrai (2782m)** which you reach approximately an hour after leaving the Ibón.

From the col the GR11 descends a short way and then contours across the slope above the Ibón de Tebarrai to reach the **Cuello de L'Infierno (2721m)**. The path down from here is steep and rocky and even in early August you may find a few patches of snow to be crossed. After half an hour you come to the Ibón Azul Alto, where there's a grassy area suitable for camping. Beyond this, the path climbs over a rocky hummock and descends across an area of boulders to the Ibón Azul Baxo where the remains of an old metal refuge stand beside the water.

Descend from the Ibón Azul Baxo towards **Ibón Alto de Bachimaña (2207m)**. Just above the lake the path climbs again and remains high above the water as it runs around the lake's west side. The trail leads you past the dam at the end of the higher lake, then past the lower lake before descending the steep hillside very rapidly in short zigzags. Despite the short distance that remains to Panticosa the rest of the walk down takes a surprisingly long time, as the GR11 climbs and falls, winding around obstacles, before making a final descent to Panticosa.

BALNEARIO (BAÑOS) DE PANTICOSA

Balneario de Panticosa was never a village but just a couple of hotels and a casino built in the nineteenth century for the thermal waters coming out of the mountains which surround them in this steep-sided bowl at the end of a valley. The owner of the hotels has decided to restore them completely, keeping only the façades, and expanding the number of rooms considerably. The hotels will not be open before the summer of 2005 and prices were not known at the time of writing, but they will be expensive and beyond the reach of most walkers.

The *Refugio Casa de Piedra* is the only option right now (☎ 974-48.75.71) but it is an excellent place to stay, a very solid old stone building with rooms made into small dormitories, each with its own shower and toilet and with tables and chairs outside amid trees, as well as views of the surrounding mountains. Both food and service here are very good, and the staff are enthusiastic. A bed costs €11, dinner is also €11 and breakfast is €4. A pint of beer costs €2 and a lunch to take away is also available. This refuge is owned by the Federation Aragonese de Montanismo (FAM) and when the old refuge is demolished by the developers, the FAM has committed to build another up in the mountains, at the Ibón Baxo de Bachimaña, ie the lower Bachimaña tarn which you would have walked past descending to Balneario de Panticosa. This is a superb location and will save walkers some 600m of vertical, both coming and going. The Casa de Piedra is guaranteed to be open in its present location for 2005, but it would be wise to check its status before leaving either Sallent de Gallego or the Refugio de Respumoso.

For a description of the GR11 beyond Balneario de Panticosa see p226.

PART 4: CENTRAL PYRENEES

Facts about the region

GENERAL DESCRIPTION

The Central Pyrenees are defined here as the area of mountains contained within the French départements of Hautes Pyrénées, Haute Garonne and Ariège and in Spain within the eastern part of Aragón and the western part Catalonia.

The central region of the Pyrenees contains the highest mountains in the range and, to a greater extent than in the eastern or western Pyrenees, it is an area defined by its topography. Each valley holds its own community, and until the building of the first roads around a century ago, these settlements were often extremely isolated. During the nineteenth century, as explorers and academics began to take an interest in the mountains, it was discovered that there were still villages here where few inhabitants spoke French. Communication was channelled through passes in the mountains, leading to localized features such as ancient market areas (Marcadau), and hospices for pilgrims and traders who were travelling through the difficult terrain (Hospice de France, Hospital de Venasque, Hospital de Vielha).

Its geographical characteristics meant that, unlike either the Western or the Eastern Pyrenees, this central section of the mountains was never a thoroughfare for other people, and thus to a great extent it was left alone. Despite this, there are still remains of the Roman presence in the valleys, where they came to mine for iron and silver. The High Pyrenees largely escaped occupation by the Moors, and thus some of the earliest examples of Romanesque church architecture appear here in the mountains.

HAUTES PYRÉNÉES, HAUTE GARONNE AND ARIÈGE

Politics and history

For much of its early history, this area was a law unto itself. Although the lowlands at the base of the mountains may have experienced a succession of rulers, the mountain people largely went their own way. Nowhere is this clearer than in the case of the Cathar sect (see p284), centred in the eastern part of the area in the 12th century. Despite the best efforts of the Catholic church, which sanctioned a crusade against its followers, Catharism took over a century to eradicate.

Historical records start with the arrival of the Romans, who fought their way through the eastern Pyrenees around 200BC and, having overcome both Gaul and Spain, colonized the area. They were largely interested in mining, and much evidence of this still remains but there are also relics around spa sites such as Bagnères-de-Luchon and Ax-les-Thermes. The spas became renowned for their healing properties from the fifteenth century onwards but it wasn't until the early nineteenth century that they became popular as resorts. Cauterets, Gavarnie, Luchon, Bigorre and Ax all became fashionable places to be seen.

By the mid-nineteenth century the mountains themselves had become the focus of attention, and alpinism increasingly became popular. This century, with the arrival of skiing (the first skis appeared in the Pyrenees around 1902), and mountaineering, the region has become increasingly well-known.

Walking in the Hautes Pyrénées, Haute Garonne and Ariège

Above all, the central Pyrenees contain variety. From the deep, well-watered valleys, one can ascend to high barren landscapes of rock and snow. Marmots, izards, and even a few bears live in these mountains, and the flora, even in the highest areas, is magnificent. While the central Pyrenees attract huge numbers of walkers during the peak holiday season, most of them tend to stay on the main paths. A little exploration away from these main routes can reveal fantastic scenery with few other people to disturb the peace.

ARAGÓN AND CATALONIA

Politics and history

The Romans started mining activities in several places but the high valleys remained largely untouched by them or, later, by the Moors. Christianity appears to have reached the mountains in the seventh and eighth centuries, and at the end of the eighth century the region came under the control of the Franks when Charlemagne created the Spanish March.

With the slow disintegration of Charlemagne's empire, and the gradual retreat southwards of the Moors, the kingdoms of northern Spain began to sort themselves out. Aragón, initially an area of the March under a nominated governor, began to emerge as a separate entity from the eighth century onwards, and from the ninth century became linked by marriage to neighbouring Navarra. Catalonia, which had remained relatively free from Muslim rule, rose to fortune under the protection of the Franks and soon became one of the most powerful states in Spain.

Even after the union of Aragón and Castille in 1479, the kingdoms of Aragón, Catalonia and Navarra retained a large degree of self-rule, and it was not for some time that border questions were settled. The exact border between Aragón and Catalonia was constantly in a state of flux, the border with France not being finalized until the 1659 Treaty of the Pyrenees. Despite this agreement,

---

❑ **Trekking in the Central Pyrenees – Highlights**
The Ordesa National Park and the Aigüestortes National Park both contain stunning scenery and are highly recommended, as is the Val d'Aran. The border area to the north of the Val d'Aran has many well-placed refuges amongst the high mountains, and there are any number of ways in which you can work your itinerary in this region.

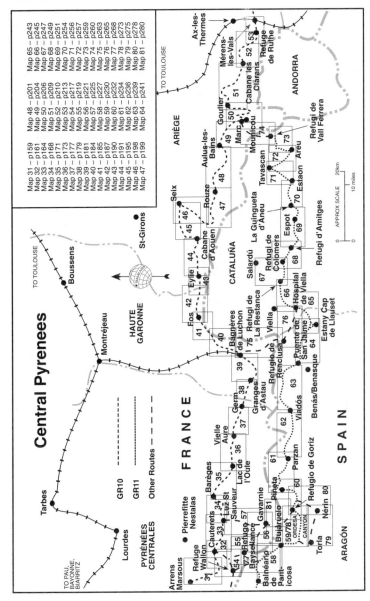

Central Pyrenees

PYRÉNÉES
CENTRALES

● Pierrefitte
 Nestalas

GR10 ————————
GR11 – – – – – – –
Other Routes – – – –

CENTRAL PYRENEES

APPROX SCALE
0   10 miles
0   20km

the ownership of the Aran valley was still in dispute as late as the Peninsular War in the early 1800s. In the twentieth century both Aragón and Catalonia were Republican strongholds in the Civil War, and the population of the villages was cut drastically when large numbers fled across the mountains.

Walking in eastern Aragón and western Catalonia

The central portion of the Spanish Pyrenees contains some of the best scenery in the whole of the range. The high mountainsides are different in character and appearance from the French Pyrenees; the colours are predominantly brown and grey, and the hills, which slope gently towards the south, are grass-covered. In Aragón, the Ordesa National Park makes a good week-long excursion, while in Catalonia, the Aigüestortes National Park and the Aran Valley provide plenty of scope for a fortnight or more of walking.

FOOD AND DRINK

Spanish Pyrenean cooking, rather like its French counterpart, is heavy on substance and energy content. Large stews and thick soups frequently feature on the menu, as do sausages such as the Catalan speciality *butifarra traidora*. There are a selection of cheeses, including *serrat* and *brossat*, and the standard drink is red wine, or water. (You may even find that wine is served at breakfast, on the dubious theory that water will weigh you down as you head off into the mountains, whereas wine will lift you up!). There is also a selection of liqueurs – in Catalonia one of the best known is Ratafia, a syrupy sweet concoction.

GETTING THERE

Getting to the Central Pyrenees

This is covered in detail on pp14-18. In outline, to get to the French Pyrenees there are **airports** in Pau and Lourdes for the western part of the region, or Toulouse for the eastern part. The nearest airport in Spain is Barcelona. By **rail**, there are direct TGV services to Pau, Lourdes, Tarbes and Toulouse. By road there are **coaches** from London to Pau, Lourdes, Tarbes and Toulouse.

Getting to the walking

To get into the hills using public transport there are various options:
● **Arrens-Marsous** (see p114 and p158) There are two buses a day between Tarbes and Arrens-Marsous (every day except Sundays and holidays). The buses go via Lourdes (bus station) and Pierrefitte Nestalas (from where there are connections to Cauterets, Luz-St-Sauveur and, indirectly, Gavarnie). From Tarbes to Arrens the journey takes one and a half hours; from Lourdes to Arrens just over one hour. The buses are operated by Salt (☎ 05.62.34.76.69, 🖹 05.62.34.76.61).
● **Cauterets, Luz-St-Sauveur, Barèges, Gavarnie** From Pau and Tarbes there are trains to Lourdes, from where there are regular bus services (running from outside the railway station) to Cauterets. All services stop at Pierrefitte Nestalas, where you can change onto a bus headed for Luz-St-Sauveur and Barèges. From Luz, there are two buses daily to Gavarnie (see p165 for details of timings).

● **Bagnères-de-Luchon** From Toulouse, there are two trains daily, via Montréjeau, to Bagnères-de-Luchon. In addition there are a further three or four services daily to Montréjeau where you can change for a connecting bus service to Bagnères-de-Luchon.

● **Aulus-les-Bains** From Pau or Tarbes you can catch a train east (from Toulouse you'll need a westbound train) to Boussens, from where it's possible to catch an SNCF bus to St-Girons. During the summer there are three buses daily from St-Girons to Aulus (€4). A taxi from St-Girons to Aulus costs €38.

● **Ax-les-Thermes and Mérens-les-Vals** There are several direct trains daily from Toulouse to Ax-les-Thermes; some also stop at Mérens-les-Vals.

Spain

● **Torla** There are two buses daily between Torla and Sabiñánigo, where there's a railway station (see p270 for more details).

● **Sallent de Gallego** There are buses daily to Jaca and Sabiñánigo, where there are railway stations and other bus connections (see p149).

Car hire

This will obviously not be ideal for most people, as it's very expensive to hire a car and then go walking for several days. However, if you want to have a flexible itinerary, it may be suitable. There are car hire services in the following towns:

● **Lourdes** Avis (☎ 05.62.42.12.97) has an office at the railway station.

● **Tarbes** Avis (☎ 05.62.34.26.76), 40 rte de Lourdes; Budget (☎ 05.62.93.91.60), 42 ave de Maréchal Joffre; Europcar (☎ 05.62.51.20.21), 54 ave Aristide Briand.

● **Pau** Avis (☎ 05.59.13.31.33), ave Didier Daurat; Budget (☎ 05.59.62.72.54), 242 ave Jean Mermoz; Europcar (☎ 05.59.92.09.09), 115 ave Jean Mermoz.

● **Toulouse** All major car hire companies have desks at the airport.

Route maps
● **Scale and walking times** All the following trail maps are drawn to a scale of 1:100,000 (10mm = 1km/0.625miles). Walking times are given along the side of each map, and the arrow shows the direction to which the time refers. Black triangles indicate the points between which the times have been taken. Note that the time given refers only to the time spent walking, so you will need to **add 30-40% to allow for rest stops**. Remember that these are **my timings** for the section; every walker has his or her own speed. With the first edition of this book, several readers commented that they found these timings on the fast side. The times are, however, consistent so you should err on the side of caution for a day or two until you see how your speed relates to my timings on the maps. When planning the day's trekking, count on between five and seven hours actual walking, and allow for an occasional rest day.

● **Up or down?** The trail is shown as a dotted line. An arrow across the trail indicates the slope; two arrows show that it is steep. Note that the arrow points towards the higher part of the trail. If, for example, you're walking from A (at 900m) to B (at 1100m) and the trail between the two is short and steep it would be shown thus: A—>>—B.

● **Refuges, gîtes and cabanes** Everywhere to stay that is within easy reach of the trail is marked. See the text for more details about each place.

● **Other information and symbols** Altitudes are given on the map in metres. Places where you can get water are shown by a 'W' within a circle.

Central Pyrenees – GR10

ARRENS-MARSOUS → REFUGE D'ILHÉOU   [MAP 31]

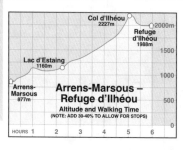

Cross the Gave d'Azun via an old arched bridge just to the south of the village centre. On the far side of the river a small track leads uphill; take a left as it forks (by the wooden arboretum sign) and follow it round and then through the top of the arboretum until it comes to a road. Join the road briefly before taking a footpath through the trees to meet the lane higher up the hillside. This time follow the lane down to the **Col des Bordères (1156m)**. Just past the sign announcing the col, a footpath leads off to the left (follow the marker closely), only to rejoin the road after a few hundred metres. Leaving it again a few metres on to follow a stream down the hill, you emerge upon the lane once more, this time leaving it below the Hanima gîte.

It soon re-emerges on a lane, then chops through woods to another lane where you turn left past some buildings, skirt around the church at Estaing and descend to meet the road (D103) running south up the Vallée d'Estaing. Just to the right, a few metres up the road, is the very smart *Camping Pyrénées Natura* which charges €22 per emplacement for two people, although it's more geared up for cars and camper vans. You can also hire a mobile home here for €40 per night. The GR10 heads directly across the road and runs south alongside the stream for 15 minutes to a point where it re-crosses the road and stream near a campsite.

After quarter of an hour along the west bank of the river, cross again and follow the road south past *Chez Place Bar and Restaurant* to the *gîte d'étape Les Viellettes* (☎ 05.62.97.14.37, 🖹 05.62.97.44.74). The gîte is open all year and charges €13 for the night or €27 for demi-pension; the farm next door sells honey. Ten minutes further south is *Camping La Pose* (☎ 05.62.97.43.10) which has basic but adequate facilities; it's €1 for emplacement and €2 per person. Opposite the campsite the GR10 again crosses to the west side of the stream, returning to the road a kilometre further on. At the top of the lane, just as Lac d'Estaing comes into view is an attractive little hotel: *Hôtel Restaurant du Lac d'Estaing* (☎ 05.62.97.06.25) is open from the beginning of May to mid-October and has rooms ranging in price from €29 to €38. The restaurant is far from cheap but the menu looks wonderful, and there is a menu du jour for around €14.

The Lac d'Estaing itself is not a place to linger as the area is generally packed with day trippers. Thankfully, few have the energy to walk more than a short way up into the hills, so the crowds are soon left behind. Five minutes' walk

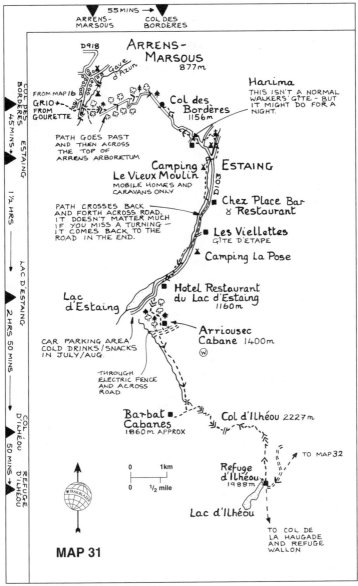

MAP 31

along the lake side and next to a sign, CABANES DU BARBAT 2H 30 & COL D'ILHÉOU 3H 45, the GR10 cuts uphill on a steep footpath through woods. After half an hour the path emerges from the trees near the **Arriousec Cabane**, which is normally locked; there's a water source near the cabane, although it might be wise to purify this water before drinking it. Ten minutes later, the GR10 crosses a rough vehicle track and heads south-east, climbing along the side of the valley. Fifty minutes' hard walking brings you to a path junction just east of the **Barbat Cabanes** and an hour beyond this, after a steep final ascent, you reach the **Col d'Ilhéou** (2227m). There's a sign here, LAC D'ILHÉOU 1H, and a conveniently grassy slope where you can collapse. The descent to the refuge is gradual and undramatic.

The **Refuge d'Ilhéou** is one of the more expensive mountain huts in the Pyrenees, which is odd since the building is accessible to four-wheel drive vehicles which should make resupply easy. The refuge has space for 32 people and charges €14 per night, €7 for breakfast, €18 for dinner, and €39 for demi-pension. A beer or other cold drink here will set you back a whacking €3 – which must be four or five times the cost price in Cauterets! There's no telephone, only a radio link in the refuge itself, but reservations can be made on (☎ 05.62.92.52.38). The refuge is named after a local lawyer and historian, Raymond Ritter, who devoted himself to writing about and promoting the Pyrenees.

REFUGE D'ILHÉOU → CAUTERETS   [MAP 32]

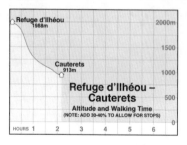

Refuge d'Ilhéou
1988m
2000m
1500
Cauterets
913m
1000
**Refuge d'Ilhéou –
Cauterets**
500
Altitude and Walking Time
(NOTE: ADD 30-40% TO ALLOW FOR STOPS)
0
HOURS 1   2   3   4   5   6

Follow the rough vehicle track downhill from the refuge for a few minutes, before turning off across the grass to the right (north). The footpath crosses the hillside and descends to meet the rough vehicle track again. The GR10 crosses the track and continues on a narrow trail across the hillside over loose rocks. At the bottom of the slope the footpath rejoins this track a few hundred metres before a bridge over the **Gave d'Ilhéou**. Just before the bridge the GR10 turns right along a clearly-marked grassy trail. After coming level with the large **parking area** on the far side of the valley, you go down the hillside to follow a fence line, and continue along a track between two fields. At the end, turn left along the road for a few metres before cutting downhill to the right, under the path of the cable car. Rejoining the road, turn right and continue downhill for 100m before yet another short cut takes you into Cauterets.

(Opposite): Throughout the Pyrenees there is a convenient network of usually excellent gîtes and mountain refuges. **Top**: Refuge Wallon/Marcadau (see p218), one of the largest in the Pyrenees. (Photo © Henry Stedman). **Bottom left**: Modern, purpose-built Refuge des Bésines, see p286. (Photo © Keith Carter). **Bottom right**: Recently opened in a converted village house, the Refugi GR-11 Estaon, see p255. (Photo ©Bryn Thomas).

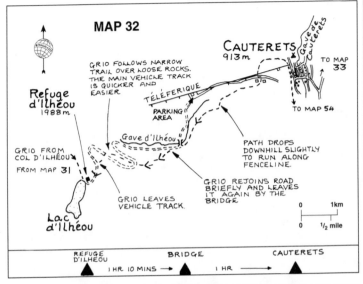

MAP 32

GRID FOLLOWS NARROW TRAIL OVER LOOSE ROCKS. THE MAIN VEHICLE TRACK IS QUICKER AND EASIER

CAUTERETS 913 m

Gave de Cauterets

TO MAP 33

TÉLÉFÉRIQUE

PARKING AREA

TO MAP 54

Refuge d'Ilhéou 1988 m

GRID FROM COL D'ILHÉOU

FROM MAP 31

Gave d'Ilhéou

PATH DROPS DOWNHILL SLIGHTLY TO RUN ALONG FENCELINE.

GRID REJOINS ROAD BRIEFLY AND LEAVES IT AGAIN BY THE BRIDGE

GRID LEAVES VEHICLE TRACK.

Lac d'Ilhéou

0   1km
0   ½ mile

REFUGE D'ILHÉOU	BRIDGE	CAUTERETS
1 HR 10 MINS →	1 HR →	

Refuge d'Ilhéou → Refuge Wallon
If you're heading for Gavarnie, or are just keen to explore the area, consider going south from the Refuge d'Ilhéou, instead of north-east towards Cauterets. By making directly for the Refuge Wallon, you can avoid Cauterets altogether and see some of the best of the scenery in this part of the Pyrenees. It takes about four hours via the Col de la Haugade (2311m) to the Refuge Wallon, and if you're feeling energetic you could carry on for a further 4½ hours to the Refuge Oulettes de Gaube. For details of the many alternative routes in the area see Excursions around the GR10 on p215.

CAUTERETS
✉ code 65110
Cauterets came to the fore in the late 19th century as a spa town. It was a fashionable place to be seen, and it attracted a cross section of society figures: musicians, artists, writers and the nobility. These days, during high season, Cauterets is just as full of visitors as it ever was in the 19th century. After the calm and solitude of walking in the

mountains, the crowded streets can be slightly bemusing but it's a good place to stock up on supplies, pick up mail and enjoy a night in a proper hotel. Because of its efficient bus connections it's also a convenient place to start or finish a walking trip.

Services
Facilities in Cauterets include several **banks** (Crédit Agricole has a cash dispenser), a

---

(**Opposite**): There are superb views from the Horquette d'Arre (2465m), see p111. (Photo © Henry Stedman).

post office (Mon-Fri 09.00-12.30, 14.00-16.30, Sat 09.00-12.00) and a self-service **launderette**. The Bibliothèque Municipal opposite the carousel has **internet access** (Tue-Sat 10.00-12.00, 15.00-19.00), charging €0.15 per minute, €3 for 30 minutes, or an hour for €5. There are numerous **shops**: there's a photographic store, a large Intersport which sells Coleman/Epigas cylinders, and an indoor market. The **tourist office** (☎ 05.62.92.50.27, 🖳 www.cauterets.com) is in the centre of town, and nearby is the **Bureau des Guides** (☎ 05.62.92.62.02) where information is available on activities including mountain biking, climbing and canyoning. The **Maison du Parc** is worth a visit if you want to find out more about the mountains. Entry is free and the well-laid-out exhibition covers flora, fauna and the traditional lifestyle of the montagnards. All captions are in French.

Just below the Maison du Parc is the wooden gare, from which **buses** depart. There are seven buses daily to and from Lourdes (€6 one way, one hour) and, during the summer, six buses daily to and from the Pont d'Espagne (25 minutes; €3.50 one way, €5 return). The Pont d'Espagne service leaves Cauterets at 08.00, 10.00, 12.00, 14.10, 16.00, 18.00 and Pont d'Espagne at 09.00, 11.00, 12.30, 15.00, 17.00, 19.00. If you're heading to Luz-St-Sauveur or Gavarnie, take the Lourdes bus north to Pierrefitte-Nestalas (€3.50, half an hour) and change there for a bus to Luz (€3.50, half an hour). For details of buses from Luz to Gavarnie, see p222. There's an SNCF booking office inside the gare (open 09.00-12.30 and 15.00-19.00) where you can book train tickets for your onward journey from Lourdes. For a **taxi**, try Taxi Bordenave (☎ 05.62.92.53.68, mobile ☎

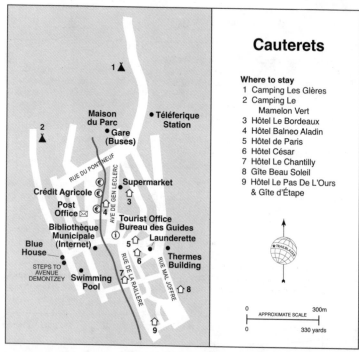

Cauterets

Where to stay
1 Camping Les Glères
2 Camping Le
     Mamelon Vert
3 Hôtel Le Bordeaux
4 Hôtel Balneo Aladin
5 Hôtel de Paris
6 Hôtel César
7 Hôtel Le Chantilly
8 Gîte Beau Soleil
9 Hôtel Le Pas De L'Ours
     & Gîte d'Étape

Maison du Parc
Téléferique Station
Gare (Buses)
RUE DU PONT NEUF
Crédit Agricole
Supermarket
Post Office
AVE DE GEN LECLERC
Tourist Office
Bureau des Guides
Bibliothèque Municipale (Internet)
Launderette
Blue House
STEPS TO AVENUE DEMONTZEY
Swimming Pool
RUE DE LA RAILLERE
Thermes Building
RUE MAL JOFFRE

TRAILBLAZER

0   300m
APPROXIMATE SCALE
0   330 yards

06. 71.01.46.86) or Taxi André Houssat (☎ 05. 62.92.61.62, mobile ☎ 06.12.91.83.19).

Where to stay

The *Hôtel Balneo Aladin* ☆☆☆ (☎ 05.62. 92.60.00, 🖳 www.hotel-balneo-aladin.com) which has double rooms starting at €131 including breakfast, is probably the best place in Cauterets. A close competitor, however, is the *Hôtel Le Bordeaux* ☆☆☆ (☎ 05. 62.92.52.50, 🖳 hotel.le.bordeaux@wana doo.fr) which has B&B from €78.

Amongst Cauterets' mid- and lower-range hotels, the friendly *Hôtel Le Pas De L'Ours* ☆ (☎ 05.62.92.58.07, 🖳 www.lepa sdelours.com) is good value with clean, pleasant double rooms from €40, and, for a small amount extra, the best buffet breakfast you're likely to come across anywhere. Another place which has been recommended is the centrally-located *Hôtel César* ☆☆ (☎ 05.62.92.52.57, 🖳 www.cesarhotel.com) which has double rooms from €36. Nearby

and right on the central square, is the *Hôtel de Paris* ☆☆ (☎ 05.62.92.53.85, 🖳 www.pe rso.wanadoo.fr/hotel.de.paris) where double rooms start at €40. There are lots of other hotels in town; the tourist office can usually assist you in finding somewhere to stay.

At the cheaper end of the scale, the best *gîte* in the town is run by Hôtel Le Pas De L'Ours; a bed in the gîte costs €15. If this is full, try the *Gîte Beau Soleil* (☎ 05. 62.92.53.52, 🖳 www.perso.wanadoo.frgite .beau.soleil/) which has a rather institutionalized atmosphere, and where they charge €20 for B&B, €33 for demi-pension.

There are two campsites close to the centre of town. *Camping Le Mamelon Vert* ☆☆ (☎ 05.62.92.51.56, 🖳 www.mamelo nvert.com) is fairly upmarket and charges €9.90 for an emplacement. *Camping Les Glères* ☆☆ (☎ 05.62.92.55.34) is more crowded and further from the centre of town; the tariff is €6 for one person and a tent, and €3 for each extra person.

CAUTERETS → LUZ-ST-SAUVEUR [MAP 33, p164]

The GR10 climbs out of Cauterets on rue Mal Joffre, heading south from the *Thermes* (thermal baths) building past the Gîte Beau Soleil to a large crucifix at a T-junction. A tap of drinking water can be found just past the crucifix.

Turn left uphill to an old thermes building with some benches affording a fine view over the town below. There's a cluster of signs by some stone steps include one pointing ahead

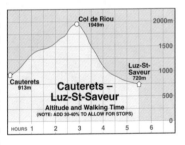

to the COL DE RIOU 3H 15; continue up the lane which in ten minutes or so becomes a loose-surfaced track. It passes a green forest hut owned by the Office National des Forêts, the path undulating at times but gaining height steadily until a hairpin bend is reached. Continue on the track and on the left a GR10 sign has been painted on a tree stump. At this point the path cuts back left and climbs up through trees, passing through a gate crudely fashioned from an old bedstead. After half an hour the path emerges from the trees by a small farm building and after some meandering climbs across open slopes to top out at the **Col de Riou (1949m)**; the wide view which opens out here is sadly marred by the skiing hardware apparent everywhere.

The GR10 departs from the col on an obvious track heading north-east but soon heads down on a footpath to the car park and ski station, deserted during the

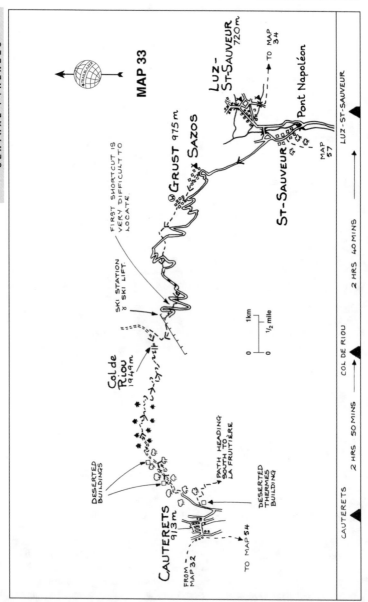

CENTRAL PYRENEES

MAP 33

Luz-St-Sauveur 720m

TO MAP 34

Pont Napoléon

St-Sauveur

MAP 57

Grust 975m

Sazos

FIRST SHORTCUT IS VERY DIFFICULT TO LOCATE.

SKI STATION & SKI LIFT.

Col de Riou 1949m

0 1km

0 ½ mile

DESERTED BUILDINGS

PATH HEADING SOUTH TO LA FRUITIÈRE

DESERTED THERMES BUILDING

CAUTERETS 913m

TO MAP 54

FROM MAP 32

CAUTERETS ◀── 2 HRS 50 MINS ──▶ COL DE RIOU ◀── 2 HRS 40 MINS ──▶ LUZ-ST-SAUVEUR

summer months. From here the path goes straight down towards Luz, crossing the road each time it meets it. The development of skiing facilities has disrupted the red-and-white waymarks but as you descend they become more evident.

After nearly two hours of continuous descent you arrive at the quiet village of **Grust** where drinking water is in abundance from a series of taps. Better still is the welcoming *Auberge Les Bruyères* (☎ 05.62.92.83.03) a restaurant/bar which also has rooms. Demi-pension costs €32. This is a nice, unsophisticated place which would make a pleasant overnight stop if you can't walk another step. Alternatively you could opt for the *Gîte d'étape Soum de l'Ase* (☎ 05 .62.92.34.79) a smallish gîte with 15 places where the tariff is €15 per night or €30 for demi-pension. There is a small kitchen for self catering and you can get drinks and sandwiches if you're just passing.

Half an hour downhill from Grust you come to Sazos where there is another gîte, *La Maisonnée* (☎ 05.62.92.96.90, 🖳 www.gitelamaisonnee.com), a friendly establishment with plenty of space (40 places) charging €26 for demi-pension. The campsite with the complicated name, *Camping Caravaneige Pyrenevasion* ☆☆☆ (☎ 05.62.92.91.54) charges €14 for two people with a tent. It is a busy, family site with a pool and can get rather crowded during August.

Luz-St-Sauveur is a further half an hour's walk down the busy road.

LUZ-ST-SAUVEUR

✉ code 65120

Luz is another of the Pyrenean spa towns which capitalized on the thermal springs and the popularity of the mountains during the late 19th century. Today, as in Cauterets, summer finds the streets crowded with tourists and the central area of the town is well supplied with camping shops, pizza restaurants and bars. It's a place to catch up on chores, and a pleasant enough place to sit in a pavement café, plan the next few days' walking and watch the world go by

Regular bus connections make it a good place to start or end a walk if you're doing the GR10 in sections.

Services

There are three **banks** (two of which have cash dispensers) near the centre of the town and a **launderette** in a side street opposite the **post office**. **Shops** near the centre include a pharmacy, a tabac which is where you buy stamps, a huge **supermarket** and several places that sell baguettes – ideal for people setting off for a day's walk. There are sports stores everywhere – Ardiden Sports, opposite the tourist office, sells

Coleman/Epigas. The **tourist office** (☎ 05. 62.92.81.60, ▤ 05.62.92.87.19) is on the central square, a few metres from the **Bureau des Guides**. The main square's the place for a beer.

Entertainments include a **cinema**, a **swimming pool** and a **nightclub**. If you're really lucky and you reach Luz on a scheduled weekend, you could always have a go at **bungee jumping** off the Pont Napoléon.

There is a regular **bus service** between Luz and Lourdes (€6 one way, one hour). To get from Luz to Cauterets, take the Lourdes bus as far as Pierrefitte Nestalas (€4, half an hour) and change there for Cauterets (€4, half an hour). Buses coming from Lourdes continue to Barèges (15 minutes) but no further. During July and August there are also two daily services to and from Gavarnie. Currently run by Transports Claude Dubie (☎ 05.62.92.48.60), they depart from Luz at 09.00 and 17.30 and from Gavarnie at 10.00 and 18.30. The journey costs €6 and takes 40 minutes; the buses make one stop, at Gèdre, halfway between Luz and Gavarnie and a possible base for a trip into the Cirque de Troumouse.

Where to stay

The area of St-Sauveur, near the church is more peaceful than the town centre but less convenient for the shops. There are a couple of reasonable hotels in this part of town: the *Crêperie Hôtel Les Templiers* ☆☆ (☎ 05. 62.92.81.52, 🖹 05.62.92.93.05) is a pleasant, friendly hotel with demi-pension from €41. In the same square is the *Hôtel Les Cimes* ☆ (☎ 05.62.92.82.03) which is more of a boarding house than a hotel but good value with rooms at €19 for B&B and €30 for demi-pension. In the bustling centre of town are two two-star hotels, both equally convenient. The first is the *Touristic Hôtel* ☆☆ (☎ 05.62.92.82.09, 🖹 05.62.92.95.41) where demi-pension costs €35 or if you'd like a balcony €40 but there is a €15 sup-

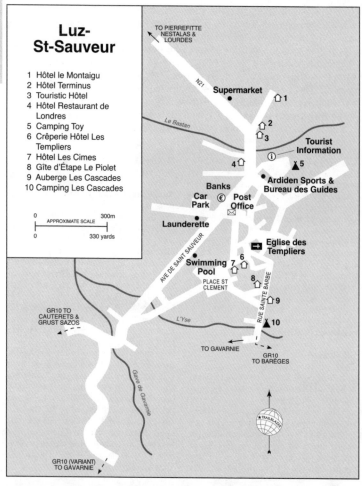

Luz-St-Sauveur

1 Hôtel le Montaigu
2 Hôtel Terminus
3 Touristic Hôtel
4 Hôtel Restaurant de Londres
5 Camping Toy
6 Crêperie Hôtel Les Templiers
7 Hôtel Les Cimes
8 Gîte d'Étape Le Piolet
9 Auberge Les Cascades
10 Camping Les Cascades

0   APPROXIMATE SCALE   300m
0   330 yards

TO PIERREFITTE NESTALAS & LOURDES

N21

Le Bastan

Supermarket

Tourist Information

Ardiden Sports & Bureau des Guides

Banks
Car Park
Post Office

Launderette

Eglise des Templiers

AVE DE SAINT SAUVEUR

Swimming Pool

PLACE ST CLEMENT

L'Yse

RUE SAINTE BARBE

GR10 TO CAUTERETS & GRUST SAZOS

TO GAVARNIE

GR10 TO BARÈGES

Gave de Gavarnie

GR10 (VARIANT) TO GAVARNIE

TRAILBLAZER

plement for single occupancy. The second, the *Hôtel Terminus* ☆☆ (☎ 05.62.92.80. 17, 🖾 05.62.92.32.89), is more modern and prices start at €40 for room with a shower.

The town's classiest hotel, *Le Montaigu* ☆☆☆ (☎ 05.62.92.81.71, 🖳 www w.hotelmontaigu.com), is a rather old-fashioned establishment on a quiet street where, if you can get a room, you will pay €65 for demi-pension if you're staying only one night. In the season they make it plain that longer stays are preferred. You'll probably have better luck at the *Hôtel Restaurant de Londres* ☆☆ (☎ 05 .62.92.80.09) which is rather old-fashioned but centrally located beside the stream. Demi-pension costs €48.

There are two gîtes to choose from, both in the quieter part of town. *Le Piolet* (☎ 05.62.92.92.67) is a no-frills place where, on entering, it feels like stepping inside someone's private house. B&B costs €14 and demi-pension, if available, €24 depending on whether enough people are staying to make it worth the owner's while to cook a meal. If not, you can eat next door at the *Auberge Les Cascades* (☎ 05. 62.92.94.14), the other gîte d'étape, less casual than Le Piolet, with 40 places. You'll pay €30 for demi-pension.

There are two campsites in Luz, the well-run *Camping Toy* ☆☆ (☎ 05.62

.92.97.56) where they charge €3.40 per adult plus €3.40 for the emplacement. Although right in the heart of where the action is, the site is quiet, orderly and above all clean. *Camping Les Cascades* ☆☆ (☎ 05.62.92.85.85) charges €6 per person, €13 for two. There's a pool and bar but the site caters predominantly for families and static caravans.

What to see

Spare a moment to look into the **Église des Templiers**, built in the 11th century and dedicated to St Andrew. Pilgrims on their way to Santiago de Compostela were traditionally welcomed here. The ruined tower which stands on a small hill overlooking Camping Toy is **Château Sainte Marie**; although it looks in reasonable shape from the town, an empty tower and a couple of walls are all that remain.

One of the local sights is the **Pont Napoléon**, a bridge which usually features somewhere on local tourist literature, and if you fancy an evening stroll it's quite impressive. If you find yourself in the area in July you may be able to catch part of the **Jazz Altitude Festival** which takes place in Luz. Even if you're not interested, try to book your place to stay in advance, as the town is packed during the festival.

LUZ-ST-SAUVEUR → BARÈGES　　　　　　[MAP 34, p168]

The GR10 leaves Luz just south of Camping Cascades. Don't go through the site but go past the entrance and down to the small bridge on the far side of which the GR10 markings point left up a path alongside the stream (these are the cascades). The path meets a minor road, crosses a bridge left and steepens through woods. About an hour after leaving Luz the path emerges from the trees

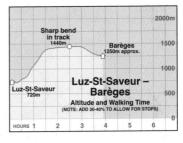

and continues climbing over the open hillside before levelling out and re-entering the woods again through the **Domaine du Gave de Pau**. This stretch of fine walking on good paths continues until a road is met rather unexpectedly. Go right, not straight across as an FFRP sign seems to suggest and stay on the road

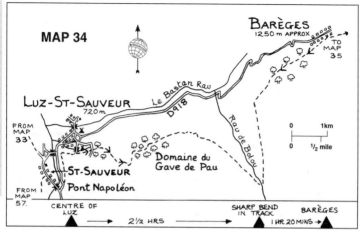

until a sign points the way to Barèges. A long walk now begins, down through trees on a path that becomes busier with strollers until, finally, you'll see the rooftops of Barèges. Debouching onto a track by the Gîte d'étape L'Hospitalet, go down some steps, turn right and Gîte d'étape L'Oasis is right in front of you.

BARÈGES
✉ code 65120

Barèges is developing rapidly as a tourist centre, particularly as a skiing mecca in the winter months. There's a thermes building for taking the water cure, plenty of accommodation and some useful shops. Cyclists begin their assault on the feared Col de Tourmalet, one of the crucial stages of the Tour de France, from here. There are cafés and restaurants, most dedicated to the pizza. During July there is a piano festival (🖳 www.pianopyrenees.com).

Services
Barèges has most things you could need except a bank, although there is now an ATM. There is a **post office**, **shops** (including a **mini-supermarket** and a **sports store**), a **cinema**, and a **swimming pool**. There's even a **paragliding school**. The **tourist office** (☎ 05.62.92.16.00) is in the centre of the village.

Where to stay
There are at least nine hotels in Barèges, of which the two best are the *Hôtel Le Central*

Landslides in Barèges
Although the village's fate as a tourist stopover may seem a little sad, life is considerably better here today than in the past. Barèges was for years cursed by the steepness of the slopes above it and the instability of the soil. In the nineteenth century the threat became so great that the village was abandoned every winter. The inhabitants only returned once the snows had disappeared, often to start digging through the rubble of the houses that had been flattened. The woods that now cloak the hillside above the village have proved successful in stabilizing the slopes.

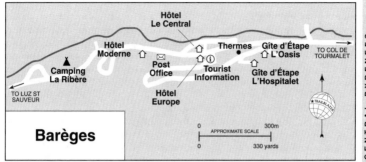

Barèges

☆☆ (☎ 05.62.92.68.05, 🖳 www.bareges
65.france.hotel.ewhr.com/hotels/hotel-cen
tral), with singles starting at €36 for demi-
pension, and the *Hôtel Europe* ☆☆ (☎ 05
.62.92.68.04, 🖳 hoteldeleurope@caramail.
com) where the rate is €42. For cheaper
accommodation, try the *Hôtel Moderne* ☆
(☎ 05.62.92.68.07, 📄 05. 62.92.36 04) –
demi-pension starting at €30-35.

There are two places with dormitory
accommodation. The *Gîte d'Étape L'Oasis*
(☎ 05.62.92.69.47, 🖳 www.gite-oasis.com)
is very pleasant and can accommodate 40
people; it costs €13 per night or €30 for
demi-pension. The couple who run it speak

excellent English and go out of their way to
be helpful. Above L'Oasis is *L'Hospitalet*
(☎ 05.62.92.68.08, 🖳 hospitalet.bareges@
wanadoo.fr), a huge old place and the first
building you come to as you reach Barèges
on the GR10. Originally a military hospital,
it seems rather forbidding. However, it's a
worthy second choice to L'Oasis and the
charges are the same.

Seven hundred metres west of the village centre is the *Camping La Ribère* ☆☆
(☎ 05.62.92.69.01, 🖳 www.laribere.com).
Facilities at the campsite include a washing
machine and tumble dryer and staying here
costs €12 for two people and a tent.

BARÈGES → LAC DE L'OULE   [MAP 35, p171]

To resume the trail after a
night in Barèges, climb up
the steps to the front of
L'Hospitalet, taking the
trail that climbs initially on
the left then drops down
briefly between cottages
before climbing again on a
footpath to a tarmac lane. It
passes a private hostel then
descends to meet the D918.
Turn right and follow the
road for about a kilometre,
heading straight on when

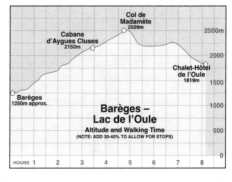

the road veers off to the right. On the left there's a café, *Auberge la Coquelle*
(☎ 05.62.92.68.15), ideal for a cold drink or a coffee before the hard work ahead.

Beyond the auberge is a large car park used by skiers in the winter but deserted in the summer months. Don't cross the car park but head right to the stream and go up the right-hand bank, heading south. To your right the D918 begins the climb to the Col de Tourmalet. This part of the trail is lacking in waymarks but by following the stream up you come to the **Pont de la Gaubie** where there is a botanical garden and a café. Go over the bridge and past the café on the road and at the first bend a cluster of signs on the right includes one that says COL DE MADAMETE 4H.

This is a busy and popular walk and on a fine day it will be crowded. Climbing steadily on a rocky track, you gain height until a succession of lovely river meadows is reached, the destination of many of the day walkers. The path winds its way up along a stream until eventually the *Cabane d'Aygues Cluses* comes into view with an idyllic lake beyond. The cabane would sleep five at a pinch but is not ideal for a night's repose. The GR10 does not in fact go all the way up to the cabane but veers right just before it.

Alternative route via Col de Barèges From here, there's an alternative and easier route to the official path. It heads south up the spur from the front door of the cabane to cross the range by the lower **Col de Barèges (2469m)**. The path then leads down to the Lac de Gourguet, passing a tin hut that's unsuitable for anything other than sheltering from the rain. The path continues south and descends steeply through old pine trees to reach the north end of Lac de L'Oule with the **Cabane de la Lude** by the shore. The cabane appears to be in permanent use but there is room for a tent in front. Fifteen minutes' walk brings you to the Chalet-Hôtel du Lac de L'Oule (see below).

Main route: GR10 via Col de Mamadète Passing the Cabane d'Aygues Cluses, head south and after half an hour's climbing you'll reach the **Lacs de Madamète**. A further 45 minutes of climbing, negotiating a couple of areas of large boulders along the way, brings you to the **Col de Madamète (2509m)** itself. The views in both directions on a clear day are spectacular; to the north you can see the observatory on the Pic du Midi de Bigorre while to the south a range of peaks unfolds. The col marks the boundary of the Réserve de Néouvielle.

The rocky path from the Col de Madamète leads down the hillside and passes round the east of the first lake. Beyond this it continues to the western end of **Lac d'Aumar** where it levels out for the first time in the day. If the weather is fine this area may well be crowded with picnickers. Some brave souls even go for a swim but the water is bitterly cold. At the far end of the lake the GR10 continues east along the side of a wooded spur with views over Lac d'Oredon. To the right, the *Chalet-Hôtel du Lac d'Oredon* (☎ 06. 23.05.72.60, 🖳 www .chalet-neouvielle.com) is a rather grand establishment which has 60 places with a choice of family rooms, doubles and dormitories for up to 10 people. Charges are €14 per night or €30 for demi-pension.

Continuing on the main route, you reach the **Col d'Estoudou (2260m)** where a sign indicates LAC DE L'OULE 1H. The path goes steeply downhill to

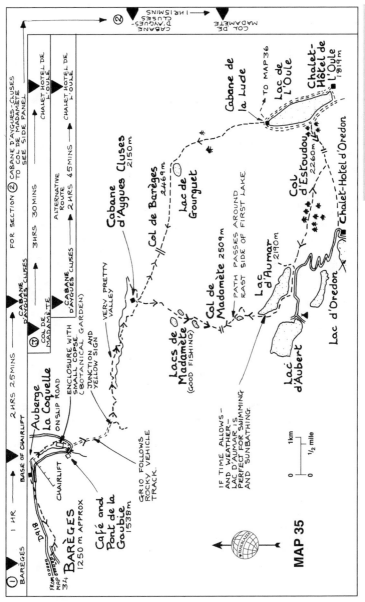

MAP 35

join the track down the western side of the lake. A ten- to fifteen-minute walk brings you to the barrage which you cross to reach the welcoming door of the ***Chalet-Hôtel du Lac de L'Oule*** (☎ 05.62.98.48.62). This is a fairly cramped establishment with one shower for 28 people, though it's friendly enough and has a bar and a nice terrace on which to while away the evening. The charges are €12.40 per night or €30 for demi-pension.

LAC DE L'OULE → VIELLE AURE/ST LARY SOULAN   [MAP 36]

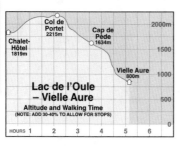

Leaving the gîte, take the lakeside path to the northern end of the lake and work up to the right (south) before climbing gently up through pine trees until a sharp change of direction forces you to veer northwards and leave the trees. The path then climbs directly up the slope passing close to the **Cabane de Bastan** (a private hut) and reaches a path junction. A profusion of red-and-white waymarkings keep you on track. From here, the variant GR10C goes north towards the Lacs de Bastan while the GR10 itself turns south.

The next section is relatively easy walking through an area reminiscent of the UK's Lake District, the GR10 now a grassy footpath which maintains height and follows the hillside south and then eastwards. After passing beneath two ski-lifts the path sinks into a dip and crosses two tiny streams. Beyond the second is a rough vehicle track which you follow right to the small car-parking area at the **Col de Portet (2215m)**.

The GR10 goes north from the car park but almost immediately swings eastwards. There are several trails across this hillside but you need the lower one – avoid staying too high but keep to a line above the twisting road that serves the ski station. The path descends gradually and then passes around the south flank of **Le Serre (2004m)** on the far side of which it follows the line of the spur eastwards, descending to a grassy col.

Cross to the south of the col and head down the hillside. There are dozens of sheep tracks which all look as though they might be the proper path but which actually contour round the slopes – while your aim is to descend them. The path comes up to a fence line which it stays with for a while until, just after a wet area, it reaches a loose-surfaced road at a sharp bend. Follow the road eastwards for about 200 metres and at the next sharp bend continue eastwards on a small footpath which descends rapidly through young woods.

After about half an hour there is a fork; you can go either way, for the tracks meet up again further down the hill. The path crosses a road and a further quarter of an hour after this it enters the quiet village of Vielle Aure (see p174).

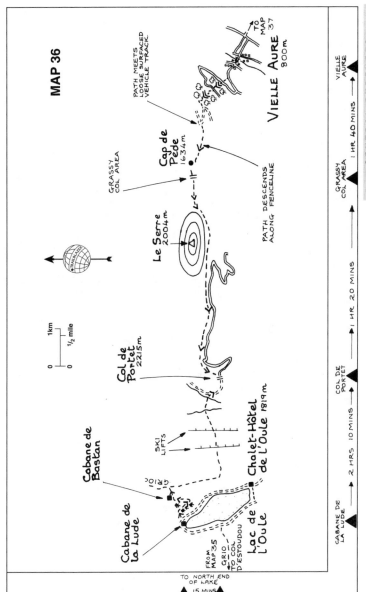

MAP 36

TO MAP 37

VIELLE AURE 800m.

PATH MEETS LOOSE SURFACED VEHICLE TRACK.

GRASSY COL AREA

Cap de Pede 1634m.

PATH DESCENDS ALONG FENCELINE

Le Serre 2004m.

Col de Portet 2215m.

1km
½ mile
0

SKI LIFTS

Cabane de Bastan

Cabane de la Lude

GR10C

Chalet-Hôtel de l'Oule 1819m.

Lac de l'Oule

FROM MAP 35

GR10 TO COL D'ESTOUDOU

TO NORTH END OF LAKE
15 MINS

CABANE DE LA LUDE ◀ 2 HRS 10 MINS ▶ COL DE PORTET ◀ 1 HR 20 MINS ▶ GRASSY COL AREA ◀ 1 HR 40 MINS ▶ VIELLE AURE

VIELLE AURE & ST-LARY-SOULAN
✉ code 65170

Vielle Aure is a peaceful village with some facilities. St-Lary-Soulan, a kilometre or so south, is a larger place.

Services
In Vielle Aure there's a **post office** and a **tourist office** (☎ 05.62.39 .50.00). **Shops** include a small épicerie and a bar/tabac which also sells bread. St-Lary-Soulan has numerous hotel and restaurants, several **banks**, a **cash dispenser**, a **pharmacy** and a **launderette**.

There are three or four **buses** daily to and from Lannemezan, one of which continues to Tarbes; Lannemezan has a railway station. Buses stop in St-Lary near the téléphérique and in Vielle Aure near the tourist office.

Where to stay
There's a decent hotel in Vielle Aure, *Hôtel Aurelia* ☆☆ (☎ 05.62.39.56.90, 🖥 www .hotel-aurelia.com), with double rooms from €36. The owners are very friendly, there's a pleasant terrace restaurant and a small swimming pool.

St-Lary-Soulan is well supplied with hotels including the plush *Hôtel Mercure* ☆☆☆ (☎ 05.62.99.50.00, 🖥 h2904@accor-hotels .com), where double rooms start at a steep €95, or you could choose B&B at €72. A better bet is the *Hôtel La Pergola* ☆☆☆ (☎ 05.62.39.40.46, 📄 05.62.40. 06.55), which has rooms from €59 for B&B and €79 demi-pension. Another good choice would be the *Hôtel Les Arches* ☆☆ (☎ 05.62.49 .10.10, 🖥 www.hotel-les-arch-es.com) a bright, modern hotel charging €53 plus €7 for breakfast and €17 for a meal.

Hôtel la Terrasse Fleurie ☆☆ (☎ 05 .62.40.76.00, 🖥 www.la-terrasse-fleurie .com) is a good middle-of-the-road hotel. It's conveniently-located with smallish but clean rooms. B&B costs €47. There is no restaurant but there are numerous places to eat close by including a crêperie, *La Galette d'Or* (☎ 05.62.40.71.62), where the food is delicious and cheap but fattening.

There are several campsites. *La Mousquère* is right on the GR10. Charges are €6.10 per person or €9.20 for two sharing a tent. There's also *Camping Autun* or you could try *Camping Municipal La Lanne* ☆☆☆☆ (☎ 05.62.39.41.58), a family-orientated site which is in the centre of St-Lary-Soulan and charges €9 for one person with tent.

VIELLE AURE → GERM

[MAP 37, p177]

Azet 1172m

Germ 1339m

Loudenville 960m

Vielle Aure 800m

Vielle Aure – Germ
Altitude and Walking Time
(NOTE: ADD 30-40% TO ALLOW FOR STOPS)

HOURS 1 2 3 4 5 6

Cross the bridge over the River Neste d'Aure in Vielle Aure and turn right and right again so that you follow a lane that runs parallel to the D116 to meet the main road (D929). The GR10 goes straight across and enters the village of **Bourisp** (no services), crossing a small bridge and swinging round to the left as it comes into the village itself. Almost immediately after the left-hand bend, turn right up a concrete track between the houses. This soon bears right then narrows to a footpath. The trail climbs the hillside to **Estensan**, a tiny hamlet where there's a water point next to the church.

Follow the lane through the village and turn left along the D225 before forking off right almost immediately along a small access lane. A few hundred

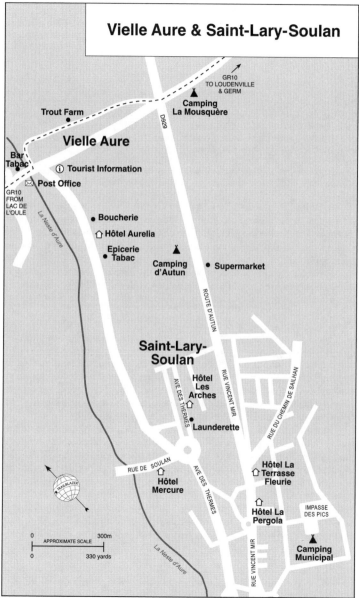

Vielle Aure & Saint-Lary-Soulan

GR10
TO LOUDENVILLE
& GERM

Trout Farm

Camping
La Mousquère

D929

Vielle Aure

Bar
Tabac

(i) Tourist Information

Post Office

GR10
FROM
LAC DE
L'OULE

La Neste d'Aure

• Boucherie

Hôtel Aurelia

Epicerie
• Tabac

Camping
d'Autun

• Supermarket

ROUTE D'AUTUN

**Saint-Lary-
Soulan**

Hôtel
Les
Arches

RUE VINCENT MIR

RUE DU CHEMIN DE SAILHAN

• Launderette

AVE DES THERMES

RUE DE SOULAN

Hôtel
Mercure

AVE DES THERMES

Hôtel La
Terrasse
Fleurie

Hôtel La
Pergola

IMPASSE
DES PICS

RUE VINCENT MIR

La Neste d'Aure

Camping
Municipal

TRAILBLAZER

0   300m
APPROXIMATE SCALE
0   330 yards

metres up the lane the GR10 bears off to the left, uphill, along a stony farm track. This gradually narrows into a footpath which meets the road briefly and then continues up the hillside to enter **Azet** (1172m).

AZET
☒ code 65170

Azet is a peaceful and attractive village; there are no shops but there are no less than three places to stay, all of which are on the lane running south from the church. *La Bergerie* (☎ 05.62.39.49.49, 🖹 05.62.40.06.31), a house with an attractive garden, offers table d'hôte and costs €22 for bed and breakfast and €30 for demi-pension. Almost opposite, the *Auberge du Col*, *Chez Marius* (☎ 05.62.39.43.97) is reached through a gate, behind which you find a charming place with a covered area of tables looking onto a yard. The charges are €18 for B&B and €30 for demi-pension. The *Gîte d'étape Azet* (☎ 05.62.39.41.44), about 50 metres down the lane from the other two, is simple but clean and has a small kitchen for self-catering. They charge €16 for B&B and €26 for demi-pension and there are 16 places in 4-bedded rooms.

The GR10 crosses in front of the church past a water fountain and leaves the village on the lane climbing north-east. After leaving the houses behind it turns up right on a steep vehicle track which bends south-eastwards and narrows to a footpath which runs almost horizontally across the hillside through an avenue of trees.

Gradually the path climbs to pass above the **Granges de Goutes**; it soon meets and crosses the road. From here to the **Col de Peyrefite** the waymarking is poor although the path is hard to miss. You follow a well-worn, earthen path parallel to and only just above the road. As it rounds a small spur the route ahead is visible all the way to the col.

Just north of the col you come to a loose-surface track which starts to lead down towards Loudenvielle. The descent eastwards is not well marked. A short way below the crest of the hill the path meets the road for the first time; cross over and go straight down through the bracken – you'll rediscover the waymarks about halfway down the slope. Where the track meets the road for the second time there is a steep bank. Head southwards above the road into the fold of the valley where there are easier places to scramble down.

On the far side of the road a track runs down the centre of the valley, to the east at first but then bending around to the north-east before coming to a path junction. Wooden signs point to Bordères and Loudenvielle but the GR10 actually takes the middle option and heads eastwards along the dry-stone wall of an old enclosure. Slightly below this enclosure it meets a cart track; follow the track to the left for a short distance before taking a right fork, marked both with yellow paint and red-and-white marks. A short way down this track you pass a house and emerge from the trees on to a patch of open hillside with a good view over the valley. Almost immediately the GR10 turns sharply right and down the steep hillside. Two-thirds of the way down there is a path junction. To the right

(Opposite): The vertiginous suspension bridge over the Gorges d'Olhadubi, see p97. (Photo © Henry Stedman).

CENTRAL PYRENEES

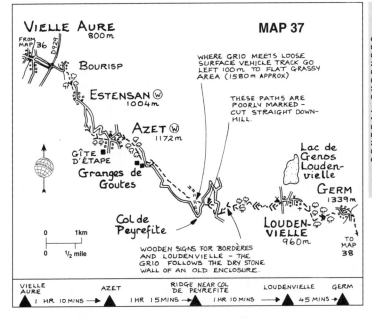

VIELLE AURE
800m
MAP 37
FROM MAP 36
D129

BOURISP

ESTENSAN Ⓦ
1004m

AZET Ⓦ
1172m

WHERE GRID MEETS LOOSE
SURFACE VEHICLE TRACK GO
LEFT 100m TO FLAT GRASSY
AREA (1580m APPROX)

THESE PATHS ARE
POORLY MARKED –
CUT STRAIGHT DOWN-
HILL.

GÎTE
D'ÉTAPE
Granges de
Goutes

Lac de
Genos
Louden-
vielle

GERM
1339m

Col de
Peyrefite

LOUDEN-
VIELLE
960m

TO
MAP
38

0   1km
0   ½ mile

WOODEN SIGNS FOR BORDÈRES
AND LOUDENVIELLE – THE
GR10 FOLLOWS THE DRY STONE
WALL OF AN OLD ENCLOSURE.

VIELLE AURE		AZET		RIDGE NEAR COL DE PEYREFITE		LOUDENVIELLE		GERM
▲	1 HR 10 MINS →	▲	1 HR 15 MINS →	▲	1 HR 10 MINS →	▲	45 MINS →	▲

the path crosses a stream, to the left it goes down some steps. Go left and after a few minutes you drop down to the *Café le Nestecafé* at the campsite entrance on the outskirts of Loudenvielle. This offers the opportunity of a cold drink and shouldn't be missed since, in spite of your efforts thus far, there is still a long way to go if you're staying at Germ. Go easy on the cold beer.

LOUDENVIELLE
✉ code 65510

Loudenvielle is a holiday village with useful facilities. In the centre of the village, there is a small group of shops including a '8 à Huit' (08.00-20.00) mini **supermarket** which is handy for stocking up on food for the next day's walk. Other shops include the usual **sports store**, a **newsagent** and a **pharmacy**. There's a Crédit Agricole **cash dispenser** and **tourist office** next to the

shops. The **post office** is a short way to the east, near the church.

The *Hostellerie des Templiers* (☎ 05 .62.99.68.03, 🖷 05.62.99.60.94) is a welcoming place and has double rooms from €42.

Camping de Pène Blanche ☆☆ (☎ 05 .62.99.68.85) charges €3 for a tent plus €3 per person. The proximity of the lake makes this a popular site with caravanners, and is likely to be busy in August.

(**Opposite**): **Top**: Refuge d'Arrémoulit and its namesake col (see p118). (Photo © Henry Stedman). **Bottom**: Many shepherds who spend their summers in cabanes in the high Pyrenees are only too happy to sell cheese to passing walkers. You may also be asked to help out with a few veterinary tasks, though! (Photo © Sarah Jane Riley).

There is still a stiff climb to **Germ,** where most people make an overnight stay thanks to the gîte d'étape and auberge in the village. There is no shop so don't forget to stock up in Loudenvielle. The GR10 goes straight through Loudenvielle where, just by the post office, a wooden sign points left up a path which leads away from the buildings. Almost immediately it turns right along a grassy track and climbs south-eastwards. The route is well-marked and there's some shade from trees but the hour's climb up to Germ is a hard slog. Where the footpath meets the road, the gîte d'étape is to the left and the auberge straight on. Both are signposted.

GERM
✉ code 65240

The ***Centre de Montagne de Germ*** (☎ 05. 62.99.65.27, 🖥 centre.germ@wanadoo.fr) is a superior gîte d'étape with its own pool. It's very pleasant and good value at €27 for demi-pension. Meals are inclusive of wine and coffee.

The only hotel in Germ is the ***Auberge de Germ*** (☎ 05.62.99.90.86, 🖥 www. auberge-de-germ.com), a small place without much character. Demi-pension is from €40 per person. The food is good, though.

GERM → GRANGES D'ASTAU   [MAP 38]

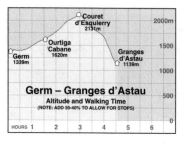

Germ – Granges d'Astau
Altitude and Walking Time
(NOTE: ADD 30-40% TO ALLOW FOR STOPS)

This is quite a short day with some wonderful scenery and a good spot for a lunch break at the Ourtiga Cabane. In the afternoon the walk down the Val d'Esquierry is a delight with butterflies and wild flowers in profusion and the chance to see some wildlife including marmots. I saw my first Pyrenean viper here.

Leaving the Auberge de Germ, the GR10 crosses the stream and takes a lane to the left with an immediate uphill gradient. At the top of the rise the track swings southwards and passes the Granges de Béderèdes. Follow the rough vehicle track as it continues south, above and parallel to the tarmac lane. Just as the track begins to descend towards the road and before a sharp switchback the GR10 turns off left onto a small footpath.

The path heads south-eastwards, running almost horizontally around the hillside. After half an hour you reach a somewhat precarious section where a landslip has taken away the path and you must be careful when crossing the steep slope. A quarter of an hour's walk beyond this you come to a clear track coming up from the right and find a water catchment pool lined with concrete. The path you meet is a GR10 variant from Loudenvielle. The main GR10 crosses the stream and climbs up left on the far side of the stream until in a further 20 minutes you reach the ***Ourtiga Cabane*** (approx 1620m). The hut is clean and has an upstairs platform for sleeping with a capacity for ten. On the door somebody has written 'Merci pour la cabane après une journée sous la pluie ça fait plaisir'.

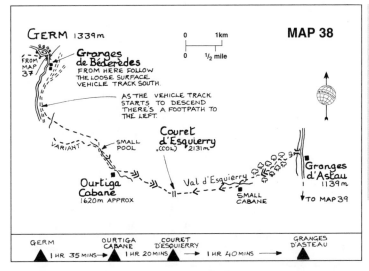

Cross the stream below the cabane and pick up the red-and-white markings on a path that climbs the hillside to the **Couret d'Esquierry (2131m)** a hard and tiring climb that is rewarded with fabulous views from the col. The ridge which runs north–south on either side of the col marks the departmental border; as you cross the col you leave the Hautes Pyrénées and enter Haute Garonne.

The walk down the Val d'Esquierry is beautiful, perfect for spotting butterflies and wild flowers and possibly wildlife. It takes about 50 minutes to reach a small *cabane* that has been much defaced with graffiti and contains a single bedstead. Below the hut the path crosses a stream and after five more minutes enters a beech wood. The steep slope is negotiated in long zigzags until the path emerges at the valley bottom, which is often filled with herds of cows. You may have become aware of the mesmerizing sound of cow bells as you descended. Sadly, in the summer the river valley will also be full of cars since this is a favourite spot for day trippers. The GR10 drops down an open hillside to a cottage then leads to the road; turn right and you reach the **Granges d'Astau (1139m)**.

The only accommodation here is the *Auberge d'Astau* (☎ 05.61.79.35.63, 📧 auberge-dastau@wanadoo.fr) a busy place with a popular bar and outdoor terrace with rooms in a separate building, the gîte. The rooms are poky and claustrophobic but adequate. The charges are €32.50 for one person demi-pension or €20 for B&B. Once the crowds of day visitors have gone home the valley is peaceful and attractive. The next-door bar, *Le Mailh d'Astau* (☎ 05. 61.79.82.17) does meals and snacks and is an alternative to eating the set meal in the gîte.

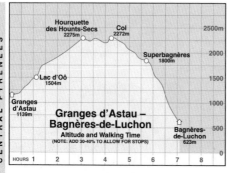

Granges d'Astau –
Bagnères-de-Luchon
Altitude and Walking Time
(NOTE: ADD 30-40% TO ALLOW FOR STOPS)

GRANGES D'ASTAU → BAGNÈRES-DE-LUCHON [MAP 39]

The GR10 passes the auberge and heads south on a loose-surfaced track, gradually gaining height and getting rougher until it becomes navigable only on foot, winding up the wooded hillside in sharp turns. After about three quarters of an hour you come to a little building rigged with a cable-and-pulley system and a set of rails running off round the hillside. Presumably this was used during the construction of the electricity installation which is tucked away below the lake. Twenty minutes further up the hill you arrive at the **Lac d'Oô (1504m),** a wonderful location with the 273m waterfall providing a spectacular centrepiece at the far end. As you reach the barrage and climb up to it there is a simple refuge to your right, reached by scrambling over boulders since you are not allowed to cross on the barrage wall. This is the ***Refuge Auberge/Bar du Lac d'Oô*** (☎ 05.61.79.12.29, 🖳 www .hebergements-de-france.com/lac-oo). It was formerly known as Chez Tintin but has dropped the name and made more of an effort to attract visitors since the last edition of this book. Demi-pension costs €38, a night's stay without meals is €18 and a meal costs €14. Camping is permitted nearby.

The path follows the edge of the lake, gaining height and making its way up a gully to the east of the waterfall. The route is obvious and well waymarked and attempts have been made to stop people taking short cuts. Just short of the **Col d'Espingo** there is a path junction which is marked by a painted sign daubed on the rocks. The GR10 does not go up to the col but breaks away left and climbs north-eastwards. The detour to the col, however, is well worth the effort since it enables one to see the lovely Lac d'Espingo and possibly visit the ***Refuge d'Espingo*** for a drink – a beer costs €2.50, understandable when you consider that it has come up on the back of a mule. The facilities are rudimentary and there are no showers. Demi-pension costs €33.

Retrace your steps to the GR10, which heads off in a north-easterly direction. This section is something of a slog: if you need encouragement take a break halfway and admire the views to the south-west. Now that you're well above the lake the glacier and snow-scattered upper slopes of Pic Belloc can be seen to their best advantage, unless it's well into August when most of the snow will have gone. Finally you top out at the **Hourquette des Hounts-Secs (2275m).** There are wonderful views from here and ahead the route of the GR10 can be seen until it disappears to the right just below the Sommet de la Coume de Bourg.

The next section is easy and a fast pace can be maintained before another sharp climb to the col (2272m) below the Sommet de la Coume de Bourg. The

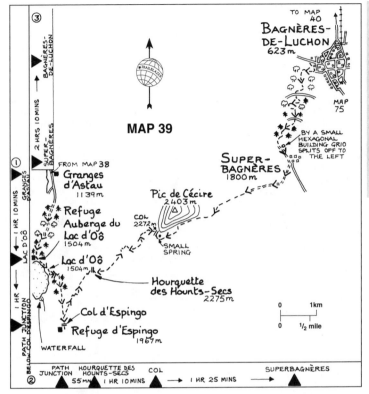

col is a popular destination for walkers, some of whom climb to the summit of the **Pic de Cécire (2403m)**. Don't rely on the small spring to the south-east of the col as it sometimes dries up in the summer.

From the col there is a descent on a narrow path around the slopes of the Pic de Cécire, gradually losing height in spite of a few sections where you have to climb, and maintaining a north-easterly direction. Soon the proximity of ski-lifts gives notice that you are nearing **Superbagnères (1800m)**. The ugly ski resort with its imposing central building is generally fairly crowded because the road running up here allows easy access to the hills. The area is popular in particular for mountain biking and paragliding. Although many of the facilities in the resort are closed during the summer, there are a couple of cafés which remain open.

If you're exhausted at this point take the **cable car** (€4.90 one way) to Bagnères-de-Luchon which is fun and quite spectacular; it takes about ten minutes. The final stretch of the GR10 to **Bagnères-de-Luchon** is all downhill but is tiring nonetheless, as you lose over 1000m of height in a very short distance.

From the resort, follow the rough road heading north-west for ten minutes, to a small hexagonal building. The GR10 passes to the left of the building along an ill-defined path which, after a minute or two, bends right to join a clear forest track. The descent from here is well marked, and is almost entirely through woods.

BAGNÈRES-DE-LUCHON
✉ code 31110

Usually referred to as simply 'Luchon', this is the Pyrenean resort town to beat them all. A quick wander down the Allées d'Étigny, past the magnificent Thermes building and the casino, show that this is still a spa town of some importance though it now owes a lot of its prosperity to skiing. It has a bustling atmosphere and the Thermes are still pulling in the customers. For the walker, Luchon suffers only from the lack of a gîte d'étape. Nonetheless, if you can stump up the cost of a hotel room for a night or two, it's an excellent place for a rest day.

Luchon is on the junction of two good walking routes (see also p262), and has all the facilities you could want.

Services
There's a **tourist office** (☎ 05.61.79.21.21, 🖳 www.luchon.com) on Allées d'Étigny, the self-styled Champs d'Elysées of Luchon, as is the **post office**. There are at least three **banks** (and cash dispensers) also on the Allées d'Étigny. Not all banks are interested in changing travellers' cheques. There are two mini **supermarkets** in the town centre, and plenty of tabacs and newsagents, an excellent **bookshop** and a **launderette**

The **railway station** is to the north of the town centre; there's one direct train daily to Toulouse, and four SNCF **buses** daily from Bagnères to Montrejeau, where you can get connections to Toulouse, Tarbes and Lourdes. The journey from Bagnères to

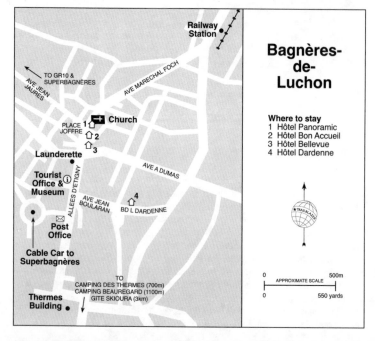

Railway Station

TO GR10 &
SUPERBAGNÈRES
AVE JEAN JAURES

AVE MARECHAL FOCH

PLACE JOFFRE 1 ✚ **Church**
2
3

Launderette

**Tourist Office &
Museum**

ALLEES D'ETIGNY

AVE JEAN BOULARAN

AVE A DUMAS

4
BD L DARDENNE

✉
Post Office

Cable Car to Superbagnères

TO
CAMPING DES THERMES (700m)
CAMPING BEAUREGARD (1100m)
GITE SKIOURA (3km)

Thermes Building

Bagnères-de-Luchon

Where to stay
1 Hôtel Panoramic
2 Hôtel Bon Accueil
3 Hôtel Bellevue
4 Hôtel Dardenne

★ TRAILBLAZER

0   500m
APPROXIMATE SCALE
0   550 yards

Toulouse via bus and train costs €18. For a **taxi**, try Farrus Voyages (☎ 05.61.79.06.78, ▤ 05.61.79.59.34) who are under contract to the British travel company Exodus; or you could try Jean-François Gerdessus (☎ 06.09.32.37.44).

Where to stay
There are plenty of places to stay in Luchon. Even during the annual Flower Festival which takes place at the end of August you'll probably find somewhere to stay, though it may be a little way out of town.

For a reasonably-priced middle-of-the-road hotel, the Belgian-run *Hôtel Panoramic* ☆☆ (☎ 05.61.79.30.90, ▤ hotel.pan oramic@wanadoo.fr) is very friendly and accustomed to walkers; the rooms are clean and pleasant if rather small. Charges are from €43.50 for B&B in a room with a shower. *Hôtel Bon Accueil* ☆☆ (☎ 05.61. 79.02.20, ▤ 05.61.79.76.83) is almost opposite the Panoramic and does B&B for €49.50 and demi-pension for €55.50. Reached through a busy pavement café is the centrally-located, no-frills *Hôtel Bellevue* ☆☆ (☎ 05.61.79.01.65, ▤ 05.61.79. 74.27 ▤ contact@hotel-luchon.com) where B&B costs €42.40 and demi-pension €50.

Further out from the centre (and consequently quieter) the *Hôtel Dardenne* ☆☆ (☎ 05.61.94.66.70, ▤ 05.61.79.62.00), near the casino, has good rooms from €35.

The nearest gîte is 3km south along the D125. The *Gîte Skioura* (☎ 05.61.79.60.59) specializes in taking groups but will also take individuals for a night. It's €15 in the dormitory and €28 for demi-pension.

The campsites are on the D125 leading south out of the town centre. Seven hundred metres from the centre is *Camping des Thermes* (☎ 05.61.79.03.85) which is rather crowded and 'residential'; it's €12 for two people and a tent.

Four hundred metres further on is *Camping Beauregard* ☆☆ (☎ 05.61.79. 30.74) which has more space and even a few real tents; it's €6 for emplacement and €6 per person with reasonable facilities.

What to see
At the southern end of the Allées d'Étigny is the imposing **Thermes building**, which was opened in 1848 on the site of the old Roman baths. Opposite the building is a statue of Baron d'Étigny himself. Unfortunately, the appearance of this central square has been spoiled by the ugly new Thermes building which stands next to its older counterpart. A visit to the **museum** is an option if you're on a rest day. It's open daily from 09.00 to 12.00 and 14.00-18.00 and houses a diverse and fascinating collection – everything from Roman masonry to old newspaper cuttings from the turn of the century. Entry is €2 per person.

BAGNÈRES-DE-LUCHON → FOS [MAP 40 p184, MAP 41, p185]

This stretch to Fos is a long one, and many people will prefer to break it up in some way, either by camping or spending a night in a cabane along the way. Alternatively some people hitch up the road to Artigue (or take a taxi: about €25) to save a lot of road walking.

Leaving Bagnères, walk north past the railway station on the avenue de Toulouse and 300 metres past the station cross the line via a small underpass.

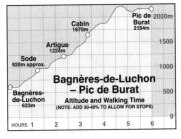

Turn left on the D125 heading out of town and after half a kilometre turn right at a roundabout towards **Juzet-de-Luchon**. Up to this point there have been few if any waymarks but they start again from here, marking the route through the

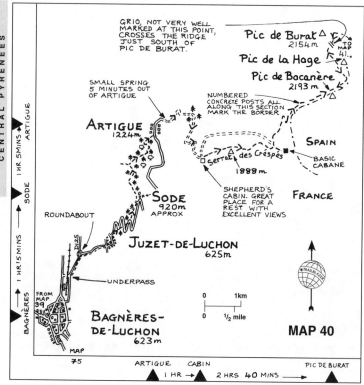

middle of the village. On the north side of Juzet the climb begins as the path heads uphill, cutting off the bends in places. After half an hour of steep climbing through woods you come to the tiny and slightly ramshackle hamlet of **Sode**. Follow the markers as the GR10 winds between the houses and take a wide, level path leading north-west out of the village. Soon the climb begins again and the path narrows considerably as it winds up through the woods. An hour and a quarter later you emerge at **Artigue (1224m)** a village with a truly ancient feel to it.

Although there is still a 500-metre climb above Artigue, it's fairly easy. Five minutes above the village there's a small spring which is a welcome chance to fill up with water. Beyond here the GR10 follows farm tracks that wind backwards and forwards across the open slopes. On a fine morning there's plenty to see: the hillside and village below are attractive and as a back drop there are the high peaks of the border. After about an hour the path reaches a small cabane just to the south-west of the **Serrat des Créspés (1888m)**, a series of deep, wooded ravines scouring the side of the hill. The hut is used by shepherds but you can take a break here and enjoy the view.

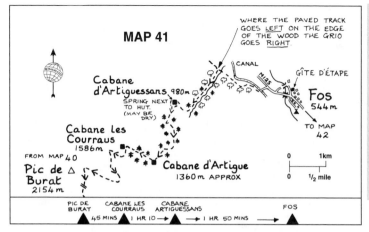

MAP 41

WHERE THE PAVED TRACK GOES LEFT ON THE EDGE OF THE WOOD THE GRIO GOES RIGHT.

CANAL

GÎTE D'ÉTAPE

Cabane d'Artiguessans 980m

SPRING NEXT TO HUT. (MAY BE DRY)

NIAS

Fos 544m

Cabane les Courraus 1586m

TO MAP 42

FROM MAP 40

Cabane d'Artigue 1360 m APPROX

Pic de Burat 2154m

0   1km

0   ½ mile

PIC DE BURAT	CABANE LES COURRAUS	CABANE ARTIGUESSANS	FOS
▲ 45 MINS →	1 HR 10 → ▲	→ 1 HR 50 MINS →	▲

Climb north-eastwards from the hut up the grassy hillside, passing to the north of the Serrat des Créspés. After half an hour you reach a plateau and some fifteen minutes later come to a tiny pond next to the track junction. (Just to the south-east of the junction there's a basic cabane that could sleep six people). Turn left and climb the hillside to the Col des Taons de Bacanère where there are the remains of an old building. From here the path follows the line of the border, passing a series of numbered marker stones en route and passing over the **Pic de Bacanère (2193m)**. The GR10 descends into a col via two more border markers then cuts back to the north-west before climbing again to cross the ridge running between the **Pic de la Hage** and the **Pic de Burat** near an area of rusty fencing. The way-marks are seriously lacking hereabouts and you have to be on your guard to avoid getting lost, particularly in the mist.

Descend on a small footpath which after 45 minutes reaches the *Cabane des Courraus* (**1586m**). The upper cabane can sleep about eight people and has a

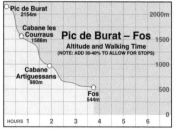

Pic de Burat 2154m

2000m

Cabane les Courraus 1586m

Pic de Burat – Fos
Altitude and Walking Time
(NOTE: ADD 30-40% TO ALLOW FOR STOPS)

1500

1000

Cabane Artiguessans 980m

Fos 544m

500

0

| HOURS | 1 | 2 | 3 | 4 | 5 | 6 |

fireplace, table and benches but it's not very clean; the lower cabane is bare inside but would provide emergency shelter if necessary. Twenty-five minutes below the cabanes is the *Cabane d'Artigue* which is quite clean though rather basic and could sleep four or five people. It's close to woods so firewood is easy to obtain. The descent continues through pine woods and after 5-10 minutes the path joins a rough road, only to leave it almost immediately down an overgrown footpath which cuts steeply down the hillside. The GR10 rejoins the loose-sur-faced road briefly before departing down a side track to the *Cabane d'Artiguessans* (**1025m**), a hut which is normally used by foresters. The spring beside the hut may be of more use to you than the hut itself although in a dry summer it may be no more than a trickle.

Near the cabane the route becomes a little difficult to locate; it runs from the south-east corner of the clearing below the hut. The path descends through trees to meet an ancient paved pathway which runs steeply down the hillside next to a rushing stream. Be careful of your footing here as the stones are extremely slippery – walking poles are a vital asset to help negotiate this section. At the bottom of the hill and just inside the edge of the wood, the GR10 leaves the paved way and turns south-eastwards. A sign here (FOS 45 MINUTES) points the way. The path through the rough woodland is poorly waymarked but leads at last and rather unexpectedly to a canal with a broad towpath. Turn right and follow the towpath to the first bridge. Cross it and soon after the track joins the busy road, the N125. Turn right along the road for a few hundred yards then cross the road to take a left-hand side road which leads between houses, crosses the river, goes right and heads with the help of small signs to the *Gîte de Fos* (see below).

FOS
✉ code 31440

There are several places to stay in Fos, although it's far from what might be called an exciting village but there's a nice gîte d'étape, *Gîte de Fos* (☎ 05.61.94.98.59). If you have problems getting through, the mobile number for Philippe, the owner, is ☎ 06.80.57.02.31. The rate is €30 for demi-pension, with the meals simple but adequate. There are self-catering facilities and you can get a beer.

Hôtel Gentilhommière (☎ 05.61.79.59.41), on the main road through the village, has rooms from €22 for B&B or €35 for demi-pension. There's a bar/restaurant here but it's closed on Sunday evenings and

all day Monday. *Camping Municipal de Fos* (☎ 05.61.79.29.28) is a pleasant site and good value – emplacement is €2.50 and it's €2.50 per person. In mid-summer it's best to book in advance. It's next to the Mairie so you could try ringing the mayor (☎ 05 61.79.41.61).

There is a **boulangerie/charcuterie** on the main road, at the south-eastern end of the village and an **exhibition centre** dedicated to the bear, greatly revered locally although the chances of seeing one are nil. It's a bit like having a centre devoted to wolves in Ambleside.

FOS → REFUGE DE L'ÉTANG D'ARAING　　　　　[MAP 42]

It will probably be too far for many walkers to complete the crossing to Eylie in a single day; it's better to take two days and book ahead for a night at the Refuge de l'Étang d'Araing.

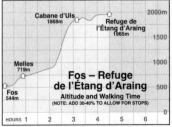

Follow the main road through the village to the bridge where a left-hand fork points to **Melles**. The GR10 sticks to the road, winding uphill without short cuts. Nobody would blame you for hitching this stretch but it would be a pity to miss the *Auberge de Crabère*

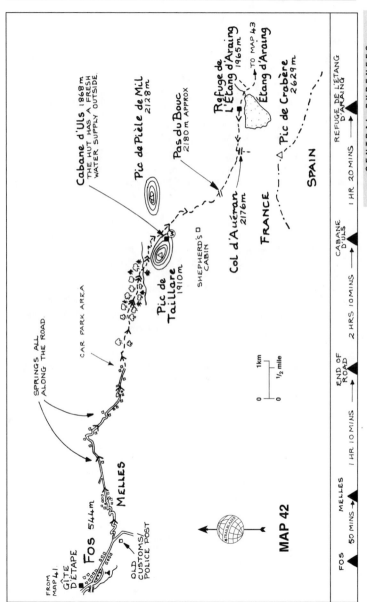

CENTRAL PYRENEES

MAP 42

FROM MAP 41.
GÎTE D'ÉTAPE
Fos 544m
OLD CUSTOMS/
POLICE POST

MELLES

SPRINGS ALL
ALONG THE ROAD.

CAR PARK AREA

Cabane d'Uls 1868m
THE HUT HAS A FRESH
WATER SUPPLY OUTSIDE.

Pic de Pièle de Mil
2128m

Pic de Taillare
1910m

SHEPHERD'S
CABIN

Pas du Bouc
2180m APPROX

Col d'Auéran
2176m

FRANCE

SPAIN

Pic de Crabère
2629m

Refuge de
l'Étang d'Araing
1965m

Étang d'Araing

TO MAP 43

REFUGE DE L'ÉTANG
D'ARAING

0   1km
0   ½ mile

FOS   MELLES   END OF   CABANE   REFUGE DE
                         ROAD   D'ULS   L'ÉTANG
                                                     D'ARAING
    50 MINS   1 HR. 10 MINS   2 HRS. 10 MINS   1 HR. 20 MINS

Bears in the Pyrenees

Until the turn of the 20th century bear hunting was a popular sport. Some of the hunters have even passed into Pyrenean folklore: it is said that one Bonnecaze of Laruns, who died in 1860, had killed 55 of the animals. Overhunting combined with deforestation saw to it that by the 1950s and 1960s numbers were so depleted as to make the recovery of the Pyrenean brown bear almost impossible.

In 1996, therefore, under a scheme to rescue the species, two female Slovenian brown bears were released into the wild above Melles. The experiment was fiercely opposed by many people whose criticisms appeared, at first, to have been justified when the bears ambled over the mountains and began slaughtering sheep in the Aran valley. Better times seemed to be ahead, when one of the bears, nicknamed Melba, produced three cubs. However, the project was dealt a crushing blow in September 1997 when Melba was shot by a hunter. There was even worse news in November 2004 when hunters in the Aspe valley killed the last native female brown bear. Among the remaining 18 bears in the Pyrenees, only two are indigenous.

(☎ 05.61.79.21.99, ✉ patrick.beauchet@wanadoo.fr) in Melles. The chef/owner is something of a celebrity and has written books about cooking; there's a range of interesting menus. If you're staying here demi-pension is €31. Out of high season they are closed on Tuesday and Wednesday.

Continue up the tarmac lane from Melles for a further 4km, always climbing but on a gentle gradient. There are springs at regular intervals and even seats. Near the end of the road is a perturbing sign which reads RANDONNEURS ATTENTION! ZONE FREQUENTÉE PAR L'OURS ... EVITEZ DE VOUS DEPLACER SEUL. NE QUITTEZ PAS LES SENTIERS BALISÉS. Your chances of seeing a bear are practically nil but it concentrates the mind.

Just past the sign is a car park. Take the concreted access track to the left (there's a sign, SAUF RIVERAINS – 'Residents only'); the lane leads just a few hundred metres to some houses where the footpath begins. The walk up to the Cabane d'Uls is very pretty but extremely hard work, with around 1000m of ascent in the space of three and a half kilometres. The trail is well waymarked and needs little description. The initial part of the climb is through woods but after crossing a stream midway the path ascends over open slopes. This area has duckboards in places over the boggier areas. Finally, after climbing the steep eastern end of the valley, the path begins to level out. After ten more minutes across grass you come to the *Cabane d'Uls* (1868m). The hut is cleanish and can sleep nine. It has a table and benches and there is a spring round the back.

From the cabane, climb south-eastwards over a small grassy col and into a much larger bowl formed by the hill tops. There's a shepherds' hut over to the right but the GR10 passes well to the east of it and it's not worth the diversion. Follow the path round the edge of the depression and then contour round the hillside to a grassy col, the **Pas du Bouc (2170m)**. Continue contouring around the side of the hill for a further quarter of an hour on a level path before arriving at the **Col d'Auéran (2176m)** where an impressive array of signs has sprouted like a man-made tree in the wilderness. The col marks the border between the Haute Garonne and the Ariège Pyrenées; to the south, the mighty **Pic de Crabère** marks the border with Spain. Climb northwards briefly and then head east down the spur to the refuge which appears below – unless you are in mist. The ***Refuge de l'Etang d'Araing*** (☎ 05.61.96.73.73, 🖥 http://refu ge-araing.apinc.org) is a modern, corrugated-tin building that looks out of place in this setting. There is a guardian in residence from mid-June to the end of September and at weekends in May, early June and October, and there's a small section which remains open for basic accommodation throughout the year. Accommodation in dormitories costs €13.50, plus €5.50 for breakfast and €13 for a mea (with vegetarian option). There is one shower for which you'll pay an extra €3 and the loos are the long-drop type. The place has a slightly authori-tarian air with rules posted up; you can't take your rucksack into the dormitory. It's a busy place and after the meal everyone retires for the night, leaving you to grope around in the darkness. If you order ahead they will get in Camping Gaz for you to pick up when you arrive.

REFUGE DE L'ÉTANG D'ARAING → EYLIE   [MAP 43, p190]

This section is shorter than usual and not unwelcome after the previous day's exertions. You should arrive in Eylie by early afternoon which will give you time for some washing of clothes and for planning how you are going to tackle the next section, which offers scant accommodation and no food.

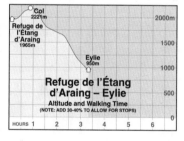

Refuge de l'Étang
d'Araing – Eylie
Altitude and Walking Time
(NOTE: ADD 30-40% TO ALLOW FOR STOPS)

Make for the barrage, cross below it and turn right (the path for the Tour de Biros goes left). As the path starts to climb you pass an empty refuge; it's pretty spartan inside but adequate for a night if you don't want to stay in the staffed refuge. Continue past some old mines and after about 45 minutes of climbing south-eastwards you reach a col (2221m) over the Serre d'Araing.

The path skirts a rocky outcrop and descends into the valley. After three quarters of an hour you reach the old mines at **Bentaillou**, and old workings are encountered for the next half hour or more. Above the main mine buildings a memorial stone commemorates three electricity workers who died here in 1960. The final descent to Eylie from here is through woods on steep tracks until the path brings you out at some houses.

A little bridge crosses the stream and signs point along a path that wends up to the houses where the guardian of the gîte lives. The GR10 runs right past the ***Gîte d'étape d'Eylie*** (☎/🖥 05.61.96.14.00). It's a well-run establishment, clean, tidy and has everything you need including a kitchen and good showers. There are two dormitories with ten places in each. Meals are taken at the house on a delightful terrace where you can spot the izards on the slopes opposite with binoculars. The couple who run the gîte are excellent hosts and you'll be

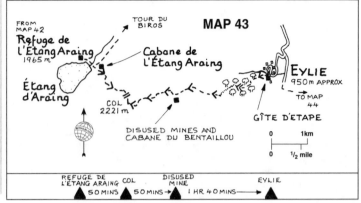

CENTRAL PYRENEES

FROM MAP 42
Refuge de l'Etang Araing 1965 m

TOUR DU BIROS

Cabane de l'Étang Araing

MAP 43

Étang d'Araing

EYLIE
950m APPROX

COL 2221 m

TO MAP 44

DISUSED MINES AND CABANE DU BENTAILLOU

GÎTE D'ETAPE

0   1km

0   ½ mile

REFUGE DE L'ÉTANG ARAING ▲ COL ▲ DISUSED MINE ▲ EYLIE ▲
50 MINS → 50 MINS → 1 HR 40 MINS →

assured of a great meal here. Accommodation costs €12 for the night, €27.50 for demi-pension and you can get a superb packed lunch for €5. Eylie has no other services except a telephone box 20 minutes down the road. A provisions van stops at Eylie between 2pm and about 2.30pm, announcing its presence with its horn and you might be lucky enough to pick up bread and possibly sausage or ham.

EYLIE → CABANE DU CLOT DU LAC → CABANE D'AOUEN [MAP 44]

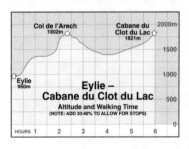

Col de l'Arech 1802m
Cabane du Clot du Lac 1821m
2000m
1500
1000
Eylie 950m
Eylie – Cabane du Clot du Lac
Altitude and Walking Time
(NOTE: ADD 30-40% TO ALLOW FOR STOPS)
500
0
HOURS 1   2   3   4   5   6

This section does not have anywhere other than the Cabane d'Aouen to spend the night. (There is an alternative offered by the GR10E variant, see pp192-3, which would give you a night's accommodation at the gîte at Bonac). If you are carrying a tent you will be all right, of course, provided you can obtain supplies from the guardian of the Eylie gîte. Turn right outside the door of the gîte and follow the narrow path that winds down to cross the river at a footbridge. The GR10 is signposted to the Col de l'Arech and climbs steadily, passing through a gate then following a stream until the path levels out, contouring through bee-heavy heather – a lovely morning's walk. In August the myrtilles (bilberries) will be in profusion. A stone hut is reached, unsuitable for anything but sheltering in bad weather, followed by a cluster of signs including one for the GR10E leading away left for Bonac.

For the main route, ignore this and go right, following the path towards the Rau de Laspe. Climb beside the stream for a few metres then cross it and make

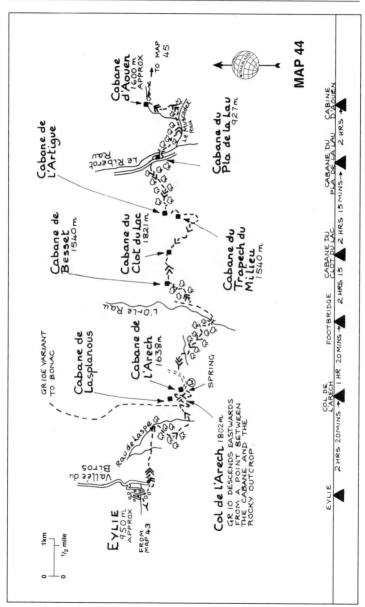

MAP 44

directly for the **Col de l'Arech (1802m)**. Once at the ridge, turn north along it towards the *Cabane de Lasplanous*. The GR10 descends from the ridge just south of the cabane, midway between the building and the rocky promontory which dominates the col. The descent to the Cabane L'Arech, accomplished in two long sweeps across the hillside, takes 20 minutes. The *Cabane L'Arech* (1638m) is a small hut with a sign outside stating that walkers can stay here only if it's not in use by shepherds. There's a spring a few metres south of the cabane.

Follow the track which leads down from the cabane and, after about 10 minutes, turn right down a tiny footpath which descends through the heather. After some minutes the path swings to the right and heads into the gully. Cross the stream, the Rau de L'Arech, and descend south-east through mature beech woods. Eventually you reach the valley bottom and the footbridge over the stream.

Cross the footbridge and go north for about 15 minutes along a level path to a wooden sign pointing the way uphill. The footpath climbs across a meadow

---

THE GR10E VARIANT
Stage 1: Eylie → Bonac

The first part of this walk is the same as the regular GR10, and is described on p190. The cluster of signs by the stone hut includes one for the GR10E variant, pointing away left for Bonac. Take this path which contours round the hillside above some old mine workings, and continue on a level path past an area of uprooted trees, the trail well marked with the red-and-white balisés. Pass through beech woods then out onto the open fell to the **Col des Cassaings (1495m)** where there is a stone hut right under the power lines. It is small but has pine benches and table and a sleeping platform on the upper deck sufficient for five.

The path continues north, negotiating a narrow ledge high above a ravine before contouring round the hillside then crossing a boggy section which has had duckboards installed for the convenience of walkers. A dense area of bracken is passed through before beech woods are encountered again, the ground thickly carpeted with old leaves. There are some undulations to the path.

The path circumvents a rocky outcrop via a series of steps then begins a long descent through beech woods on a well waymarked trail. Through the trees to the west is the Valley du Biros and the village of Rozes. After passing two barns, neither suitable for sleeping in, you come to a sign pointing the way to Bonac. A stony, narrow path continues down the hillside, passing derelict buildings to meet a broad track above a lake. Follow the track and the trees open out to a recreation area used by motor homes and fishermen. Turn right over the river, pass a washing station and cross the road. The gîte is opposite the church. This is the *Relais Montagnard* (☎ 05.61.04 .97.57) where the accommodation is clean and orderly if a little eccentric. Demi-pension is €35. There are no kitchen facilities but the food's good. The proximity of the church is no problem since the clock does not chime between 10pm and 8am.

Bonac doesn't have a shop so it would be as well to ask them to do a packed lunch (*un picnic*) for the day's march.

The next gîte (Gîte d'étape de la Bouche) is two and a half hours away at Tournac as a sign on the bridge indicates, so if you have anything left in your legs it is really worth considering carrying on if only to reduce the next day's considerable distance.

and enters the trees, making a steady ascent. Eventually it passes through the upper treeline and rises over grassy slopes to the *Cabane de Besset* (1540m). The tiny hut is in excellent condition, immaculately clean, with plates and cutlery and a saw for cutting wood. The view from the front of the hut is superb and there's a spring a few metres from the door. At a real push it could sleep four or five.

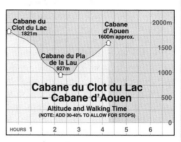

Forty minutes' more climbing up steep grassy slopes brings you to the *Cabane du Clot du Lac* (1821m), which is very basic and could sleep only two people. There appears to be no water supply nearby. On the way down from the cabane, the *Cabane du*

🐐 THE GR10E VARIANT
Stage 2: Bonac → Esbints

Leaving the gîte, go north past the municipal shelter between houses to a narrow path that climbs beside a stream to a sign pointing to Balacet. The sunken path rises to meet a larger track and continues through beech trees. Go right when you meet another track to meet the D704, which you keep to through the villages of **Balacet** and **Uchentein**, neither of which has any facilities. Leaving the villages, you turn off the road at a sign on the left pointing to Bordes, following a good path in an easterly direction which forks right and then descends more steeply. You meet and cross over a lane, and meet a second lane at a bend, with a sign telling us that Bonac is two hours away. Cross a bridge to enter the village of **Bordes-sur-Lez**. There's a gîte d'étape at Tournac, a short way away: *Gîte d'étape de la Bouche* (☎ 05.61.04.72.12) has 20 places, where demi-pension costs €35. This is a delightful spot with a quiet garden and a swimming pool. The trail from Bordes-sur-Lez is a little confusing but the waymarks are faithful and there to be followed if you're careful. Cross the bridge in the village and turn right up a lane to where a path on the right points to La Bouche (the gîte d'étape). Cross a stream and climb up the other side, keeping right at the top then left, climbing through steep woodland. Cross a fast watercourse by a concrete building and go left along the watercourse to meet a road. The gîte d'étape is opposite.

The path goes right in front of the gîte and enters woods, generally following the line of the watercourse although leaving it at times as the path meanders. Crossing a road by a house, turn back left up a bank and then steeply down to level out through woods and rejoin the watercourse, the walking thankfully dead level along the concrete edge. To the north-east you can clearly see the village of Ayet in the lovely Vallée de Bethmale. The path meets a T-junction with Ayet to the left. Turn right up a cart track that climbs and loses height at times but maintains a south-easterly direction towards Lac de Bethmale. In a further hour you come to a road busy with day trippers and a sign pointing left, LAC 1050M. At a small lake go right and follow the forest trail to the warden's cabin where there's a tap for drinking water and an open-sided shelter where you could spend the night in an emergency. The **Étang de Bethmale** is likely to be thronged with picnickers during August.

The variant rejoins the main GR10 here. See p194 for details of the path from here.

Trapech du Milieu (1540m) soon becomes visible below. Getting to it takes some time, however, as the GR10 makes a long detour to the south-east, almost to the banks of the stream, before it turns back northwards towards the cabane. The hut is dark and dirty; it could take four or five people. There's a spring just behind the building. Twenty-five minutes further down the hill is the *Cabane de l'Artigue* which is smaller and in no better condition; two or three people at most could fit into this one. From here, descend alongside the stream, Le Trapech Rau, through woods to the bottom of the valley. The area is a popular picnic spot so it may be packed with cars. Passing quickly through the mêlée, turn south-east along the river, Le Riberot Rau, to the *Cabane du Pla de la Lau* (927m). The location is excellent but the hut is not one of the best. The ugly concrete building has three rooms, two of which are suitable for sleeping in. One of these could take two people and the other could sleep four.

Cross the footbridge near the cabane and follow the river south-eastwards up the valley before turning eastwards along the bank of its tributary, Le Muscadet Rau. The path climbs through trees, alongside the waterfalls and white water of the Muscadet: it's a very attractive scene. The path finally leads away from the river and the trees and heads up the valley of the Rau d'Aouen. After some further steep climbing, you reach the *Cabane d'Aouen* (1600m approx). It's an ugly but functional hut, newly made out of concrete breeze blocks. The smaller room is left unlocked, and there's space here for only two people. There's a water supply via a hosepipe but a little investigation showed that the source was actually open to contamination in an area heavily grazed by sheep. You should purify the water before drinking it.

CABANE D'AOUEN → SEIX [MAP 45]

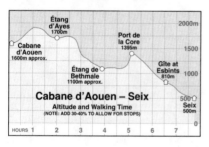

From the Cabane d'Aouen, climb to a wooden signpost just below the top of the ridge. Follow the level path north-west across the hillside, which soon brings you to the **Tuc de Lazies** (near spot height 1883m on the map). The GR10 heads due east from the col, losing a little height and then rising again to pass just to the north-east of the **Pic de Crabère**. The **Étang d'Ayes**, visible below, is reached after about 25 minutes. Go north-east from the lake along the hillside and climb slightly to the **Col d'Auédole** (1730m), below which is the *Cabane du Clot d'Eliet*. The cabane is very basic and dirty, but could sleep about five people if necessary.

At this point there's a choice. The GR10 proper descends north-westwards and makes a loop via the **Étang de Bethmale**, an attractive lake which is popular with picnickers. The variant heads almost directly east, retaining its height and passing across rocky terrain before reaching the Port de la Core. A notice at

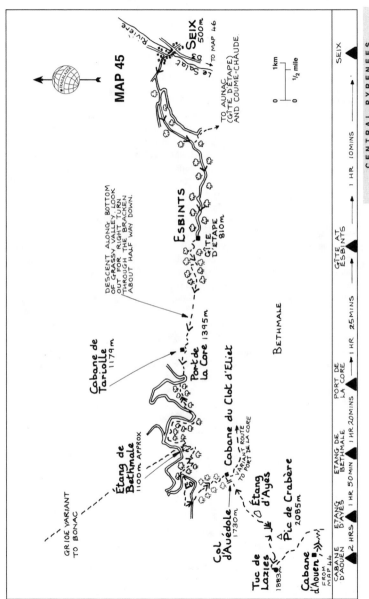

MAP 45

GR 10E VARIANT
TO BONAC

Étang de
Bethmale
1100 m APPROX

Col
d'Auédole
1730 m

Tuc de
Lazies
1883 m

Étang
d'Ayes

Pic de Crabère
2085 m

Cabane
d'Aouen
FROM
MAP 44

Cabane du Clot d'Eliet

VARIANT ROUTE
TO PORT DE LA CORE

Cabane de
Tariolle
1179 m

Port de
La Core
1395 m

BETHMALE

DESCENT ALONG BOTTOM
OF GRASSY VALLEY LOOK
OUT FOR RIGHT TURN
THROUGH THE BRACKEN
ABOUT HALF WAY DOWN.

ESBINTS

GÎTE
D'ÉTAPE
810 m

TO AUNAC
(GÎTE D'ÉTAPE)
AND COUME-CHAUDE.

Le Salat Rivière

SEIX
500 m

TO MAP 46

0   1km
0   ½ mile

CENTRAL PYRENEES

▲ CABANE D'AOUEN	▲ ÉTANG D'AYES	▲ ÉTANG DE BETHMALE	▲ PORT DE LA CORE	▲ GÎTE AT ESBINTS	▲ SEIX
2 HRS	1 HR 50 MIN	1 HR 20 MINS	1 HR 25 MINS	1 HR 10 MINS	

the Port de la Core warns walkers not to use this route in stormy or wet weather. The main GR10 goes steeply downhill through beech woods. It crosses a rough road and then leaves the trees briefly to make a long zigzag across the open hillside. After re-entering the woods it meets the road again and follows it to the right for a short distance before heading downhill to the left. The footpath leads down to the lake, emerging by the Refuge Forestier de Bethmale. The house is not for use by walkers but there's an *open-sided shelter* on the eastern edge of the lake which might be useful for cover from cloudbursts.

Take the footpath leading uphill beside the shelter; after four or five minutes it levels off and contours around the hillside, heading north at first and then swinging southwards. Finally it descends to join the road just below an area of heavy-duty steel netting, erected to catch boulders tumbling down the hillside. Follow the road for several minutes and then take the clearly signposted footpath to the right and climb through the woods to the **Port de la Core (1395m)**.

Leave the col on a clear path heading diagonally down the hillside in an easterly direction through bracken to the **Cabane de Tariolle (1179m)**, a large cleanish hut capable of sleeping 8-10 people with more below the sleeping platform. Descend the grassy slope on a well-marked path, looking out for a turning to the right some way below the cabane to arrive at the small *Gîte d'Esbints* (☎ 05.61.66.86.83, 🖥 gila.francischevillon@wanadoo.fr) run by the redoubtable Gila Chevillon and her son whom many walkers have had cause to bless. They are a mine of information and you can consult them about the trail. A fantastic place, perched on the hillside with farm animals snuffling about, the accommodation consists of one large dormitory with ten places, with a single flush toilet out back and two showers off the well-equipped kitchen downstairs. The meal is taken in the farmhouse round a communal table and the food is outstanding and the wine plentiful. A night's stay costs €10.50 and demi-pension €26. Gila will make you a packed lunch for €5 although the town of Seix is only about an hour downhill and you can get all the supplies you want there.

An alternative to staying at the gîte is to continue to **Aunac** and those walkers who intend missing Seix might consider doing this. The *Gîte La Souleille d'Aunac* (☎ 05.61.66.82.15. 🖥 pyreneesanes@free.fr) charges €13 for a night or €33 for demi-pension. The turning where you leave the road to follow the GR10 heads south-east towards Coume-Chaude, 25 minutes walk below Esbints. For Seix, stay on the road to a T-junction, turn right and walk down the hill into the town; continuing down the lane you'll come to Seix some three-quarters of an hour later.

SEIX

✉ code 09140

Seix is a charming town; a stopover here makes a pleasant change to life on the trail although it's a bit short on accommodation.

The *Auberge de Haut Salat* ☆ (☎ 05. 61.66.88.03, 🖥 www.ariege.com/haut-salat) on the central square is a friendly place; single rooms with shower and WC start at €25 and are comfortable and clean. Demi-pension costs €31. The restaurant is good value. The main hotel, the Mount-Vallier, was closed and for sale in August 2004. There are two campsites to the north of Seix, 1.5–2km from the town centre, the best of which is *Camping Le Haut-Salat* (☎ 05.61.66.81.78, 🖥 www.ariege.com

/campinghaut-salat). **Shops** include a mini-supermarket, a tabac and a boulangerie. The **tourist office** (☎ 05.61. 96.52.90) is on the central square, and the **post office** is just to the north-east. There is a **bank** but this tiny branch of Crédit Agricole has inconvenient opening hours: Monday 14.00-16.00 and Thursday 09.30-12.00 and 14.00-16.00. There's no cash dispenser. If you find yourself in need of cash at other times, remember that post office branches can change money or travellers' cheques.

There are two local **taxi** services (☎ 05.61. 66.81.79 or ☎ 05.61.66.86.10). These may be useful since to resume the GR10 entails some road walking which you may wish to avoid. This can be done by taking the taxi up to Couflens. It costs €17 or so.

SEIX → ROUZE

[MAP 46, p198; MAP 47, p199]

If you decide to rely on your feet, walk south from the centre of Seix on the D3 road to rejoin the GR10 near **Coume-Chaude**. Half a kilometre beyond the bridge, where the road bears sharply left, the GR10 goes right over a small bridge and along the lane past the hamlet of **Couflens de Betmajou** – not to be confused with the other Couflens. The lane is level initially but soon begins to climb and after a while the tarmac surface gives way to loose stones. Eventually the track comes to an end by a footbridge and a building. A sign CABANE D'AULA 3H points the way up a footpath.

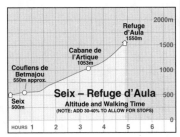

Seix – Refuge d'Aula
Altitude and Walking Time
(NOTE: ADD 30-40% TO ALLOW FOR STOPS)

Follow the footpath up the pretty, wooded valley. Twenty-five minutes beyond the sign there's a building which might do as a shelter in an emergency. An hour or so later the path leaves the trees, emerging into a huge open area near the **Cabane de l'Artigue (1053m)** which is kept locked.

From the cabane the path begins to climb more steeply, heading south-west towards the end of the valley and then ascending through the trees to reach a cirque, in the middle of which is the **Refuge d'Aula (1550m)**. The hut is large but fairly spartan inside and quite dirty; the first room has an upstairs large enough for two people while the second room has nine bunks and lots of extra floor space. Firewood can be found in the woods by retracing your steps a short way.

The GR10 zig-zags up the hillside south-east of the refuge to a col (1980m approx) on the far side of which it descends to the **Étang d'Areau**. The cabane next to the lake is private, as is the **Cabane d'Areau** which you pass lower down. Below this second building, the path briefly cuts down the grassy slope and then follows the rough road to the **Col de Pause (1527m)**. From the col, most of the descent to Couflens is along the road although the GR10 takes a few short cuts. Just west of Couflens is the **Camping Les Bourriès** (☎ 05.61.04

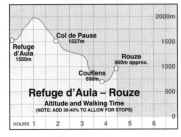

Refuge d'Aula – Rouze
Altitude and Walking Time
(NOTE: ADD 30-40% TO ALLOW FOR STOPS)

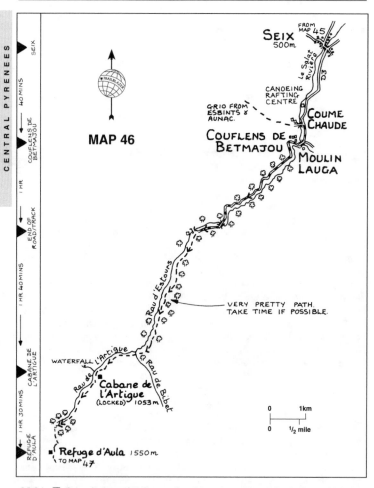

MAP 46

VERY PRETTY PATH.
TAKE TIME IF POSSIBLE.

Rau d'Estours

WATERFALL

Rau de l'Artigue

Rau de Bibet

Cabane de l'Artigue (LOCKED) 1053m

Refuge d'Aula 1550m
TO MAP 47

SEIX 500m

FROM MAP 45

Le Salat Rivière

D3

CANOEING RAFTING CENTRE

GR10 FROM ESBINTS & AUNAC.

COUME CHAUDE

COUFLENS DE BETMAJOU

MOULIN LAUGA

0 — 1km
0 — 1/2 mile

TRAILBLAZER

SEIX — 40 MINS
COUFLENS DE BETMAJOU — 1 HR
END OF ROAD/TRACK — 1 HR 40 MINS
CABANE DE L'ARTIGUE — 1 HR 30 MINS
REFUGE D'AULA

.85.84, ✉ fermelesbourries@wanadoo.fr), a *'camping à la ferme'* which has fairly basic facilities. The charge is €4.50 and they sell essential foodstuffs.

A kilometre further east along the lane is **Couflens**: there are no facilities here. Go north through the village and after about 400m there's a sign on the right by a small gate by a house pointing the way to the gîte at Rouze. Thirty-five minutes' climb beside the stream brings you to the *Gîte d'Etape de Rouze* (**969m**; ☎ 05.61.66.95.45, ✉ gîte.rouze@waika9.com). The gîte is in a separate building next to the farmhouse with superb views westwards towards the Col de Pause. Among the attractions here are the excellent home-made cheeses and a

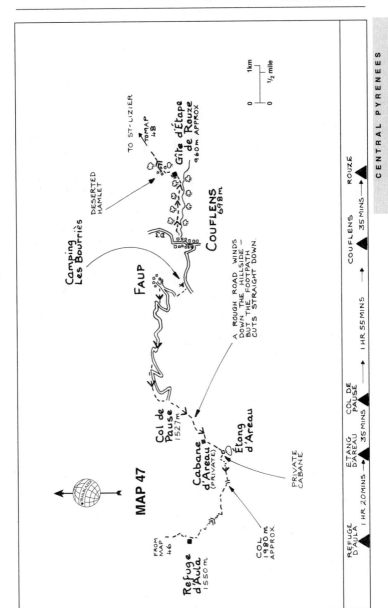

CENTRAL PYRENEES

MAP 47

FROM MAP 46

Refuge d'Aula 1550 m

COL 1980 m. APPROX.

Cabane d'Areau (PRIVATE)

Étang d'Areau

PRIVATE CABANE

Col de Pause 1527 m

A ROUGH ROAD WINDS
DOWN THE HILLSIDE —
BUT THE FOOTPATH
CUTS STRAIGHT DOWN.

Camping Les Bourriès

Faup

DESERTED HAMLET

COUFLENS 698 m

Gîte d'Étape de Rouze 960 m APPROX

TO ST-LIZIER

TO MAP 48

0   1km
0   ½ mile

REFUGE D'AULA		ÉTANG D'AREAU		COL DE PAUSE		COUFLENS		ROUZE
◀	1 HR 20MINS ▶	◀	35 MINS ▶	◀	1 HR 55 MINS ▶	◀	35 MINS ▶	◀

visit to the fromagerie is a must. The gîte has 14 places and charges €11 for the night or €29 for demi-pension. They do a packed lunch for €6. Even if you're just passing through you can still get a beer. There is a well-equipped kitchen area and an outside table under a lovely almond tree.

ROUZE → AULUS-LES-BAINS [MAP 48]

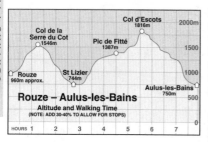

From the gîte, climb steeply on a sunken footpath through the woods, passing two deserted hamlets. It's a pretty stiff climb but also shady and you emerge from the trees just below the **Col de la Serre du Cot (1546m)**.

Two paths head away from the col in a north-easterly direction. Take the lower one which soon enters the woods and winds down the hillside to meet a vehicle track running along the valley floor. Turn left along the track and follow it as it winds its way down to the road where you go right for **St Lizier (744m)**. Walk into the village where the activity centres round the campsite and the public swimming pool. ***Camping Municipal d'Ustou*** (☎ 05.61.66.92.21, 🖳 www.ustou.info) charges rates of €2.37 per person and €2.84 per emplacement. The well-stocked shop sells camping gaz and Epigas. In the square is a bar with outside tables across the road from it but no accommodation.

The GR10 heads along the road going south and just past the last building turns left across an old footbridge. Almost immediately there's a track junction; turn right and follow a narrow path along the valley south to where the path up to Fitté departs to the left.

For **Bidous** carry on along the stream, passing a number of farm buildings to arrive at a bridge across the stream. Turn right across it and the gîte is opposite. The ***Gîte L'Escolan*** (☎ 05.61.96.58.72, 🖳 www.gite-ariege-pyrenees.com) is an old-fashioned building with swings in the garden for children and a busy, bustling air about it due to its popularity. It would be essential to book in the holiday season. In fine weather they lay the table outside and everyone eats together. The rooms are rather small, every inch of space being taken up with beds. Demi-pension in a dormitory is €32 and in a single room €35. It's open year-round. After the gîte, cross back over the bridge and re-trace your steps beside the stream to where a signpost points up right to the Col de Fitté.

The climb starts steeply and does not relent. All you can do is grit your teeth and keep going and you'll get there in the end, your efforts at last rewarded by emerging at the **Col de Fitté**. From the ridge, the modern ski resort of Guzet-Neige is clearly visible across the valley, disfiguring the hillside. Turn south-east for a couple of hundred metres to where the GR10 begins to climb again, striking directly up the next hill and passing by the base of a pole which stands

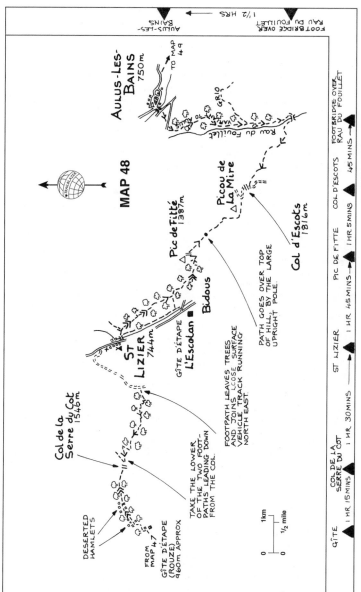

AULUS-LES-BAINS 1½ HRS
RAU DU FOUILLET
FOOTBRIDGE OVER

MAP 48

AULUS-LES-BAINS 750m

TO MAP 49

Rau du Fouillet

GRIO

Pic de Fitté 1387m

Picou de La Mire

Bidous

Col d'Escots 1816m

PATH GOES OVER TOP OF HILL, BY THE LARGE UPRIGHT POLE.

ST LIZIER 744m

GÎTE D'ÉTAPE L'Escolan

FOOTPATH LEAVES TREES AND JOINS LOOSE SURFACE VEHICLE TRACK RUNNING NORTH EAST.

Col de la Serre du Cot 1546m

TAKE THE LOWER OF THE TWO FOOT-PATHS LEADING DOWN FROM THE COL.

DESERTED HAMLETS

GÎTE D'ÉTAPE (ROUZE) 960m APPROX

FROM MAP 47

0   1km
0   ½ mile

GÎTE
COL DE LA SERRE DU COT — 1 HR 15 MINS
ST LIZIER — 1 HR 30 MINS
PIC DE FITTÉ — 1 HR 45 MINS
COL D'ESCOTS — 1 HR 5 MINS
FOOTBRIDGE OVER RAU DU FOUILLET — 45 MINS

on the top. In mist you might miss it. The path skirts round the south of the next hill, the Picou de la Mire and arrives among the skiing superstructure on the **Col d'Escots (1816m)**.

Immediately apparent among the jumble of signs and advertising boards is the **Restaurant d'Altitude** (☎ 05.61.04.96.08) where you can get meals, snacks or just a coffee or beer or both. It seems rather out of place but I bet skiers love it. Having sampled its hospitality or walked right on by, continue south-east across the hillside as the GR10 undulates, so much so that at times one feels as though one is gaining and not losing height. This feeling continues after crossing the footbridge over the Rau de Fouillet in a wonderful blind bowl among the hills where the path turns north and seems to maintain height, running parallel to the stream and passing numerous small waterfalls.

After about 45 minutes you reach a fork; those wanting to break their journey at **Aulus-les-Bains** take the left fork while the GR10 proper takes the right. For Aulus, the path descends through woods and meets the road twice and then a third and last time. Turn left and walk over the bridge into the main square of Aulus, where you'll find the tourist office directly in front of you.

AULUS-LES-BAINS
✉ code 09140

Aulus is a small town with enough facilities to make it tempting as a stopover although it somehow seems to promise more than it delivers. Like many holiday towns, it is thronged in the height of the season and dead the rest of the year.

The swankiest hotel is the **Hostellerie de la Terrasse** ☆☆☆ (☎ 05.61.96.00.98) where demi-pension costs €54. The riverside terrace looks nice and menu prices seem quite reasonable with plenty of local specialities but the general impression is that they are not in a hurry to take walkers during the main season. Hôtel de Beauséjour opposite was closed and for sale in August 2004. The other hotel option is the **Hôtel Les Oussailles** ☆☆ (☎ 05 61.96.03.68, 🖳 www.ariege.com/les-ous sailles) where single rooms start at €45.50.

There are two gîtes: the long-established and spooky **Gîte d'étape Le Presbytère** (☎ 05.61.96.02.21) in the centre of the village charges €12 for the night and €23 for demi-pension. Walkers praise the new showers and toilet and the food is said to be good. Better still is the newly-opened **La Goulue** (☎ 05.61.66.53.01) which is a model of its kind. Spotlessly clean, lovingly run in an extraordinary old building that used to be a dance-hall, the food is excel-

lent, the vegetables coming from the owners' own garden. A night's stay costs €12 and demi-pension a reasonable €32 including wine at the table. Full marks for La Goulue and long may they flourish. There's a pleasant restaurant/bar, **La Cascade**, beside the river just along from the Hostellerie de la Terrasse where a beer goes down well and the meals are of the pizza type but are tasty.

Also near the centre of the village is the **Camping le Couledous** ☆☆☆ (☎ 05. 61.96.02.26, 🖳 couledous@wanadoo.fr) which charges €3.10 per person and €3.10 for emplacement. Aulus also has a **tourist office** (☎ 05.61.96.01.79) a **mini-supermarket** and a **launderette** as well as a **paper shop/bookshop** with an exhaustive supply of maps and guides; it also sells Camping Gaz, stamps and telephone cards. There are also a **boulangerie** and an **épicerie** which open – and close – early. There is no ATM and no bank in Aulus, the nearest being in Seix 15km away.

A **bus service** operates between St Girons (nearest point for SNCF buses) and Aulus. The service, running three times a day, is operated by Cars Antras (☎ 05.61.66.08.87) and costs €4 one way. Taxis are going to be expensive since they have to come from Seix.

AULUS-LES-BAINS → MOUNICOU [MAP 49, p204]

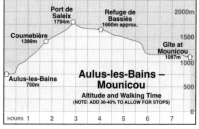

Those intent on walking to Mounicou are in for a day of about nine or ten hours including stops. An alternative would be to break the journey at the Refuge de Bassiès, quite a workable option if you'd prefer two short days

From the main square in Aulus go north-east along the street containing the Hôtel Les Oussailles and follow the road out of the village. Beyond the houses you come to a road junction where traffic coming from the town makes its way up to Coumebière which is where you are heading; so if you want to avoid the next hour and three quarter's trudge you could try hitching a lift. Failing that, cross the road and take the cart track opposite which before long joins the road again higher up. Cross the road and continue uphill on a wooded path; after a while it becomes less steep and follows along the hillside, still climbing.

After about three kilometres the GR10 emerges at a huge parking area known as **Coumebière (1399m)** where there is an interpretation board and a picnic table of bizarre design. People park here for the easy walk up to the **Port de Saleix (1794m)** tackled by families with young children and dogs. You're unlikely to be alone on this stretch during the holidays.

From the Port de Saleix col the GR10 turns right (due south) and climbs the steep slope, a half-hour of hard going until the path levels out at the plateau where the tiny lake, **Étang d'Alate**, is found, a lovely spot to have a picnic and bathe one's feet in the icy water. The path rises over a rocky area and at the top the view down to the **Étangs de Bassiès** presents a magnificent prospect. As you descend the narrow path you can make out the *Refuge de Bassiès* (1650m; ☎ 05.61.64.89.98) like an alien spaceship below you to the right, with a small pool beyond where people from the refuge go to bathe. A night's stay here costs €10.50, breakfast is €13 and demi-pension €28.50. Showers are an extra €2. If you're just passing through you can get coffee or a beer and they can do you a sandwich too. Like most of the refuges, it closes at the end of September.

The refuge is actually a few hundred metres off the GR10 trail which follows the lakes south-east on a rocky path along the northern side. The last lake has a dam from which point the path begins to descend, gradually at first, past the remnants of some old buildings before dropping more steeply for about an hour, passing two water sources and eventually arriving at a path junction. From here, Auzat is 45 minutes' walk to the north-east (signposted) while the GR10 turns right (south) for Marc and Mounicou.

This next section is almost like walking along the road since it follows a watercourse high above the valley for about three quarters of an hour. Just beyond, where it meets a water tower, the path joins the road. Turn left and stay

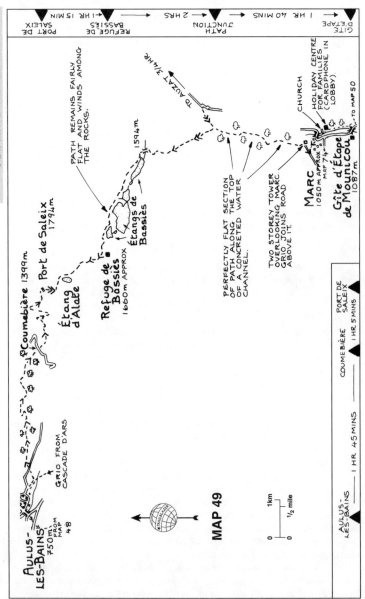

CENTRAL PYRENEES

MAP 49

GÎTE D'ÉTAPE ← 1 HR 40 MINS → PATH JUNCTION ← 2 HRS → REFUGE DE BASSIÈS ← 1 HR 15 MIN PORT DE SALEIX

PORT DE SALEIX 1794m

Coumebière 1399m

Étang d'Alate

Refuge de Bassiès 1660m APPROX

Étangs de Bassiès

1594m

PATH REMAINS FAIRLY FLAT AND WINDS AMONG THE ROCKS.

TO AUZAT 3¼ HR

PERFECTLY FLAT SECTION OF PATH ALONG THE TOP OF A CONCRETED WATER CHANNEL.

TWO STOREY TOWER OVERLOOKING MARC. GR10 JOINS ROAD ABOVE IT.

CHURCH

HOLIDAY CENTRE FOR FAMILIES (CARDPHONE IN LOBBY).

MARC 1050m APPROX MAP 74

TO MAP 50

Gîte d'Étape de Mounicou 1087m

AULUS-LES-BAINS 750M FROM MAP 48

GR10 FROM CASCADE D'ARS

1km
0

½ mile
0

AULUS-LES-BAINS —— 1 HR 45 MINS —— COUMEBIÈRE —— 1 HR 5 MINS —— PORT DE SALEIX

Auzat and Vicdessos

For those not continuing along the GR10, **Auzat**, a small town dominated by a huge factory, is seven kilometres down the road. Three kilometres beyond it is **Vicdessos**, which is much prettier, and which boasts a **tourist office** (☎ 05.61.64.87 .53), **bank** (Credit Agricole), **cash dispenser**, **pharmacy**, and a handful of **shops** and cafés. The nearest railway station is in Tarascon sur Ariège. According to the guardian of the Refuge du Pinet there is a daily bus from Marc to Tarascon which leaves Marc at 06.30, but it would be wise to confirm this with another source before dragging yourself out of bed at such an hour. Alternatively you could try to hitch a ride down to Auzat/Vicdessos, or you could phone a taxi (there's a pay phone in the holiday centre). For taxis, try **Transports Bernard Pujol** in Vicdessos (☎ 05.61.64.88.02).

Once you get to Vicdessos there's a daily **bus** service to Tarascon, which again leaves at a horribly early hour. A taxi from Vicdessos to Tarascon costs about €17.

on the road for a few minutes before leaving it at a footpath on the left which leads down to Marc. Down some steps to some houses you'll notice an advertisement announcing honey for sale. This is a private house which also does *accommodation* (☎ 05.61.64.83.86) and you may want to try them: it's the only other option to the gîte which is twenty minutes further away and rather eccentric.

If you have decided on the gîte, go down to the road and turn left, following the road down to the church before turning right up past a holiday centre. Indeed, Marc seems to be one large holiday centre; over a new footbridge on the right is a swimming pool but not for casual visitors as I was informed, rather sniffily. Continue on a rising path beside the stream to where a road bridge is reached. The *Gîte de Mounicou* (☎ 05.61.64.87.66) is run by Mme Eugénie Denjean who keeps the café, walkers being accommodated in a building through a passageway and up some steps from her house. You'll get a beer and wine but no meals are available at the gîte; a night here will cost €11. It's clean enough, has a well-equipped kitchen, the welcome is warm and the beer cold.

Some thought needs to be given here to providing for the next two days, foodwise. There are no shops in Marc or Mounicou and it would entail a hitch down the road to Auzat to visit a shop. The next night will be OK because there are two gîtes in Goulier but after that it will take two days to reach Mérens-les-Vals with nowhere to buy food.

MOUNICOU → GOULIER [MAP 50, p206]

Cross the river via the road bridge and walk a short way south along the lane. The GR10, signposted to the left, climbs steeply from the tarmac for about 35 minutes before levelling out and heading northwards. After a further 25 minutes you pass the hut at **Prunadière** (1600m approx), a reasonably large *shelter* with room for at least five or six people. There's a small (and possibly unreliable) water source next to the cabane. The GR10 continues almost level along the wooded hillside for

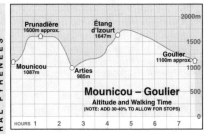

another 1500m before reaching the end of the spur and beginning to descend. At the bottom of the hill, the path passes straight through the hamlet of **Arties (985m)** to the road, where there is a tap with drinking water. Turn right (south) along the lane, and follow it as it climbs gently up from the valley bottom. After half an hour, next to some buildings you pass a sign, GOULIER 3H 30, pointing uphill to the east. Although the timing on this is questionable, this short cut, shown on the IGN map, appears worth considering if you're in a hurry. The climb is, however, particularly steep and exhausting, so if you're not in any great rush the longer route is more enjoyable.

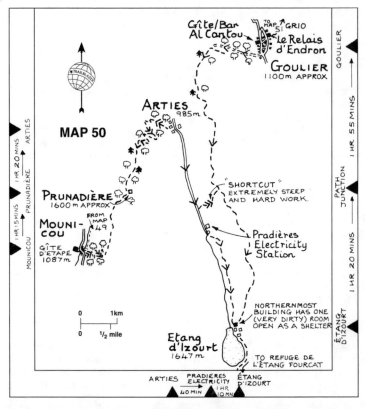

Ten minutes south of the sign, you come to the electricity installation at **Pradières**. Take the left fork, past the power station itself, and after about five minutes the lane doubles back to the left to a small parking area. From here the GR10, well signposted, continues as a footpath. It's about an hour's climb to the **Étang d'Izourt (1647m)** where there are a number of abandoned buildings at the northern end of the lake. The first building you come to has a large and very dirty room open as a shelter. The GR10 climbs very briefly and then settles into a long, gradual descent northwards. After an hour and twenty minutes you reach a path junction, at the top of the short cut mentioned earlier. Continue along the hillside, eventually rounding the spur to another junction, where you take the left-hand path. The footpath soon turns into a broad track which descends through the woods to the village of **Goulier (1100m)**.

GOULIER

Thoroughly recommended is the excellent *Gîte Al Cantou* (☎ 05.61.64.81.84, 🖥 al.ca ntou@wanadoo.fr). The gîte, which is in the centre of the village, is well laid out, with individual beds, good washing facilities and a well-equipped little kitchen. The warmth of the welcome is what really makes this place great, though. Demi-pension is €34 and there is a small bar on the ground floor. Just above the village is the other gîte, the modern *Relais d'Endron* (☎ 05.61. 03.87.72, 🖥 www.pyrenees-gites.com). It seems to be planned more as an activity centre, with lots of information about

what's on in the area. Accommodation is either in the gîte which has nine beds or in individual rooms. Demi-pension is €32 in the dormitory, or €36 in a private room. The night only in the dormitory is €12. There are no shops in Goulier.

Whichever gîte you choose, get them to make you up a packed lunch for the next day. Better still, see if you can get down to Vicdessos (see box p205) to stock up with money and food: you are going to need food tomorrow night since there is no access to a cooked meal until the Refuge de Rulhe, 45km away.

GOULIER → SIGUER → REFUGE LES CLARANS [MAP 51, p209]

This is best split into two days: the first a short day (four hours) from Goulier to Siguer but you're probably due for one after the last two long, hard days. Regrettably, there is no shop in

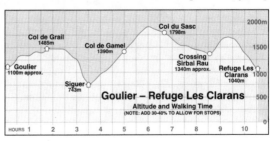

either Goulier or Siguer and supplies in your rucksack may be getting low unless you made a trip to Vicdessos (see box p205).

Goulier to Siguer From the Relais d'Endron, go up north-eastwards through the village and after a quarter of an hour the GR10 passes a spring. Just beyond this the route-marking needs careful attention as the trail makes its way up to the **Col de Risoul (1330m)** just south of the Pic de Risoul. Turn south-eastwards and follow a level footpath which runs just above a loose-surfaced road. After 25 minutes you reach a path junction where the GR10B variant runs off to the south-west while the GR10 main route goes north-east.

The track climbs slightly and crosses the **Col de l'Esquérus (1467m)** and then turns south-east along the hillside above a forest road. It soon descends and joins the road which it follows to the **Col de Grail (1485m)** where there is a *forester's hut* which walkers can use. It is tidy enough and has room for three and there is a water point here. Go along the track behind the hut for a minute or two before turning right on a level footpath which heads north-east. After about 35 minutes the path joins a broad track which leads to a tarmac lane. Follow the lane down to **Lercoul**; the GR10 goes through the village and continues on a footpath which descends steeply to **Siguer**.

Siguer has no accommodation other than the *Accueil Randonneur* which has been set aside for walkers to stay in for free. You cannot book and there are no cooking facilities. There is a toilet, wash basin and shower, six bunks and a table and chairs. The room is administered by the Mairie and if you need to ring to check on anything the telephone number is ☎ 05.61.05.65.45.

Siguer to Refuge les Clarans From Siguer, climb directly uphill east crossing the road twice to **Gesties (958m)**. There's a water fountain in the village but nothing else. Pass through the village and continue uphill, maintaining the easterly direction on a tiny, steep path which is not very well waymarked. It reaches the Col de Gamel (1390m) and continues to the Col du Sasc but the route is unclear and the faint path soon peters out in long grass and bracken. The direction is south-west and the easiest option is to keep close to the edge of the woods on your left as the GR10 runs along much the same line.

Provided it isn't misty you should soon see the triangulation point on the top of the **Pla de Montcamp (1904m)**; the GR10 passes over the top of this hill and descends south-south-eastwards. The waymarks come back in evidence here and every second rock is plastered with red and white paint as you head down to the shepherd's hut at the **Col du Sasc (1798m)**. This is the *Cabane du Besset d'en Haut* and has room for three if need be.

Go south-east around the top of a small valley and then follow the route-markings eastwards. The GR10 crosses a dirt road and descends past another shepherd's hut to the refuge of *Courtal Marti (1812m)*. This tiny shelter could accommodate two people at the most and is not a place to spend the night if you can help it. From Courtal Marti the path continues down through undergrowth into the small valley to the south, at the bottom of which is the *Cabane de Balleydreyt (1600m)* which is now a ruin. Cross the stream just below the cabin and follow it north-eastwards down into the wooded valley of the **Sirbal Rau**.

❏ **Walking times on trail maps**
Note that on all the trail maps in this book the times shown alongside each map refer only to time spent actually walking. Add 30-40% to allow for rest stops.

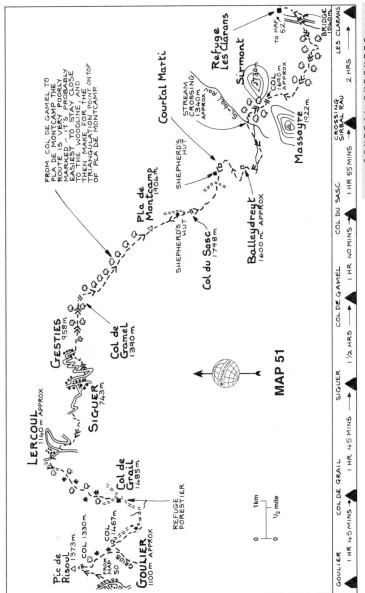

MAP 51

FROM COL DE GAMEL TO
PLA DE MONTCAMP THE
ROUTE IS VERY POORLY
MARKED — IT'S PROBABLY
EASIEST TO STAY CLOSE
TO THE WOODLINE, AND
THEN MAKE FOR THE
TRIANGULATION POINT ON TOP
OF PLA DE MONTCAMP

Refuge les Clarans

TO MAP 52

BRIDGE 1040m

Sirmont 1730m

COL 1600m APPROX

Massoure 1922m

STREAM CROSSING 1340m APPROX

Courtal Marti

SHEPHERD'S HUT

Balleydreyt 1600m APPROX

Pla de Montcamp 1904m

SHEPHERD'S HUT

Col du Sasc 1798m

SHEPHERD'S HUT

GESTIES 958m

Col de Gamel 1380m

LERCOUL 1140m APPROX

SIGUER 743m

Col de Grail 1485m

REFUGE FORESTIER

COL 1467m

COL 1330m

Pic de Risoul 1373m

GOULIER 1100m APPROX

FROM MAP 50

0   1km

0   ½ mile

GOULIER | COL DE GRAIL → | SIGUER → | COL DE GAMEL → | COL DU SASC → | CROSSING SIRBAL RAU | LES CLARANS
1 HR 45 MINS | 1 HR 45 MINS | 1½ HRS | 1 HR 40 MINS | 1 HR 55 MINS | 2 HRS

CENTRAL PYRENEES

From the stepping stones across the Rau, climb steeply through beech woods to the grassy col south of Sirmont. The path swings southwards, enters the woods and then makes a long and steep descent to reach the **road bridge** (1040m) over the **Aston Rau**. Cross the bridge and immediately turn left up a footpath which leads after five or ten minutes to a large clearing, on the north-west side of which is the *Refuge les Clarans* (1100m). There is room for four in the cabin and at a pinch the adjoining barn could also provide shelter. The road runs north to the village of Aston where there is a *campsite*.

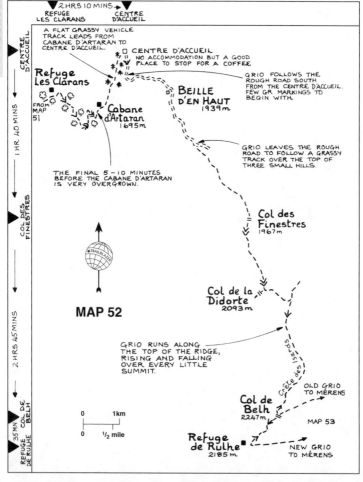

2 HRS 10 MINS →
REFUGE   CENTRE
LES CLARANS   D'ACCUEIL

A FLAT GRASSY VEHICLE
TRACK LEADS FROM
CABANE D'ARTARAN TO
CENTRE D'ACCUEIL.

CENTRE D'ACCUEIL
NO ACCOMMODATION BUT A GOOD
PLACE TO STOP FOR A COFFEE

GRIO FOLLOWS THE
ROUGH ROAD SOUTH
FROM THE CENTRE D'ACCUEIL.
FEW GR MARKINGS TO
BEGIN WITH.

Refuge
Les Clarans

BEILLE
D'EN HAUT
1939m

FROM
MAP
51

Cabane
d'Artaran
1695m

GRIO LEAVES THE ROUGH
ROAD TO FOLLOW A GRASSY
TRACK OVER THE TOP OF
THREE SMALL HILLS.

THE FINAL 5 – 10 MINUTES
BEFORE THE CABANE D'ARTARAN
IS VERY OVERGROWN.

Col des
Finestres
1967m

TRAILBLAZER

Col de la
Didorte
2093m

MAP 52

GRIO RUNS ALONG
THE TOP OF THE RIDGE,
RISING AND FALLING
OVER EVERY LITTLE
SUMMIT.

Crête des Isards

OLD GRIO
TO MÉRENS

Col de
Belh
2247m

MAP 53

0   1km
0   ½ mile

Refuge
de Rulhe
2185m

NEW GRIO
TO MÉRENS

1 HR. 40 MINS   COL DES FINESTRES   2 HRS 45 MINS   35 MN COL DE BELH   REFUGE DE RULHE

CENTRE D'ACCUEIL

REFUGE LES CLARANS → REFUGE DE RULHE [MAP 52]

Although both are named as refuges, the Refuge de Rulhe is a properly-run establishment with a guardian, meals, sleeping accommodation and beer, which will be something to look forward to after the rather cheerless hut which is the Refuge les Clarans. However, to guarantee that there is space, it would be wise to make a phone call and book a place.

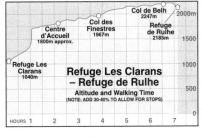

From the clearing by the refuge, follow an overgrown but clearly-marked path up the valley to the south-east. The gradient is initially fairly gentle but after about half an hour the path turns directly uphill and becomes much steeper. About 45 minutes later the path begins to level out and passes through an extremely overgrown area of head-high bushes. If it's been raining or there's a heavy dew, prepare to get soaked, as the needle-like leaves retain a lot of water. Some people seem to have a skin allergy to these plants which are known as *Cystisus scoparius*; struggling through them and getting wet could leave you scratching for the rest of the day so it would be wise to put on your waterproofs first. Just beyond the bushes you come to the ***Cabane d'Artaran*** (**1695m**). It's in good condition and has two rooms; the smaller one could sleep five while the larger room has a picnic table and could sleep three or four more if necessary. There is a water source available about ten minutes away to the north-east.

Walk north-north-east along a grassy vehicle track and after half an hour you'll reach the ***Centre d'Acceuil du Plateau de Beille***, a restaurant built for skiers although it remains open all year. There's no accommodation but it's a good place to stop for a coffee or a snack; opening hours are 09.30-18.00. The GR10 goes past the building and follows the prominent vehicle track southwards – markers are a bit scarce at this point but you just have to stick to the track. After half an hour you pass the **Cabane de Beille-d'en-Haut (1939m)** which has not been available for walkers for several years. After a further 25 minutes, where the vehicle track bears left, the GR10 continues south along a grassy track. Waymarking is rather widely spaced but the track takes you all the way to the **Col de Finestres (1967m)**.

Climb up the ridge to the south of the col and then descend slightly before climbing again past the **Col de la Didorte (2093m)**. From here, head south-east briefly and then south along the top of the ridge which leads to the Crête des Isards. This section is quite tiring as the path climbs and falls over every hummock. Eventually you reach the **Col de Belh (2247m)**. There's little to mark it except a sign pointing south-west towards the refuge which you reach after another half-hour of toil. The ***Refuge de Rulhe*** (2185m; ☎ 05.61.65.65.01, 🖳 www. rulhe.com) is a modern place with a capacity of 53 places in rooms of 2, 4, 5 and 6 beds plus a dormitory sleeping 10. Demi-pension is €27 or it's €10 for the night only. The grandly-named *assiette et panier du randonneur* (packed lunch to you) costs €8. A shower costs an extra €4. There's a guardian in residence from May to the end of September but out of season they keep part of the building open for use by walkers.

REFUGE DE RULHE → MÉRENS-LES-VALS [MAP 53]

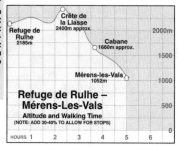

A yellow sign near the refuge building points the way onwards towards Mérens-les-Vals: MERENS 5H 30. Follow the GR10 waymarks eastwards towards the **Col des Calmettes (2318m)**. Keep on the left slope as the path passes over the left side of the col. Beyond the col the going becomes very slow as the GR10 passes north of the first small tarn then runs around the southern shore of the **Étang Bleu**, across an area of rocks and large boulders. The route indicated on older 1:50,000 IGN maps shows the GR10 passing north of the Étang Bleu but the southern shore is more direct. Finally, the path climbs very steeply up a grass track to the **Crête de la Lhasse (2439m)**.

Go east for a short distance before doubling back and descending into the valley to the south-east. Follow a clear path downhill passing above the **Étang de Comte** and into the valley bottom to the north-east of the lake. Here there is a tiny *cabane*; it has no door and the inside of the building is bare and dirty but it would serve as a temporary shelter. The level grassy area beside the Rau de Mourgouillou is popular with day-trippers and consequently the path down the valley to the north-east is well trodden. About half an hour beyond the cabane join an unsurfaced road leading down from a car park and a few minutes later take a footpath away from the road again. After a further 40 minutes you reach **Mérens-les-Vals (1052m)**.

MÉRENS-LES-VALS
✉ code 09580

Mérens makes an obvious starting or finishing point for a walk along part of the GR10, because of its easy access by rail; direct trains from Toulouse pass through en route to La-Tour-de-Carol. There are few facilities – there's a small **shop** on the main road and a **post office** (which doesn't change money). The *Gîte d'étape Le Soula* (☎ 05.61.64.32. 50, 🖹 05.61.64.02.75) is slightly above the village. Walkers rate it as one of the best along the GR10, partly for the clean and smart accommodation, but mostly for the

excellent food. It's €10.50 per night, €26.50 for demi-pension. You can camp for €2.70 per person and €1.90 per emplacement. The Hôtel/Bar Rouaix and the Auberge de Jeunesse, which is signposted from the road, are both now closed.

One kilometre south of the village is the *Camping Ville de Bau* (☎ 05.61.02. 85.40, 🖹 05.61.64.03.83), which has a small shop on site; the tariff is €2.40 per person and €2.50 for emplacement.

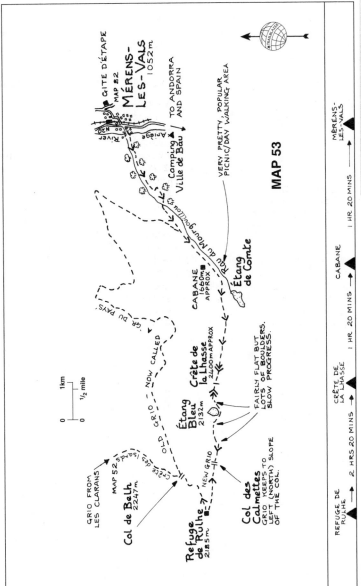

MAP 53

CENTRAL PYRENEES

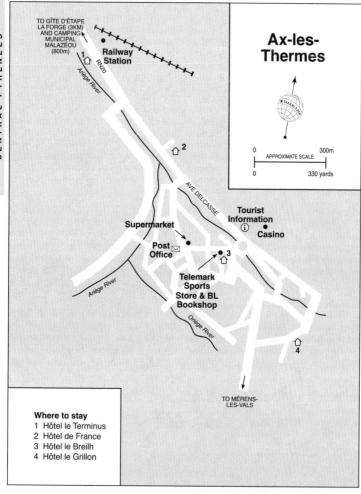

Where to stay
1 Hôtel le Terminus
2 Hôtel de France
3 Hôtel le Breilh
4 Hôtel le Grillon

AX-LES-THERMES

✉ code 09110

Ax-Les-Thermes is eight kilometres north of Mérens. Whereas Mérens has few facilities, Ax has plenty. It's a busy town seemingly choked with traffic in the season but away from the main thoroughfares it has a lot of charm. Known, like many Pyrenean towns, for its thermal springs, there's always plenty to see and it would make a good centre for touring the area and for winter sports. It is also ideal as the starting or finishing point if you are doing the GR10 in stages, being well served by trains from Toulouse.

Services

Ax has three **banks** with cash dispensers. **Shops** include two food stores, a good bookshop, pharmacy, photo shop and two newsagents. The **tourist office** (☎ 05.61.64.60.60, 💻 www.vallees-ax-com) is near the centre of town and the staff speak some English. **Telemark Sports** (💻 www.telemark-pyrenees.com), which sold Coleman Epigas, was up for sale in August 2004.

There are six **trains** a day between Mérens and Ax on the line to Tarascon and Toulouse. The journey takes about 15 minutes and costs €4.50 one way. There's also a night service to Paris Austerlitz leaving Ax at 21.30. There are also a couple of **buses** which depart from the bus stop opposite the shop. If all else fails, hitching the few kilometres down the road is easy.

Where to stay

Ax has plenty of reasonably-priced hotels. Most convenient for the station – since it's right opposite – is the *Hôtel Le Terminus* (☎ 05.61.64.20.55, 💻 contact@axhotelterminus.com) which promises '*chambres calme*' which they are, since they're situated mostly at the back away from the main road, looking out on the river. The rooms are reasonably comfortable and you'll pay €48 for demi-pension. The food's good too.

The best of the rest is the *Hôtel le Grillon* ☆☆ (☎ 05.61.64.31.64, 💻 www.hotel-le-grillon.com) which is slightly away from the bustle of the town centre; double rooms start at €44 for demi-pension or €42 for two people sharing a double room, plus €6.50 for breakfast. Similar in terms of price and standard, *Hôtel de France* ☆☆ (☎ 05.61.64.20.30, 💻 www.valleesax.com/html/partenaires/hdefrance/acceuil.htm) where the charges are €40 for demi-pension and €45 for two sharing; and the *Hôtel le Breilh* (☎ 05.61.64.24.29, 💻 www.ariegehotellebreilh.com), a friendly establishment with slightly-cramped accommodation. A room with breakfast costs €38 but there is no restaurant.

There is a gîte d'étape, *La Forge* (☎ 05.61.03.67.95, 🖹 05.61.03.68.09) at Ascou, 3km outside Ax. It has room for €40, a kitchen and decent showers and demi-pension costs €33 or it's €14 for a night in the dormitory without meals.

About one kilometre north-west of the station is the *Camping Municipal Malazéou* (☎ 05.61.64.69.14) where they charge €6 per person and €6 for emplacement.

Ax has practically wall-to-wall restaurants and cafés: pizza reigns supreme. Try *La Creperie* on the main square where they do a great omelette for €7.80.

Excursions around the GR10

CAUTERETS → REFUGE WALLON   [MAP 54, p217]

There are several options for the southern route out of Cauterets although the most direct route, along the avenue Demontzey, is occasionally closed because of the danger of rockfalls. An alternative route (marked on the 1:50,000 map) runs along the eastern side of the valley towards La Fruitière, while another option is simply to walk up the road to La Raillère. A fourth is to take the bus to Pont d'Espagne, and start walking from there: for bus details see the Cauterets section.

The route via avenue Demontzey is both the most pleasant and the quickest route and is therefore recommended but you should check that it is open before venturing onto the path. To get to the start of the avenue from the centre of town, walk up the steps just to the north-west of the swimming pool by the large blue house. There's a large modern sculpture of a bird halfway up, which is hard

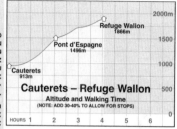

CENTRAL PYRENEES

Cauterets 913m

Pont d'Espagne 1496m

Refuge Wallon 1866m

2000m
1500m
1000m
500m
0

Cauterets – Refuge Wallon
Altitude and Walking Time
(NOTE: ADD 30-40% TO ALLOW FOR STOPS)

HOURS 1 2 3 4 5 6

to miss, and a yellow sign, LA RAILLÈRE 0H 40 & PONT D'ESPAGNE 2H 15, at the bottom. Above the steps, the path climbs the hillside in a few long gentle zigzags before heading off southwards. This shady 2km stretch of path, known as avenue Demontzey, is named after the Inspector General of Waters and Forests, Prosper Demontzey (1831-1898), who was responsible for a drive to replant huge areas of woodland in the Pyrenees.

At the end of the avenue go past a building which until recently housed the Thermes, and follow the road (the upper one, on your right) on to the tiny village of **La Raillère**. Just before the bridge over the river leading to the Centre du Rhumatologie is a yellow sign pointing to the right: CHEMIN DES CASCADES; PONT D'ESPAGNE 1H 30. From here the path, waymarked with those familiar red-and-white painted marks, climbs steadily for an hour and a half beside a series of impressive waterfalls to the **Pont d'Espagne (1496m)**. The area around the bridge is generally packed with people, and the most prominent building is the *Hôtellerie du Pont d'Espagne* (☎ 05.62.92.54.10) where food and drink are served, and rooms are available from €30. Follow the well-beaten trail a little beyond the waterfall and you'll arrive at the bottom of the *telesiège* (chair lift) de Gaube. For information on the route up to the Lac de Gaube, and the Refuge de Bayssellance beyond it, see p218.

Circuit des Lacs

According to the signs, the tour is supposed to take six and a half hours. If you leave your rucksack at Refuge Wallon (see p218) and carry only a light day pack, the walk can be accomplished in more like five hours. There are few route markers along the way, but the path is well trodden and would be hard to miss; at the two points where the path divides there are clear signs.

From the refuge go north-west, leaving the small **chapel** on your left. After climbing the rocky slope above Wallon for 20-25 minutes you come to the first track junction and sign. The climb continues for a further half hour or so until you reach **Lac Nère**. It's a desolate scene: clear blue water, bare rock and a chaos of boulders. Quarter of an hour beyond Lac Nère is the **Lac du Pourtet**, which is of a similar appearance. Throughout this part of the climb there are good views south and south-east towards Vignemale.

When almost at the northern end of the Lac du Pourtet, the path bears east, away from the lakeside and starts to descend steeply. From here the route is all downhill; halfway down, near the **Lacs de l'Embarrat**, you pass the junction with the path heading towards the **Lac d'Ilhéou**, and eventually after a steep and rocky descent you arrive at the **Gave du Marcadau**.

The return journey to Refuge Wallon takes about an hour and is as described above, in the main body of the text.

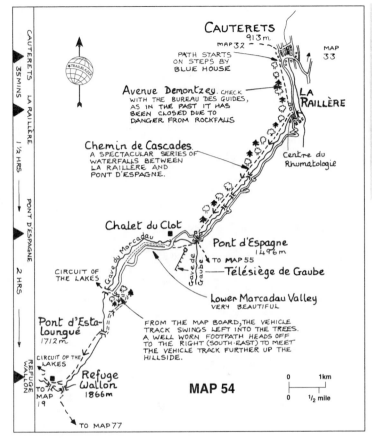

CAUTERETS
913m
MAP 32
MAP
33

PATH STARTS
ON STEPS BY
BLUE HOUSE

LA
RAILLÈRE

Avenue Demontzey. CHECK
WITH THE BUREAU DES GUIDES,
AS IN THE PAST IT HAS
BEEN CLOSED DUE TO
DANGER FROM ROCKFALLS

Chemin de Cascades
A SPECTACULAR SERIES OF
WATERFALLS BETWEEN
LA RAILLÈRE AND
PONT D'ESPAGNE.

Centre du
Rhumatologie

Chalet du Clot

Gave du Marcadau

Pont d'Espagne
1496m

TO MAP 55

Télésiège de Gaube

Gave de Gaube

CIRCUIT OF
THE LAKES

Lower Marcadau Valley
VERY BEAUTIFUL

Pont d'Esta-
loungué
1712m

FROM THE MAP BOARD, THE VEHICLE
TRACK SWINGS LEFT INTO THE TREES.
A WELL WORN FOOTPATH HEADS OFF
TO THE RIGHT (SOUTH-EAST) TO MEET
THE VEHICLE TRACK FURTHER UP THE
HILLSIDE.

CIRCUIT OF THE
LAKES

Refuge
Wallon
1866m

TO
MAP
19

MAP 54

0   1km
0   ½ mile

TO MAP 77

CAUTERETS 35 MINS LA RAILLÈRE 1½ HRS PONT D'ESPAGNE 2 HRS REFUGE WALLON

From here, two paths head up the Marcadau valley, on either bank of the Gave du Marcadau – it doesn't much matter which one you take. After only a few hundred metres you pass a building on the right. The ***Chalet du Clot*** (☎ 05. 62.92.61.27, 📠 05.62.92.07.93) is a bar/restaurant/refuge, with room for 40 people. Bed and breakfast costs €16 or it's €27 for demi-pension.

Beyond the Chalet, the Vallée du Marcadau is very pretty. After half an hour you reach a mapboard, and next to it a sign: CIRCUIT DES LACS 6H 30, REFUGE WALLON-MARCADAU 1H 30. Follow the vehicle track as it bends left into the trees, and just past a tiny parking area take a footpath to the right. This climbs a short way, before rejoining a large track to head south-west.

After 25 minutes you come to a footbridge, the **Pont d'Estaloungué (1712m)**, to the south of which is a large open area: the remains of a lake which has become silted up. The footpath onwards is unmistakable and after 50 minutes or so you reach the Refuge Wallon (1860m approx).

Refuge Wallon/Marcadau (☎ 05.62.92.64.28) is one of the largest refuges in the French Pyrenees. This area of the Pyrenees is very popular and Wallon, which is also known as Refuge Marcadau, can easily get booked out. In summer, with a guardian and several helpers it can take 115 people, and some die-hard mountain walkers complain that it's more of a hotel than a refuge. Summer accommodation is in a mixture of dormitories and private rooms. It costs €13.50 to stay the night in a dormitory, or €6.75 for CAF members, or there's a €2.50 per person supplement if you want a private room. The evening meal costs €14.70. Washing facilities consist of a few handbasins.

Next to the refuge is a tiny **chapel**, built in the 1960s. Every year on 5th August the chapel is the destination of a pilgrimage in memory of those who have been lost in the mountains.

CAUTERETS → REFUGE BAYSSELLANCE [MAP 55]

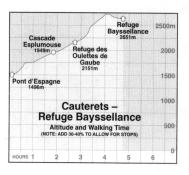

[Includes high section – see warning on pp19-20] From Cauterets to the Pont d'Espagne is as described in the section above. Once at the bridge, follow signs for the Lac de Gaube, and climb the well-trodden track up the eastern side of the Gave de Gaube. The rocky path climbs through an area of mature pine trees, and after three quarters of an hour, reaches the northern edge of the **Lac de Gaube (1725m)**. There's a *café/bar* (open beginning of June to the end of October).

Follow the path around the west side of the lake, and past a flat grassy area which is popular with picnickers. From here the trail starts to climb and soon passes the *Cabane du Pinet*, a bare hut which could sleep five or six people.

> **The English Couple**
> The Lac de Gaube became assured of a place in Pyrenean folklore when, in 1832, it was the scene of a much-publicized accident. The newly-wed Pattisons, out from England on their honeymoon, hired a rowing boat. Their brief excursion was to end in their deaths, drowned in the lake. This tragic event so caught the imagination of other visitors that a plethora of stories soon grew up. In one the couple had formed a suicide pact, in another the husband slipped overboard and his wife, failing to see him surface, chose to follow him. For several years the lake itself was an attraction because of the accident, rather than anything else.

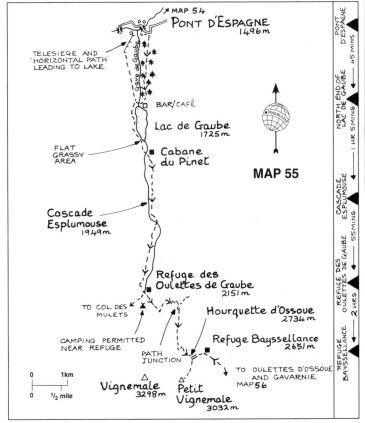

MAP 54
PONT D'ESPAGNE
1496m

TELESIEGE AND
'HORIZONTAL PATH'
LEADING TO LAKE.

BAR/CAFÉ

Lac de Gaube
1725m

Cabane
du Pinet

FLAT
GRASSY
AREA

Cascade
Esplumouse
1949m

MAP 55

Refuge des
Oulettes de Gaube
2151m

TO COL DES
MULETS

Hourquette d'Ossoue
2734m

CAMPING PERMITTED
NEAR REFUGE

Refuge Bayssellance
2651m

PATH
JUNCTION

TO OULETTES D'OSSOUE
AND GAVARNIE
MAP 56

0   1km
0   ½ mile

Vignemale
3298m

Petit
Vignemale
3032m

PONT D'ESPAGNE — 45 MINS
NORTH END OF LAC DE GAUBE — 1 HR 5 MINS
CASCADE ESPLUMOUSE — 55 MINS
REFUGE DES OULETTES DE GAUBE — 2 HRS
REFUGE BAYSSELLANCE

CENTRAL PYRENEES

Half an hour further up the hill is the **Cascade Esplumouse (1949m)**. Above the waterfall, the path continues to climb gradually for another fifty minutes or so to the refuge (2151m). The *Refuge des Oulettes de Gaube* (☎ 05.62.92.62.97) is situated at the base of Vignemale and has an excellent view of the mountain. Camping is possible on a large flat area below the building. Accommodation in the refuge costs €13.50 for the night, or €32.50 for demi-pension.

Near the refuge, a sign points the way onwards towards the Refuge Bayssellance: HOURQETTE D'OSSOUE 2H. Approximately three quarter of an hour's climb up the steep and rocky trail above the refuge, there's a path junction, and approximately fifty minutes beyond this you reach the **Hourquette d'Ossoue (2734m)**. In the mornings and early afternoons you may well find it crowded, as it's a popular excursion to climb from here to the top of Petit Vignemale (3032m).

The path up Petit Vignemale is not difficult and takes about half an hour. The *Refuge Bayssellance* (2651m) (☎ 05.62.92.40.25), a space-age-looking building, is visible just below the col and is only ten minutes' walk down the track; it has places for 58 people but gets booked out in mid-season. It's usually open from May to the end of September and at weekends in April and October is the weather allows. Accommodation in the refuge costs €17 for the night, or €35 for demi-pension.

REFUGE BAYSSELLANCE → GAVARNIE [MAP 56]

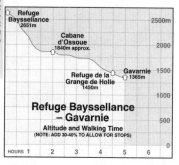

Refuge Bayssellance 2651m — 2500m
Cabane d'Ossoue 1840m approx. — 2000
Refuge de la Grange de Holle 1450m — Gavarnie 1365m — 1500
— 1000
Refuge Bayssellance – Gavarnie
Altitude and Walking Time
(NOTE: ADD 30-40% TO ALLOW FOR STOPS) — 500
HOURS 1 2 3 4 5 6 — 0

[Includes high section – see warning on pp19-20] The path descends rapidly from the refuge, with magnificent views. After twenty minutes you pass the **Grottes Bellevue**: three caves, hewn out of the rock, which have been extended with some brickwork.

After a further hour of descent you arrive at the western end of the plateau, the **Oulettes d'Ossoue**. Cross the stream by a small footbridge, and walk across the plateau for 30-35 minutes to arrive at the barrage, and the (often locked) *Cabane d'Ossoue* (1840m approx). According to the yellow sign next to the cabane it's two hours' walk to Gavarnie if you follow the rough road.

The GR10 crosses a small footbridge just below the barrage and comes to another sign: CABANE DE LOURDES 0H 30 & GAVARNIE 2H 45. Most of the walk from the barrage is very pleasant on an almost horizontal path along the hillside. The *Cabane de Lourdes* had one room open (space for four people) when I passed; the basic *Cabane de Saus Dessus* is thirty five minutes further along the way. Half an hour beyond this, the path begins a gradual descent and soon reaches the road.

Count Henry Russell (1834-1909)

Henry Killough Russell, born to an Irish father and French mother, is one of the great characters in Pyrenean history. After completing his studies, he embarked on a series of travels which even today seem impressive. He toured North America and lived with the Sioux Indians; he journeyed across Siberia from Moscow to Peking before the railway was built; he crossed the Gobi Desert and visited, among other countries, Japan and Australia. He eventually returned and settled in the Pyrenees, where he developed something of an obsession with Vignemale, the highest peak in the French Pyrenees (hence the title of the recent biography, *The Man who Married a Mountain*, see p31). In 1888 he succeeded in renting the Glacier d'Ossoue on a 99-year lease, and he subsequently had three caves carved in it, so that he could stay up on the mountain during the summer. His book *Souvenir d'un Montagnard* is one of the classic Pyrenean texts but is hard to come by nowadays.

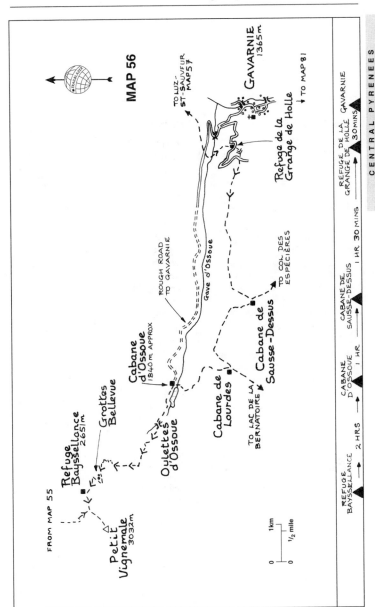

MAP 56

GAVARNIE
1365m.

TO LUZ-
ST-SAUVEUR MAP 57

TO MAP 81

Refuge de la
Grange de Holle

ROUGH ROAD
TO GAVARNIE

Gave d'Ossoue

TO COL DES
ESPÉCIÈRES

Cabane d'Ossoue
1840 m. APPROX

Cabane de
Sausse-Dessus

Cabane de
Lourdes

Oulettes
d'Ossoue

TO LAC DE LA
BERNATOIRE

Grottes
Bellevue

Refuge
Bayssellance
2651m.

Petit
Vignemale
3032m.

FROM MAP 55

0 _____ 1km
0 _____ ½ mile

CENTRAL PYRENEES

REFUGE
BAYSSELLANCE ──▶ 2 HRS

CABANE
D'OSSOUE ──▶ 1 HR

CABANE DE
SAUSSE-DESSUS ──▶ 1 HR. 30 MINS

REFUGE DE LA
GRANGE DE HOLLE ──▶ 30 MINS

GAVARNIE

The GR10 goes straight across the road and cuts down the hillside towards the *Refuge de la Grange de Holle* (☎ 05.62.92.48.77, 🖹 05.62.92.41.58). Accommodation in the refuge is €12.20 for the night, and €26.70 for demi-pension. The refuge (1450m) is an ideal place to stop if you're following the GR10 and aren't too bothered about not staying in Gavarnie itself, since the GR10 turns northwards from here avoiding the village altogether.

Twenty minutes' further down the road brings you into **Gavarnie** (1365m).

GAVARNIE

✉ code 65120

Gavarnie must be the best known village in the Pyrenees. The breathtaking cirque, with its soaring cliffs and the 423m waterfall has attracted visitors from around the world since the village first became accessible.

Today, Gavarnie is as popular as ever and hosts a drama festival in early summer with the cirque as the backdrop. It's a good place to start or finish a trip and has enough shops to make it worth a stop to stock up on supplies. Many people, however, will find the crowds, donkey rides and souvenir shops a little too much and will move on quickly.

The office of the Parc National des Pyrénées shares a building with the Mairie. There are a few exhibits and books, and the staff can answer questions. It's worth a visit just to see the stuffed vultures. The small church has 12th-century origins and a small wooden statue inside which pilgrims en route to Santiago de Compostela would sleep underneath in veneration. Nowadays, only tour buses of pilgrims to nearby Lourdes come to pay their respects, but the church is certainly worth looking at.

Services

There's no bank but the **post office** can change cash or travellers' cheques and has a cash machine outside. There's also a cash machine (not always accessible) next to the Mairie. The **tourist office** (☎ 05.62.92 49.10, 🖳 www.gavarnie.com) is now at the northern entrance to the village. They will call around the hotels if you need a room.

Shops in the village include a mini supermarket, boulangerie and newsagent. The supermarket sells some packed things individually, of great convenience for walkers, and will make you sandwiches to go. Two shops, La Cordée and the sports shop

opposite the supermarket, LaPorte, sell Coleman/Epigas, though you have to rummage behind the stuffed toys. The sports shop also sells Editorial Alpina maps of the Spanish Pyrenees. Near the campsite, at the southern end of the village is **CRS mountain rescue service** (☎ 05.62.92.48.24).

Buses run from the bus stop in front of the tourist office. Buses to Luz cost €5 and times vary according to season but the school bus continues to provide a service outside of peak season, on schooldays. From Luz there are regular buses to Lourdes, via Pierre-fitte-Nestalas where you can change for Cauterets.

Where to stay

The top hotel in Gavarnie is the *Grand Hôtel Vignemale* ☆☆☆ (☎ 05.62.92.40.00, 🖹 05.62.92.40.08, 🖳 www.hotel-vignemale.com), €97/154 for singles/doubles. The two-star hotels are fairly run of the mill, the largest and most successful being *Hôtel le Marboré* ☆☆ (☎ 05.62.92.40.40, 🖹 05.62.92.40.30) which has rooms from €52, and its own bar/pub, Le Swan, to make Brits feel at home. There are several other hotels prices lower than this, all of which are fine: *Hôtel Le Taillon* ☆☆ (☎ 05.62.92.48.20), *Hôtel L'Astazou* ☆☆ (☎ 05.62.92.48.07), *Hôtel des Cimes* ☆☆ (☎ 05.62 92.48.13) all charge around €35 for a double room. Worth a special mention is the *Compostelle Hôtel* ☆☆ (☎ 05.62.92.49.43), a friendly place run by Mme Laporte, where clean, pleasant double rooms start at €36. It's next to the church, so raised above the village a little and with nice views, though the beds are all very soft, which may or may not be what you like.

There are two gîtes. *Gîte Oxygène* (☎ 05.62.92.48.23) is a modern, soulless place with beds for €12, demi-pension €28. *Gîte Auberge La Gypaète* (☎ 05.62.92.40.61), behind and below the tourist office, does good business, with demi-pension for €23-26. All dorms have showers and toilets and in the cooler months, a log fire is usually burning. There are no self-catering facilities, but otherwise the place is fine.

Other options are the several chambres d'hôte in the village; they usually have an excellent atmosphere, though modern conveniences may be lacking. Mme Passet-Cumia, just over the road from the tourist office, has beautiful large rooms with windows on both sides and a balcony overlooking the river for €50, but you have to go downstairs to use the shared bathrooms. *La Chaumière*, the first or last business in the village, on the way out to the Cirque, has only two rooms but it's a good place to sit and look at the mountains and have a drink at the same time.

Camping La Bergerie (☎ 05.62.92.48.41) is run by the friendly Mme Sacaze and has a pleasant position next to the river. It costs €2 per person, and €1.80 per tent. The position is excellent, at the quiet end of the village with views towards the Cirque, but there is no shade if you fancy a rest day there. Meals are available in the little café/bar and a hot shower costs an extra €1.50.

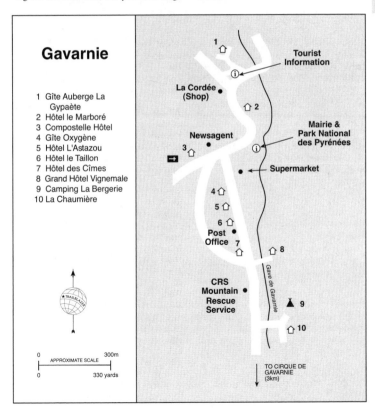

Gavarnie

1 Gîte Auberge La Gypaète
2 Hôtel le Marboré
3 Compostelle Hôtel
4 Gîte Oxygène
5 Hôtel L'Astazou
6 Hôtel le Taillon
7 Hôtel des Cîmes
8 Grand Hôtel Vignemale
9 Camping La Bergerie
10 La Chaumière

1
Tourist Information
La Cordée (Shop)
2
Mairie & Park National des Pyrénées
Newsagent
3
Supermarket
4
5
6
Post Office 7
8
Gave de Gavarnie
CRS Mountain Rescue Service
9
10

★TRAILBLAZER

0   300m
APPROXIMATE SCALE
0   330 yards

TO CIRQUE DE GAVARNIE (3km)

CENTRAL PYRENEES

GAVARNIE → LUZ-ST-SAUVEUR [MAP 57]

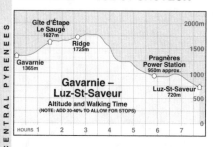

To get back onto the GR10, follow the road north-west out of Gavarnie to the first sharp switchback. Take the small lane (signposted 8 BARRAGE D'OSSOUE) which runs westwards and soon crosses the **Gave d'Ossoue**. Twenty minutes' walking brings you to a yellow sign pointing the way to LE SAUGUÉ 1H. The path climbs gradually across the hillside before rounding the spur and heading north, past several farm buildings; eventually you join a rough road which leads to the gîte. The **Gîte d'étape Le Saugué** (**1627m**, ☎ 05.62.92.48.73) is an attractive thatched building; there are two dormitories, a small kitchen for self-catering, and a large dining area. It's open from May to September and accommodation here costs €12 for the night; demi-pension is €25. Camping (€3) is permitted on the lawn next to the gîte, but only for those on foot and only for one night.

From the gîte, continue north, to a point where the track swings left into the side valley. Just past the corner, the GR10 takes a poorly-marked turning and cuts up the embankment on the left along a small footpath. Follow the path to a **footbridge**, on the far side of which it turns north-east and climbs again. This part is poorly marked, and the multitude of small tracks made by people and animals can be confusing. Keep a careful eye out for markers.

The path slowly climbs to the ridge, becoming steeper as it nears the top. Soon, the power station at Pragnères comes into view, and after a further 20 minutes' climbing you reach a level area where the path turns west, heading into the valley of the Gave de Cestrede. The descent across the side of the valley is almost entirely through the trees of the **Sapinière de Bué**.

Near the bottom of the valley, the GR10 turns back on itself and veers east, soon passing above a small parking area which is at the end of a rough road leading down the valley. Although the GR markers indicate that the route continues down the footpath, there have been landslips on this section and the path may still be impassable. It is wiser, therefore, to cut down to the car park and follow the rough road downhill for approximately 900 metres to a point where the GR10 crosses it. Rejoin the GR10 at this point as it heads down to the left of the road, into the valley. After a 10-15 minutes you cross a small footbridge and continue down the valley to a group of houses on a tarmac lane. Turn left, and follow the lane to the main road (D921) opposite the **Pragnères power station**. Turn left along the D921 and follow it for 1.5 kilometres to the **Camping St Bazerque** ☆☆ (☎ 05.62.92.49.93). The campsite is uninspiring but adequate; it costs €3 per person and €3 for emplacement and there's a small bar.

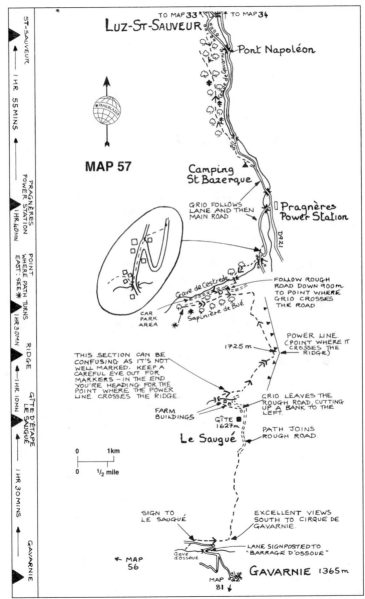

CENTRAL PYRENEES

MAP 57

LUZ-ST-SAUVEUR

TO MAP 33 TO MAP 34

Pont Napoléon

Camping St Bazerque

Pragnères Power Station

GRIO FOLLOWS LANE AND THEN MAIN ROAD

D921

Gave de Cestrède

FOLLOW ROUGH ROAD DOWN 900m TO POINT WHERE GRIO CROSSES THE ROAD

CAR PARK AREA

Sapinière de Bué

POWER LINE (POINT WHERE IT CROSSES THE RIDGE)

1725 m

THIS SECTION CAN BE CONFUSING AS IT'S NOT WELL MARKED. KEEP A CAREFUL EYE OUT FOR MARKERS — IN THE END YOU'RE HEADING FOR THE POINT WHERE THE POWER LINE CROSSES THE RIDGE.

FARM BUILDINGS

GRIO LEAVES THE ROUGH ROAD, CUTTING UP A BANK TO THE LEFT.

GÎTE 1627m

Le Saugué

PATH JOINS ROUGH ROAD.

0   1km
0   ½ mile

SIGN TO LE SAUGUÉ

EXCELLENT VIEWS SOUTH TO CIRQUE DE GAVARNIE.

LANE SIGNPOSTED TO "BARRAGE D'OSSOUE"

← MAP 56

Gave d'ossoue

MAP 81 ↓

GAVARNIE 1365m

ST-SAVEUR

1 HR 55 MINS

PRAGNÈRES POWER STATION

1 HR 40 MIN

POINT WHERE PATH TURNS EAST: SEE ✱

1 HR 30 MIN

RIDGE

1 HR 10 MIN

GÎTE D'ÉTAPE LE SAUGUÉ

1 HR 30 MINS

GAVARNIE

Beyond the campsite, the GR10 parallels the main road via a narrow and overgrown footpath, soon reaching a **tiny hamlet**. From here, the path climbs on wooded tracks until you reach a summit with a rough wooden cross, the **Croix de Sia**. From here you go down to St-Sauveur; the final descent is on a steep footpath which enters St-Sauveur near the Thermes building. It's a fifteen-minute walk to the centre of **Luz-St-Sauveur** (see p165 for more information).

For a description of the GR10 beyond Luz, see p167.

Central Pyrenees – GR11

The GR11 route through the Central Pyrenees contains some of the best walking in the entire range. Quite apart from the fantastic scenery of the Ordesa National Park, the GR11 also passes through the beautiful Maladetta region, and continues through the Aigüestortes National Park. While travel to and from the region from the Spanish side of the mountains may not be ideal, it's easy to pick a route that starts and ends in France, crossing over a high mountain pass at each end to join and leave the GR11. Possible itineraries include:

● Tour of the Ordesa National Park, starting at Cauterets and ending at Gavarnie (4-7 days) (see p269);

● GR11 through the Aigüestortes National Park, starting at Bagnères de Luchon and ending at Mounicou (14-17 days).

For the GR11 route through the Western Pyrenees (as far as Panticosa) see p121.

BALNEARIO/BAÑOS DE PANTICOSA → BUJARUELO   [MAP 58]

Baños de Panticosa – Bujaruelo
Altitude and Walking Time
(NOTE: ADD 30-40% TO ALLOW FOR STOPS)

[Includes high section – see warning on pp19-20] Walk up the steps beside Casa Belio and follow the clear GR markings which lead left to a stony path. The path, well marked and easy to follow, climbs the steep hillside gradually via long, gentle zigzags. After walking for an hour or so you'll leave behind the grass and the few pine trees while the path continues to climb through a moonscape of bare rock. Two hours after starting from Panticosa you'll reach the dam of the **Ibón de Brazato (2360m)**. The path remains level around the north shore of the lake for five minutes and then climbs steeply across a scree slope to reach the top of a spur. On the far side of the spur the GR11 contours around the side of a bowl, high

CENTRAL PYRENEES

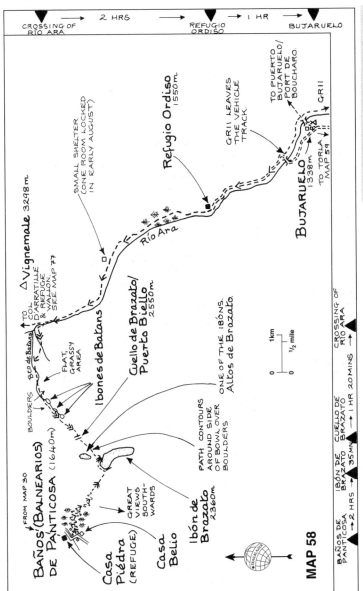

CROSSING OF RÍO ARA → 2 HRS → REFUGIO ORDISO → 1 HR → BUJARUELO

△ Vignemale 3298 m.

SMALL SHELTER (ONE ROOM LOCKED IN EARLY AUGUST)

Refugio Ordiso 1550m.

GR11 LEAVES THE VEHICLE TRACK.

TO PUERTO BUJARUELO/ PORT DE BOUCHARO.

BUJARUELO 1338m.

TO TORLA MAP 59

GR11

Río Ara

TO COL D'ARRATIULLE & REFUGE WALLON, SEE MAP 77

Bco de Batans

FLAT, GRASSY AREA

Ibones de Batans

Cuello de Brazato/ Puerto Biello 2550m.

BOULDERS

ONE OF THE IBÓNS, Altos de Brazato.

PATH CONTOURS AROUND SIDE OF BOWL OVER BOULDERS

(FROM MAP 30)

BAÑOS (BALNEARIOS) DE PANTICOSA (1640m)

Casa Piédra (REFUGE)

Casa Belio

GREAT VIEWS SOUTH-WARDS

Ibón de Brazato 2360m.

1km
0
0   ½ mile

CROSSING OF RÍO ARA →

CUELLO DE BRAZATO → 1 HR 20 MINS

IBÓN DE BRAZATO → 35 MNS

BAÑOS DE PANTICOSA → 2 HRS

AUSTRALIASIA

MAP 58

above another lake. The slope is covered with boulders, so there's no path as such but the paint markings on the rocks are enough to keep you on track and lead you up to the **Cuello de Brazato (2550m)**. Looking east from the col you have an excellent view of the imposing shape of Vignemale (3298m).

Head straight down from the col on an indistinct path which is hard to pick out at times, although the route markings are generally adequate. The path passes to the left (north) of the three **Ibones de Batans**, crossing several areas of boulders. Below the third lake the path crosses the stream and descends a small gully, again mostly across boulders. Below the gully you pass a flat grassy area (possible for camping in late summer) and continue to descend eastwards, crossing the Barranco de Batans two or three more times and staying close to it before descending finally into the Ara valley. Follow the Río Ara downstream for a few minutes before crossing to join the path on the far bank.

Follow the footpath down the valley. After about 45 minutes you come to a small, empty *shelter* with two rooms (one of which seems permanently locked). The hut is far from clean but would do for an overnight stop. An hour further down the valley, at the end of a rough road, is the *Refugio Ordiso* **(1550m)**, a tiny building which looks (and smells) as though it has been used as a sheep shelter. Follow the rough road down from the refuge, and then take the marked trail along the east side of the river to the old bridge of **Bujaruelo**.

BUJARUELO

Bujaruelo is no more than a refuge/albergue/campsite, with another campsite and some cabins half an hour's walk down the road. The first you come to is *Camping San Nicolas* (☎ 974-48.63.12). Being privately owned, you get good coffee and slightly better meals than at a regular refuge and a dormitory that was described as being like a hotel – in contrast to the packed dormitories at Refugio de Goriz – and the refuge staff here are generous and friendly too.

The campground at San Nicolas is a large field which is also shared by a few cows, so campsites need to be chosen with care. Campers have their own toilets and showers, which are functional enough, and there is a washing machine and tumble drier for use at €4.20.

Camping costs €3.20 per person and per tent, half board at the refuge is €24, but if you share a room for four, half board is still only €26.

Dinner is €10, but drinks are extra. Unusually for a Spanish breakfast, they serve bread and will bring more if you ask, just as they do in France.

Should you want fractionally more comfort, the campground down the road, *Camping Valle de Bujaruelo* ☆☆ (☎ 974-48.63.48, 🖳 www.campingvalledebujaruelo), is a more tended, manicured sort of place, with grassy terraces for camping running up above the road. There is a restaurant and bar with a pretty patio to sit out on. A set-menu dinner is €11. The small **shop** has the puncture-type Camping Gaz cartridges. Hard-core walkers invariably choose Camping San Nicolas for its 'mountain hut' atmosphere, but campers would have a pleasant time at either place. Cabins are available at Camping Valle de Bujaruelo for €19-32 for a double, with triples and quads available too; campers pay €3.40 per person and per tent.

BUJARUELO → REFUGIO DE GORIZ [MAP 59/78, p230]

If you are staying at Camping San Nicolas it is a short walk back to the bridge if you want to cross the river and continue on the GR11. The track on the right bank and the GR11 on the left bank run parallel until Puente de los Navarros. The GR11 runs through woods undisturbed by cars, but if you choose to follow the wide vehicle track down the valley, it saves time and allows good views and easy walking. Either route would be a good choice.

At the **Puente de los Navarros** a red-and-white GR marker on the stonework indicates the way under an arch of the bridge and down a footpath. A sign here points the same way: Camino Viejo a Ordesa. A short way down here the path crosses a bridge and beyond it comes to a junction. The GR11 heads eastwards, climbing up into the Ordesa valley. (If you're going to Torla follow the path south until it emerges near the Camping Río Ara, just below the town).

Following the GR11 route eastwards, the path climbs at a steady but easy gradient through trees with occasional excellent views to the left. After about an hour you come to the Cascada Tomborrotera and ten minutes beyond this the Cascada Abelos. Just beyond the second waterfall you pass a turning to the left, leading to the Puente Luciano Briet (there's a monument and plaque to Briet, who was the first person to champion the cause of the Ordesa area). You can either cross this bridge and walk up the road to the car park area or, better, continue along the same bank of the river for a further 20 minutes until another sign points you left across a bridge to 'aparcamiento'. Cross the river via this bridge and arrive at the car park area. There's a bar/restaurant here, with a water point and toilets nearby.

The GR11 leaves the car park heading eastwards on the path towards the Refugio de Goriz. After about an hour you pass the **Cascada de Arripas**, and there's a water point at the side of the path. Ten minutes beyond this there's a fork; go left, following signs: Gradas de Soaso. The section above here, running past a series of low waterfalls and clear blue pools, is perfect for picnicking and sunbathing. Nearly two hours beyond the fork in the track, you reach the eastern end of the canyon, the **Circo de Soaso (1760m approx)**, where a tiny bridge crosses the stream just below an impressive waterfall, **Cascada de Cola de Caballo**. For those who have a good head for heights, just to the right of the waterfall (north-east of the bridge) a chain has been fixed to the rocks to facilitate the climb up this direct but very steep route to the Refugio de Goriz. Most people, however, go for the easier option and take the main path which winds up the scree slope to the east, before heading north

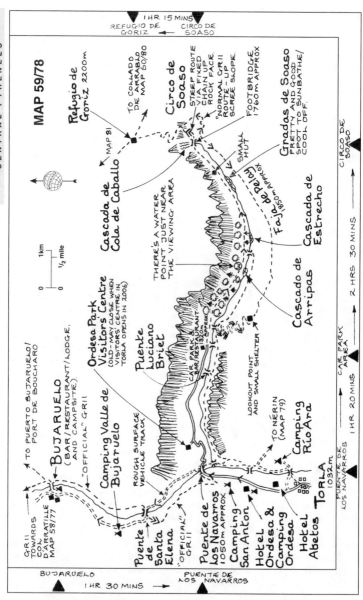

MAP 59/78

to join the other path just above the cliff. A further three-quarters of an hour's climbing brings you to the refugio (2200m).

The ***Refugio de Goriz*** (☎ 974-34.12.01) is very popular and you should book in advance if you're visiting during peak season (mid-July to mid-August), or make an effort to turn up as early in the afternoon as possible. In the evening the area around the refuge is often crammed with tents, too. The refuge has a guardian in residence all year, and has 90 places; charges are €11 per night, €12.10 for the evening meal and €4.10 for breakfast. Some provisions are sold at the refugio, including pasta, chocolate and puncture-type camping gaz cylinders.

REFUGIO DE GORIZ → CIRCO DE PINETA   [MAP 60, p232]

[Includes high section – see warning on pp19-20] The section from Goriz to the Circo de Pineta is a long one, albeit through spectacular scenery.

From the refuge, head south-east along a level and clearly-marked path for twenty minutes or so, before climbing to the **Collado de Arrablo (2329m)**. From the col continue south-eastwards across a grassy plateau before reaching a very steep descent. The path crosses a couple of grassy ledges with steep sections between

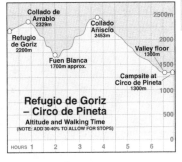

them before crossing the Barranco Arrablo and heading down a very steep slope to arrive at **Fuen Blanca**. There's a tiny *stone shelter/hut* here (for use only as a last resort; it could take no more than two or three people but it may soon be renovated as have been the other shelters in the region). The Fuen Blanca area, with a string of small waterfalls along the Río Vellos and with steep canyon walls on either side, is extremely beautiful and a popular camping spot.

Just below the level of the small stone shelter the GR11 crosses the stream via a footbridge and the heads north-eastwards climbing up the valley at a fairly steep gradient. The path remains on the east side of the stream throughout the climb and just before reaching the top it turns sharply right and heads south-east for 10 minutes, contouring round to reach the **Collado Añisclo (2453m)**.

The descent from the col is very steep and hard work (there's a drop of approximately 1200m to the valley floor) so allow plenty of time and energy. From the col, the parador, refuge and campsite can be seen far below but the markers must be followed carefully as the path, precipitous as it is, winds around the mountainside to avoid cliffs. Initially (for the first hour or so) the path goes almost straight down, zigzagging in short sharp turns. After about an hour you come to a junction where there's a sign pointing left to the Faja Tormosa. Don't take this turning, but continue on the main path as it slowly

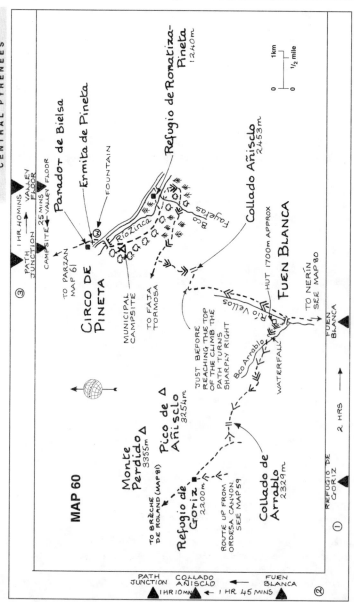

bends to the right and contours around the mountainside before going down into pine trees. Several fallen trees and three or four steep sections which need to be scrambled down make the descent somewhat time-consuming. Approximately 1¹/₂ hours below the path junction and sign, the path crosses the Barranco Fayetas. Continue the descent for a further half hour before arriving at the valley floor.

Just before the path finally flattens out at the bottom of the valley, the GR11, not very well signed, goes left on a path along the base of a cliff. It doesn't matter much if you miss this turn; the alternative path continues across an open grassy meadow and meets the GR11 in the trees on the far side. From here the GR11 winds through a small wood before emerging on a stony riverbank. A sign here points the way (right) to the Refugio de Ronatiza-Pineta, which is some five minutes' walk to the east, across the stream. The GR11, however, continues towards the north-west, without crossing the stream, and after a further quarter of an hour arrives at the campsite.

Pineta

The Pineta area has little in the way of facilities.

The large hotel which can be seen from the Collado Añisclo is the *Parador de Bielsa* ☆☆☆ (☎ 974-50.10.11; 🖹 974-50.11.88, 🖳 www.parador.es). It's a very smart place which is generally fully booked and is probably beyond most walkers' budgets anyway. In mid-summer (July and August) a single room here costs €91.42 and doubles go for €114.28. While the hotel itself is probably too costly to be of interest, if you have some extra cash to spare you could consider splashing out on a meal in the restaurant. The menu for €25 seems expensive but the food is wonderful and a beer or two beforehand on the terrace, with its superb view of Monte Perdido, is

the perfect way to relax after the day's walking. Non residents should try to get to the restaurant relatively early (ie 20.00, when it opens) to ensure that there's a table.

Refugio de Ronatiza-Pineta (☎ 974-50.12.03), built in 1997, is open all year. A place in the dormitory costs €11, dinner is €9.40 and breakfast is €3.60.

The municipal **campsite** is extremely popular and generally very crowded, possibly because, although there's a charge for staying there (€1.65 for a tent and €1.95 per person), very often the collector doesn't seem to turn up. The down side of this is that the facilities are very basic (cold showers and some smelly toilets). There's a small **bar** where sandwiches and snacks are for sale.

CIRCO DE PINETA → PARZÁN   [MAP 61, p234]

From the campsite entrance, walk up the road towards the hotel and follow the route markers around the back of the Ermita de Pineta, passing between the ermita and the water fountain. The clearly-marked path climbs steeply for half an hour through trees before meeting a vehicle track. The path short cuts directly uphill between the loops of the track, finally meeting it again at

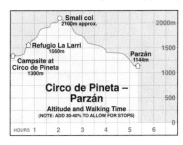

Circo de Pineta – Parzán

Altitude and Walking Time
(NOTE: ADD 30-40% TO ALLOW FOR STOPS)

CENTRAL PYRENEES

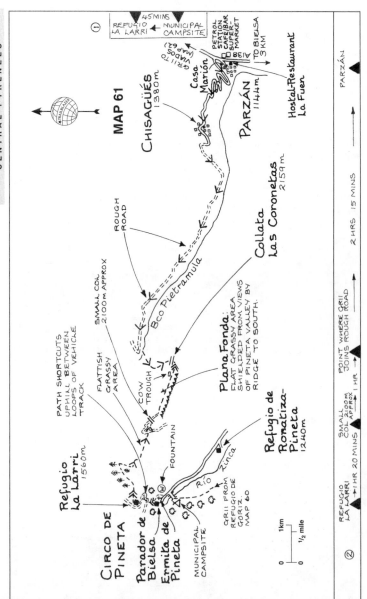

MAP 61

Refugio La Larri 1560m

Circo de Pineta

Parador de Bielsa

Ermita de Pineta

Municipal Campsite

Refugio de Ronatiza-Pineta 1240m

Path shortcuts uphill between loops of vehicle track

Small col 2100m approx

Flattish grassy area

Cow trough

Fountain

Rio Zinca

GR11 from Refugio de Goriz. Map 60

Plana Fonda: flat grassy area shielded from views of Pineta valley by ridge to south.

Rough road

Bco Pietramula

Collata las Coronetas 2159m

Chisagüés 1380m

Casa Marión

Grito Viados (Map 62)

Petrol station Cafe/bar Super-market

A138

Bielsa

To Bielsa 3 km

Parzán 1144m

Hostal-Restaurant La Fuen

Refugio la Larri   45 mins
Municipal Campsite

① Refugio la Larri
1 hr 20 mins

Small col 2100m approx
1 hr

Point where GR11 joins rough road
2 hrs 15 mins

Parzán

0   1km
0   ½ mile

a grassy plateau and following it (left) to **Refugio La Larri (1560m)**. The refuge building is now used as a cowshed and is unsuitable for walkers.

The GR11 swings right here and begins to climb steeply. After a half-hour's ascent across an almost bare hillside with only a few trees, the trail enters an area of pine trees and the climb becomes even steeper for about 10 minutes. At the top of this the path emerges at a flatter area and then follows a small gully up to a grassy plateau. Head roughly south-east across the grass until after quarter of an hour you come to a vehicle track. Go right along the track for a few metres, then turn off left up a gully to reach a small **col (approx 2100m)**.

The GR11 descends gently from the small col and continues south-eastwards across the **Plana Fonda**, a flat grassy area screened from views of the Pineta valley by a rocky ridge along the right-hand side. After 10 minutes you pass a cow trough and then follow a distinct path climbing the slope north-eastwards to the **Collata las Coronetas (2159m)**. The route down from the col, mainly over grass, swings from north-west through to north-east before crossing the Barranco Pietramula and coming to a rough mountain road. Follow this all the way to Parzán. After about $1^{1}/_{2}$-2 hours the road passes through the tiny hamlet of Chisagüés, and the loose surface gives way to tarmac. Beyond the hamlet the lane descends the hillside in long zigzags for 3.5km to meet the main road next to the village of Parzán (1144m).

Parzán

There's not much to Parzán but it does offer the chance to stock up on supplies and the possibility of somewhere to stay for the night. On the main road, *Hostal-Restaurant La Fuen* (☎ 974-50.10.47, 🖳 www. montep erdido.com/lafuen) seems to be more of a holiday home than a hotel but could be worth trying (€36/48 for doubles/triples; breakfast extra) – book in advance.

Otherwise up in the village there are a couple of houses which advertise 'habitaciones' (rooms to rent). Look for the signboards: *Casa Marión* (☎ 974-50.11.90) charges €20/26 for a double/triple. For breakfast you'll need to visit the **café** (open 08.00 to 21.00 daily) by the petrol station on the main road where there's also a tiny but very well-stocked **supermarket**.

PARZÁN → REFUGIO DE VIADÓS [MAP 62, p236]

From the petrol station, walk north up the main road for just over a kilometre to a turning off to the right, signposted LAGO DE URDICETO 11. Take this turning down across the bridge and follow the mountain road as it climbs south-south-eastwards. From here the GR11 follows the rough road almost as far as the Collata Chistau with only a couple of short deviations.

After about an hour the track passes a flattish grassy area with two

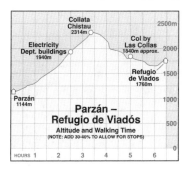

Collata
Chistau
2314m — 2500m

Electricity
Dept. buildings
1940m

Col by
Las Collas
1840m approx. — 2000m

Refugio
de Viados — 1500m
1760m

Parzán
1144m — 1000m

**Parzán –
Refugio de Viadós**

Altitude and Walking Time
(NOTE: ADD 30-40% TO ALLOW FOR STOPS) — 500

0

HOURS 1   2   3   4   5   6

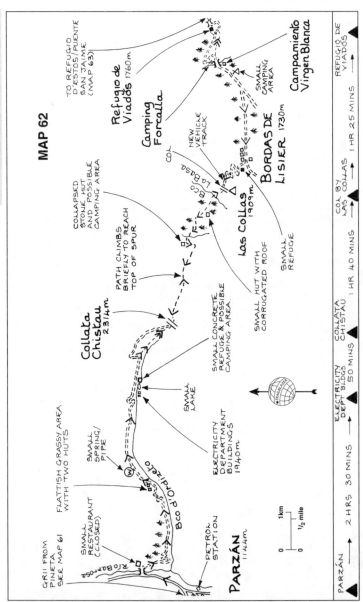

MAP 62

huts (the first possible spot to camp since leaving Parzán); about ten minutes beyond this there's a spring on the left-hand side of the path. An hour or so above the huts the GR11 leaves the rough road briefly to climb past the buildings of a small hydroelectric station. Just above these buildings there's a tiny *refuge* which could sleep two or three people, as well as a grassy area which is suitable for camping.

From the refuge, continue uphill along the vehicle track for a further half hour until the road makes a sharp switchback to the left. Here the GR11 splits away on a footpath which continues straight up the valley, level at first and then climbing directly towards the col. The footpath rejoins the rough road a few metres before reaching the **Collata Chistau (2314m)**.

From the col, follow the obvious path leading eastwards, which descends for quarter of an hour across a bare hillside before climbing briefly again to reach the top of a spur. The path descends along the top of the spur for 10 minutes before swinging left (north) and leading down to a grassy area where there's a stone hut, the roof of which has collapsed. Go down past the hut, and you'll soon cross the Barranco Montarruego and pass through an area of pine trees. Just beyond the trees, on the right, a small hut with a corrugated roof offers possible shelter for three people. The path continues to descend through pine trees before crossing a stream and climbing for five minutes to reach a small col just to the north of Las Collas.

Despite the maps showing this part of the GR11 as a footpath there is actually a vehicle track here which zigzags down the hillside. The remains of the GR11 footpath can still be seen but they are now blocked with fallen trees, so it's easiest to follow the vehicle track. Approximately quarter of an hour after leaving the col you pass, on the right, another tiny hut with space for 3-4 people. Just below this you arrive at a junction with a more permanent rough road which runs east–west past the **Bordas de Lisier (1730m)**. Follow this rough road eastwards as it descends into the valley where it meets an earthen road running along the valley floor. There's an information board here and a GR11 sign pointing north-east up the road towards Viadós.

Follow the road and after five minutes you pass a fairly basic *camping* area. There's a building here with some rudimentary washing facilities. Five minutes further up the road you pass a youth camp, the Campamiento Virgen Blanca. Just beyond this the road crosses a bridge and swings around to the right to pass *Camping Forcalla*, a small campsite with adequate facilities and a bar/café. Beyond the campsite the rough road winds up the hillside but the GR11 shortcuts between the loops on a well-worn path. Above a parking area the GR11 climbs again, crosses a ridge and descends to the refuge (1760m). The *Refugio de Viadós* (☎ 974-50.61.63, 🖥 www.refugiosyalbergues.com/viados) is a lovely place to stay. It's immaculately clean and from the benches outside the door there's a fantastic view across the valley to the impressive peaks around Pico Posets (3375m). It's €7 for a bed, €11 for supper and €4 for breakfast. The refuge is open from around mid-June to late September and at some weekends outside this period.

CENTRAL PYRENEES

REFUGIO DE VIADÓS → PUENTE DE SAN JAIME [MAP 63]

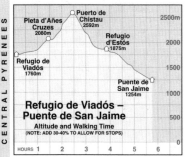

CENTRAL PYRENEES

Refugio de Viadós –
Puente de San Jaime
Altitude and Walking Time
(NOTE: ADD 30-40% TO ALLOW FOR STOPS)

[**Includes high section – see warning on pp19-20**]   Head down a narrow footpath from the refuge and, on reaching the vehicle track below, follow it left across the bridge. The track almost immediately narrows to a footpath, and runs eastwards through the middle of a cluster of old stone barns. After a few minutes it meets another path and a sign next to the junction points the way: REFUGIO D'ESTOS 4H 30. Continue along the footpath which heads north-east across the side of the valley, climbing at a gentle gradient. After approximately three quarters of an hour the path turns directly uphill and the climb is very steep for five minutes before you turn north-eastwards again, continuing on a gradual ascent.

Quarter of an hour beyond this, the Río Zinqueta d'Añes Cruzes curves north-eastwards through a tiny gorge and the GR11 follows it closely, climbing steeply alongside the gorge. Having reached the top of the ravine the path leads down into the **Pleta d'Añes Cruzes (2080m)**, a small bowl in which there is a stream junction and, next to it, a sign: COLLADO DE ESTOS 1H 30. The GR11 crosses two streams before starting to climb eastwards up the south slope of the valley of the Barranco El Puerto. After a tiring ascent the path levels off slightly near the top and finally reaches the **Puerto de Chistau/d'Estós (2592m)**.

Descend from the col on a steep, narrow path running across the valley side. On reaching the valley bottom the path crosses the course of the Barranco d'Estós (which is dry by mid-/late summer) a couple of times before finally crossing to the north bank of the Río Estós, where it remains, running parallel to the river down the valley. Approximately an hour after leaving the col, the path climbs slightly away from the river and soon arrives at the refuge (1875m). The *Refugio d'Estós* (☎ 974-55.14.83, 🖳 www.refugiosyalbergues.com/estos) is a large place (space for 185 people) which is open all year. It costs €11.50 for the night, €12 for an evening meal and €4 for breakfast.

Beyond the refuge, the GR11 descends briefly before following a shady and level path through pine trees. After 20 minutes it descends again to cross a footbridge over the river. Just beyond the bridge the path joins a vehicle track which is, with one small exception, followed all the way to Puente de San Jaime. Five minutes' walk down the track there's a brief diversion to the left, where the GR11 takes a short cut across a loop of the vehicle track. Actually the short cut probably takes longer than remaining on the vehicle track, so it's hardly worth it.

Approximately 45 minutes after starting down the vehicle track you pass, on the right, *Cabana Santa Ana*, which appears to be open for use by walkers. Ten minutes beyond this the track crosses a bridge over the river and 20-30 minutes later you'll arrive at the parking area just above **Puente de San Jaime (1254m)**.

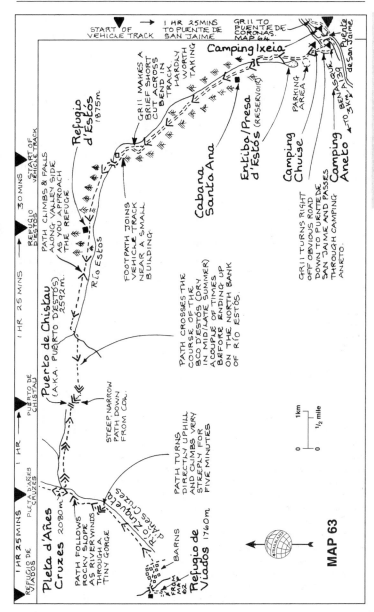

CENTRAL PYRENEES

START OF → 1 HR 25MINS
VEHICLE TRACK TO PUENTE DE
SAN JAIME

GRILL TO
PUENTE DE
CORONAS.
MAP 64

Camping Ixeia

Puente
de San Jaime

Refugio
d'Estós
1875m.

GRILL MAKES A
BRIEF SHORT
CUT ACROSS
BEND IN
TRACK.

HARDLY
WORTH
TAKING.

PATH CLIMBS & FALLS
ALONG VALLEY SIDE
AS YOU APPROACH
THE REFUGE

Entibo/Presa
d'Estós (RESERVOIR)

Camping
Chuise

TO BENASQUE A139
←TO BENASQUE 3KM

Cabaña
Santa Ana

Camping
Aneto

FOOTPATH JOINS
VEHICLE TRACK
NEAR A SMALL
BUILDING.

GRILL TURNS RIGHT
OFF OBVIOUS ROAD
DOWN TO PUENTE DE
SAN JAIME AND PASSES
THROUGH CAMPING
ANETO.

Río Estós

Puerto de Chistau
(A.K.A. PUERTO D'ESTÓS)
2592 m.

PATH CROSSES THE
COURSE OF THE
BCO D'ESTÓS (DRY
IN MID/LATE SUMMER)
A COUPLE OF TIMES
BEFORE ENDING UP
ON THE NORTH BANK
OF RÍO ESTÓS.

STEEP NARROW
PATH DOWN
FROM COL.

Pleta d'Añes
Cruzes 2080m.

PATH FOLLOWS
ROCKY SLOPE
AS RIVER WINDS
THROUGH A
TINY GORGE

Río Añes Cruzes

Barranqueta

PATH TURNS
DIRECTLY UPHILL
AND CLIMBS VERY
STEEPLY FOR
FIVE MINUTES

BARNS

FROM
MAP 62

Refugio de
Viadós 1760m.

0 ___ 1km
0 ___ ½ mile

MAP 63

Puente de San Jaime

The area around the Puente de San Jaime is a popular holiday spot with three campsites. Other facilities, including hotels and shops, are available in the village of Bénasque, 3km down the road.

Just below the parking area, the *Camping Chuise* (€3.20 per person; €3.20 per tent) has a slightly jaded appearance but it's perfectly adequate and considerably quieter than its enormous neighbour. Beyond Camping Chuise the GR11 leaves the road and passes, via a rough road and then a footpath, down to the enormous *Camping Aneto* (☎/🖺 974-55.11.41, 🖳 www.camp inganeto.com). The campsite has excellent facilities including a large bar/restaurant, a well-stocked supermarket (puncture-type gas cylinders only), washing machines and swimming-pool. Camping costs €4.38 per person and €4.38 per tent, and there's also an albergue which charges €14.44 for a bed for the night. The staff at reception sell maps and have information on local activities and transport. Just beyond the Puente de San Jaime is *Camping Ixeia* (☎ 974-55.21.29, €3.20 per person, €3.20 per tent).

There's currently a **bus service** running three or four times a day from Bénasque to the area of La Besurta, just below the Port de Bénasque/Vénasque and the Refugio de la Renclusa (see p264). The bus service stops at, among other places, Puente de San Jaime and the Hospital de Benasque.

PUENTE DE SAN JAIME → ESTANY CAP DE LLAUSET [MAP 64]

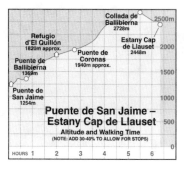

Refugio d'El Quillón 1820m approx.
Puente de Ballibierna 1369m
Puente de San Jaime 1254m
Puente de Coronas 1940m approx.
Collada de Ballibierna 2728m
Estany Cap de Llauset 2448m

Puente de San Jaime – Estany Cap de Llauset
Altitude and Walking Time
(NOTE: ADD 30-40% TO ALLOW FOR STOPS)

HOURS 1   2   3   4   5   6

[Includes high section – see warning on pp19-20] This section is far from ideal because it doesn't have any accommodation at the end of it. Alternatives include stopping overnight in or near the small refugio at Puente de Coronas, or continuing beyond Estany Cap de Llauset to stop overnight in or near the Refugio d'Angliós. If you don't have a tent, the problem with either of these options is that the refuges could well be already occupied when you get there.

Cross the stone footbridge, the Puente de Cubera, in the middle of Camping Aneto, and turn left along the river bank, passing under the road bridge. Beyond the bridge the GR11 joins a rough road running north-north-east, past Camping Ixeia. Just below the dam of the Embalse de Paso Nuevo the rough road doubles back sharply to the right and the GR11 leaves the track, short-cutting uphill for ten minutes. Where it meets the track again, turn left and follow the road past the reservoir, over the Puente de Ballibierna to a track junction where there's a sign: VALLEBIERNA GR11.

Go up the rough road which soon leads past a concrete water container on the right. Just past the container the GR11 splits away from the track, climbing very steeply for quarter of an hour through an area of large pine trees. Where the path rejoins the vehicle track, turn right and follow the track, which climbs at a constant and fairly easy gradient. After almost an hour you pass the *Refugio*

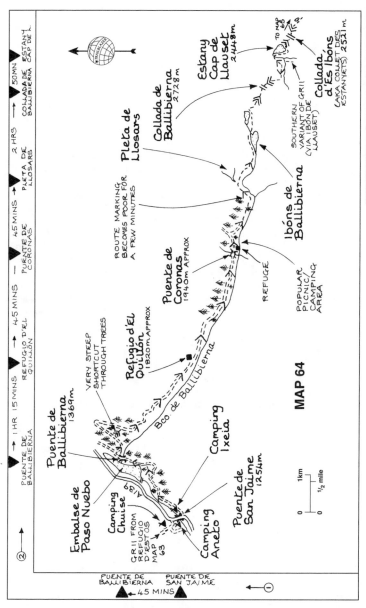

d'El Quillón, almost hidden up a steep bank on the left; it could sleep six or seven people. After a further 45 minutes you come to the **Puente de Coronas (1940m approx)** and, just beyond it, the *refuge*. The building is in good condition, contains an emergency SOS radio and can sleep 12 people on two tiers. The area around the refuge is popular both as a picnic area and for camping.

Follow the wide, stony track eastwards from behind the refuge building. After about seven minutes, at a fork, clear GR markings direct you to the right. Beyond this the path becomes narrower, rockier and steeper. Approximately half an hour after leaving the refuge the route temporarily becomes less well marked; keep an eye out for a few cairns which assist. Soon you arrive at a flat grassy area, the **Pleta de Llosars**. This is shown on the map as marshy ground, but in late summer it's possible to camp here. Cross the Barranco de Llosars and climb up the steep rocky slope to reach the lower of the Ibones de Ballibierna. The GR11 goes around the north side of the lower lake, crosses the rocky area between the two lakes and passes around the southern side of the upper lake. A stream feeding the upper lake provides a possible water source. From the edge of the second lake the climb to the col takes a fairly direct route (the paint markers are faded and can be hard to spot), first up a grassy path and then across boulders in the last part of the climb. Finally you arrive at the **Collada de Ballibierna (2728m)** from which there are magnificent views to the east and west.

The descent from the col starts directly down towards the Estany Cap de Llauset, which can be seen below. A short way down from the col, however, the path swings right, heading south to a flattish area before descending eastwards alongside a stream which soon meets the outflow coming from the Estany Cap de Llauset. At this point the path divides – one route of the GR11 going north and the other south. Both routes are clearly marked on the rocks. This description follows the north route.

The north route runs across an area of boulders then crosses the stream coming from the lake above and climbs to the side of the **Estany Cap de Llauset (2448m)**. Although camping is probably not strictly allowed here, the grassy western shore of the lake provides a suitable overnight spot.

ESTANY CAP DE LLAUSET → HOSPITAL DE VIELLA   [MAP 65]

[Includes high section – see warning on pp19-20] The GR11 heads around the western side of the Estany Cap de Llauset and then climbs across boulders to the **Collada d'es Ibóns (2521m)**. The descent from the col is via a steep rocky path, and then across boulders to the edge of the first of the Estanys Cap d'Angliós. From here the GR11 runs around the south side of the first two lakes and then crosses an area of boulders to pass around the north side of the third lake before finding a grassy path which leads down to the refuge.

The *Refugi d'Angliós* (2220m), a tiny wooden shelter with only four bunks, is open for use by anyone (including shepherds – so you may find it already full). Below the refuge the GR11 circles around the edge of the Estany Gran and descends quite steeply along the side of the small gully below it. It levels out slightly through an area of pine trees before descending very steeply through

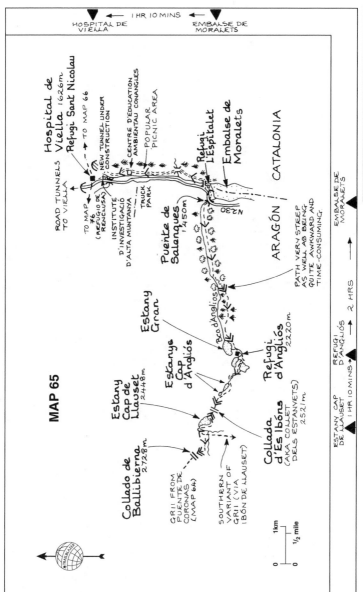

MAP 65

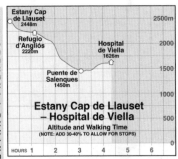

Estany Cap de Llauset 2448m
Refugio d'Angliós 2220m
Puente de Salenques 1450m
Hospital de Viella 1626m

Estany Cap de Llauset – Hospital de Viella
Altitude and Walking Time
(NOTE: ADD 30-40% TO ALLOW FOR STOPS)

2500m
2000m
1500m
1000m
500m
0
HOURS 1 2 3 4 5 6

mixed coniferous and deciduous woods. This section is very awkward and time-consuming. After $1^1/2$-$1^3/4$ hours of descent from the refuge the gradient lessens and the path descends gently through deciduous woods to the north end of the **Embalse de Moralets**. The route markers invite the walker to ford the stream above the road bridge, the **Puente de Salenques (1450m)** but it's easier to cross via the bridge and walk up the tarmac for 200-300m to a parking area. Just to the south on the dam's edge is the *Refugi L'Espitalet*. Near the road, it's in very poor condition with windows smashed out but does offer some shelter and a fireplace.

At the north end of the parking area, a small concrete bridge crosses a stream. Cross the bridge, passing as you do so from the province of Aragón into the province of Catalonia, and turn left, heading north along the rough vehicle track. The track initially runs close alongside the stream, at first as a stony cart track and then across grass. About 10 minutes later the path climbs a little to cross a concrete footbridge and then descends again to run alongside the river. A short way beyond this it passes a large and popular picnic area and then the large Centre d'Education Ambientau Conangles (refuge for groups only).

By now you may be becoming aware of the sounds of construction up the valley: this is the new €128-million tunnel being excavated through the Pyrenees. EU tunnel-safety regulations have made the winding old tunnel inefficient to operate: trucks must queue in the large parking areas before going through in convoy. Until the new tunnel opens in 2007 the surrounding area will continue to be blighted with noise and dust. The Hospital de Viella church and the *Refugi Sant Nicolau* (1626m, see p267) are right by the new tunnel entrance.

HOSPITAL DE VIELLA → REFUGI DE LA RESTANCA [MAP 66]

(For the linking stage from Bagnères-de-Luchon, see p262) If you're short

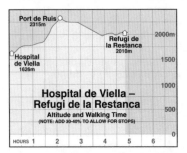

Port de Ruis 2315m
Refugi de la Restanca 2010m
Hospital de Viella 1626m

Hospital de Viella – Refugi de la Restanca
Altitude and Walking Time
(NOTE: ADD 30-40% TO ALLOW FOR STOPS)

2000m
1500m
1000m
500m
0
HOURS 1 2 3 4 5 6

of time this section could be combined with the next stage to Colomers. This stage takes about $4^1/2$-5 hours and after a long but fairly gentle climb to the Port de Rius it's pretty much all downhill to Restanca.

From the Hospital de Viella the route is well defined with the familiar red-and-white paint-markings. A sign points the way along the path running eastwards from the refuge (REFUGI DE LA RESTANCA 4H 40) and after a few

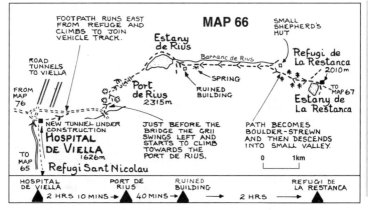

CENTRAL PYRENEES

HOSPITAL DE VIELLA	PORT DE RIUS	RUINED BUILDING	REFUGI DE LA RESTANCA
2 HRS 10 MINS →	40 MINS →	2 HRS →	

minutes you start to pick up the route markers. These become increasingly clear as the GR11 joins a vehicle track which you follow eastwards into the Vall de Conangles.

Just before a small **bridge** across the Barranc de L'Hospital, the path heads left and the climbing begins. The path zigzags back and forth and about two hours after leaving the refuge, you reach the **Port de Rius (2315m)**, from which there is an excellent view westwards towards the Tuc de Mulleres.

Follow the path to and around the northern edge of the **Estany de Rius**. The shores of the lake are boulder-strewn, and the scene is somehow both attractive and extremely desolate. From the eastern end of the lake the path starts to descend gently into the valley below, passing a ruined building and soon afterwards a tiny spring. Finally, just before passing above a **shepherd's hut**, the GR11 turns south-east and climbs gently across the hillside. As it rounds the spur it passes through an area of rocks and then descends into a valley.

The climb up the far slope of the valley is short but steep and follows roughly along a line of telegraph poles. At the top of the climb the path crosses the ridge and soon the **Estany de la Restanca** and the refuge (2010m) come into sight below. Walk down the hill and across the barrage to get to the refuge. The *Refugi de la Restanca* (☎ 608-03.65.59, 🖳 www.restanca.com) is a large and rather ugly building, with 80 beds. The guardians are friendly and the place is generally very well run. It costs €11.60 for the night, €2 for a hot shower, €13.50 for dinner, €4.90 for breakfast and they'll make you up a picnic lunch for €8.25. Visa cards and MasterCards are accepted and there's a phone here.

REFUGI DE LA RESTANCA → REFUGI DE COLOMERS [MAP 67, p247]

[Includes high section – see warning on pp19-20] Take the path which climbs rapidly up the hillside to the south-east. After 25 minutes you come to a small plateau and the **Estanh deth Cap deth Port**, a pretty little lake with a good area

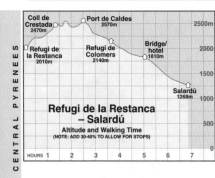

CENTRAL PYRENEES

Coll de Crestada 2470m

Port de Caldes 2570m

2500m

Refugi de la Restanca 2010m

Refugi de Colomers 2140m

Bridge/hotel 1810m

2000m

1500m

Salardú 1268m 1000m

Refugi de la Restanca – Salardú

500

Altitude and Walking Time
(NOTE: ADD 30-40% TO ALLOW FOR STOPS)

0

HOURS 1   2   3   4   5   6   7

for camping on its north shore, although it's sometimes bugged with mosquitoes. Follow the markers around the north-eastern edge of the lake and climb through an area of boulders to the **Col de Crestada (2470m)**, from which there's a good view south over Estany des Monges. The GR11 continues south-eastwards, crossing a grassy bowl and climbing a small ridge from which you can see, in the valley below, the Estany des Mangades and the Estany del Port de Caldes.

After a steepish descent into the valley, the painted markings lead you between the two lakes and up the rocky slope on the far side to the **Port de Caldes (2570m)**. Head straight over the pass and down the other side; the footpath is steep in places but after about half an hour it levels out into an attractive route alongside the stream. Following the path and stream as they turn north you soon reach the *Refugi de Colomers* (2140m; ☎ 973-25.30.08, no credit cards). The refuge is small (40 places) but attractive and is a popular destination for day trippers. It costs €10.90 for the night and €13.50 for dinner. Camping is permitted nearby. A new refuge building is under construction a few hundred metres round the lake and is due to open around 2006.

There are several places in the Aran valley where you can pick up supplies. **Viella/Vielha** is the largest town in the valley, and **Espot** (see p252) also has a few shops; there's a store in the campsite in **La Guingueta d'Àneu** (see p253), and there are several shops in the nearby village of **Esterri d'Àneu**. Alternatively you could choose to head down from Colomers 14km to **Salardú**.

SALARDÚ

Salardú is about 14 weary kilometres down the road from Colomers. Unless you have your own mobile phone, there's nowhere from which to phone for a taxi (☎ 610-29.45.56, approx €20 to Salardú), so the only option apart from walking is to try hitching a lift from the main parking area, one hour below the refuge. The park does, however, operate a minibus service (€3.50, July-Sep daily 09.00-18.30) between the main parking area and just below the refuge.

From the refuge, descend below the barrage and follow the clear footpath northwards. After 25 minutes you arrive at the rough road (where the minibus waits) which leads down towards Salardú. Turn right and follow the road; after half an hour

it passes through a large parking area. Half an hour later it crosses a small bridge, near the hotel, *Banhs de Tredos* ☆☆☆ (☎ 973-25.30.03, ☐ www.banhsdetredos.com). Built on the site of some hot springs, this spa hotel charges €138.67-166.24 for a double including breakfast, spa and sauna – a lot of money to stay in a comfortable but rather characterless building. Dinner (€18 for main dishes) is, however, very good.

After a further 1¾ hours' walk down the lane you come to Salardú.

Services

From June to September, the **bank** is open 08.15-14.00 Monday to Friday (presumably the opening hours are reduced outside this period), and there's a cash dispenser outside the building. There's a small **supermarket**, a **bakery**, a **pharmacy** and even an open-air public **swimming-pool** (€3). The **tourist office** (☎ 973-64.51.97, 🖥 www.aran.org) is in a tiny wooden hut by the car park; they can give details of accommodation throughout the Aran valley. If you need to see a **doctor**, try the place opposite Era Trobada Café, which is open 12.00-

14.00 daily. The nearest **hospital** (☎ 973-64 00.04) is in Viella. The **taxi service**, though far from cheap, is useful to avoid the trudge back to Colomers: between the bank and Hotel Colomèrs lives Manel Paba (☎ 610-29.45.56) and there's also Sergio Gallardo (☎ 610-30.99.95). The next nearest taxis are in Viella: try Ignacio Gallardo (☎ 629-31.43.34) or Javier Martinez (☎ 609-38.69.68) who has an Espace-type van (up

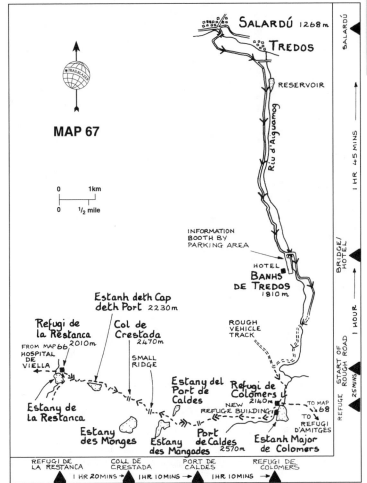

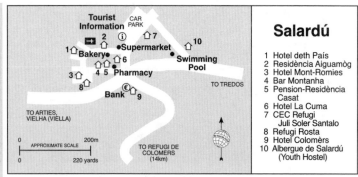

Salardú

1 Hotel deth País
2 Residència Aiguamòg
3 Hotel Mont-Romies
4 Bar Montanha
5 Pension-Residència
    Casat
6 Hotel La Cuma
7 CEC Refugi
    Juli Soler Santalo
8 Refugi Rosta
9 Hotel Colomèrs
10 Albergue de Salardú
    (Youth Hostel)

to eight passengers). He charges about €55 to make the trip up to just below Colomers. There are nine **buses** daily between Salardú and Viella; the journey takes 20 minutes.

Where to stay
There's a good range of reasonably-priced accommodation in Salardú. The smartest place is *Hotel Mont-Romies* ☆☆ (☎ 973-64.58.16, 🖥 973-64.45.39), on the Plaça Major. Double rooms start at €87.74 (including breakfast). On the edge of the village, *Hotel Colomèrs* ☆☆ (☎ 973-64.45.56, 🖥 www.hotelcolomers.com) is highly recommended. The owners are very friendly and there are lovely views from the bar downstairs. Singles/doubles are €37.45/ 74.90. *Hotel deth País* ☆☆ (☎ 973-64.58.36) is very comfortable but perhaps a little lacking in character; doubles start at €51.36 (including breakfast) in July, rising to €68.48 in August. *Hotel La Cuma* ☆☆ (☎ 973-64.50.17, 🖥 973- 64.58.48) is also modern and charges similar prices to Hotel Pais though rates rise to €80.25 in August.

Just around the corner from La Cuma is the *Residència Aiguamòg* (☎ 973-64.54.96), a pretty old house, the inside of which has been completely modernized. A good place to stay, it's €27/55/66/77 for a single/double/triple/ quad (€30/60/72/83 in July/ August), including breakfast.

Coming down in price, in the lane running east from the Plaça Major are two little places. The *Bar Montanha* (☎ 973-64.41.08) has doubles from €33. Almost next door, the *Pension-Residència Casat* (☎ 973-64.50 56) has doubles from €36.

Refugi Rosta (☎ 973-64.53.08, 🖥 6.58.14) has private rooms (€24 for media-pensión) and dormitory accommodation (€17 with breakfast in the café here). *CEC Refugi Juli Soler Santalo* (☎/🖥 973-64 .50.16) is open between June and October and offers basic accommodation run by friendly people. A bed in a four-bedded room costs €15 (€29.40 media-pensión); a bed in the dormitory is €10 (€25 media-pensión). Breakfast is €4.40. There's also the large youth hostel, *Albergue de Salardú Era Garona* (☎ 973-64.52.71, 🖥 www.to juva.com). A bed with breakfast costs €18.10/21.60 for under/over 25 year olds; there are 2-/3-/4-bedded rooms.

REFUGI DE COLOMERS → REFUGI D'AMITGES   [MAP 68]

[Includes high section – see warning on pp19-20] Cross the barrage and follow the path as it dips down into the bowl just north-east of the dam; it then climbs eastwards up a short, steep slope to pass over a col. From here the path heads southeast, remaining level and passing a succession of idyllic lakes. Some 50 minutes after leaving the barrage you pass the southern end of Estanh Obago and start to

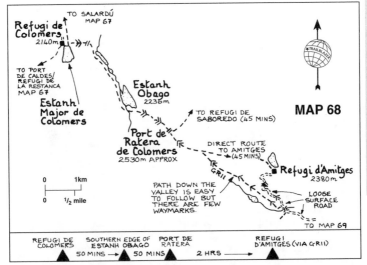

climb to the **Port de Ratera** (2530m approx). The steep ascent is made considerably easier by the fact that the path is well-trodden and weaves back and forth maintaining a manageable gradient. In the middle of the col a sign points towards the *Refugi de Saboredo* (☎ 973 -25.30.15), 45 minutes away.

Descend south-eastwards from the col to a grassy shoulder where there's another sign. The direct path to the Refugi d'Amitges is signposted to the left, while the arrow to the right points to Estany de Sant Maurici (via the GR11). It is possible to follow the GR11 and then double back to the refuge, but it's not a great idea as the path loses a lot of height which you then have to regain by climbing the very steep vehicle track. (If you do follow the main GR11, towards Estany de St Maurici, don't be surprised to find that it is poorly marked until you get about halfway down the valley. The path isn't hard to follow, but for some reason, almost all the markings disappear for a while.) If you're taking the direct path to Amitges, follow the yellow marker posts away from the grassy shoulder. As you come around the corner, stay high above the area of moraine, which is both difficult and time-consuming to cross. *Refugi d'Amitges* (**2380m**; ☎ 973-25.01.09, 🖥 www.amitges.com) is a large modern building with all comforts; it's €11.50 for a bed, €5 for breakfast, €13.50 for lunch or dinner and €8 for a packed lunch. There's a public phone.

REFUGI D'AMITGES → LA GUINGUETA D'ÀNEU [MAP 69]

CENTRAL PYRENEES

Refugi d'Amitges 2380m
2000m
Espot 1320m approx.
1500
La Guingueta d'Àneu 940m
1000
Refugi d'Amitges – La Guingueta d'Aneu
500
Altitude and Walking Time
(NOTE: ADD 30-40% TO ALLOW FOR STOPS)
0
HOURS 1 2 3 4 5 6

Much of the day's walk is on roads and vehicle tracks so this is not the most interesting of the sections in this circuit. The countryside is attractive but less dramatic than on the previous sections. Despite this, Espot is a good place to stop for a break and beyond here, as you pass out of the National Park, you suddenly have the countryside almost entirely to yourself.

From the Refugi d'Amitges, follow the vehicle track downhill to join the GR11. Despite what is shown on some maps, the GR11 follows the track all the way to the eastern end of the **Estany de Sant Maurici**, passing en route the ruins of a large roofless old building which used to be a military barracks. With excellent views over the lake, it would make a perfect refuge though it would need to have a lot of money spent on it to make it habitable.

An hour's walking brings you to the edge of the lake where there's a small **information booth** with a few displays and some leaflets about the national park. For those in a hurry to get to Espot, there's a regular service up and down the hill in Land Rovers during the summer months; it's €4 per person and stops running around 20.00.

On the south side of the lake, under the huge shape of Gran Encantat, is *Refugi Ernets Mallafré* (2000m; ☎ 973-25.01.18). There's room for 28 people and an extension was recently added with a cold shower and loos. The refuge is open from 1 June to 30 September: it costs €10.90 for the night and €12 for the evening meal.

The path running towards Espot on the southern bank of the Riu Escrita has suffered from avalanche damage and is hard to follow, so the only option is to take the vehicle track eastwards. Ten minutes after leaving the refuge, you pass the **Chapel of Sant Maurici** where there's a shelter: a small unlocked room with a fireplace. Five minutes beyond the chapel the track joins the tarmac road. Follow the road for ten minutes until, by a small cabane, the GR11 heads off on a grassy footpath. After quarter of an hour there's a junction. The path to the right descends to a footbridge across the river, while the GR11 climbs slightly from the junction and continues along the northern slopes of the valley on a wide track.

After about forty minutes, the GR11 crosses the river at the **Pont de Suar** and continues down to Espot on the road. En route you pass *Camping Vora Park* (☎ 973-62.41.08, 🖳 www.voraparc.com), a pleasant and peaceful campsite with its own shop, bar, restaurant and pool. Charges are €4.40 per person and €4.40 per tent, and the campsite is open from June to the end of September. Quarter of an hour further down the road at the start of Espot village is *Camping Solau* (☎ 973-62.40.68), where the tariff is €4 per person and €4 per tent. There's a poorly-stocked shop and a bar.

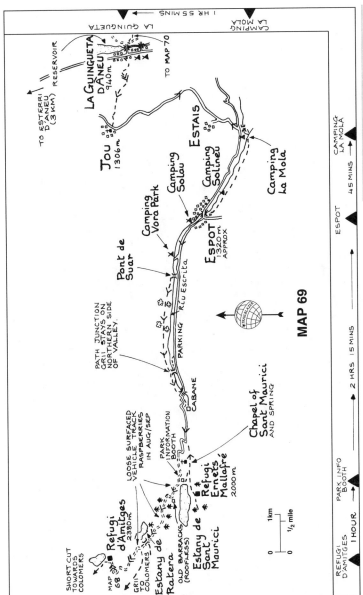

CENTRAL PYRENEES

MAP 69

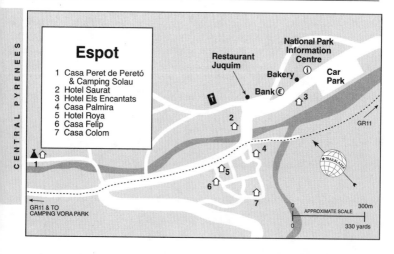

ESPOT

The village of Espot is enjoying a rebirth as a tourist centre and is consequently well-stocked with hotels, restaurants and shops. The tiny La Caixa **bank** is open from Monday to Friday 11.00-14.00, but there's also a cash dispenser. The **National Park Information Centre** is open 09.00-13.00 and 15.30-18.45, June to September.

The top hotels often have generous special offers if business is slow, which it can be outside the busiest time: mid-July to late August and over the winter ski season. The best place to stay is *Hotel Saurat* ☆☆ (☎ 973-62.41.62, 💻 www.hotelsaurat .com). Peak season prices are €72/107 for a single/double room and breakfast or €84.53/132.68 for media-pensión. *Hotel Roya* ☆☆ (☎ 973-62.40.40, 📠 62.41.44) is a little cheaper but not so well placed. Finally, *Hotel Els Encantats* ☆☆☆ (☎/📠

973-62.41.15, 💻 www.hotelencantats.com) is a stylish new hotel with a spa. It's €64.20/96.30 for single/double and breakfast or €77.04/121.98 for media-pensión. There are four Cases de Pagès: *Casa Colom* (☎ 973-62.40.10) is highly recommended. It's self-catering and charges €17 per person per night. It's run by two friendly ladies, has a well-equipped kitchen and is open year-round. *Casa Felip* (☎ 973-62.40.93) charges €15, is equally friendly and all rooms have a shower; breakfast is available for €5. *Casa Palmira* (☎ 973-62.40.72) is a much larger and slightly impersonal place where they charge €23.40 per person with breakfast or €35 for media-pensión. *Casa Peret de Peretó* (☎ 973-62.40.68) is attached to *Camping Solau* and has apartments for four or six people; they charge €17 per person.

From the centre of Espot, the GR11 goes east down an alley and follows a grassy vehicle track. After about 15 minutes, *Camping Solineu* (☎ 973-62.40.01, €4.40 per person, €4.40 per tent) is on the left by the river. Another 20 minutes brings you to a path junction, where a signpost points left to: ESCALÓ. Follow the path downhill, cross the river and climb to the road near the entrance to *Camping La Mola* (☎ 973-62.40.24). The campsite has a shop, café and bar and a few apartments for rent, generally for a minimum of two days. The campsite is open from mid-June to the end of September and charges €4.40 per person, €4.40 per tent.

From the campsite, the GR11 follows the minor road north-eastwards all the way to **Jou**. The village is pretty but has no shops or other facilities. A clearly marked footpath leads downhill from Jou to **La Guingueta d'Àneu**.

LA GUINGUETA D'ÀNEU

Despite being so small La Guingueta has several places to stay, although it does straddle a busy main road. The best of these is the very friendly *Hotel Poldo* ☆☆ (☎ 973-62.60.80, 🖹 62.63.85), which boasts a swimming pool and a good restaurant. A single/double room here costs €53.50/74.90. Opposite is the *Hostal Orteu* (☎ 973-62.60.86), a bar restaurant which has double rooms available for €42.80. *Pensio/Fonda Abril* (☎ 973-62.60.89) charges €32.12 for a double. Breakfast is €3.20. At *Hostal Cases* (☎ 973-62.60.83), a double room (with a real bath as well as a shower) costs €31. Breakfast is €3.30.

There are two large campsites in the hamlet, both of which have pools. *Nou Camping* (☎ 973-62.60.85, 🖳 www.noucamping.com) charges €4.40 per person and €4.40 per tent; it's very smart and has a

well-stocked shop, restaurant/bar, mountain-bike hire and laundry service; it's open summer only. *Camping Val d'Aneu* (☎ 973-62.63.90) charges €4 per person and €4 per tent, and also has a restaurant and bar; it's open from Easter to the end of November.

Jordi Cases Taxi (☎ 659-10.45.75) operates from Hostal Cases. Alsina Graells (☎ 932.65.68.66) operates **buses** daily to Barcelona (5½ hours) and Lleida (3 hours). There is a daily bus service to Llavorsi (the local transport hub).

The nearest **shops** (apart from campsite shops) are 3km north (along the road) from La Guingueta, in **Esterri d'Àneu**. There are two supermarkets, a well-stocked chemist, a post office and an outdoor adventure centre. There's **internet access** at the library from 17.00.

LA GUINGUETA D'ÀNEU → ESTAON   [MAP 70, p254]

Now that the refuge in Estaon has opened it's possible to do this fairly short section without a tent. However, as the refuge (see p255) is very small you should book ahead. It is quite possible to continue beyond Estaon to Lleret or even Tavascan but you'll need to make a very early start, as it's a long section.

From La Guingueta, the GR11 crosses the **concrete bridge** to the east side of the reservoir and turns right

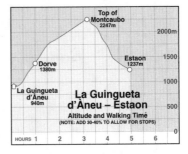

(southwards) down the vehicle track. Despite the route shown on the IGN map (which has it that the path follows a road/track to Dorve) the GR11 actually leaves the rough road within a couple of minutes. The footpath up to the left is marked only by a cairn but after some 200 metres the first red-and-white waymarks appear. The steep climb to **Dorve**, best undertaken in the early morning when the hillside is in shade, takes about an hour. Almost all the houses in the attractive little hamlet are deserted. It's a lovely shady spot to stop for a rest; the houses are

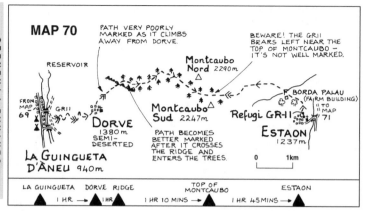

MAP 70

PATH VERY POORLY MARKED AS IT CLIMBS AWAY FROM DORVE.

RESERVOIR

BEWARE! THE GR11 BEARS LEFT NEAR THE TOP OF MONTCAUBO – IT'S NOT WELL MARKED.

Montcaubo Nord 2290m

FROM MAP 69 GR11

BORDA PALAU (FARM BUILDING)

Montcaubo Sud 2247m

Refugi GR11

TO MAP 71

DORVE 1380m SEMI-DESERTED

PATH BECOMES BETTER MARKED AFTER IT CROSSES THE RIDGE AND ENTERS THE TREES.

ESTAON 1237m

LA GUINGUETA D'ÀNEU 940m

0   1km

| LA GUINGUETA | DORVE | RIDGE | TOP OF MONTCAUBO | ESTAON |
| ▲ 1 HR → | ▲ 1 HR → | ▲ 1 HR 10 MINS → | ▲ 1 HR 45 MINS → | ▲ |

in remarkably good condition and there's a picturesque **chapel** dedicated to San Bartolomé. There's a **water fountain** next to the path as you enter the village.

The route marking, which up to this point has been excellent, becomes much less clear above the village. It's not easy to spot the faded paint splashes as the rocky hillside is covered with low vegetation and criss-crossed by animal tracks. If in doubt, climb north-eastwards, making your own loops across the hillside; the markers will be picked up again eventually. Once at the ridge, the GR11 enters a shady pine forest and the path becomes well marked again, adopting a gentler gradient. The climb to the top of **Montcaubo** is still quite steep in places but at least there's the shade, and the views, when they come, are excellent.

At the top of the climb, and just to the south of Montcaubo Nord, the GR11 suddenly bends left and begins its descent. It's easy to miss the turning, not least because another path continues across the hilltop in a straight line. The *other* path is indicated with yellow-and-white paint markings. Take note! These are not some strange local alternative to the proper GR waymarks.

Catalonia's vanishing mountain communities

Estaon is a lovely little place – an example of an old mountain village being given new life. Many of the houses have been restored and the narrow alleys between them are lined with flower baskets and banks of flowering shrubs. It is one of the lucky villages – although it has a permanent resident community of fewer than 20 people, it's undergoing a rejuvenation at the hands of city dwellers. People from Barcelona, in particular, are buying up the houses and undertaking massive refurbishment – a process you see in villages throughout the Spanish Pyrenees.

The village emptied in the 1960s when factory work in the cities offered well-paid employment and an easier alternative to the harsh mountain life. In a way, though, the ruin had started before this. In the 1930s many of the local Romanesque churches were stripped of their artefacts by collectors, and the villages were further ravaged by the effects of the Civil War.

The descent to **Estaon** is long and in some places steep (1000m of height is lost in a little over 3km). It's well marked, however, and after about 1³/4 hours you come to the village. Open year-round, ***Refugi GR-11 Estaon*** (☎ 973-62.32.87, 🖳 www.refugigr-11estaon.com) has just 12 places and charges €10 for a dorm bed and €15/22 for bed and breakfast/media-pensión. There's also one double room. Perhaps more accommodation will open in the village but until that happens the next nearest place to stay is in Lleret some 3¹/2 hours further along the GR11.

The **Church of St James**, below the village, is definitely worth a visit; the key is kept by a neighbour near the large house named Casa Pau, by the refugi. Although the church has a venerable and time-worn appearance (it dates from the 18th century), in the centre of the village are the remains of a much older structure. The chapel, which was dedicated to Saint Eulalia, dates from the 12th century. The early frescos that used to adorn the walls of the chapel are now kept in various museums.

ESTAON → TAVASCAN   [MAP 71, p256]

Follow the road eastwards away from the village. At the bridge over the Ribera d'Estaon, ignore the GR markings alongside the stream (this was the old route), and continue on the road a little further to find the vehicle track which runs north up the valley. Eventually it narrows to a footpath, which continues along the peaceful and shady valley bottom. About an hour after leaving Estaon, you pass **Bordes**

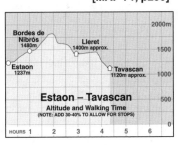

Estaon – Tavascan
Altitude and Walking Time
(NOTE: ADD 30-40% TO ALLOW FOR STOPS)

de Nibrós, a collection of farm buildings. A couple of minutes beyond the hamlet, the path makes a sudden right turn, doubling back on itself and starting up the hillside. After 10-15 minutes on a good footpath, you come to the **ruins** of a large old barn. The route marking becomes a little vague above here but it's no great problem, and after a further half hour of climbing you'll reach the top of the **ridge** (1820m approx).

From here, the GR11 actually follows a route quite different from that marked on the IGN map. Cross straight over the ridge and head directly down the hillside on a steep earthen path. Near a sign, LLERET, AINETO, TAVASCAN, the GR11 joins an old cart track which winds down the hillside to **Lleret**. Only a handful of houses in the village are occupied, one of which is a casa de pagès, ***Casa Rabassó*** (☎ 973-62.32.12, 🖳 rabasso@terra.es). It would make a good place to stay: the house is beautiful, the owner is very friendly and Lleret has a wonderful sleepy atmosphere to it. The tariff is €35.12 per person for media-pensión. There are two water points in the village.

Leave the village on the rough access road and at the first sharp bend, 200-300 metres from the houses, continue northwards on a footpath. The junction is

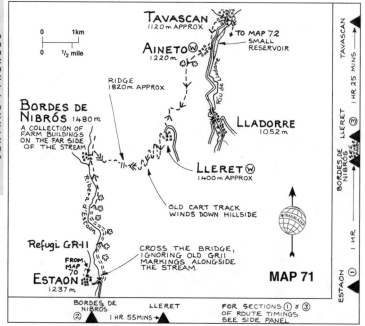

not well marked, so keep an eye out for the path and the paint-markers. The footpath climbs initially and then levels out heading northwards along the valley side. It's an easy route although in a couple of places you need to watch your footing.

After about an hour you come to **Aineto**, where there is a water point. Quarter of an hour beyond Aineto you reach **Tavascan**.

TAVASCAN

There are four places to stay in Tavascan. The *Hotel Llacs de Cardós* ☆ (☎ 973-62.31.78, 🖳 www.llacscardos.com) is a comfortable place where a single/double with breakfast costs €41.16/62.06 (although if business is slow they may be prepared to give you a much better price). Separate but under the same management is the plush *Hotel Estanys Blaus* ☆☆☆ beside the river; with breakfast a single/double room is €58.72/97.18.

Hotel Marxant (☎ 973-62.31.51, 🖳 62. 30.39) is cheaper than either of these and good value: media-pensión costs from €34.24 per person.

At *Casa Feliu* (☎ 973-62.31.63) the rooms are fairly small and basic but the price isn't bad: media-pensión costs €26.75 per person if you have a room with common bathroom. The owner claims that she serves the best local food in the village.

CENTRAL PYRENEES

The nearest campsite, *Camping Serra* (☎ 973-62.30.17), is 2km past Lladore.

Tavascan has a well-stocked **shop** and there's a public **swimming pool** just north of the church. There's a small **tourist kiosk** here too.

The **church** is well-worth looking into; the key is kept behind the bar in the Hotel Llacs de Cardos. Also interesting is the ancient **bridge**, west of the church. Just by the bridge is a large mulberrry tree that fruits profusely in late August.

TAVASCAN → ÀREU   [MAP 72]

Cross the Riu de Lladore via the bridge near the church and begin a steep climb. Soon the footpath settles into a pattern of regular turns up the hillside, through a young wood of beech, birch, hazel and oak. After 35 minutes there's a painted sign on a rock beside the path indicating a fountain to the right of the trail; it's possible that there's a spring slightly further away from the path but there's no sign of any water source. The

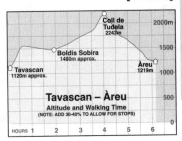

Tavascan – Àreu
Altitude and Walking Time
(NOTE: ADD 30-40% TO ALLOW FOR STOPS)

Coll de Tudela 2243m — 2000m
Boldis Sobira 1480m approx. — 1500m
Àreu 1219m — 1000m
Tavascan 1120m approx.
500
0
HOURS 1 2 3 4 5 6

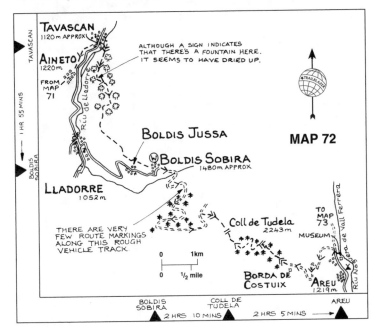

MAP 72

TAVASCAN 1120 m APPROX

AINETO 1220m

FROM MAP 71

Riu de Lladore

ALTHOUGH A SIGN INDICATES THAT THERE'S A FOUNTAIN HERE. IT SEEMS TO HAVE DRIED UP.

↑TRAILBLAZER

BOLDIS JUSSA

BOLDIS SOBIRA 1480m APPROX

LLADORRE 1052m

THERE ARE VERY FEW ROUTE MARKINGS ALONG THIS ROUGH VEHICLE TRACK

Coll de Tudela 2243m

TO MAP 73

MUSEUM

Riu de Vall Ferrera

Riu Noguera de Vall Ferrera

0 1km
0 ½ mile

BORDA DE COSTUIX

ÀREU 1219m

1 HR 55 MINS — TAVASCAN / BOLDIS SOBIRA

BOLDIS SOBIRA   2 HRS 10 MINS   COLL DE TUDELA   2 HRS 5 MINS →   ÀREU

area directly above this point is poorly marked; go straight uphill across the grass to find the markers again. After just over an hour's ascent, the path levels out and contours around the hillside, passing above **Boldis Jussa** and entering **Boldis Sobira**, a sleepy little village with several fountains.

From Boldis Sobira, the route to the **Coll de Tudela** is simple but bears no relation to that shown on the IGN 1:50,000 map. The GR11 leaves the village heading eastwards along a rough vehicle track, which you follow for the next 1-1¹/₂ hours. The track itself takes a different route from that shown on the map, and the GR markings are, in some places, hundreds of metres apart. No matter, stay on the track. Towards the top of the climb with the coll almost in sight, the track follows a long leg eastwards. After a tight left bend and then entering a right bend to head northwards, you'll find the markers suddenly reappearing to the right, indicating the way up a rocky path which runs straight up the hillside. This area is fairly overgrown, and following the trail up to the coll is tricky. Once you reach the coll, however, the view is superb. To the west are the high rocky peaks of the Aigüestortes; to the east are the peaks of Andorra. The rolling grassy hill tops of the Pallars Sobira region contrast with the land on either side.

Despite the fact that you have to lose around 1000m in height to get down to Àreu, it's a surprisingly easy descent – much of it through shady pine woods and on gently-sloping footpaths. After about an hour, you reach the two barns of **Borda de Costuix**, and join a vehicle track which leads down to **Àreu**.

ÀREU

The only hotel in Àreu is *Hotel Val Ferrera* (☎ 973-62.43.43, 🖥 www.hotelvallferrera.com); the rooms are comfortable and prices for media-pensión start at €48.23. There are several casas de pagès, including *Casa Besoli* (☎ 973-62.44.15) where doubles costs €25, and media-pensión is €36 per person. At the far northern edge of the village, *Casa Gallardó* (☎ 973-62.43.44) is a lovely old house with double rooms from

€19.50. Nearby, *Camping Pica d'Estats* (☎ 973-62.43.47) is pleasant and shady, and the swimming pool and bar make it all the more enticing. The tariff is €4.40 per person and €4.40 per tent; non residents can use the pool for a small fee. The campsite is open from Easter-October.

Àreu has a small **shop** and, north of the campsite, a **museum and mill** (July-Sept 11.00-13.00 and 17.00-19.00; €3).

ÀREU → REFUGI DE VALL FERRERA   [MAP 73]

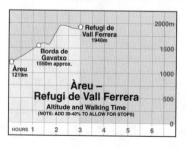

Walk north from the village to rejoin the GR11 and continue along the road as it parallels the Ríu Noguera de Vall Ferrera. The tarmac lane soon turns into an unsurfaced track and the GR markings become increasingly rare. Just over 3km from the village, the track crosses the river. A short way north of the bridge, a sign (ROUTE VIA PLA DE BOET TO PORT DE BOET) marks the spot where the

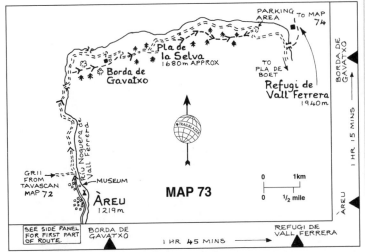

GR11 turns right up a footpath through birch and pine trees. The footpath climbs through the trees and then passes along the grassy hillside, near the two barns of the **Borda Gavatxo**.

Beyond the barns, the GR11 rejoins the vehicle track near a sharp right-hand bend. Follow the track around the bend and on up the hill, past the **Pla de la Selva**. Three-quarters of a kilometre beyond the Pla, the GR11 heads off to the right along a well-marked footpath. The path climbs, quite steeply at times, through pine woods. After some minutes it widens into a new logging track which soon starts to descend, passing an open area with a track junction. Half a kilometre beyond this, the GR11 again heads off to the right on a footpath, which soon leads downhill to join the main vehicle track (marked on the map) near a small parking area.

As the vehicle track swings south-eastwards towards the Pla de la Boet, there's a tiny area set aside for camping and a sign pointing left: REFUGI DE VALL FERRERA. After another ten minutes you come to the refuge (1940m). The *Refugi de Vall Ferrera* (☎ 973-62.43.78) was built in 1935. At a squeeze, 30 people can fit into the tiny dormitory. The refuge has a guardian from June to October; the tariff is €11.60 per night, €13 for supper, and €4.20 for breakfast.

REFUGI DE VALL FERRERA → MARC [MAP 74, p260]

[Includes high section – see warning on pp19-20] The route to Marc via the Refuge du Pinet is excellent. It's mountainous, pretty and it provides the option of climbing up one, two or even three peaks of over 3000m en route. It's also a fairly long and tiring (though very satisfying) day, so an early start is recommended.

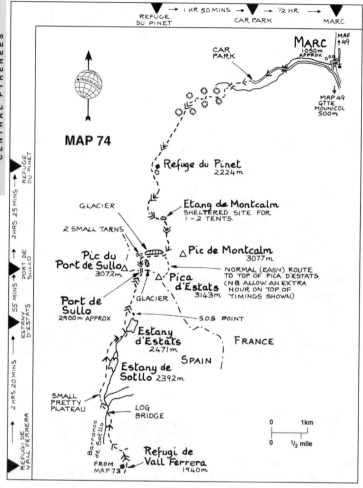

MAP 74

CENTRAL PYRENEES

REFUGE DU PINET — 1 HR 50 MINS → CAR PARK → ½ HR → MARC

MARC 1050m APPROX

CAR PARK

MAP 49

MAP 49 GÎTE MOUNICOL 500m

Refuge du Pinet 2224m

Etang de Montcalm
SHELTERED SITE FOR 1 - 2 TENTS.

GLACIER

△ Pic de Montcalm 3077m

2 SMALL TARNS

NORMAL (EASY) ROUTE TO TOP OF PICA D'ESTATS. (NB ALLOW AN EXTRA HOUR ON TOP OF TIMINGS SHOWN)

Pic du Port de Sullo△ 3072m

△ Pica d'Estats 3143m

Port de Sullo 2900m APPROX

GLACIER

SOS POINT

FRANCE

Estany d'Estats 2471m

SPAIN

Estany de Sotllo 2392m

SMALL PRETTY PLATEAU

LOG BRIDGE

0 ___ 1km
0 ___ ½ mile

Barranco de Sotllo

FROM MAP 73

Refugi de Vall Ferrera 1940m

REFUGE DU PINET ↑ 2 HRS 25 MINS ↑ PORT DE SULLO ↑ 55 MINS ↑ ESTANY D'ESTATS ↑ 2 HRS 20 MINS ↑ REFUGI DE VALL FERRERA

Next to the Refugi de Vall Ferrera is a sign: PICA D'ESTATS 5H. Follow the path almost straight up the hill for 15 minutes to a junction where another sign points left. The trail is well trodden and easy to follow; it heads west and then swings northwards, contouring around the hillside and soon following the valley above the Barranc de Sottlo. After a short scramble down a rocky outcrop, the trail leads to a **log bridge** over the Barranc, beyond which is a **small plateau** where several streams meet. At the north end of the plateau, as the path starts to climb again, there is a metal plaque fixed to one of the rocks: three ice axes and a rope make up the simple design. Follow the path above the plaque and soon you reach the **Estany de Sottlo**, which has a flat grassy area at its northern end, ideal for camping (it's also possible to camp at the southern end, which has far less space but is much more sheltered). Continue up to the **Estany d'Estats**, from which, with the Pica d'Estats towering above, you have a clear

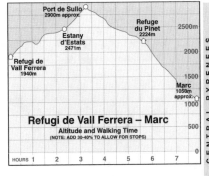

view of the climb to the **Port de Sullo**. Passing around the west side of the Estany, the path passes an SOS point on a rocky mound and then begins its climb, heading straight up the very steep shale slope towards the Port. From the northern end of the lake up to the Port is approximately an hour's climb.

Your effort is rewarded by excellent views at the top. Immediately west of the Port is the **Pic du Port de Sullo (3072m)**, while to the east is the **Pica d'Estats (3143m)**. The direct route from the Port to the top of the Pica requires considerable scrambling/climbing and is best not attempted by those who are inexperienced. Most walkers follow the easier route to the top, going past the **Pic de Montcalm (3077m)** and approaching the Pica d'Estats from the north-east.

From the Port, head down towards the **small tarn** which you can see below. Although a path leads eastwards only a short way below the Port, it's better to ignore this and continue down until you are just above the tarns (as you get lower down, a second one comes into view). Finding a suitable spot, scramble east over the ridge and cross the rocks below the steep glacier beyond. The path can now be seen heading directly east, climbing beside a long glacier which stretches down the valley. Follow this route up to a small cirque below the Pic de Montcalm and the Pica d'Estats, from which ascent to either is easy. To the north, the way to the Refuge du Pinet is prominently marked with circles of yellow paint on the rocks.

The descent to Pinet is steep and rocky. Halfway down you pass the **Étang de Montcalm**, which has a suitably sheltered area at its western end where you could pitch a tent. Forty minutes later you come to the refuge (2224m). *Refuge de l'Étang Pinet* (☎ 05.61.64.80.81, 🖥 www.refugedupinet.com) is a modern and rather ugly building which can take 55 people. The tariff is €13 for the night, €32 for demi-pension. There are facilities for self-catering and it's possible to camp beside the refuge. It's open from 1 June to 30 September.

The descent from Pinet is on a clear path waymarked with yellow paint. It takes a little over 1½ hours to get down to the car park and a further half-hour along the road to Marc. For information on accommodation in **Marc** and **Mounicou** see p205, and for facilities in **Auzat** and **Vicdessos** see p205.

GR10–GR11 route link
Bagnères-de-Luchon to Hospital de Viella

This two-day section from Bagnères-de-Luchon to Hospital de Viella will not be possible in early summer (due to snow), or in bad weather (due to problems with route finding). The second day in particular is extremely arduous – requiring a very early start, some hard walking and a reasonable head for heights. Having said all this, the section is worth considering as it passes through a wonderful area (the Maladetta Region) and links up with a great stretch of the GR11 through the Aigüestortes National Park. If you can get past the tough first couple of days, the route provides a challenging but excellent two-week itinerary.

BAGNÈRES-DE-LUCHON → REFUGIO DE LA RENCLUSA [MAP 75]

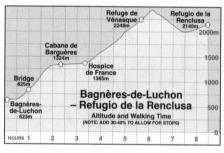

Refuge de Vénasque 2248m
Refugio de la Renclusa 2140m
Cabane de Barguères 1324m
Hospice de France 1385m
Bridge 825m
Bagnères-de-Luchon 623m

Bagnères-de-Luchon – Refugio de la Renclusa
Altitude and Walking Time
(NOTE: ADD 30-40% TO ALLOW FOR STOPS)

HOURS 1 2 3 4 5 6 7 8

2000m
1500
1000
500
0

[Includes high section – see warning on pp19-20] Many would advise cutting out the first part of this section by taking a taxi (approx €20, 20 mins) or hitching a lift to the Hospice de France, as the walk up to the Hospice is mainly along roads and tracks. For diehard pedestrians, however, the route is easy to follow. From the centre of Luchon, follow the road (D125) south out of the town past the campsites. After half an hour, as the road begins to climb, you pass *Gîte Skioura* (☎ 05.61.79.60.59), a friendly place which specializes in groups, though they'll take individual walkers, too. There's a kitchen area for self-catering, and meals are also available by prior arrangement; it costs €12 for the night. One hundred metres further up the road is *Auberge de Castel Vielh* (☎ 05.61.79.36.79), a tiny place set in a delightful garden. There are only three (double) rooms here, ranging in price from €40 to €55, but one gets the impression that people don't really come here for the accommodation – the food's the thing. The Menu Castel-Vielh at €29 looks mouth-watering and local dishes are a speciality.

Another half-hour's walking up the road brings you to a **bridge** over the river. Immediately on the far side of the bridge, a footpath goes off to the left. Follow this uphill for a couple of hundred metres and then follow the yellow pointer, No 20. The path climbs across the hillside in a south-easterly direction, eventually swinging eastwards. After an hour and twenty minutes it levels out and comes to the *Cabane de Barguères*. The hut is in regular use by foresters and is consequently in good condition; there is space for four people.

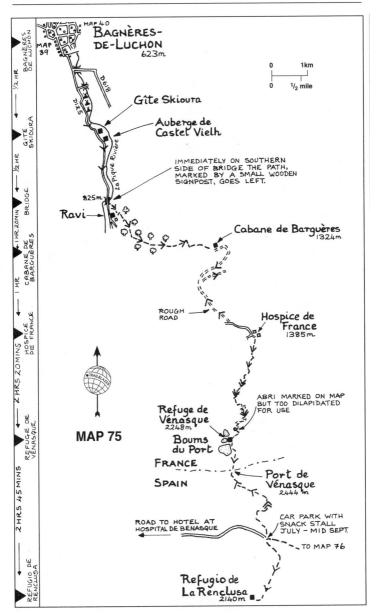

CENTRAL PYRENEES

MAP 40

BAGNÈRES-
DE-LUCHON
623m

MAP 39

D618

D125

Gîte Skioura

Auberge de
Castet Vielh

La Pique Rivière

IMMEDIATELY ON SOUTHERN
SIDE OF BRIDGE THE PATH,
MARKED BY A SMALL WOODEN
SIGNPOST, GOES LEFT.

825m

Ravi

Cabane de Barguères
1324m

ROUGH
ROAD

Hospice de
France
1385m

ABRI MARKED ON MAP
BUT TOO DILAPIDATED
FOR USE

Refuge de
Vénasque
2248m

Boums
du Port

FRANCE

SPAIN

Port de
Vénasque
2444m

CAR PARK WITH
SNACK STALL
JULY – MID SEPT.

ROAD TO HOTEL AT
HOSPITAL DE BENASQUE

TO MAP 76

TRAILBLAZER

MAP 75

0   1km
0   1/2 mile

Refugio de
La Renclusa
2140m

½ HR   BAGNÈRES-DE LUCHON

½ HR   GÎTE SKIOURA

½ HR   BRIDGE

1 HR 20MIN   CABANE DE BARGUÈRES

1 HR   HOSPICE DE FRANCE

2 HRS 20MINS   REFUGE DE VÉNASQUE

2 HRS 45 MINS   REFUGIO DE RENCLUSA

From the hut, follow a large forestry track east to the end of the valley, and then south-west around the hillside. After about a kilometre it is joined by another, larger track; turn right and follow this steeply downhill. On reaching a junction with the tarmac road, turn left and walk up to the **Hospice de France**, which you come to about an hour after leaving the cabane. There's little to see at the hospice. Three ruined houses stand just above the car park and there's a monument to those who escaped across the mountains during the war. The area is popular with day walkers and picnickers.

The climb to Refuge de Vénasque (2248m) is long and steep but at least the stream running down the centre of the valley means that water is available throughout the walk. *Refuge de Vénasque* (☎ 05.61.79.26.46) is a small place that, with the addition of the tent next to the building, can sleep 25 people. They charge €12 for the night, and €14 for an evening meal; camping is permitted (though there's not much space) next to one of the nearby lakes. It's open from early June to mid-September – even if to open it they have to dig it out of the snow first.

From the refuge, it's a 25-minute walk up to the gap in the ridge which constitutes the **Port de Vénasque (2444m)**. Passing through the narrow gap is rather like entering another world; suddenly the views on the French side of the mountains seem tame in comparison with the dramatic scenery of the Maladetta massif. You can see below you the car park at the end of the road from the Hospital de Bénasque; beyond it, and slightly to the right, the Refugio de la Renclusa is visible, midway up the opposite mountain side.

The path heads south initially before veering south-east along the top of a steep slope. It eventually descends in a series of zigzags to the road below. Turn left to the car park, where there is a snack stall in the summer months and from which there's a regular bus service running down to Bénasque. A large path, way-marked with yellow and white paint, runs south-eastwards. It soon veers south-west, and climbs the hillside to the *Refugio de la Renclusa* (2140m; ☎ 974-55.21.06). They charge €11.50 for the night, €12 for dinner and €4 for breakfast.

REFUGIO DE LA RENCLUSA → HOSPITAL DE VIELLA [MAP 76]

❏ **Weather alert**
This section should be tried only in good weather and with plenty of time (locals recommend a 07.00 start or earlier); not only is it a fair distance, but the path can be hard to locate in some places, necessitating extra time for route-finding. The descent from the Col de Mulleres involves a steep scramble/climb down from a ridge, unsuitable for those who dislike heights. It could be dangerous in poor conditions. Having said all this, if weather permits, the walk has lots to recommend it: spectacular views, peaceful valleys and varied scenery.

[**Includes high section – see warning on pp19-20**] From the refuge, walk back down almost to the car park and follow the sign pointing to FORAU D'AIGUALLUT. After 35 minutes you arrive at the **Forau d'Aiguallut**, a spectacular chasm where a rushing stream tumbles down a waterfall and disappears underground. From here the water passes through a maze of limestone tunnels to emerge in the next valley, where it joins the River Joeu and becomes a tribu-

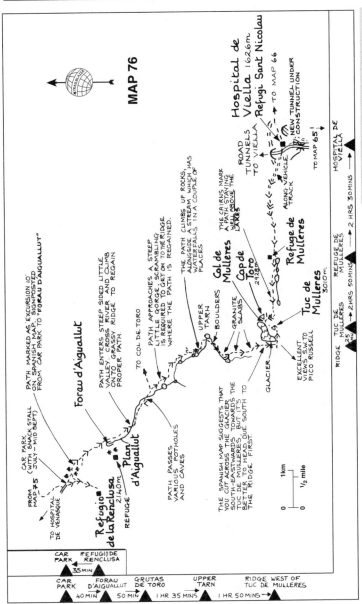

MAP 76

CENTRAL PYRENEES

PATH MARKED AS 'EXCURSION 10' ON SPANISH MAP, SIGNPOSTED FROM CAR PARK TO "FORAU D'AIGUALLUT"

Forau d'Aiguallut

PATH ENTERS STEEP SIDED LITTLE VALLEY, CROSS RIVER AND CLIMB ONTO GRASSY RIDGE TO REGAIN PROPER PATH.

CAR PARK (WITH SNACK STALL JULY - MID SEPT)

FROM MAP 75

TO HOSPITAL DE VENASQUE

Refugio de la Renclusa 2140m.

REFUGE

Plan d'Aiguallut 2140m.

REFUGE

PATH PASSES VARIOUS POTHOLES AND CAVES

TO COL DE TORO

PATH APPROACHES A STEEP LITTLE GORGE, SCRAMBLING IS REQUIRED TO GET ON TO THE RIDGE WHERE THE PATH IS REGAINED

THE PATH CLIMBS UP ROCKS, ALONGSIDE A STREAM, WHICH HAS WATERFALLS IN A COUPLE OF PLACES

UPPER TARN

BOULDERS

GRANITE SLABS

Col de Mulleres

Cap de Toro 2928m.

THE CAIRNS MARK A PATH STAYING WELL ABOVE THE LAKES

Refuge de Mulleres

Tuc de Mulleres 3010m.

GLACIER

EXCELLENT VIEWS S.W. TO PICO RUSSELL

THE SPANISH MAP SUGGESTS THAT YOU CUT ACROSS THE GLACIER SOUTH-EASTWARDS TOWARDS THE TUC DE MULLERES, BUT IT'S BETTER TO HEAD DUE SOUTH TO THE RIDGE FIRST.

Hospital de Viella 1626m.

Refugi Sant Nicolau

TO MAP 66

ROAD TUNNELS TO VIELLA

NEW TUNNEL UNDER CONSTRUCTION

ALONG VEHICLE TRACK

TO MAP 65

HOSPITAL DE VIELLA

0   1km
0   ½ mile

RIDGE TUC DE MULLERES → 25 → 2 HRS 30 MINS

REFUGE DE MULLERES → 2 HRS 30 MINS

CAR PARK   REFUGIO DE RENCLUSA
← 35 MIN →

CAR PARK   FORAU D'AIGUALLUT   GRUTAS DE TORO   UPPER TARN   RIDGE WEST OF TUC DE MULLERES
← 40 MIN → ← 50 MIN → ← 1 HR 35 MINS → ← 1 HR 50 MINS →

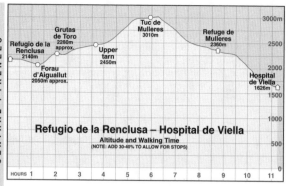

Refugio de la Renclusa – Hospital de Viella
Altitude and Walking Time
(NOTE: ADD 30-40% TO ALLOW FOR STOPS)

tary to the Garonne. There's a small *refuge* hidden just behind the trees to the west. The path follows the eastern side of the grassy **Plan d'Aiguallut** to the southern edge of the plateau, where it approaches the steep-sided entrance to the Valleta de la Escaleta. Cross to the southern bank of the torrent (easier said than done if the water is high) and then scramble up the side of the gully to find a path a short way above the stream. Follow the track south-eastwards into the valley, and you soon pass the Cova de la Escaleta and Grutas de Toro. To your left at this point is the **Col de Toro**. The area has a dense population of marmots and they can be seen all along the route.

Climbing still to the south-east, the path, marked by tiny cairns, leads into a steep-sided little valley where it comes to an apparent dead end. Scramble a few metres up the rocks to find a path slightly higher up, and continue south-eastwards. Low cairns assist with route-finding as the track is at times clearly visible and at other times practically non-existent. Follow the route past two small tarns, before climbing south-south-east across a rocky scarp, next to a rushing stream with waterfalls. The water issues from an upper tarn, to which the path climbs, passing across the stream just at the point where it comes from the tarn.

At this point the path changes direction and climbs up a gully heading south-west before crossing an area of large boulders. On the far side of the boulders is a weird but beautiful landscape, as the route, marked only by a few tiny cairns, crosses enormous sloping plates of granite. The path passes within a few hundred metres of another tarn and then heads south, parallel to a stream.

Soon the vague line of cairns brings you up just to the west of the **Tuc de Mulleres (3010m)**, a rounded boulder-covered summit with an iron cross on top. Before climbing the Tuc, take time on the ridge; there's a magnificent view south-west across the Valle de Salenques to Pico Russell (3205m). Despite the fact that a path is shown on the map, there's no real route up to the top of Tuc de Mulleres; clamber across the boulders as best you can. The iron cross has a box below it with a notebook for walkers to record their visit. Again, the views are stunning.

The eastern side of the ridge leading to the Col de Mulleres is near vertical, so stick to the western side above the glacier as you move towards the col – there are a few cairns here which take a suitable line. You need to go almost to the northern end of the col to find the point to cross – looking down, you can see a route which has been much used. Great care needs to be taken when descending this part; there are good foot and hand holds, but it's very steep. Even in July there may be snow at the bottom of the scramble down; again great care is required as the slope is steep and there are rocks at the bottom.

From the area just below the col, follow the cairns, which lead east, staying high above the lakes below. Eventually the cairns lead down to the valley bottom near the easternmost lake. On a spur above the tarn is the **Refuge de Mulleres**, a bright orange metal shelter that can sleep twelve people. Note that the position of the refuge is incorrectly shown on the Editorial Alpina map.

The path continues its steep descent down the valley, becoming increasingly clear and easy to follow. You'll now be aware of a massive building project below you – the new tunnel through the Pyrenees to Viella. When you reach the lower valley, join a vehicle track which leads directly to the refuge. The **Refugi Sant Nicolau** (☎ 973-69.70.52) can sleep 49 people in the huge dormitory in the basement. It's a comfortable place with a good restaurant/bar on the ground floor. Bed and breakfast costs €12, and media-pensión is €21.50. The refuge is open every day from 30 June to 15 September; the rest of the year it is basically open Tuesday to Sunday though it does close occasionally, so check in advance. For a local taxi phone ☎ 629-31.43.34.

For the continuation of the walk through Aigüestortes region, see p244.

Ordesa National Park (Spain)

Spain's Ordesa region, just across the border from Gavarnie, contains some of the most spectacular scenery in the Pyrenees. The Ordesa Canyon, carved by glacial action up to a million years ago, is justifiably the most famous feature but the narrow Añisclo Canyon is just as impressive and is considered by many to be much prettier. Monte Perdido, at 3355m the third highest peak in the Pyrenees, dominates the area, while the Brèche de Roland (see p122), a jagged hole in the frontier ridge between France and Spain, is a landmark of legendary status. A combination of the wonderful scenery and the fact that the weather is generally more stable on the Spanish side of the mountains means that a visit to the Ordesa region, whether by itself or as part of a longer itinerary, is highly recommended.

There are, of course, many ways to do this. The GR11 passes through the region anyway but for those not intending to follow the GR11, the route suggested below is a four- to seven-day circuit which starts from Refuge Wallon and arrives back in France, via the Brèche de Roland, at Gavarnie. If you have the time, and particularly if you're carrying a tent (and thus have some flexibility over accommodation) it's worth allowing at least six days. Each of the four stages of the circuit outlined here involves a very long day's walking. (Note, too, that both the Col d'Arratille, at the start of the circuit, and the Brèche de Roland, at the end of the circuit, are high passes that may not be passable without proper equipment in the early summer.)

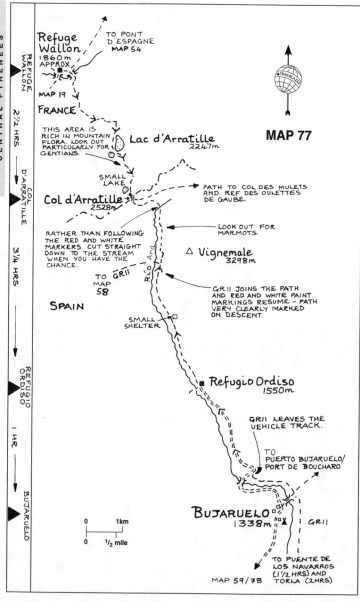

CENTRAL PYRENEES

REFUGE WALLON — 2½ HRS — COL D'ARRATILLE — 3¼ HRS — REFUGIO ORDISO — 1 HR — BUJARUELO

TO PONT D'ESPAGNE
MAP 54

Refuge Wallon
1860m
APPROX

MAP 19

FRANCE

THIS AREA IS RICH IN MOUNTAIN FLORA. LOOK OUT PARTICULARLY FOR GENTIANS.

Lac d'Arratille
2247m

SMALL LAKE

Col d'Arratille
2528m

PATH TO COL DES MULETS AND REF DES OULETTES DE GAUBE.

MAP 77

LOOK OUT FOR MARMOTS.

△ Vignemale
3298m

RATHER THAN FOLLOWING THE RED AND WHITE MARKERS CUT STRAIGHT DOWN TO THE STREAM WHEN YOU HAVE THE CHANCE.

TO GRII
MAP 58

SPAIN

GRII JOINS THE PATH AND RED AND WHITE PAINT MARKINGS RESUME – PATH VERY CLEARLY MARKED ON DESCENT.

RÍO ARA

SMALL SHELTER

Refugio Ordiso
1550m

GRII LEAVES THE VEHICLE TRACK.

TO PUERTO BUJARUELO/ PORT DE BOUCHARO

BUJARUELO
1338m

GRII

0   1km
0   ½ mile

TO PUENTE DE LOS NAVARROS (1½ HRS) AND TORLA (2 HRS)

MAP 59/78

REFUGE WALLON → TORLA (VIA ARA VALLEY)　　[MAP 77]

[Includes high section – see warning on pp19-20] Just to the east of the Refuge Wallon a sign points the way towards the Col d'Arratille (LAC D'ARRATILLE 1H 30; COL D'ARRATILLE 2H 30). From here the path heads across a footbridge and starts to climb south-eastwards. The trail, which also links with the Col des Mulets and the Refuge des Oulettes de Gaube beyond, is popular in high season, so try to make an early start; it's a beautiful walk and best enjoyed without crowds.

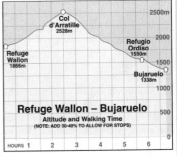

Refuge Wallon – Bujaruelo
Altitude and Walking Time
(NOTE: ADD 30-40% TO ALLOW FOR STOPS)

Beyond the Lac d'Arratille the gradient steepens and the final part of the climb to the col involves picking your way through boulders and then crossing the steep slope above a small lake. (This section will be hazardous for walkers without proper equipment if there is still snow, so in early summer it's worth asking the guardian at Wallon whether the col is passable before starting out.)

Approximately 2¹/₂ hours after leaving the refuge you reach the **Col d'Arratille (2528m)**. The Ara valley, with Vignemale on the far side, lies before you. In sharp contrast with the landscape to the north of the col, the valley slopes gently down towards the south; it seems strangely deserted after the busy trails around Wallon. The route down from the col, clearly indicated with red-and-white paint marks, makes a wide loop towards the Col des Mulets. You can save a little time by cutting down the slope when the opportunity arises and crossing the stream to join the footpath on the eastern bank of the Río Ara.

Follow the footpath down the valley. After 1¹/₂-2 hours you come to a small, empty *shelter* with two rooms (one of which may be locked). The hut is far from clean but would do for an overnight stop. An hour further down the valley, at the end of a rough road, is the *Refugio Ordiso* **(1550m)**, a tiny building which looks (and smells) as though it has been used as a sheep shelter. Follow the rough road down from the refuge and then take the marked trail along the east side of the river to the old bridge of Bujaruelo. The GR11 continues on the east bank; cross the bridge for the two campsites below.

Bujaruelo is no more than a refuge/albergue/campsite and lies another 30 minutes down the road. The first you come to is *Camping/Refuge San Nicolas* (☎ 974-48.64.12). Camping costs €3.20 per person and €3.20 per tent in a large field which is also shared by a few cows. At the refuge, half board is €24 in a dormitory that was described as being like a hotel in contrast to the packed dormitories at Refugio de Goriz. In a room for four, half board is €26. Dinner is €10. There's a washing machine and tumble drier for use at €4.20.

Should you want fractionally more comfort, *Camping Valle de Bujaruelo* ☆☆ (☎ 974-48.63.48), half an hour's walk down the road, is a more manicured sort of place. Cabins are available for €19-32 (2-4 people) and campers pay €3.40

per person, €3.40 per tent.There is a restaurant and bar with a pretty patio to sit out on and a set-menu dinner is €11. The small shop has Camping Gaz cartridges.

Three and a half kilometres below the campsite is the main road and the **Puente de los Navarros (1050m approx)**, which is just below the entry to the national park. The rooftops of Torla can be seen to the right, down the valley.

There are two ways to get to Torla. You can either walk straight down the road (approximately 40 minutes), or follow the attractive footpath which heads down the valley along the side of the river (³/₄ hour to 1 hour). If you're taking the old path, a red-and-white marker on the arch of the bridge indicates the way, and there's also a sign: CAMINO VIEJO A ORDESA. A short way down the path you come to a junction; continue southwards until the path brings you out just below the town, next to the Camping Río Ara.

If you're heading down the road, after quarter of an hour you come to the *Camping San Anton* ☆☆ (☎ 974-48.60.63) where there's a shop and bar/restaurant; the tariff is €3.70 per person and €3.70 per tent. Ten minutes further south you come to *Hotel-Camping Ordesa* (☎ 974-48.61.25, 🖹 48.63.81), a large complex. During high season, the hotel has double rooms from €51.29 with breakfast, and a space in the campsite costs €3.65 per person and €3.65 per tent. Campers can use the hotel swimming pool. Just beyond the hotel you come to **Torla**.

TORLA

A pretty village with a relaxed atmosphere and plenty of good facilities, Torla is a great place to take a break. However, in mid-season it can get very crowded so you should book accommodation in advance.

Services

Shops in Torla include several mini-supermarkets, two camping stores (one of which sells Coleman/Epigas) and a pharmacy. There are two **banks** with cash dispensers. The **post office**, through an unmarked door near the main square, is open 09.00-11.00 on weekdays; if you want to send a parcel, note that they accept only small ones. There's a small **internet centre** nearby. It's only open 19.00-21.00 but you're allowed free access for 30 minutes. The **tourist office** is on the main square and is open daily (closed Monday morning) during the season. For more information see 🖥 www.ordesa.net.

There's are two **buses** daily (60 mins) between Torla and Sabiñánigo (where there's a railway station). Buses leave Torla at 15.30 and 20.00, and depart from Sabiñánigo at 11.00 and 18.30. There is also one daily bus between Torla and L'Ainsa, leaving Torla at 12.00 and leaving L'Ainsa

at 14.30; again the journey takes an hour. From the start of July to mid-October (and at Easter) a useful bus service runs between Torla and the car-park area in the Ordesa Canyon (stopping en route to drop off and pick up at the Visitors' Centre, although when the new Visitors' Centre opens in 2006 it may no longer stop at the old centre). The service runs at 06.00, 7.00, 08.00 then at roughly every 15 minutes until 19.00 (18.00 in September and October). It costs €3.10 for a return ticket.

Taxi Bellavista (☎ 974-48.61.53) operates from Hostal Bellavista. They use Espace-type vans, so if there are several of you it becomes a viable option. A taxi to Nerín costs around €50. Other taxi operators include **Taxi J Lardiés** (☎ 616-72.25.31) and **Taxi J Soler** (☎ 974-48.62.43).

There are numerous **places to eat**. Most restaurants offer a menu del día from around €11 which includes three courses, bread and wine. The menus are all posted outside the restaurants.

Where to stay

Probably the best hotel is *Hotel Villa de Torla* ☆☆ (☎ 974-48.61.56, 🖹 48.63.65),

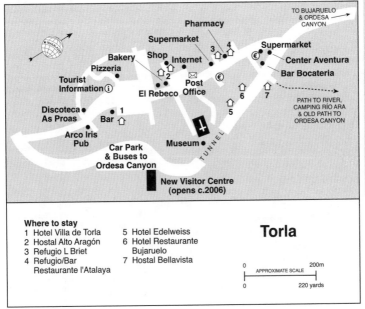

Where to stay
1 Hotel Villa de Torla
2 Hostal Alto Aragón
3 Refugio L Briet
4 Refugio/Bar Restaurante l'Atalaya
5 Hotel Edelweiss
6 Hotel Restaurante Bujaruelo
7 Hostal Bellavista

Torla

0 _____ 200m
APPROXIMATE SCALE
0 _____ 220 yards

---

on the central square, which has singles/doubles for €37.45/58.85 (avoid Room 110: the double glazing is no match for the noise at turning-out time from Discoteca As Proas.) Several other hotels are similar in standard and price: *Hostal Bellavista* ☆☆ (☎ 974-48.61.53, 🖳 www.bellavistaordesa .com) has doubles for €48.15; *Hotel Restaurante Bujaruelo* ☆ (☎ 974-48.61.74, 🖳 www. torla.com) has singles/doubles for €32.10/40.66; *Hotel Edelweiss* ☆☆ (☎ 974-48.61.73, 📄 48.63.72) charges from €32.10/ 52.96 singles/doubles. *Hostal Alto Aragón* (☎ 974-48.61.72) is good value: there are singles/doubles with attached bath from €28.89/37.45, breakfast included. Some rooms are in the building opposite.

For budget accommodation, *Refugio L Briet* (☎ 974-48.62.21, 🖳 www.refugioluci enbriet.com) is recommended. It takes its name from the French explorer who studied and photographed this part of the Pyrenees. It's very clean and modern and excellent

value at €8.50 for a dormitory bed. They also have three private rooms (a double, a triple and a four-bedded room) but no self-catering facilities. *Refugio/Bar/Restaurante l'Atalaya* (☎ 974-48.60.22) has similarly-priced accommodation.

Several campsites have already been mentioned above, but the nearest to Torla is the *Camping Río Ara* ☆☆ (☎ 974-48.62.48) which is situated in a peaceful shady area near the river. There's a shop and bar/restaurant; the tariff is €3.63 per person and €3.63 per tent.

What to see

There's an **ethnographic museum** (€1, open 11.00-14.00, 18.00-21.00 daily except Monday morning) with a small but interesting display of old photos and implements. The **church** nearby is quite plain inside apart from three grand baroque *retablos*. A new national park **Visitors' Centre** opens in 2006 beside the car park. Until then the display will remain in its old building, inconveniently located several kilometres away at the entrance to the canyon. The Torla–Ordesa park bus service stops there and entry is free. The displays cover the geology, flora and fauna, and the local history and culture of the area.

Activities in the area include climbing, horse riding, mountain biking, rafting and caving. For information try the tourist office or contact a local company such as **Compañia Guias de Torla** (☎ 974-48. 64.22, 🖳 www.guiasdetorla.com).

Entertainment in Torla is limited but there's sometimes live blues in the **Bar/Restaurant l'Atalaya**, or you could pay a visit to **Discoteca As Proas**, which opens at midnight.

THE ORDESA CANYON   [MAP 78/59]

Many walkers visit the Ordesa Canyon en route to or from the Refugio de Goriz. Another option, however, if you're staying in Torla, is to do a one-day circuit. It's a fairly long day, but if you leave your gear in Torla and carry only a light day sack, it's a very enjoyable walk. Alternatively, if you want to spend more time in the canyon itself and less time getting there, you could use the excellent bus service which runs between Torla and the car park in the canyon.

The walk up to the canyon from Torla is highly recommended. From near the Hostal Bellavista, take the path leading down towards Camping Río Ara. On the far side of the river bridge, and just below the entrance to the campsite, take the large path which runs north along the side of the river. Various signs in Torla and along the path point the way: CAMINO DE TURIETO ORDESA. After 15-20 minutes the path forks, the right fork being marked as the CAMINO TURIETO and the left fork PUENTE DE LOS NAVARROS, VALLE DE BUJARUELO. Go right, following the red-and-white markers of the GR11, which has come down from Bujaruelo.

The path climbs at a steady but fairly easy gradient through the trees, which provide welcome shade. As the path swings eastwards into the entrance of the canyon, there are excellent views northwards towards the old Visitors' Centre (see p271). Approximately half an hour after leaving the fork in the path, you pass the impressive **Cascada Tomborrotera** which is visible from a small viewing platform, and ten minutes beyond this you come to the **Cascada Abelos**. Just beyond this second waterfall there's a fork in the trail. The left-hand path leads down to the **Puente Luciano Briet**, beside which there's a monument to the French naturalist. It's probably better not to cross the river here, but if you have time to spare, wander down to the bridge and admire the view up the canyon.

Continuing along the south side of the river, the path is now wide and level and runs through mature woods which provide plenty of shade. Twenty minutes beyond the Puente Luciano Briet, you come to a sign pointing left across the river towards the car park ('aparcamiento'), where there are a few useful facilities including a *restaurant/bar*, **toilets**, a **drinking fountain**, and **buses** back to Torla.

CENTRAL PYRENEES

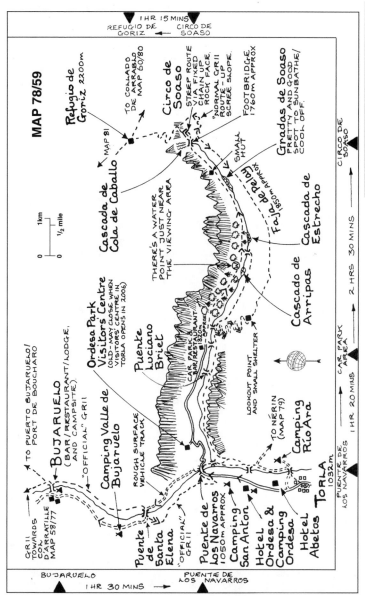

MAP 78/59

IHR 15 MINS
REFUGIO DE GORIZ ← CIRCO DE SOASO

Refugio de Goriz 2200m

TO COLLADO DE ARRABLO MAP 60/80

TO Collado de Arrablo MAP 81

Cascade de Cola de Caballo

Circo de Soaso

STEEP ROUTE VIA FIXED CHAIN UP ROCK FACE.

"NORMAL" GRII ROUTE - UP SCREE SLOPE.

FOOTBRIDGE 1760m APPROX

SMALL HUT

Gradas de Soaso
PRETTY AND GOOD SPOT TO SUNBATHE/COOL OFF.

CIRCO DE SOASO

Faja de Pelay 1850m APPROX

THERE'S A WATER POINT JUST NEAR THE VIEWING AREA

Cascada de Estrecho

Cascada de Arripas

0 ____ 1km
0 ____ ½ mile

Ordesa Park Visitors Centre
(OLD-MAY CLOSE WHEN VISITORS' CENTRE IN TORLA OPENS IN 2006)

Puente Luciano Briet

CAR PARK/CAR PARK RESTAURANT 1320m APPROX

CAR PARK AREA

LOOKOUT POINT AND SMALL SHELTER

ROUGH SURFACE VEHICLE TRACK

Camping Valle de Bujaruelo

Bujaruelo
(BAR/RESTAURANT/LODGE AND CAMPSITE).

"OFFICIAL" GRII

TO PUERTO BUJARUELO/ PORT DE BOUCHARO

GRII TOWARDS COL D'ARRATILLE MAP 58/77

Puente de Santa Elena

"OFFICIAL" GRII

Puente de Los Navarros 1050m APPROX

Camping San Anton

Hotel Ordesa & Camping Ordesa

Hotel Abetos

Torla 1032m

TO NÉRIN (MAP 79)

Camping Río Ara

PUENTE DE LOS NAVARROS

IHR 20 MINS → 2 HRS 30 MINS

BUJARUELO

PUENTE DE LOS NAVARROS
IHR 30 MINS →

IHR 30 MINS →

CIRCO DE SOASO

The route from the eastern end of the car park is well signposted and the circular tour of the canyon begins and ends here. There is, however, a choice – which direction to complete the circuit? On either side of the Río Araza two main paths follow the valley floor as far as the Puente de Arripas, where the path on the north side of the river becomes the only option. Running high around the south side of the canyon, however, is the Faja de Pelay, a promontory some two thirds of the way up the canyon wall, from which there are spectacular views. If you walk up the valley floor and then back along the Faja de Pelay you find yourself climbing slowly but constantly for two thirds of the route, then completing a level section along the Faja, before descending very steeply to the car park. If you do it the other way around there's a long and incredibly steep climb to begin with, after which it's all either level or downhill. The description here is of the first option.

It doesn't much matter whether you take the path on the south or north side of the river for the first part of the walk – both are shady and very pleasant. If you take the southern path, after about forty minutes you come to the **Puente de Arripas** at which point you are forced to cross the river and join the northern route. The (northern) path climbs steadily from here, gaining height above a series of waterfalls until, about an hour's walking beyond the Puente de Arripas, you come to the **Gradas de Soaso**, a series of low waterfalls and clear blue pools which provide a perfect place to stop for a break. Approximately an hour beyond the Gradas, you reach the eastern end of the canyon, the **Circo de Soaso (1760m)**, where a tiny bridge crosses the stream just below an impressive waterfall, **Cascada de Cola de Caballo**.

North-east of the bridge, a chain has been fixed to the rocks to facilitate the steep climb towards the *Refugio de Goriz* (see p231). (There's also an easier path to the refugio, which runs up the scree slope to the right). The path to the Faja de Pelay, however, is much less strenuous and runs south-west, climbing gradually up the hillside. The path soon levels off, continuing around the side of the valley horizontally while the bottom of the canyon sinks away below. There are superb views westwards towards the mouth of the canyon and across to the towering walls on the far side. At the western end of the Faja de Pelay, the descent into the canyon begins near a large and decrepit refuge building, marked on the map as 'Ref y Mirador'. It takes an hour to get down the unrelentingly steep path to the car park. From the Circo de Soaso back to the car park via the Faja takes about $3^{1}/4$ hours. In all, the circuit starting from and returning to the car park has taken about 6-$6^{1}/2$ hours.

TORLA → NERÍN   [MAP 79]

This section from Torla to Nerín is not going to be a highlight of anyone's trip; it's a thirsty, tiring walk, almost entirely along a single rough road, and there's a large uphill section to begin with. It does get you to Nerín, however, which is the ideal starting point for a hike up the Añisclo Canyon, and walking over the tops of hills is a lot better than walking down the road, which is the only alternative. If you wish to avoid all or part of this section, consider taking a taxi (see p270).

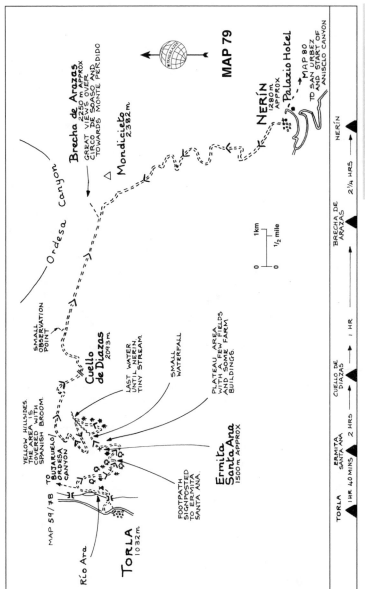

CENTRAL PYRENEES

MAP 79

Brecha de Arazas
2250 m APPROX
GREAT VIEWS OVER
CIRCO DE SOASO AND
TOWARDS MONTE PERDIDO

△ Mondicieto
2382 m.

Ordesa Canyon

Nerín
1280 m.
APPROX

Palazio Hotel

MAP 80
TO SAN URBEZ
AND START OF
ANISCLO CANYON

SMALL
OBSERVATION
POINT

Cuello
de Diazas
2043 m.

LAST WATER
UNTIL NERÍN.
TINY STREAM.

SMALL
WATERFALL

PLATEAU AREA
WITH A FEW FIELDS
AND SOME FARM
BUILDINGS.

YELLOW HILLSIDES.
THE AREA IS
COVERED WITH
SPANISH BROOM.

TO
BUTARUELO/
ORDESA
CANYON

MAP 59/78

Ermita
Santa Ana
1500 m APPROX

FOOTPATH
SIGNPOSTED
TO ERMITA
SANTA ANA.

Río Ara

TORLA
1032 m.

TORLA ◄ 1 HR 40 MINS ► ERMITA ◄ 2 HRS ► CUELLO DE ◄ 1 HR ► BRECHA DE ◄ 2¼ HRS ► NERÍN
SANTA ANA   DIAZAS   ARAZAS

0   1km
0   ½ mile

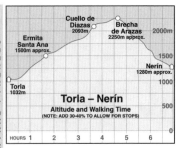

CENTRAL PYRENEES

From Torla, follow the footpath over the old river bridge and go left along the track which passes below the Camping Río Ara. After about twenty minutes, the vehicle track bends sharply right and the footpath continues towards Ordesa. Follow the vehicle track, which starts to climb the hillside. After forty minutes you pass a rough sign: STA ANA. The little path is rather overgrown and presumably forms an alternative route to the Ermita, for some twenty minutes further up the vehicle track you reach the **Ermita Sta Ana** (1500m approx) anyway.

Up to this point, if you've started at a reasonable hour, the trees and the steep slopes above the path will have provided welcome shade. From here, however, there is little in the way of shelter from the sun. Five minutes beyond the Ermita there's a small waterfall and twenty minutes later you cross the same stream further up the hillside. This is literally the last water until Nerín. Ensure that you are carrying at least two litres, as the entire walk from here is exposed to the sun and is arid and dusty.

Another hour and a half of climbing brings you to the **Cuello de Diazas (2093m)**, from which there are good views west to Mondiciero (2296m) and south into the Valle de Vío. Ten minutes further east along the track you get a glimpse of the Ordesa Canyon, where a break in the rocks allows a footpath to a **small observation point**.

Fifty minutes later, there's a better view as a grassy vehicle track leads across the hillside to the **Brecha de Arazas**. The view from anywhere around here is unbelievable: way below you, you can see people on the Faja de Pelay, and as far below again, walkers on the path alongside the Río Araza. The view of the Circo de Soaso with Monte Perdido towering above it is memorable. From the Brecha de Arazas, it's about 2^1/4 hours down the rough road to **Nerín**. (For details of the bus service from here to Nerín, see p277.)

Ramond de Carbonnières

The first ascent of Monte Perdido was masterminded by Frenchman Ramond de Carbonnières, one of the great figures in Pyrenean history. Following a stay in Barèges in 1787, Ramond became fascinated with the mountains. In 1789 he published *Observations faites dans les Pyrenées*, and over the following years he travelled widely, recording details of all aspects of Pyrenean life. After several attempts to scale Monte Perdido, he finally succeeded on 10 August 1802; in the same year he published his account of the feat in *Voyage au Mont Perdu*. Ramond's contribution to scientific knowledge of the mountains was commemorated in 1865 by the formation of the Société Ramond – an organization dedicated to intellectual enquiry about the Pyrenees. There is also a flower named after him – *Ramondia Pyrenaica*.

NERÍN

Nerín, a tiny, pretty hamlet of 10-15 houses, has somehow avoided the fate that has befallen some of its neighbours (such as Sercué) which have simply been abandoned. In summer a substantial part of Nerín's income must come from tourism, both from the walkers who stay in the lodges here and from the day trippers who use the coach service up to the Brecha de Arazas. In winter it's a different matter: only one family remains in the hamlet year-round.

There are three places to stay in Nerín. First up, the *Palazio Hotel Restaurante* (☎ 974-48.90.02, 🖳 www.hotelpalazio. com), on the edge of the village, opened recently. Rooms have attached baths and they charge €70.62 for a double with breakfast. In the village, *Añisclo Albergue* (☎ 974-48.90.10, 🗒 974-48.90.08) is run by a friendly family, has a good selection of walking books and a big terrace facing east towards the mountains around Ainsa. A bed in the clean and modern dormitories (four-, five- and eight-bedded) costs €7.50, or it's €21 for media-pensión. It's open year-round. *Pensión el Turista* (☎ 974-48.90.16) is slightly less welcoming, but has the attraction that the proprietress speaks French (which makes reservation easier if your Spanish isn't too hot). They charge €38 for a double room (€4 for breakfast).

For those who are feeling terminally lazy, a bus service runs three times a day from Nerín up the rough road to the Brecha de Arazas (near **Mondicieto (2382m)**. The idea is that this takes day walkers up to the same level as the Refugio de Goriz, so that they can walk to the refuge around the top of the canyon without having to climb any hills. The bus currently leaves Nerín at 07.00, 10.00 and 15.00; the 10.00 and 15.00 services will also bring walkers back to the village from the Brecha; there is a late service at 20.00 to bring walkers down to Nerín.

NERÍN → REFUGIO DE GORIZ   [MAP 80, p278]

On the lane leading east out of the village there's a signpost and a map board showing all the local paths. The GR15 is the one you want; the actual signpost points down into the stony valley and simply reads: SERCUÉ, AÑISCLO. The path is easy to follow, and after 45 minutes you come to the deserted village of **Sercué (1160m)**. One house is in use, but the other buildings are all in vari-

ous states of ruin. Just above the houses is a flat grassy area which would be good for camping, though the village might be a little too spooky for most people.

Twenty minutes' walk beyond Sercué you come to the lip of the canyon, from which a steep but well-made path descends to the main trail along the valley floor. Heading north along the canyon, the scenery gets progressively more attractive, with waterfalls, clear pools and a tiny spring en route.

About half an hour past the spring, the path starts to climb steeply, zigzagging up the hillside, eventually levelling out when it has gained enough height to pass over the top of the cliffs. After a further three quarters of an hour you come to **La Ripareta (1405m)**, a perfect spot for a break. The river edge is

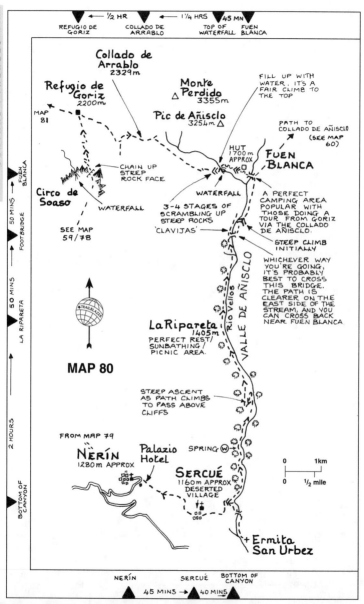

CENTRAL PYRENEES

← ½ HR ← 1¼ HRS 45 MN ▶

REFUGIO DE GORIZ   COLLADO DE ARRABLO   TOP OF WATERFALL   FUEN BLANCA

Collado de Arrablo 2329m

Refugio de Goriz 2200m

MAP 81

Monte Perdido △ 3355m

Pic de Añisclo 3254m △

FILL UP WITH WATER. IT'S A FAIR CLIMB TO THE TOP

PATH TO COLLADO DE AÑISCLO (SEE MAP 60)

HUT 1700 m APPROX

FUEN BLANCA

CHAIN UP STEEP ROCK FACE

Circo de Soaso

WATERFALL

WATERFALL

3-4 STAGES OF SCRAMBLING UP STEEP ROCKS 'CLAVIJAS'

A PERFECT CAMPING AREA POPULAR WITH THOSE DOING A TOUR FROM GORIZ VIA THE COLLADO DE AÑISCLO.

STEEP CLIMB INITIALLY

SEE MAP 59/78

WHICHEVER WAY YOU'RE GOING, IT'S PROBABLY BEST TO CROSS THIS BRIDGE. THE PATH IS CLEARER ON THE EAST SIDE OF THE STREAM, AND YOU CAN CROSS BACK NEAR FUEN BLANCA.

VALLE DE AÑISCLO

Río Vellos

La Ripareta 1405m PERFECT REST/ SUNBATHING/ PICNIC AREA.

MAP 80

STEEP ASCENT AS PATH CLIMBS TO PASS ABOVE CLIFFS

FROM MAP 79

NERÍN 1280m APPROX

Palazio Hotel

SPRING Ⓦ

SERCUÉ 1160m APPROX DESERTED VILLAGE

0   1km
0   ½ mile

Ermita San Urbez

← 50 MINS FUEN BLANCA
← 50 MINS FOOTBRIDGE
← 50 MINS LA RIPARETA
← 2 HOURS
BOTTOM OF CANYON

NERÍN   SERCUÉ   BOTTOM OF CANYON
▲ 45 MINS → ◀ 40 MINS ▲

lined by an area of flat rock and grass: just right for a spot of sunbathing.

From La Ripareta, continue up the valley along a narrow and sometimes indistinct footpath, which runs through the trees. After about 50 minutes you come to the **footbridge** marked as *pasarela* on the map. Although a path is shown (on the Editorial Alpina map) as continuing on the west bank of the stream, it is not recommended. Having passed over a short stretch of *clavijas* (a cable and some iron pins to enable walkers to traverse a vertical bit of rock) the path becomes hard to follow and then peters out completely. Whichever route you take, therefore, it's best to cross here to the eastern bank of the stream, where a clear path winds northwards towards **Fuen Blanca**.

On the far side of the bridge, the narrow path climbs steeply at first, before levelling out and running across the side of the canyon to arrive at Fuen Blanca. Opposite the tiny footbridge at Fuen Blanca is a ***stone shelter***. The area is beautiful with little waterfalls and pools, and impressive mountains on all sides. It's a popular camping spot, and many walkers use it as a stopover. The shelter is picturesque but only for use as a last resort; it's extremely dirty and could take no more than two or three people.

From this hut, the route to the Refugio de Goriz is clearly indicated with the red-and-white waymarks of the GR11. After 3/4 hour of steep climbing, the path crosses the stream above the waterfall. Fill up here, as there's more climbing to come. The trail now rises in three or four stages, mounting to a grassy ledge, crossing it and then climbing again. Finally you reach a grassy plateau, and you'll see the **Collado de Arrablo (2329m)** ahead; the river runs almost next to the path, and there's another chance to get water. Having reached the col, the path starts to head south-west; within a short distance, you take an obvious turning to the north-west and follow the path to Goriz.

Refugio de Goriz (☎ 974-34.12.01) is very popular, and you should book in advance if you're visiting during peak season (mid-July to mid-August), or make an effort to turn up as early in the afternoon as possible. In the evening the area around the refuge is often crammed with tents, too. The refuge has a guardian in residence all year, and has 90 places; charges are €7 per night, €12 for the evening meal and €3.60 for breakfast. Some provisions are sold at the refuge, including pasta, chocolate and puncture-type camping gaz cylinders.

REFUGIO DE GORIZ → GAVARNIE   [MAP 81, p280]

[Includes high section – see warning on pp19-20] This section over the Brèche de Roland and down to Gavarnie is not especially difficult but it is quite arduous and should definitely not be attempted in bad weather. The route is unmarked apart from a few low cairns and there are areas where, even in reasonable visibility, it is easy to lose the way amongst the rocks. Equally, in early summer there may still be a fair amount of snow around the south side of the Brèche, and it's worth asking for advice from the guardian at the Refugio de Goriz about whether the Brèche is passable for walkers.

From Goriz, follow the well-worn track along the hillside to the west of the refuge, as it climbs to a small ridge. Scramble up the rocks and continue in a

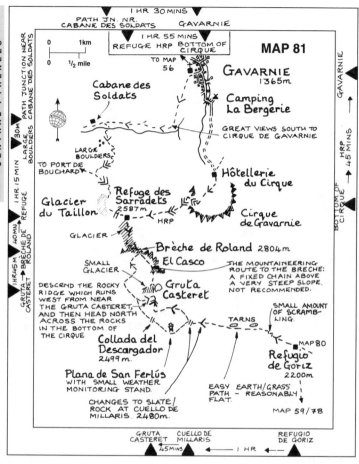

westerly direction along a mostly level and grassy track to the **Cuello de Millaris** (2480m approx). From the bare and desolate hummock of the col, you'll see in front a large flat area, the **Plana de San Ferlús**. Most of it is completely bare, covered with small rocks, while the southern part is grassy and has a weather-monitoring stand. You have a choice here between the adventurous route near the Gruta Casteret, or the more straightforward route which is advisable in bad weather. This latter, easier route bears slightly to the left but basically heads for the next col, where you can stop again and take a good look up at the Brèche and get your bearings. A line of cairns leads down off the col diagonally to the right, then climbs directly towards the Brèche, occasionally zigzagging to avoid the need for scrambling. On the next patch of level ground, facing the Brèche, it is clear that you will climb up from the left and not go straight up the loose rock. There is barely any scrambling necessary.

The more challenging route leads to, but does not commit you to, the mountaineering route, which features chains bolted to the rock for support in places. A path marked by tiny cairns leads off to the right, and contours around the

northern side of the bowl. Gradually it climbs the hillside and, as it starts to bend northwards, it steepens, leading towards the **Gruta Casteret** (see below). The actual route is very indistinct; keep an eye out for the cairns which lead you up a steep scramble to a rocky promontory just to the south of the cave (although the mouth of the cave remains out of sight until you're very close to it). As you reach the promontory, the frontier ridge suddenly comes into view, and you can see to the north two prominent gaps in the ridge. The left of these has a pillar of rock standing in the middle of it, while the right one is simply a huge rectangular breach in the chain. This latter is the **Brèche de Roland (2804m)**.

From here it's possible to continue up and around the promontory to get to

---

Gruta Casteret

In July 1926, Norbert Casteret, one of France's leading speleologists, set out on an expedition looking for caves with his wife, mother and brother. Catching a brief glimpse of what appeared to be the opening of a cavern, they struggled up a snow slope towards it, half expecting that they would find only another overhang. The cave, however, complete with a 'a river of ice ... from the bowels of the mountain' was beyond their wildest dreams.

Casteret's account of their initial exploration makes modern caving techniques look positively wet. 'Pushed by Martial, wielding my pick, and holding the candle in my teeth, I finally managed to scramble to the top. I started to crawl up a flattened tube in the thick ice, white as porcelain; but at each attempt an air-current trumpeting through the tunnel blew out the candle...'

Turning back only because the candle was about to run out, Casteret had to wait a month until he and his wife could return to have another look – again by candlelight. 'Our first step was to explore the huge hall which we had glimpsed a month before. Its vast roof was all in one piece, spanning an ice-field with an estimated area of three thousand three hundred and fifty square yards ... Huge blocks off the ceiling were set in ice which was so clear that we could see tiny pebbles frozen six or seven feet deep. Cracks in the vault furnished a considerable influx of ice to feed the lake. The largest of these streams filled a vertical cleft and formed a translucent cascade sixty or eighty feet high. Its top was lost to sight'.

the cave; the entrance is accessible to all walkers but in order to go into the cave you'll need to be properly equipped. The best route towards the Brèche, however, involves descending again, down the rocky ridge which runs westwards. There's no defined path, but from the vantage point near to the cave you should be able to pick out a route down the ridge. Having descended, you then need to head north across the bottom of the cirque, finally ascending the relatively straightforward slope directly below the Brèche. (For those with a strong head for heights, a **high path** runs under the vertical walls of El Casco, with the aid, in places, of a steel cable. Considerable care, and proper equipment is required: the scree and snow slopes are extremely steep and slippery).

The descent from the Brèche to the Refuge des Sarradets (also called the Refuge de la Brèche Rolande) takes 30-40 minutes, and is across the Brèche glacier. In mid-summer, although many people carry an ice axe, there's little need for one; a stick is useful, however, to give a little extra stability. The *Refuge des Sarradets* (2587m; ☎ 05.62.93.37.20) has 60 places and charges €12 for the night and €12 for an evening meal. The refuge, like other huts around Gavarnie, gets heavily booked in the summer.

There are two ways down to Gavarnie from the refuge:

The HRP route The HRP route, which runs eastwards into the Cirque de Gavarnie, has the twin advantages of being both less busy and of having spectacular views. Although it's shown in dots on the IGN map it's not difficult; the path can, however, be slippery after rain. Some easy scrambling is required in three or four places. Following this route, it takes about 1¾ hours to get to the bottom of the cirque; ten minutes' walk further down is the Hôtellerie du Cirque. There is no accommodation here, and the whole area is generally packed during the summer. Follow the rough road which runs to the left of the hôtellerie for three kilometres to arrive in Gavarnie. For details of where to stay and information on facilities in Gavarnie see p222.

The alternative route Most walkers doing the trek between Gavarnie and the Refuge des Sarradets follow this route, rather than the HRP path. From the refuge follow the clear path running north-westwards for a few minutes to the adjacent col. On the far side of the col the path descends steeply to pass below the Glacier du Taillon. About twenty minutes after leaving the refuge, there's a fork, with the path to the Port de Boucharo heading west and the path towards Gavarnie starting a steep descent beside the meltwater streams coming from the glacier. The path is difficult to pick up in places but soon becomes clearer.

About 1¼ hours below the refuge the path comes to a small level area with three or four huge boulders, where some flat grass provides an ideal camping spot. From here the path descends for half an hour to meet the main trail coming down from the Cabane des Soldats which can be seen to the left. At the path junction there's a yellow sign pointing back up the hillside: REFUGE DE LA BRÈCHE 2H 15. Follow the main trail eastwards until, after about 40 minutes, the path swings north-eastwards to begin the descent to Gavarnie. A further half hour's walking brings you to Gavarnie.

PART 5: EASTERN PYRENEES

Facts about the region

GENERAL DESCRIPTION

The area dealt with here is entirely on the French side of the border, in the département of Pyrénées Orientales (Eastern Pyrenees). This area, which starts just to the east of Mérens-les-Vals is distinctive in several ways. There is a noticeable climatic change as you move towards the Mediterranean. The short, violent thunderstorms of the high mountains give way to more consistent, calmer weather. Good news as this may sound, it also means that trekking in this part of the Pyrenees can be a hot and dusty experience – carry plenty of water!

The landscape alters as you move east, too. Andorra, the Aran Valley and the high mountains to the west of Mérens soon become memories. As you cross the border from Ariège to Roussillon and approach the Étang de Lanoux, the differences start to become obvious. The huge shallow valleys of the Lacs de Lanoux and Bouillouses are in contrast to anything so far experienced along the GR10, and the meandering course of the Têt River is a surprise. The Pic du Carlit (2921m) and the Pic Canigou (2784m) are the last mountains of any size on the way east. Within five or six hours of descending from Canigou you find yourself in Arles-sur-Tech, which sits at only 282m.

With the change of altitude and climate, there is a marked change in lifestyle. The remote world of the montagnard is left behind, and everywhere the plains start to close in. Villages are no longer slate-roofed mountain hamlets perched on hillsides but groups of red-tiled, whitewashed houses huddled in the valleys. The Eastern Pyrenees, like their western counterparts, have been a traditional access route to the peninsula, so there is a variety of influences at play.

Politics and history

The Roussillon region, which encompasses the Pyrénées Orientales, has one of the richest cultural histories of any part of the Pyrenees. In 218BC Hannibal passed through here, and the Romans later used this access route to get into the peninsula for themselves. The slopes of Canigou still have the traces of Roman

> **Trekking in the Eastern Pyrenees – Highlights**
> While there are plenty of places to see away from the walking trail, your choices are rather limited if you are on foot. **Mont-Louis** is extremely impressive and makes a great stopover for the night. Likewise, the abbey in **Arles-sur-Tech**, with its miraculous Holy Tomb is well-worth seeing. A visit to the old Cathar stronghold at **Montségur** is also most interesting but you'd need to hire a car.

The Cathars
The Cathar sect is believed to have originated around the tenth century, probably in the Balkans. Over the ensuing years it spread through Europe and by the twelfth century had arrived in south-west France.

Cathar doctrine held that the material world was corrupt and worthless, and that salvation depended on escaping a cycle of reincarnation which tied the soul to an earthly existence. A pure life, and the blessing or consolation given by a priest just before death were the keys to freeing the soul and its return to God.

The Cathars had fundamental doctrinal differences with the Catholic Church and these combined with an alarming spread of Catharism prompted swift action. In 1209, the Pope sanctioned a crusade in which many notable Crusaders like Raymond of Toulouse refused to take part. Nevertheless a period of random violence was unleashed as a band of northern nobles, led by Simon de Montfort the Elder, ravaged the country. For a brief period from 1216 to 1224 the Languedoc dignitaries managed to regain their property. In 1226, however, a further crusade took place, accompanied by the work of the Inquisition which hunted down individual members of the Cathar priesthood. By this stage, many of the remaining Cathar priests had withdrawn to the protection of the the fortress at Montségur.

On 16 March 1244, the fortress eventually fell, and 225 Cathars who refused to renounce their faith were burnt alive below the walls of the castle.

iron mines, and the remains of the Via Domitia which connected the Iberian peninsula to Rome show the importance of the area as a natural corridor. After the Roman departure, when the nation states of Europe were beginning to take shape, the foothills of the Eastern Pyrenees were home to the Cathars (see above). This ill-fated Christian sect pursued a teaching of non-violence but was brutally suppressed in a persecution sponsored by the Catholic Church. The most famous reminder of them is the castle at Montségur, north of Ax-les-Thermes.

This area has not always belonged to the French. In 1213, Peter II, King of Aragon and Count of Barcelona, intervened on behalf of the Cathars, and for many years Roussillon was a Catalan province. Having been exchanged during a series of treaties in the latter half of the fifteenth century, the area was finally given to France in 1659, under the Treaty of the Pyrenees.

Walking in the Eastern Pyrenees

The Eastern Pyrenees are not the most interesting part of the range for walking but they have their attractions. Settled weather is one obvious bonus, and there's also the pleasant prospect of finishing a walking trip at the Mediterranean, where you can relax and sunbathe to recuperate. The Pic du Canigou (2784m) is fun to climb and the sections from Mérens to the Lac des Bouillouses, from Mont-Louis to Mantet and from Refuge de Mariailles to Cahlet de Cortalets are very attractive.

GETTING THERE

Getting to the Eastern Pyrenees

This is covered in detail in Part 1 (see pp14-18). In outline there are airports in Toulouse and Perpignan, and to the south of the border there is also an airport

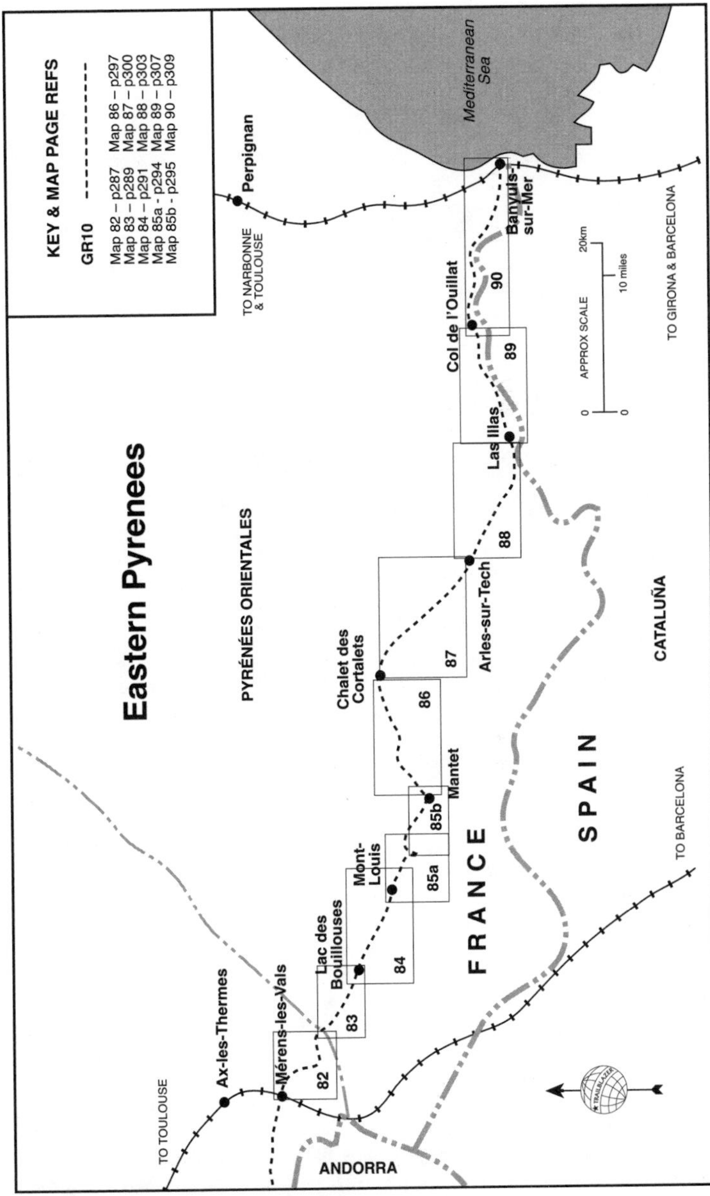

Eastern Pyrenees

PYRÉNÉES ORIENTALES

EASTERN PYRENEES

KEY & MAP PAGE REFS

GR10 -------------

Map 82 – p287   Map 86 – p297
Map 83 – p289   Map 87 – p300
Map 84 – p291   Map 88 – p303
Map 85a – p294   Map 89 – p307
Map 85b – p295   Map 90 – p309

Mediterranean Sea

Perpignan

TO NARBONNE & TOULOUSE

Banyuls-sur-Mer

Col de l'Ouillat

90

89

Las Illas

88

TO GIRONA & BARCELONA

APPROX SCALE

0   20km
0   10 miles

Arles-sur-Tech

87

Chalet des Cortalets

86

CATALUÑA

Mantet

85b

SPAIN

Mont-Louis

85a

Lac des Bouillouses

84

FRANCE

83

Mérens-les-Vals

82

Ax-les-Thermes

TO TOULOUSE

TO BARCELONA

ANDORRA

in Barcelona. By rail, there are direct TGV services from Paris to Toulouse, and by coach, there's a summer service from London to Perpignan.

Getting to the walking

Getting into the mountains is particularly easy because of the direct access to both Mérens-les-Vals and Banyuls-sur-Mer. Mérens is on the line from Toulouse to La Tour-de-Carol, and there's even a direct train from Paris. It's also possible to get a direct train from Paris to Banyuls.

Le Petit Train Jaune (see box, p289) also provides a scenic route up into the mountains, from Villefranche-de-Conflent via Prades and Font Romeu, to La Tour-de-Carol. In addition to these services, both Mont-Louis and Arles-sur-Tech are served by buses which connect to Perpignan.

Eastern Pyrenees – GR10

MÉRENS-LES-VALS → REFUGE DES BÉSINES [MAP 82]

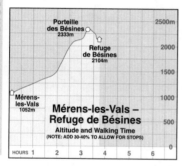

EASTERN PYRENEES

This is one of the shorter sections though the super-fit can continue to Lac des Bouillouses. Leave the gîte d'étape on the lane that passes in front, going up past the church which, along with much else in the village, was burnt to the ground by Spanish bandits in 1811. The tower which still stands is thought to date from the tenth or eleventh century. Go right at the phone box and right again over the bridge where there is a water source, a shelter and a bench. Pass between buildings and go left up a stony path which climbs to the **hot springs** with two small pools. The path climbs steadily up the valley and you pass on a rock a plaque inscribed: 'Alain Mugnier, décedé subitement dans cette vallée, 9/8/1998'.

After an hour and a half or so you cross a small footbridge and the ascent continues on the other side of the stream. Half an hour beyond this the path turns sharply south-south-west by a sign indicating that the refuge is two and a half hours away. A steep climb to the Porteille des Bésines, visible ahead, now begins. After a further 35-40 minutes the route levels out at a small lake then climbs again beyond the tarn, where a short stiff climb brings you to the **Porteille des Bésines (2333m)**. You reach the **refuge** (2104m), which can be seen as you begin to descend from the col, after a further forty minutes.

The *Refuge des Bésines* (☎ 05.61.05.22.44) can sleep 60 in eight dorms. It's clean and modern with a friendly guardian; demi-pension is €31.20, and a hot shower is €3. It closes at the end of September though one room is kept

MAP 82

EASTERN PYRENEES

MÉRENS-LES-VALS	PORTEILLE DES BÉSINES	COLL DE COMA D'ANYELL	PORTELLA DE LA GRAVA
→ 3 HRS 15 MINS →	2 HRS 15 MINS →	1 HR 35 MINS →	

open all winter but without water or electricity. The small ***cabane*** at the north end of the lake is an alternative if the refuge is full.

REFUGE DES BÉSINES → LAC DES BOUILLOUSES [MAPS 82-83]

From the front of the refuge the path descends nearly to the stream before turning east to make its way up the valley, the waymarks clear and frequent. A signpost after half an hour points the way to the Coll de Coma d'Anyell, though before it there is a series of lovely clearings with scattered pines that are great

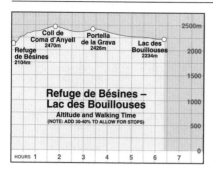

Refuge de Bésines –
Lac des Bouillouses
Altitude and Walking Time
(NOTE: ADD 30-40% TO ALLOW FOR STOPS)

for camping. The gradient steepens as you come to some areas of large boulders. Approximately 1¹/₂ hours after leaving the refuge, you arrive at the **Coll de Coma d'Anyell (2470m)**, where the path crosses from Ariège into the département of Pyrénées Orientales. The view from the col comes as something of a surprise. After the high and bare mountains to the west of Mérens, the Étang de Lanoux sits in a huge, shallow bowl. With its rounded, boulder strewn slopes and the apparent emptiness of the scene, the lake and its surroundings seem almost enchanted. (A ten-minute detour southwards at this point brings you to the *Cabane du Solà*, a tiny shelter available for use by walkers).

The route descends on an easy path to the northern end of the lake where there's a choice of paths. The most clearly-marked one, with red-and-white flashes, is in fact the GR7 which turns north and should be avoided. The direction of the less prominent GR10 is east. If, after leaving the junction, you don't arrive at the shepherd's hut, the small **Cabane de Rouzet**, you know you've gone wrong. The hut is reserved for shepherds so is no place for an overnight stop. From the cabane, cross an open plain where mouflons are sometimes seen – I saw a herd of about 30 when I last came this way. The gradual climb to the **Portella de la Grava** (Porteille de la Grave; 2426m) begins and you soon reach it.

The GR10 heads down from the col into the wide, flat-bottomed valley below. Although the landscape is not dramatic in the same way as the mountains that have been left behind, it's extremely pretty, and the walk down to the **Lac des Bouillouses** is one to be savoured. As the GR10 approaches the north-west corner of the lake, a yellow sign points the walker southwards. About three quarters of an hour later you come to the barrage.

LAC DES BOUILLOUSES

There's plenty of accommodation near the lake. On the western side of the barrage is a huge building that houses the gîte d'étape *Le Bones Hores* (☎ 04.68.04.24.22, 📧 04.68.04.13.63). Built to house the athletes training for the Mexico Olympics, it was sold off in sections so that the gîte occupies only part of the building – they have only two dormitories and four rooms open. A night in the dormitory costs €29 for demi-pension or, if you want your own room with bath and WC, €44. There's a supplement of €9.50 for single occupancy. The

food is good but the place can get very busy since it's accessible by road.

Cross the barrage to reach the *Auberge du Carlit* (☎ 04.68.04.22.23, 🖥 www.aubergeducarlit.free.fr) which has friendly staff, a pleasant terrace to enjoy a beer and a choice of accommodation. You can opt to stay in the hotel in a private room or stay in the gîte in a separate wooden building across the car-parking area. Demi-pension in the small hotel is €37, in the gîte, €27. They remain open all year. Slightly further down the hill is the CAF's own *Chalet*

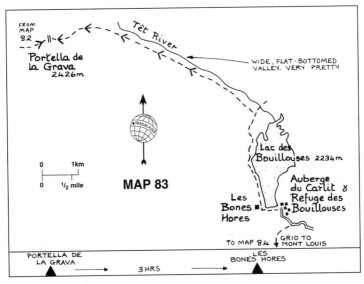

Refuge des Bouillouses (☎ 04.68.04.20.76) which has a rather institutional air about it. It holds 42 people, charges €30 for demi-pension and closes at the end of September, leaving just a small shelter open for winter walkers. It has a fireplace and a table and benches with an inner bunk room sleeping ten. In the summer months a *navette* (bus) runs from the lake to Font Romeu in the valley – convenient if you need supplies.

LAC DES BOUILLOUSES → MONT-LOUIS [MAP 84, p291]

Leave the lake by the road that passes the CAF refuge and stay on it for five minutes before crossing a plank bridge, where the GR10 departs into the trees on the right. In about 20 minutes the trail reaches a small lake, **Estany de la Pradella**, where there are good flat areas for camping and a small *cabane* with room for about four people. Cross the stream opposite the cabane and follow the broad path around the south side of the lake, a lovely walk in the morning sunshine.

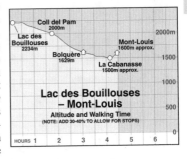

The path enters pine woods and you soon begin a rocky descent, coming to a fork with the right-hand path signposted to the Coll del Pam and the left, the GR10 and the correct route, to Bolquère. Descend on the rocky path through firs and in 20 minutes you'll pass under a **chairlift**, with a ski station below you on the left. Continue descending, crossing a cattle grid to reach a track where the trail divides again. The GR10 to Bolquère is signposted to the right. The path soon takes a right down a narrow trail that passes by some of the ski chalets that are sprouting up in this whole area. Cross a clearing and reach the main road, the busy D618, which you cross over to take the less busy D10C opposite. Stay on the road till a small path cuts away right, leading down to the road again on the outskirts of Bolquère where more chalets abound. This is a place where practically every house seems to be a second home.

BOLQUÈRE

Bolquère wins no prizes for being attractive but there's accommodation and a small shop here which might come in handy. Off-season, Sunday is a day not to be visiting though, with everything closed.

Both *Hôtel/Restaurant l'Ancienne Auberge* ☆ (☎ 04.68.30.09.51) and *Lassus Hôtel/Café/Restaurant* ☆ (☎ 04.68.30.09 .75) are quiet and have doubles from €38.

The cheapest place in the village is the spartan *Chez Guillamo* (☎ 04.68.30.15.82) which has single rooms from €12 and doubles from €24.

The gîte d'étape is *Les Ramiers* (☎ 04 .68.30.37.48, 🖳 les.ramiers@wanadoo.fr); it has 33 places and charges €33 for demi-pension.

Continue through the village and remain on the road. Just before the **Col de la Perche (1579m)**, on the right is a station of the famous **Petit Train Jaune** (see below). You could catch this delightful train either west from here to Latour-de-Carol or east to Villefranche de Conflent, from where a change of train would take you to Perpignan. In other words, you could begin or end a walk here. The col itself is a busy junction on a main road with thundering traffic. It does, how-

Le Petit Train Jaune

One of the most delightful tourist attractions in the Cerdagne is the Little Yellow Train and for walkers on the GR10 a diversion to travel on it makes a welcome alternative to trekking. The line runs for 63km from Villefranche-de-Conflent to La Tour du Carol and meets the GR10 in two places, at Bolquère and Mont-Louis. It remains open all year in spite of heavy winter snows which are dealt with by fixing a snow plough to the front. Bolquère is in fact the highest station on the line at 1593m.

Operated by the SNCF, the French National Railway Company, the line was started in 1903 and completed in 1927. It is powered by electricity delivered by the third rail similar to trains on the London Underground and there are thankfully three separate braking systems. The train seems to literally cling to the rocks high above gorges and ravines and is a marvel of engineering which includes 19 tunnels and two major viaducts. The middle carriage is open to the sky and is usually the first one to fill up since the panoramic views are spectacular. It is great fun to sit among the happy crowds and listen to the banter. It's also the place to be if you are a keen photographer.

As well as providing a terrific excursion for tourists the railway has a serious purpose, too, since it is the only lifeline for the people who live in the remoter villages which may otherwise be cut off during the worst of the winter snows.

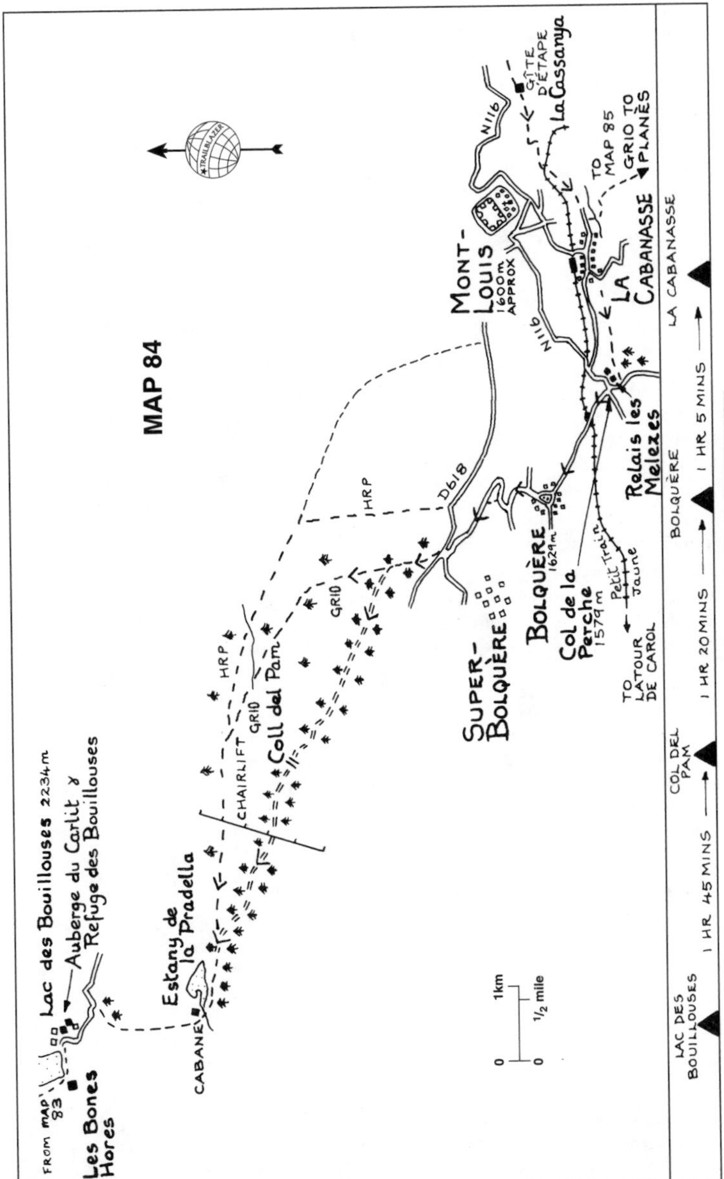

MAP 84

FROM MAP 83

Les Bones Hores

Lac des Bouillouses 2234m.

Auberge du Carlit & Refuge des Bouillouses

Estany de la Pradella

CABANE

CHAIRLIFT

HRP

GR10

Coll del Pam

HRP

GR10

SUPER-BOLQUÈRE

Bolquère 1624m

Col de la Perche 1579m

Petit Train

TO LATOUR DE CAROL

GR10

Db18

HRP

MONT-LOUIS 1600m APPROX

N116

N116

GÎTE D'ÉTAPE

La Cassanya

TO MAP 85

GR10 TO PLANÈS

LA CABANASSE

Relais les Melezes

Petit Train Jaune

LA CABANASSE

0   1km
0   ½ mile

ever, have a gîte d'étape and a hotel side by side, though both are right on the main road and likely to be noisy. The *Relais Les Melezes* (☎ 04.68.04.22.85) provides gîte accommodation for €42 for demi-pension. The hotel, *Le Catalan* (☎ 04.68.04.21.83), is more of a roadhouse, its garish red-and-yellow sign attracting coaches rather than walkers.

At the crossroads, cross over the hectic N116 and take the D33 opposite for a couple of hundred metres. Turn left on a cart track and walk along what is an ancient Roman trackway all the way down to **La Cabanasse**. At the centre of the village there's a good restaurant, *La Cerdagnole* (☎ 04.68.04.14.06) and a number of useful facilities including a post office, public toilets, a telephone box and some shops but nowhere to stay. The grocery is excellent and opens on Sundays even during the off-season. The Train Jaune also stops here.

To get to **Mont-Louis** take the left fork out of La Cabanasse and walk up the road.

MONT-LOUIS
✉ code 66210

There are two hotels within the fort (see box below). *Hôtel Taverne-Bernagie* (☎ 04.68.04.23.67, 🖳 info@bernagie.fr) is quite comfortable, with double rooms from €53; the hotel has its own upmarket pizza restaurant next door. *Hôtel Restaurant Lou Baillou* (☎ 04.68.04.23.26), with double rooms from €50, also looks good and the restaurant has been recommended by just

---

🦌 The Fortress of Mont-Louis

The Pyrenees are rich in reminders of the past, from the Roman Via Domitia to the Cathar fortress at Montségur. No monuments have survived so well, however, as the fortresses which the French constructed during the seventeenth century to bolster the border with Spain. Louis XIV's famous military architect was Sébastien le Prestre de Vauban (1633-1707) and examples of his Pyrenean work can be found as far apart as Bayonne in the Basque Country, and Le Perthus, near the Mediterranean coast. Vauban built for war; subtlety didn't come into it: his citadels were constructed to last, with unbelievably thick walls made of huge blocks of stone. Mont-Louis has outer and inner walls, a moat, and a triple main gate. All that, of course, is before you get to the citadel, which contained all the essentials to survive a long siege.

It isn't hard to see why the French chose this site for one of their eastern fortresses – the hill top commands a view across the Col de la Perche, one of the most accessible corridors through the Pyrenees. What is surprising is how short a time it took to build: work started in 1679 and the fort was completed in 1681. The testimony to the workmanship lies in the fact that after more than 300 years, the place looks pristine, and it's easy to imagine that it will look just as good after another three centuries.

Although the walled town is open to the public, the citadel remains the preserve of the military, housing a French commando training centre. There's a marked route which you can take around the walls, provided you stay on the path and don't touch any of the training gizmos that are lying around. Part of the fun of following the path is trying to figure out how all the apparatus is used. There are ropes, pulleys, bungees, steps, ladders and jumps – let your imagination run wild as you try to figure out how the unfortunate trainees tackle this nightmare assault course. The citadel is interesting, too.

The walking tour takes about forty minutes, and you can pick up the trail by the gendarmerie, within the walled town.

about every good food guide. Set menus start from €23. Outside the fort, the *Hôtel Le Clos Cerdan* (☎ 04.68.04.23.29, 🖂 04.68.04.23.79) has zero atmosphere but is very comfortable and you get free use of the swimming pool in the evening; double rooms cost from €53 for bed and breakfast and most people eat at one of the restaurants in town.

Shops inside the fort include a pharmacy, a tabac and a small food store. There is a **bank** of sorts, a tiny branch of Crédit Agricole which is open only on Tuesday and Thursday, 13.30-15.30. There's a **cash dispenser** on the corner of the Hôtel le Clos Cerdan. There is also a small **tourist office** (☎ 04.68.04.21.97).

MONT-LOUIS → REFUGE DU RAS DE LA CARANÇA → MANTET
[MAP 85a, p294; MAP 85b, p295]

This is another long section, which might be better split into two parts, with a stopover at the Refuge du Ras de la Carançà.

Stage 1: Mont-Louis → Refuge du Ras de la Carançà From the fort walk back down

Mont-Louis – Mantet
Altitude and Walking Time
(NOTE: ADD 30-40% TO ALLOW FOR STOPS)

Coll Mitja 2387m · Coll del Pal 2294m · Pla de Cédeilles 1911m · Refuge de l'Orry 1810m · Mont-Louis 1600m approx. · Refuge du Ras de la Carança 1830m · Mantet 1540m approx. · La Cabanasse 1500m approx.

to the centre of La Cabanasse, go through the village past a turning on the right and take a path leading south away from the village. After crossing a little stream the GR10 runs across fields to the tiny settlement of **Planès**. Opposite the Mairie is the gîte d'étape, *Le Malaza* (☎/🖂 04.68.04.83.79), a nice clean establishment run by two women. They have two dormitories sleeping 18 altogether, and five rooms of 1, 2 and 3 beds. Demi-pension is €26 in the dormitory or €30 in a room. A picnic for the next day is €7. Opposite Le Malaza is another gîte called *Bethanie* (☎ 04.68.04.38.16) – at least it's run on gîte lines but is not mentioned in any of the gîtes guides. It has showers, just two toilets and costs €38 for demi-pension. The food is said to be good but in season it takes groups and you could be sharing your accommodation with hordes of teenagers. What's more, two GR10 walkers told me that they were asked for a deposit on arrival – unknown throughout the entire trail.

The GR10 leaves Planès and above the houses you come to a junction where a yellow sign points the way to a forestry track heading south-east. After one of those long climbs with which you will have become all too familiar the path climbs through pine woods to reach the **Pla des Cédeilles (1911m)**.

The path heading down from the Pla is narrow and, at times, steep. It emerges eventually in the valley bottom beside a stream which you cross via a small footbridge near a tiny stone shelter. Three hundred metres north of the footbridge on the east bank of the stream is the *Refuge de l'Orry* (**1810m**). The hut can sleep

MAP 85a

LA CABANASSE	PLA DE CÉDEILLES	REFUGE DE L'ORRY	COLL MITJA	REFUGE DU RAS DE LA CARANÇA
1 HR 35 MINS	1 HR 10 MINS	2 HRS 15 MINS	50 MINS	

6-8 people but it is often occupied by shepherds or hunters, so don't rely on its being available. It's also currently none too clean.

Walk north from the refuge along a large track which slopes downhill through pine trees. After about 1500m turn right at a sign for Coll Mitja and

Crossing the Mountains – 1937

In December 1937, **Laurie Lee** crossed the Eastern Pyrenees on foot, to join the International Brigade, fighting with the Republicans in the Spanish Civil War. *In A Moment of War*, he recalls his arrival at a Spanish farmhouse: ' "He's come to join us", said one of the youths; and that set them off again, and even the girl lifted her gaunt head and simpered. But I was pleased too, pleased that I had managed to get here so easily after two days' wandering among peaks and blizzards. I was here now with friends. Behind me was peace-engorged France. The people in the kitchen were a people stripped for war – the men smoking beech leaves, the soup reduced to near water; around us hand-grenades hanging on the walls like strings of onions, muskets and cartridge-belts piled in the corner, and open orange-boxes packed with silver bullets like fish. War was still so local then, it was like stepping into another room.'

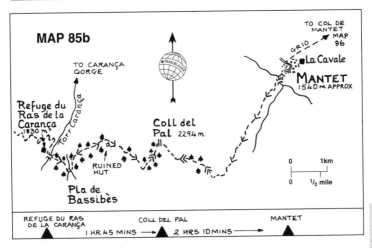

after five minutes you come to a stone shelter and penned area where you turn right across a stile. From here the GR10 breaks off to the right and climbs steeply to the **Els Collets d'Aval (1996m)**. It doesn't matter too much if you miss the turning: the rough vehicle track which you're on takes about an hour to climb to the same point.

The ascent from Els Collets d'Aval to the **Coll Mitja (2367m)** is steep and takes nearly an hour too, passing a small **spring** which often spills over onto the path. From the col a stony path leads down to the refuge (1830m) which you reach in a further 50 minutes. The *Refuge du Ras de la Carança* (☎ 04 .68.04.13.18) has room for 30 people during the summer, when a guardian is in residence, and 19 in the winter when she's not. It's quite basic, with only one toilet in a hut at the back, yet the refuge still gets full during the season perhaps because it's cheap at €21 for demi-pension. It's better, perhaps, to camp in the area 100m from the refuge where there are fireplaces and a great communal atmosphere. You can still eat at the refuge for about €12.

Stage 2: Refuge du Ras de la Carança → Mantet Cross the bridge south of the refuge and climb eastwards on the track. The waymarks have been repainted and are easy to spot. Having reached a flat open area, the **Pla de Bassibès**, where you have to hop across several small streams, the path re-enters the pines and heads north and then east. Finally, near a ruined hut, you begin the steep climb to the **Coll del Pal (2294m)**.

From the col the path initially heads south-east, contouring around the hillside, but soon begins its descent eastwards down a small footpath. Gradually the GR10 swings north-eastwards and, after coming down along the side of a valley, you arrive at the village of **Mantet**. Cross a bridge and go up a paved lane into the village.

MANTET

✉ code 66360

There are three places to stay in Mantet. On the left of the steep lane is the gîte d'étape *Chez Richard* (☎ 04.68.05.60.99, 🖥 richard. cazenove@wanadoo.fr) where demi-pension costs €27. Clean and well-run, this is a superior gîte and the people are friendly and helpful.

The second option is the *Auberge Le Bouf tic* (☎ 04.68.05.51.76) on the road below La Cavale. Demi-pension costs €33 and you'll need to phone in advance to ensure a room as there isn't much space.

Finally, above the village is *La Cavale* (☎ 04.68.05.57.59, 🖥 www.la-cavale.fr), an equestrian centre with a small gîte and a few chambres d'hôte. The rooms cost from €38 and demi-pension in the dormitory is €27. The food is very good indeed and wine is included.

MANTET → REFUGE DE MARIALLES → CHALET DES CORTALETS
[MAP 86]

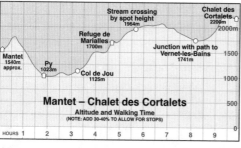

Mantet – Chalet des Cortalets
Altitude and Walking Time
(NOTE: ADD 30-40% TO ALLOW FOR STOPS)

Stage 1: Mantet to Refuge de Marialles

Go up through the village past the auberge and take the track on the right that passes La Cavale.

There is a path on the left that climbs up the hillside following a line of telegraph poles and leads to the **Col de Mantet (1761m)**. From the col go downhill on a steep, rough path that descends to Py, crossing the road several times.

Py is a sleepy red-roofed village with a small *gîte d'étape* (☎ 04.68.05 .58.38, demi-pension €32) and a *café/restaurant* below it with a very, very small épicerie.

The GR10 continues out of the village on the lower of the two roads heading east. After a few minutes a yellow sign marks the turn-off to the right. Cross the bridge over the river and follow the lane north for 500m before turning off on another footpath to the right. This climbs the hillside to a promontory with a good view down over the town of Sahorre and across to the Tour de Goa on the opposite hilltop. The path turns sharply south-east from here and descends to cross the valley before climbing to the **Col de Jou (1125m)**. The col is a veritable crossroads of paths with cars parked everywhere and signs sprouting up all over the place. You can reach **Casteil** and its small hotel, *Le Molière* (☎ 04.68.05.50.97, 🖥 www.lemoliere.com), in half an hour – ideal for anyone wanting to take a break from the trail. Demi-pension costs €45 and the food is excellent. If you need a **taxi** from here you could try Jean-Claude Cullel (☎ 04.68.05.64.61).

To continue on the GR10 from the Col de Jou, go uphill on a broad track, liberally signposted. The path through pine woods soon narrows and gradually the gradient lessens till you meet a dirt road which you follow for five minutes.

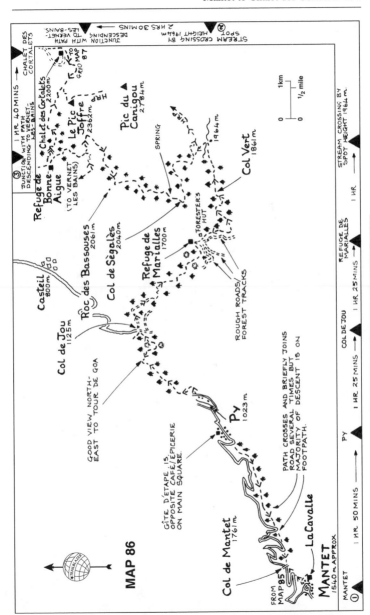

MAP 86

EASTERN PYRENEES

The GR10 descends slightly then climbs again beside a watercourse to meet a track. To the left is the *Refuge de Marialles* (☎ 04.68.05.57.99, 🖳 mjordron neau@wanadoo.fr), currently run by the president of the Refuges Association, the redoubtable Marie-Josée Ordronneau, an invaluable source of information and a superb hostess. Her meals are brilliant and it is a rule of the house that the same plate is used for all courses to save on washing up. Demi-pension costs €29 and there's space for 55 people. She closes for her own holiday in January. Sometimes she will read a story after the evening meal, a nice touch which walkers greatly appreciate.

If you climb the rocky outcrop behind the refuge you can see an extraordinary series of rocky pinnacles where Egyptian vultures have been known to nest. Gazing upon this extraordinary scenery is a great way to spend an evening.

Stage 2: Refuge de Marialles to Chalet des Cortalets

From the refuge, climb up along the line of the fence to the car park area and follow the waymarks right (south) beside a water channel on a narrow path through the trees. Go through a gate, cross the stream via a new bridge then up through a further four gates to the **Col Vert (1861m)**. This is a beautiful walk with views down to Saint-Martin du Canigou, a lovely thirteenth-century abbey.

The path comes to a **stream crossing** (near spot height 1964m on the map), turns north and in 15 minutes comes to the junction with the HRP route. Turn right to climb the summit of the Pic du Canigou (2784m), or left to stay on the GR10, a pleasant, shady and level route around the mountainside that at times crosses boulder fields on terraced walkways. At the **Col de Segalès (2040m)** there is a yellow sign and five minutes beyond the col there's a good spring.

The path continues level for another half-hour to a shoulder next to the **Roc des Bassouses (2061m)**; from here it turns sharply east and starts to descend, levelling out briefly a quarter of an hour later before continuing to drop, still on a clear, well-waymarked path. At the bottom of this descent the path joins a dusty vehicle track where a yellow sign points right for the GR10. Stay on the vehicle track and in fifteen minutes you come to the *Refuge de Bonne-Aigue* (1741m), a turf-roofed hut occasionally used by walkers. The water supply is unreliable here.

Beyond the hut the path leaves the vehicle track on an easily-missed path to the right, climbing up east through the trees on a zig-zag course. The climb to just below the Pic Joffre takes about an hour and a quarter and at altitude 2250m joins the path coming down off Canigou, turning left for the Chalet des Cortalets.

Follow the well-made path for about 15 minutes down past a small lake to reach the *Chalet Refuge des Cortalets* (☎ 04.68.96.36.19), which is open from mid-May to the end of September though there is a winter bunkhouse with water and electricity and a fireplace. The main refuge is large, with space for 111 people, and accessible by car, though it does lie many miles from the main road. Demi-pension in a dormitory is €31. You can opt to stay in the bunkhouse where the cost for a place is €9 but it's very basic. Try to book in advance, particularly if you're planning to stay during a weekend, as the Pic du Canigou is a popular destination for weekend walkers. Alternatively, camping by the lake is free.

CHALET/REFUGE DES CORTALETS → ARLES-SUR-TECH
[MAP 87, p300]

From the refuge, follow the vehicle track northwards, a tedious walk until you reach the **Ras del Prat Cabrera (1739m)** where the GR10 goes straight ahead onto a footpath and the vehicle track bears away left. The path goes south-west, remaining almost level around the hillside. At the end of the valley (**La Carnisserie** on the map) the GR10 turns eastwards, still remaining level but

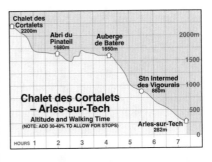

now running through trees, to the *Abri du Pinateil* (**1680m**), a very basic wooden shack with room for 6-8 people. The path begins to go downhill from here and after a further 35 minutes passes a *foresters' hut*, which has been renovated in the last few years and has room for at least eight people.

Just beyond the hut the path begins to climb steeply. It levels out briefly after a quarter of an hour and then climbs again to the **Col de la Cirère (1731m)**. A wide loose-pebble path leads down from the col initially but within minutes the surface is grass. The GR10 heads down past a ruined hut to join the rough road which can be seen below. Follow the road for nearly a kilometre until you reach the *Auberge de Batère* (☎ 04.68.39.12.01), a large place with a bar/restaurant, chambres d'hôte and a gîte d'étape. Accommodation in the gîte is €16 in a single room, €13 per person in a double, and a meal in the restaurant will cost about €13, drinks extra. Reports on the food vary from good to excellent!

From the auberge, follow the road downhill for about ten minutes to the **Col de la Descarga (1393m)**. The GR10 drops down into the gully just to the left of the low hilltop and follows a line of waymarks. The path gradually becomes better defined and runs down a steep hillside past rusting cables – the remains of iron-mining operations. After half an hour's steep descent the GR10 joins an earthen vehicle track which continues downhill to a ruined building (**Stn Itermed des Vigourais** on map). From here most of the descent is on footpaths, much of it along the line of an old cable lift. The GR10 briefly joins vehicle tracks in three or four places but soon leaves them again for the footpath to Arles-sur-Tech.

ARLES-SUR-TECH
✉ code 66150

Arles' most famous sight is La Tombe Sainte (see box p301), the Holy Tomb which rests in the courtyard of the eleventh-century Benedictine abbey in the centre of the town. A visit to the abbey is worthwhile, with the cloisters a beautiful and tranquil spot. Facilities in Arles include the **tourist office** (☎ 04.68.39.11.99), which doubles as the ticket office for the abbey, a **post office**, **cash dispenser** (Crédit Agricole) and several **shops** including a well-stocked **Spar**. There are eight **buses** a day to Perpignan.

EASTERN PYRENEES

EASTERN PYRENEES

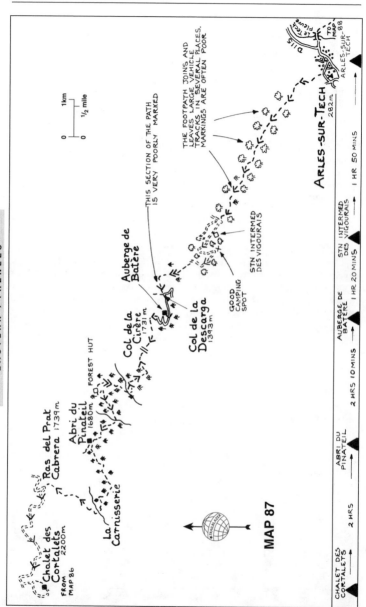

THIS SECTION OF THE PATH IS VERY POORLY MARKED

THE FOOTPATH JOINS AND LEAVES LARGE VEHICLE TRACKS IN SEVERAL PLACES. MARKINGS ARE OFTEN POOR.

Auberge de Batère

Col de la Cirère 1731m.

Col de la Descarga 1343m.

GOOD CAMPING SPOT

STN INTERMED DES VIGOURAIS

ARLES-SUR-TECH 282m.

Ras del Prat Cabrera 1739m.

Abri du Pinateil 1680m. FOREST HUT

La Carnisserie

Chalet des Cortalets 2200m. FROM MAP 86

MAP 87

0   1km
0   1/2 mile

CHALET DES CORTALETS	ABRI DU PINATEIL	AUBERGE DE BATÈRE	STN INTERMED DES VIGOURAIS	ARLES-SUR-TECH
2 HRS	2 HRS 10 MINS	1 HR 20 MINS	1 HR 50 MINS	

La Tombe Sainte

This marble coffin, believed to date from the fourth century, is held by many to be miraculous: despite the fact that it is covered with a lid the sarcophagus is constantly filled with water, which many claim has healing properties. Popular belief links this mysterious quality to the fact that, during the tenth century, the coffin was used to store the holy relics of two Christian martyrs, St Abdon and St Sennen. The bones, which had been brought to Arles from the catacombs in Rome, were subsequently removed and placed in silver reliquaries but the coffin soon gained a reputation for producing the inexplicable flow of water. Over the centuries there have been several official enquiries none of which could explain the phenomenon. More recently, attempts to account scientifically for the production of the water, estimated at 500-600 litres per year, have also been unsuccessful.

Water is regularly drawn off for distribution to those who request it, and during the Saints' feast day, on 30 July, large quantities are taken from the coffin to be given to supplicants. Anthony Fitzherbert's book, *A Coffin of Clear Water*, which is on sale in the town book shop, goes into greater detail about the mystery.

The big problem for walkers is the dire lack of accommodation in Arles-sur-Tech. There is one hotel, the faded *Hôtel les Glycines* ☆☆ (☎ 04.68.39.10.09, 📠 04.68.39.83.02) which aspires to be quite upmarket but doesn't entirely live up to expectations. Rooms are reasonably comfortable; prices start at €40 for a single or €50 for a double.

You could try the chambre d'hôte, *La Couvent Sana* (☎ 04.68.83.92.09, 💻 j.bertran@wanadoo.fr) which is outstandingly good. The rooms sleep three but can be taken as a single for €45 for the night, with the meal taken with the family in their house for €17. To find it, follow the GR10 south from the main car park by the bus station and climb uphill to a sign for the Stade Fontaine des Bois. Five minutes beyond this, La Couvent Sana is on the left down a gravel drive.

If you have a tent *Camping du Riuferrer* ☆☆ (☎ 04.68 39.11.06, 📠 04.68.39.12.09) lies near the sports centre; prices are €5 per person and €5 for an emplacement.

If you need a **taxi** in Arles, call VSL Taxis (☎ 04.68.39.08.95).

ARLES-SUR-TECH → MOULIN DE LA PALETTE → LAS ILLAS [MAP 88, p303]

The section from Arles to Las Illas is quite a long one, with a fair amount of climbing; there are few places to get water en route, so ensure that you have enough. It's now possible to split this section into a very short day and a longer one and stay at the gîte, Moulin de la Palette.

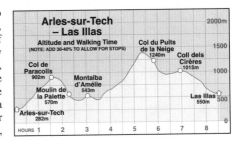

EASTERN PYRENEES

> **Eating out – Pyrenean style**
> For the walker with a basic knowledge of plants, the Pyrenean woodlands har-
> bour the wherewithal for a delicious meal. I spent a day walking with a
> Frenchman who really knew his stuff. On the way up through low-bushed slopes we
> feasted on *myrtilles* (bilberries), and on the way down the opposite hillside we
> stopped several times to sample *fraises sauvages* (wild strawberries) and *framboises*
> (raspberries). Passing through the next section of beech wood I was chastised round-
> ly for failing to notice a series of mushrooms that were right next to the path and invit-
> ed to dinner to share the boxful that we collected.
>   Mushroom collecting is, of course, a passion on both sides of the border, and if
> you're walking in the Pyrenees in late summer or early autumn you are likely to find
> the woods patrolled by locals with large wicker baskets full of fungi. To be a suc-
> cessful collector – and the competition is strong – requires both skill and experience,
> and I couldn't hope to compete with this depth of knowledge. I did, however, make
> one vital discovery. The *mûres* (blackberries) along the final section of the GR10
> (around Arles-Sur-Tech and Las Illas) are quite the largest and best tasting I've ever
> come across. Over the period of two days, progress towards the Mediterranean was
> considerably slowed, not only by the need to feast on blackberries, but the urge to
> munch the huge *châtaignes* (chestnuts) that lay everywhere.

Stage 1: Arles-sur-Tech → Moulin de la Palette

From the large car park in Arles behind the bus station, take the path leading
from the east corner of the square behind the public toilets and cross the long
footbridge over the River Tech. Go up a concrete lane to where, at a corner, the
GR10 departs on the right up a rocky stream bed, where there's a gap in the
fence that's too narrow for anyone with a rucksack on their back. Turn left and
climb steadily along the edge of a field to re-enter woods through another narrow fence gap.

Previous reports of this section of the trail told of dreaded diversions and
deviations but the route is now straightforward and well-marked. Basically, the
GR10 ascends the rocky bed of a stream. In rain, with the stream in spate, there
could be problems but in dry weather it's a breeze. Continue climbing through
chestnut woods, the walk now shady and cool. High up, the path divides with
the GR10 forking right while the left fork heads to Amélie-les-Bains. After a
further ten minutes you reach the **Col de Paracolls (902m)**, a narrow gap
between rocks with an odd assortment of signs; follow the one pointing to the
Moulin de la Palette.

Descend gradually through woods and in twenty minutes pass a dilapidated ruin with a pantiled roof. The waymarking improves dramatically with the
odd post ringed with the red-and-white balises. Descend through chestnut
woods to a small stream which you must ford. Signs on the trees warn that this
is private property.

After crossing the stream the path descends under high-tension wires to
reach the river which you cross on stepping stones. Turn left along the far side
of the river and up an embankment to the road, then left again to the honey farm,

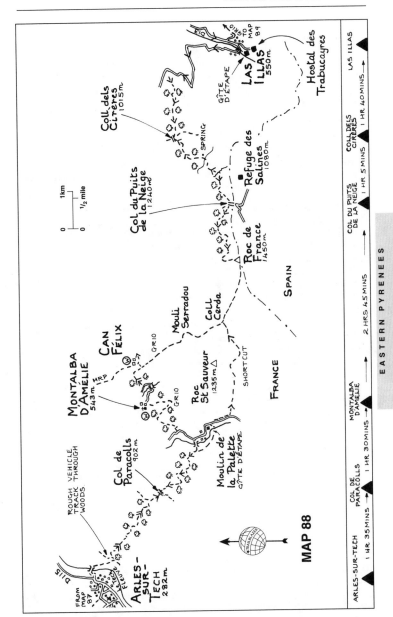

MAP 88

Moulin de la Palette (☎ 04.68.83.91.77, 🖳 chinaud@libertysurf.fr), the nicest little gîte d'étape you're ever likely to see. The accommodation is above the shop that sells all kinds of honey products. It comprises one room for four, a dormitory that sleeps 12 and a room that sleeps four in bunks. There is a day room and kitchen facilities. Demi-pension costs €30, you can camp for €4 and a packed lunch costs €7. You can have a tour round the farm and see how honey is made. This place one of the gems of the GR10.

Stage 2: Moulin de la Palette → Las Illas

There are two options on leaving the Moulin. The GR10 takes the path via Montalba d'Amélie. An alternative suggested by the owner of the gîte is to save an hour or so by following a path that goes directly east to join the GR10 at Coll Cerda. This is a sensible alternative for those who are either short of time or getting tired.

Option 1: GR10 via Montalba d'Amélie Turn left from the gîte and follow the D53b road for 500m then take the path on the right that starts to climb immediately. In an hour you come to **Montalba d'Amélie (543m)**, a hamlet consisting of a scattered handful of buildings including a tiny chapel, and there's a water point beside the road.

From Montalba d'Amélie the GR10 no longer goes via Coll del Ric as described in previous editions of this book and shown on the IGN map. It takes a more direct route via Mouli Serradou and Coll Cerda as far as the Roc de Frausa/Roc de France.

Leave Montalba d'Amélie heading south-west into the forest, crossing several small ravines as the path goes around the side of the mountain. After about three-quarters of an hour the gradient lessens: pass the ruined sawmill of **Mouli Serradou** and climb south on a path to reach **Coll Cerda (1058m)**.

Option 2: Short cut avoiding Montalba d'Amélie Turn right from the gîte and follow the road for 500m until, with a large house on the right, a track forks off left and runs parallel to the road. Twenty minutes after leaving the gîte d'étape, at a bend where cars are parked, a path goes off left by an ancient sign: ROC DE FRAUSA. The path climbs up along the valley, first north-east then veering east, with the path waymarked in blue.

Coming to what appears to be a private estate – to judge by the fence around it – with an unusual gate, head past the strange, half-built house and continue to follow the blue waymarks. After two more gates you leave this property and come to a ruined building set high on a promontory.

The path then climbs a steep open hillside to gain the **Coll Cerda (1058m)** where you rejoin the GR10.

(Opposite): The cloisters at the abbey church Sainte-Marie, Arles-sur-Tech, were constructed in the late 13th century. The abbey is best known for La Tombe Sainte (see p301), a fourth-century sarcophagus which miraculously produces a supply of water said to have healing powers. (Photo © Keith Carter).

From **Coll Cerda** the path continues on a rising gradient on the right bank of the river. On the edge of the forest cross the stream and climb through bleak woods to the Collado de Saint-Marti (1426m), where you follow the border between France and Spain for 500m and continue on to the **Roc de France (Roc de Frausa)**. From a promontory below this peak you can see, for the first time, the Mediterranean. The trail now resumes its old course and is clearly waymarked as far as the **Col du Puits de la Neige (1240m)**. The col is a broad open area with signs in profusion including one pointing to the *Refuge des Salines*, 25 minutes away to the south-east.

Follow the path that leaves the col in a north-easterly direction under the large rocky outcrop. Descend for about twenty minutes, then skirt under some massive crags to cross a small rocky gully before climbing up the far side. Twenty minutes later you pass a tiny **spring** and then briefly join a forestry track, before a sharpish ascent brings you to the **Coll dels Cirères (1015m)**, with Las Illas, according to the sign, 1 hour 50 minutes away. The first 45 minutes of the descent is on footpaths and vehicle tracks, the path cutting corners until it reaches the road, where you should turn right to reach a junction. Signs point left to Maureillas-Las-Illas, though turn right to the village.

LAS ILLAS

✉ code 66400

Las Illas is a quiet, tidy village with two places to stay. The *gîte d'étape* (☎ 04.68.83.23.93) is next door to the Mairie, a telephone box right outside. It is up there among the cleaner and more pleasant gîtes on the GR10, charges €11 per night, and is run by Mme Martinez who lives about 50 metres down the road. No food is available and the place closes between the end of September and the beginning of April.

The highly-recommended *Hostal des Trabucayres* (☎ 04.68.83.07.56) is a friendly bar/restaurant/hotel just up the road from the gîte. Rooms are available from €32.50 demi-pension, the food is good (and available to non-guests too) and the terrace is just the place to relax with a cold beer.

If the gîte and the hotel are full, your only recourse would be to go down the hill to Maureillas and stay there.

LAS ILLAS → COL DE L'OUILLAT [MAP 89, p307]

The GR10 heads north-east out of Las Illas on the D13 Maureillas road, turning right after less than five minutes up a small tarmac lane which weaves uphill for 45 minutes to the **Col du Figuier (685m)**. Follow the road north-eastwards from here as it gently climbs and falls, eventually becoming

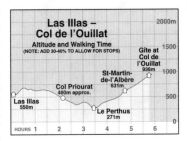

EASTERN PYRENEES

(Opposite) Top: Banyuls-sur-Mer (see p310), on the Mediterranean coast, is the finishing point for the GR10 and HRP High Level Route. Relax, sunbathe and celebrate your achievement! (Photo © Douglas Streatfeild-James). **Bottom**: The weather turns on the Port de Caldes (see p246); looking back west. (Photo © Bryn Thomas).

an earthen vehicle track. After one and a half hours you'll arrive at the **Col de Priourat (459m)**. There is a boundary stone (No 565) here. The GR10 continues downhill and at a sharp left-hand bend departs to the right on a footpath, climbing east. Meeting a track, turn right and continue to a road which you should follow past a farm and some Roman ruins to the **Fort de Bellegarde** which dominates the little valley. The Roman presence here depended on the Via Domitia which, with the Via Aurelia, joined Rome to its Iberian outposts. Continue uphill past a small seventeenth-century military cemetery and the gate of the fort, which was built by Vauban. The fort is open 10.30-12.30, 14.30-18.30 daily. Entry is €3 and there are various art exhibitions during the high season.

A short way beyond the fort you walk down into **Le Perthus**. Opinions vary about this place but whatever its attractions as a bargain shopping centre, it holds little appeal to the walker. The border with Spain runs down the main street and the shops and supermarkets are all on the left where the applicable tax rate is the Spanish 5.5% rather than the French 19.6%. Hordes of French turn off the motorway to buy their booze, fags and fuel there so the streets are thronged; the poor backpacker, however, looks sadly out of place. There are plenty of places to eat and a few hotels too – try *Chez Grand Mère* (☎ 04.68.83.60.96) where the demi-pension rate is €40.

Go north along the main street and turn right onto the D71 just before the large car park. Continue under the massive **motorway flyover** to begin a long

---

The évadés

During the Second World War, the mountains to the south-west of Perpignan were extensively used (as were almost all parts of the Pyrenees) to smuggle évadés (escapees) into Spain. George Millar's account of his escape brings to life the extreme arduousness of such a journey. Millar crossed successfully only on the third attempt; his first attempt having been dogged by bad luck, and his second ruined by an incompetent guide. Finally, led by a wiry old Spaniard, and accompanied by a group of unfit American airmen, it appeared that the end was in sight.

'...we moved on slowly to what he said was the last slope. It was very steep, and the snow was deeper and softer. The four weak Americans were all in grave difficulties. Fritz and I had to divide all that they carried between us ... The guide and his assistant did nothing to help. They only got angry, screaming at us and jabbering in fast, incomprehensible Catalan...

[Gable] collapsed finally. Fritz and I tried everything we could think of, praise, vilification, encouragement, massage, wine from the Spaniard's skin, alcohol from Fritz's little bottle. The big man would not move. Tears oozed from his eyes. "Leave me to die, you fellows. I can't go on".

What the group had not been told was that even having reached the border, after two nights' walking, there were still many miles to be covered to escape the clutches of the Spanish border guards, who might send them back. Finally, they made it to a small farmhouse, and the guide knocked on the door:

'A thin, nondescript Spaniard came forward, said in French that he was from the British Consulate in Barcelona, and asked us to fill in our particulars, rank, regiment, etcetera, on a paper he carried...'.   (*Horned Pigeon*, George Millar, London, 1946)

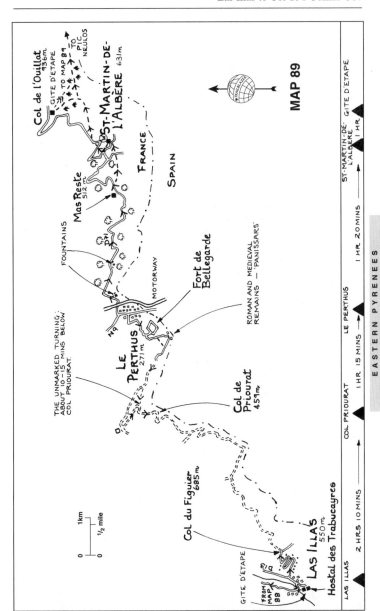

MAP 89

Col de l'Ouillat 936m.
GITE D'ETAPE
TO MAP 89
TO PIC NEULOS
ST-MARTIN-DE-L'ALBÈRE 631m.
FRANCE
SPAIN
Mas Reste 512m.
FOUNTAINS
MOTORWAY
Fort de Bellegarde
Le Perthus 271m.
ROMAN AND MEDIEVAL REMAINS - 'PANISSARS'
Col de Priourat 459m.
THE UNMARKED TURNING: ABOUT 10-15 MINS BELOW COL PRIOURAT.
Col du Figuier 685m
Las Illas 550m.
Hostal des Trabucayres
GITE D'ETAPE
FROM MAP 88
1km
½ mile
0

EASTERN PYRENEES

LAS ILLAS — 2 HRS 10 MINS — COL PRIOURAT — 1 HR 15 MINS — LE PERTHUS — 1 HR 20 MINS — ST-MARTIN-DE-L'ALBÈRE GITE D'ETAPE — 1 HR

uphill trek on tarmac of about four and a half kilometres. Near the building of **Mas Reste** you pass under an old archway; beyond, turn uphill through trees on an old cart track, then circle round the hillside to the buildings of **St-Martin-de-l'Albère**. After a day with few pleasant views, this is a great place to take a break, sit on the church steps and look back across the valley.

The GR10 follows the road away from St-Martin-de-l'Albère but soon cuts uphill on a footpath. After several minutes' climbing, cross the road up to the Col de l'Ouillat and up the spur, heading at first through trees and then across open grass. Near the top of the spur there's a path junction: the right-hand path takes you to the Pic Neulos, while the **Col de l'Ouillat (963m)** is 20 minutes' away up the left-hand path. The gîte d'étape here is *Chalet de l'Albère* (☎ 04 .68.83.62. 20). It gets a lot of tourists during the day but quietens down in the evenings. Demi-pension costs €31. The food is good and the balcony has great views back to the Pic du Canigou. A yellow sign here says BANYULS 8H, PIC NEULOS 1H.

COL DE L'OUILLAT → BANYULS-SUR-MER   [MAP 90]

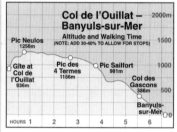

Leave the gîte and take the path that goes uphill through woods until, after 15-20 minutes, you reach a junction with two wooden signs. You want the path to the left which joins the road at the **Col/Roc des 3 Termes (1100m)**. This leads up to the massive radio transmitter on **Pic Neulos (1256m)** which is protected by no less than three layers of high-security fencing. Pass to the left of the station, work your way round behind it and then head south-east, descending through wide-ly-spaced trees to the ridge below. The path reaches a concrete bunker set into the hillside – a cattle trough. Slightly down to the left is a picnic area and a **water fountain**. Keep ahead, not on the track but on the grass, maintaining a level line as far as a *cabane* which has a sign on it reading Tanynareda (Tagnarède in French). It's clean inside, with space for about 10 people, and has a well-used fireplace with a supply of wood.

The waymarks are tricky to locate along this next section but with care you should be able to keep to the trail. From the cabane the path rises to a small summit then descends alongside a fence to meet a track where a smart new signpost of a kind seldom seen on the GR10 tells you that it is 22.3km to Port Bou – totally useless information for those of us on the way to Banyuls, which it fails to mention. The narrow path enters beech woods again and in three-quarters of an hour emerges onto a rocky ridge.

Climb on a well-marked path to a hilltop. A sign reads COL DES GASCONS 3HR10MIN. Descend on a badly-eroded path through scattered holly and juniper bushes; soon the path levels out and becomes easy. It is important here not to

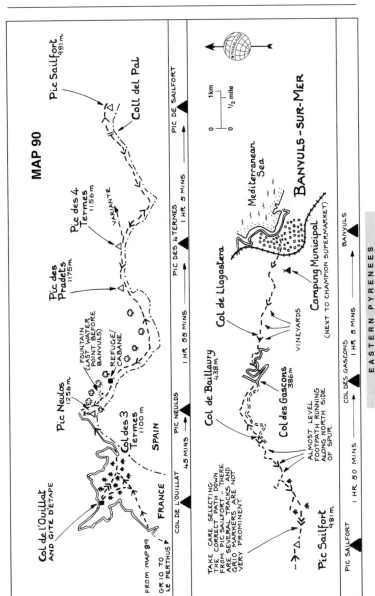

MAP 90

drift too far to the left (west) and not to lose height. Above all, avoid entering the trees which several small paths seem to invite. An hour from the last-mentioned sign, climb to the rocky top of **Pic Sailfort** (Pic Sallfort; 981m) from which you get the first view of Banyuls itself, still a long way off, with an entire range of hills between you and it.

The path off Sailfort is crucial and not all that obvious. From the rocky outcrop of the Pic you need to find a way down, heading due east down the prominent spur. It looks impregnable but is in fact quite easy and there are waymarks. The descent is steep and at times the right way down has to be worked out as if you're in a maze. Eventually, however, the gradient eases and you meet a path running along the north side of the ridge and under power lines to meet a dusty track at the **Col de Baillaury** (438m).

A sign points to the elusive Col des Gascons and you must climb again on a narrow path up to a small coll. Over the other side, continue on a terraced path that contours the hillside, passing a large, ruined building and crossing a number of streams to drop down suddenly to the road and a car parking area. This is the **Col des Gascons (386m)**. The GR10 takes to the road but leaves it at intervals, cutting corners, until joining it again at the **Col de Llagastera** where there is a *table d'orientation*. A sign says BANYULS 1HR 20MIN – nearly there now.

Leave the road for a track and for the next hour you walk through vines, a very pleasant experience. Winding down the slope and cutting back on yourself, make your way down to the red roofs of Banyuls and the blue sea beyond. Reaching the outskirts of the town by the railway tracks, go through a tunnel not designed for pedestrians and along past Les Palmiers holiday centre. Turn left at the road, left again at the next junction and follow the road to the seafront.

BANYULS-SUR-MER
✉ code 66650

Banyuls is the archetypal French Mediterranean town – sunny, relaxed and full of holiday-makers. Allow a day here to celebrate your achievement; there's very little to do but eat, drink, swim and sunbathe – wonderful!

Services
Banyuls has most services you could want. There are two **banks** and plenty of **shops**. The **tourist office** (☎ 04.68.88.31.58, 💻 ot.banyuls@banyuls-sur-mer.com) is on the seafront. There's a large **post office**, and the **tabac** opposite it is licensed to change money, a service it provides all week except Sunday afternoons. If you need a **taxi**, call Transport Patrick (☎ 04.68. 88.57.60).

If you're looking for a souvenir of your trip, buy a bottle or two of the local wine. The town is full of shops selling both Banyuls wine and other regional varieties. Banyuls wine is described as *vin doux naturel* and is rather different from anything else you may have tried. It's quite thick and sweet and tastes rather more like a light port than wine; when you ask if it should be drunk before the meal or after, they will tell you both! A bottle will cost between €9 and €15 but it's a must.

Where to stay
There is no shortage of hotels but during August they can get booked up and those with vacancies may be reluctant to take people for a single night. Book ahead if you can. One of the smartest is *Le Catalan* ✩✩✩ (☎ 04.68.88.02.80, 🖷 04.68.88.16 .14) up on the hill to the east of the town

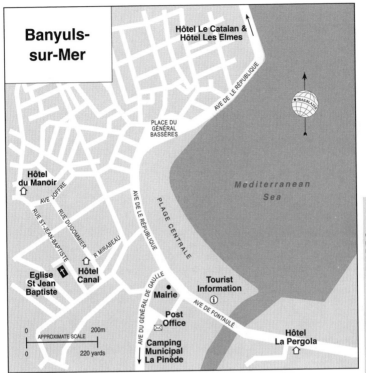

Banyuls-
sur-Mer

Hôtel Le Catalan &
Hôtel Les Elmes

AVE DE LE REPUBLIQUE

PLACE DU
GÉNÉRAL
BASSÈRES

Mediterranean
Sea

Hôtel
du Manoir

AVE JOFFRE

RUE ST-JEAN-BAPTISTE

RUE DUGOMMIER

AVE DE LA RÉPUBLIQUE

R. MIRABEAU

PLAGE CENTRALE

Eglise
St Jean
Baptiste

Hôtel
Canal

AVE DU GÉNÉRAL DE GAULLE

Mairie

Tourist
Information
ⓘ

AVE DE FONTAULE

Post
Office

0   200m
APPROXIMATE SCALE
0   220 yards

Camping
Municipal
La Pinède

Hôtel
La Pergola

EASTERN PYRENEES

with a private pool and a seriously good restaurant and wine list. Demi-pension costs €73 but after a celebratory meal with wine and a few drinks you'll be up around the €100 mark.

Good two-star choices would be *Les Elmes* ☆☆ (☎ 04.68.88.03.12, 🖳 hotelle-selmes@wanadoo.fr) with demi-pension from €64, or *La Pergola* ☆☆ (☎ 04 .68.88.02.10) where a room with a sea view costs €46.50, but it closes at the end of September.

Two cheaper options are the pleasant, relaxed *Hôtel du Manoir* ☆ (☎ 04.68 .88.32.98), near the station, where demi-pension costs €34; and *Hôtel Canal* ☆ (☎ 04.68.88.00.75, 🖳 hotelcanal@aol.com),

conveniently situated in a narrow street just back from the seafront and with a good restaurant serving local specialities. Demi-pension starts at €33 but for a room with shower and WC you can pay up to €60.

Camping Municipal La Pinède ☆ (☎ 04.68.88.32.13, 🖳 camp.banyuls@ban yuls-sur-mer.com) is about a kilometre from the centre of town near the big Champion supermarket. It charges €4 per person and €4 per emplacement. The other big site, Camping Le Stade near the sports stadium, is apparently reserved mainly for groups.

APPENDIX: FRENCH AND SPANISH

As with travel to any part of the world, time spent learning the local language is well worth while. People instantly become more prepared to help, and to share a joke (even if it happens to be at your expense!). In the Pyrenees you can get by without speaking anything other than English but a little effort will open a lot of doors. The following short selection of useful words and phrases in no way replaces the need for a phrase book.

Some phrases	French	Spanish
Good morning	*Bonjour*	*Buenos dias*
Good evening/good night	*Bonsoir*	*Buenas noches*
Hi! / Goodbye	*Salut! / Au revoir*	*¡Hola! / Adiós*
Help!	*Au secours!*	*¡Socorro!*
How are you?	*Comment allez-vous?*	*¿Como esta?*
Well, thank you	*Très bien, merci*	*Bien gracias*
Do you speak English?	*Vous parlez anglais?*	*¿Habla usted inglés?*
I don't understand	*Je ne comprends pas*	*No entiendo*
How much is it?	*C'est combien?*	*Cuánto es?*

General vocabulary		
Open / closed	*ouvert / fermé*	*abierto / cerrado*
Bank	*banque* (f)	*banco* (m)
Cash dispenser (ATM)	*distributeur de billets*	*cajero automático*
Post office	*poste* (f)	*oficina de correos* (f)
Rucksack	*sac à dos* (m)	*mochila* (f)
Shop	*magasin* (m)	*tienda* (f)
Today / tomorrow	*aujourd'hui / demain*	*hoy / mañana*
Tourist office	*Syndicat d'initiative* (m)	*oficina de turismo* (f)

Directions		
left	*gauche*	*izquierda*
right	*droite*	*derecha*
straight on	*tout droit*	*todo recto*
Where is ...?	*Où est ...?*	*¿Dónde esta ...?*
near	*près*	*cerca*
far	*loin*	*lejos*
Is it far to ...?	*C'est loin pour aller à ...?*	*¿A cuánto está ...?*

Trekking		
col	*col* (m)	*collado* (m)
farm	*ferme* (f)	*borda* (f)
hut	*cabane* (f)	*cabaña* (f)
lake	*étang* (m), *lac* (m)	*lago* (m), *estany* (m)
map	*carte* (f)	*mapa* (m)
pass	*pas* (m), *port* (m)	*puerto* (m)
path	*chemin* (m), *sentier* (m)	*senda* (f), *camino* (m)
plateau	*pla* (m)	*meseta* (f)
shelter	*abri* (m)	*abrigo* (m)
slope	*pente* (f)	*cuesta* (f)
stream	*gave* (m), *ruisseau (abbrevrau)* (m)	*arroyo* (m)
summit	*cîme* (f), *sommet* (m)	*cima* (f)
valley	*vallée* (f), *val* (m)	*valle* (m)

	French	**Spanish**
Accommodation		
Accommodation	*hébergement* (m)	*alojamiento* (m)
Camp-site	*camping* (m)	*camping* (m)
Full (booked out)	*complet*	*completo*
Full board	*pension* (f)	*pensión completa* (f)
Half board	*demi-pension* (f)	*media-pensión* (f)
Overnight stay	*nuitée* (f)	*noche* (f)
Room	*chambre* (f)	*habitación* (f)
Food and drink		
beer	*bière* (f)	*cerveza* (f)
bill	*addition* (f)	*cuenta* (f)
bread	*pain* (m)	*pan* (m)
breakfast	*petit déjeuner* (m)	*desayuno* (m)
cheese	*fromage* (m)	*queso* (m)
coffee	*café* (m)	*café* (m)
dessert	*dessert* (m)	*postre* (m)
dinner	*repas* (m), *dîner* (m)	*cena* (f)
egg	*oeuf* (m)	*huevo* (m)
fish	*poisson* (m)	*pescado* (m)
lunch	*déjeuner* (m)	*comida* (f)
meat	*viande* (f)	*carne* (f)
milk	*lait* (m)	*leche* (f)
sandwich	*sandwich* (m)	*bocadillo* (m)
snack	*casse-croûte* (m)	*bocado* (m)
tea	*thé* (m)	*té* (m)
vegetables	*légumes* (m)	*verduras* (f)
water	*eau* (f)	*agua* (f)
wine	*vin* (m)	*vino* (m)

Numerals

	French	**Spanish**		**French**	**Spanish**
1	*un/une*	*uno/una*	20	*vingt*	*veinte*
2	*deux*	*dos*	21	*vingt et un*	*veintiuno*
3	*trois*	*tres*	22	*vingt-deux*	*veintidós*
4	*quatre*	*cuatro*	30	*trente*	*treinta*
5	*cinq*	*cinco*	40	*quarante*	*cuarenta*
6	*six*	*seis*	50	*cinquante*	*cincuenta*
7	*sept*	*siete*	60	*soixante*	*sesenta*
8	*huit*	*ocho*	70	*soixante-dix*	*setenta*
9	*neuf*	*nueve*	71	*soixante et onze*	*setentiuno*
10	*dix*	*diez*	75	*soixante-quinze*	*setenticinco*
11	*onze*	*once*	80	*quatre-vingts*	*ochenta*
12	*douze*	*doce*	90	*quatre-vingt-dix*	*noventa*
13	*treize*	*trece*	95	*quatre-vingt-quinze*	*noventicinco*
14	*quatorze*	*catorce*	100	*cent*	*cien/ciento*
15	*quinze*	*quince*	150	*cent-cinquante*	*cien cincuenta*
16	*seize*	*dieciséis*	200	*deux cents*	*doscientos*
17	*dix-sept*	*diecisiete*	1000	*mille*	*mil*
18	*dix-huit*	*dieciocho*	5000	*cinq mille*	*cinco mil*
19	*dix-neuf*	*diecinueve*	1,000,000	*un million*	*un millón*

INDEX

For refuge names see under Refuge/Refugi/Refugio.
*Map references are in **bold** type.*

318 Index

TRAILBLAZER'S BRITISH WALKING GUIDE SERIES

We've applied to destinations which are closer to home Trailblazer's proven formula for publishing definitive route guides for adventurous travellers. Britain's network of long-distance trails enables the walker to explore some of the finest landscapes in the country's best walking areas and they are an obvious starting point for this series. These are guides that are user-friendly, practical, informative and environmentally sensitive.

● **Unique mapping features** In many walking guidebooks the reader has to read a route description then try to relate it to the map. Our guides are much easier to use because walking directions, tricky junctions, places to stay and eat, points of interest and walking times are all written onto the maps themselves in the places to which they apply. With their uncluttered clarity, these are not general-purpose maps but fully-edited maps **drawn by walkers for walkers**.

● **Largest-scale walking maps** At a scale of just under 1:20,000 (8cm or 3^1/$_8$ inches to one mile) the maps in these guides are bigger than even the most detailed British walking maps currently available in the shops.

● **Not just a trail guide – includes where to stay, where to eat and public transport** Our guidebooks are a complete guide, not just a trail guide. They include: what to see, where to stay, where to eat: pubs, hotels, B&B, camping, bunkhouses, hostels. There is detailed public transport information for all access points to each trail so there are itineraries for all walkers, both for hiking the route in its entirety and for day walks.

Coast to Coast	**Pennine Way**
Cornwall Coast Path	**Pembrokeshire Coast Path**
Hadrian's Wall Walk (in preparation)	**The Ridgeway** (in preparation)
North Downs Way (in preparation)	**South Downs Way**
Offa's Dyke Path	**West Highland Way**

*'The same attention to detail that distinguishes its other guides has been brought to bear here'. **The Sunday Times***

Trekking in Corsica *David Abram*
1st edition, 320pp, 74 maps, 48 colour photos
ISBN 1 873756 63 1, £11.99, Can$26.95, US$18.95

A mountain range rising straight from the sea, Corsica holds the most arrestingly beautiful and diverse landscapes in the Mediterranean. Among the many trails that penetrate its remotest corners, the GR20, which wriggles across the island's watershed, has gained an international reputation. This guide also covers the best of the other routes.

*'Excellent guide'. **The Sunday Times***

Dolomites Trekking – AV1 & AV2 *Henry Stedman*
2nd edn, 256pp, 60 trail maps, 13 town plans, 30 colour photos
ISBN 1 873756 83 6, £11.99, Can$29.95, US$19.95

The Dolomites region of northern Italy encompasses some of the most beautiful mountain scenery in Europe. This new edition features selected routes including Alta Via I, Alta Via II, and other trails, plus detailed guides to Cortina, Bolzano, Bressanone and 10 other towns. Also includes full colour flora section and bird identification guide.

TRAILBLAZER GUIDES – TITLE LIST

Adventure Cycling Handbook	1st edn late 2005
Adventure Motorcycling Handbook	5th edn Apr 2005
Australia by Rail	5th edn out now
Azerbaijan	3rd edn out now
The Blues Highway – New Orleans to Chicago	2nd edn out now
China by Rail	2nd edn Aug 2005
Coast to Coast (British Walking Guide)	1st edn out now
Cornwall Coast Path (British Walking Guide)	1st edn out now
Good Honeymoon Guide	2nd edn out now
Inca Trail, Cusco & Machu Picchu	2nd edn out now
Indian Rail Handbook	1st edn late 2005
Hadrian's Wall Walk (British Walking Guide)	1st edn mid 2006
Japan by Rail	1st edn out now
Kilimanjaro – a trekking guide	1st edn out now
Mediterranean Handbook	1st edn out now
Nepal Mountaineering Guide	1st edn Aug 2005
New Zealand – The Great Walks	1st edn out now
North Downs Way (British Walking Guide)	1st edn mid 2006
Norway's Arctic Highway	1st edn out now
Offa's Dyke Path (British Walking Guide)	1st edn out now
Pembrokeshire Coast Path (British Walking Guide)	1st edn out now
Pennine Way (British Walking Guide)	1st edn out now
The Ridgeway (British Walking Guide)	1st edn mid 2006
Scottish Highlands – The Hillwalking Guide	1st edn July 2005
Siberian BAM Guide – rail, rivers & road	2nd edn out now
The Silk Roads – a route and planning guide	1st end out now
Sahara Overland – a route and planning guide	2nd edn out now
Sahara Abenteuerhandbuch (German edition)	1st edn out now
South Downs Way (British Walking Guide)	1st edn out now
South-East Asia – The Graphic Guide	1st edn out now
Tibet Overland – mountain biking & jeep touring	1st edn out now
Trans-Canada Rail Guide	3rd edn out now
Trans-Siberian Handbook	6th edn out now
Trekking in the Annapurna Region	4th edn out now
Trekking in the Everest Region	4th edn out now
Trekking in Corsica	1st edn out now
Trekking in the Dolomites	2nd edn Sep 2005
Trekking in Ladakh	3rd edn out now
Trekking in the Moroccan Atlas	2nd edn May 2005
Tuva and Southern Siberia	1st edn late 2005
West Highland Way (British Walking Guide)	1st edn out now

For more information about Trailblazer, for where to find your nearest
stockist, for guidebook updates or for credit card mail order sales visit:

www.trailblazer-guides.com

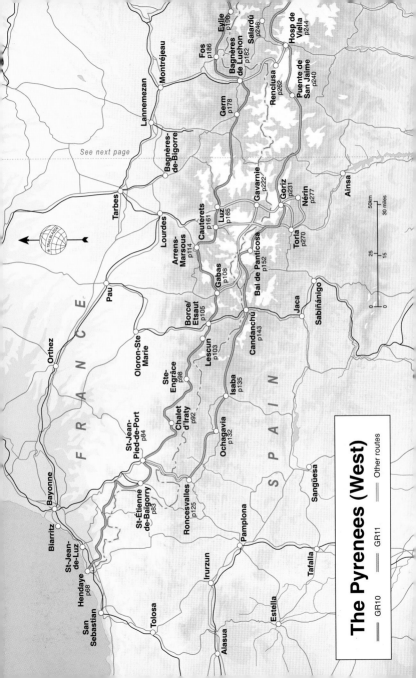

The Pyrenees (West)

— GR10   — GR11   — Other routes

San Sebastian

Biarritz

Bayonne

St-Jean-de-Luz

Hendaye p68

Orthez

Pau

Lourdes

Tarbes

Lannemezan

Montréjeau

Bagnères-de-Bigorre

See next page

Tolosa

Alasua

Irurzun

Pamplona

Tafalla

Estella

Sangüesa

Sabiñánigo

Jaca

Ainsa

Oloron-Ste Marie

St-Jean-Pied-de-Port p84

St-Étienne-de-Baïgorry p83

Roncevalles p125

Chalet d'Iraty p92

Ste-Engrâce p98

Lescun p103

Borce/Etsaut p105

Gabas p108

Arrens-Marsous p114

Cauterets

Luz p165

Germ p178

Fos p186

Eylie p190

Bagnères-de-Luchon p182

Salardú p246

Hosp de Vielha p244

Puente de San Jaime p240

Renclusa p262

Goriz p231

Nérin p277

Gavarnie p222

Torla p270

Bal de Panticosa p152

Candanchú p143

Isaba p135

Ochagavia p132

F R A N C E

S P A I N

50km

30 miles

0

0

15

25

25

30

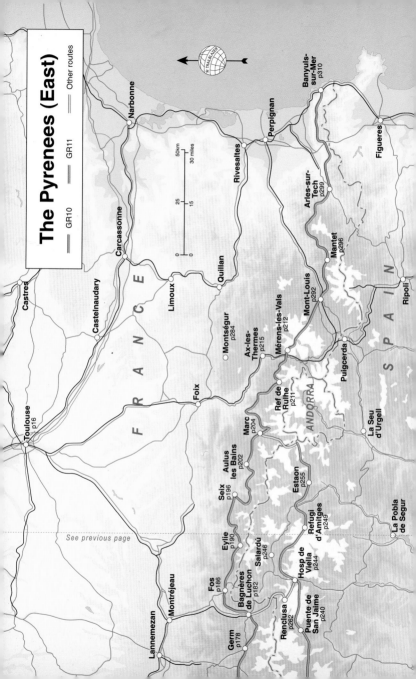

The Pyrenees (East)

— GR10 — GR11 — Other routes

★ TRAILBLAZER ★

FRANCE

Castres

Castelnaudary

Carcassonne

Narbonne

Toulouse p16

Foix

Limoux

Quillan

Rivesaltes

Perpignan

Narbonne

Banyuls-
sur-Mer
p310

Figueres

Ripoli

SPAIN

Montségur p284

Ax-les-
Thermes
p215

Mérens-les-Vals
p212

Mont-Louis
p292

Arles-sur-
Tech
p299

Mantet
p296

Ref de
Ruhle
p211

ANDORRA

Puigcerda

La Seu
d'Urgell

Marc
p204

Aulus
les Bains
p202

Seix
p196

Estaon
p255

Refugi
d'Amitges
p249

La Pobla
de Segur

Eylie
p190

Salardú
p246

Hosp de
Vielha
p244

Fos
p186

Bagnères
de Luchon
p182

Renclusa
p262

Puente de
San Jaime
p240

Germ
p178

Lannemezan

Montréjeau

See previous page

50km

30 miles

0   15   25   30 miles
0   25   50km